COLLINS GUIDE TO
TREE PLANTING
AND
CULTIVATION

COLLINS GUIDE TO

TREE PLANTING

AND

CULTIVATION

———

H. L. EDLIN

COLLINS
St James's Place, London

First Edition 1970
Second Edition 1972
Third Edition 1975
Reprinted 1976
Reprinted 1980

*For Stuart
and Angela*

ISBN 0 00 219159 8

Made and printed in Great Britain by
William Collins Sons & Co. Ltd, Glasgow

Contents

PART I: TENDING TREES

PART II: CHOOSING TREES

Text figures

All text figures were drawn by Malcolm Atkins, from sketches by the author.

Illustrations

Why Plant Trees?

———————

PEOPLE to-day plant trees for many reasons. The profits that can arise, after a wait of a few years, from raising fruit trees are clear enough. So, too, is the money yield from a timber crop, though here the waiting period is much longer. Yet the majority of tree planters expect no direct cash return for their effort and expense. They simply seek to make their surroundings more pleasant to live in. Before we consider what trees to plant, or how to plant them, we should consider the benefits that trees can bring.

Trees are good to look at. They grow naturally in shapes and curves that reflect natural forces, since their trunks and branches support a great weight in the face of the wildest winds. At the same time they display a multitude of leaves well placed to catch every ray of sunlight. The towering green dome that we admire in the oak or the beech, or the slender pyramid of a spruce tree, has comely outlines even when at rest. Yet they are seldom motionless, as any artist or photographer who has tried to depict trees will know. Each breeze, each gust of wind, changes their shape in some subtle fashion, and a great gale will bend their supple trunks in an ever-changing harmony of movement.

Likewise the sun will work upon each tree's crown a mobile pattern of light and shadow. Clouds drifting across the sky will create spells of shade, allowing the deep recesses of the foliage to be seen in their truer greens. Then a blaze of sunlight will strike reflections from the sunward surfaces, causing shadows elsewhere to define more firmly the tree's depth of form. All the time the angle of the sun will be changing, so giving a different emphasis to each sweep of the foliage. Taking wind and sun together, we can say that a tree rarely looks the same for more than an hour at a time. It is this variety of appearance, found only in living organisms, that gives to trees their unique visual appeal.

We can add to this hourly change the greater changes caused by the march of the seasons. In a broadleaved tree, the fresh green of the newly-budding leaves strikes a welcome note in spring, and leads on through the rich hues of summer to the glorious auburn and russet colours of the fall of the leaf, in the fall of the year. The intricate tracery of leafless twigs in winter has an airy beauty to match the rich green tapestry of the midsummer foliage.

Foliage alone is not the full appeal of a growing and living tree. It has bark in view at all seasons, and it may bear magnificent spring blossoms or a gay decoration of autumn fruits. In midwinter, hoar frost or clinging snow may give it another transient loveliness as every feature glistens in its brief bright white outline.

All these effects can be gained only from a living tree. Think, if you can bear it, of an artificial tree, or a tree poster, set up to give the same visual effects, and you will realise at once what a hopelessly inadequate substitute that would be.

Trees make good screens. They can effectively shut out the view of an unsightly building, but more usually they are planted to relieve the hard straight lines of modern architecture. Most garden plots have straight fences, and the curves of a growing tree relieve the rigidity of a rectangular layout. If you used a man-made screen instead of a tree, you would simply extend the oppressive pattern of straight lines and flat surfaces. Further, your artificial screen would need repeated painting and repair, whereas a tree replaces its own dead tissue as it grows. The most it needs is an occasional judicious pruning.

Besides shutting off unpleasant views, tree screens keep out unwanted noise and dust. No artificial outdoor barrier has the same deadening effect on sound, or slows the wind so well to the point when dirt is not carried across it.

As windbreaks, trees have the tremendous advantage that they check the force of the wind without causing eddies. They act as a brake on the air currents, in contrast to solid barriers that simply deflect the air streams. And of course they renew themselves indefinitely, filling up any gaps that arise in their leafy screenwork.

When shade from strong sun is needed, there is nothing to equal a tree. It is the cheapest large-scale parasol that we can produce, and the only kind that will last two hundred years without renewal. It will also give a good measure of protection from rain and snow, and prove a useful screen against the short, sharp spring frosts that can do so much harm to tender plants in a garden. Trees can thus keep us cooler in summer, drier when it rains, and warmer when brief frosts strike or an easterly wind blows keenly.

These manifold benefits from well-sited trees are not imaginary. They can be measured with the usual scientific apparatus that gauges wind speed, temperature, air pollution, and sound. Those wealthy Victorian landowners who surrounded their mansions with tall ornamental trees, and their home farms with shelterbelts, were not doing so simply for show and decoration. They definitely created houses and gardens that were more pleasant to live in, and farmsteads that were more profitable, than any in a treeless landscape.

Another attraction of tree planting springs from the long life-span of the individual tree. Whether we own mature oaks or sycamores, or simply admire them on the properties of others, we inherit from an earlier generation. Some were planted by the fathers of those now living, others by their grandfathers, and many by still earlier generations.

Soon after the Royal Scottish Forestry Society had celebrated its own one hundredth anniversary, a group of its members were shown the butt of an old Scots pine tree, felled on the Queen's estate at Balmoral. It was a sobering thought that this tree was three times as old as the Society! Since it was a seedling in the year 1640, it had lived for over 300 years, through the reigns of sixteen monarchs and one Commonwealth. Such links with the past lead us to cherish great trees. No matter how skilled we may become, we cannot create them in our own lifetime.

The opposite side to this lies in the thought that the trees we plant ourselves will delight future generations beyond our own. Unless we are still youngsters, we do not plant for our contemporaries but for our children, and for our grandchildren. Some of the trees we plant will become centenarians, and a few may stand for two or three centuries, to be seen and admired by people whose way of life may be very different from our own. To take an actual example of a planter's foresight bridging the centuries, in 1803 Lord Nelson visited the Forest of Dean in Gloucestershire and made strong and firm recommendations that more oaks should be planted for the building of warships. The work was duly done, and though steel and steam succeeded timber and sail in the Royal Navy, oak from Nelson's trees was actually used, in the 1939-45 war, for the building of the wooden minesweepers that swept magnetic mines from the vital approaches to our seaports.

Some of us are privileged to plant many trees, as the owners, designers or managers of woodlands, parks or highways. Such people, who plant trees every year, will naturally study methods and aims intensively, and add a store of experience as they go on. Those who plant fewer trees, more occasionally, have an even greater need to make sure of their ground before they start. Nobody wants to plant the wrong tree, or the right tree in the wrong place. Failures are expensive, mistakes last a long time, and look more obvious as they grow larger. If you make a blunder with a flower bed, you can rip the offending plants out and put a happier selection in next year. You just can't do that with your trees, so you must plan for many years of rewarding growth, right from the outset.

Great stores of knowledge are held by experts who can help you to plan your work aright. I say "stores" advisedly, for hitherto there has been no common pool. On the scientific side we have the botanists and the timber technologists, along with plant pathologists and experts on soils and insect pests. On the practical side stand the nurserymen, the foresters, and the tree surgeons, each knowing a lot about his own craft and a little, but only a little, about a few related ones. Landscape architects, who contribute an artistic leaven to many planting schemes, are expected to appreciate all these woodland skills. The newcomer, and the amateur, can easily become bewildered by it all. So my earnest aim in the text that follows is to open the way to sound tree planting based on modern methods and the latest of scientific thought.

It would be unhelpful to draw any strict line round what we may, or may not, regard as a "tree", in so general a study of planting. Fruit growing is a specialised profession, and the raising of rose trees is a craft on its own; yet both these arts—though there is little space to discuss them here—call for the same kinds of skills and knowledge as the raising of timber trees or ornamental shrubs. The man who sets out to raise a dwarf conifer in his rockery, or even a Japanese miniature tree in a pot, is handling the same kind of plant life as the forester who puts out several hundred spruce each day on a hillside, all destined to yield sawmill timber or paper pulp.

Few of those who read this book will wish, themselves, to become expert seed collectors, grafters, or tree surgeons. But everyone with an inquiring mind and an interest in plant life will wish to know how these jobs are done, and to judge when they may need to seek the help of an expert. Tree tending opens fresh viewpoints in many directions, such as the history of rare kinds brought from the farthest forests of the earth to grace our gardens. The simpler and commoner tasks are within the reach of all, while every knowledgeable landowner or land manager needs to know a little about the more complex jobs, if only to assess their necessity and probable cost.

Therefore I have planned this book to meet the needs of those who wish to plant trees for future enjoyment, or for the future needs of timber users; and also for those who have to maintain the older and grander trees that have been entrusted to their care.

PART ONE

TENDING TREES

1. How Trees Live and Grow

To raise trees successfully you must have an understanding of the life processes that support them. These are complex, but as they are the same for every kind you are likely to deal with it is worth while to master them. Those who know their botany will realise that the main features are the same as those in lesser plants, but it is surprising how few know the essential distinguishing feature found only in the *woody* plants, that is, the trees, shrubs, and woody climbers.

THE CAMBIUM AND ITS WORK

The key feature in the life of woody plants is called "secondary thickening", because it follows on the first or "primary thickening" of each stem that occurs when it first arises from a bud. The mechanism of it lies in a marvellous layer of cells called the *cambium*, which is found just beneath the tree's bark and bast tissues. This cambium is a continuous sheath of living cells that extends all round the trunk and every branch of every woody plant, all the way from ground level to the topmost twig. Though very thin itself, it is responsible for the whole of the thickening of a tree's stem after its first year's start. It works in a curious way, by forming fresh wood tissue on its *inner* side. This means that, however stout a tree trunk may become, the cambium always remains on the outside of the true wood, just below the bast and bark, for year by year it pushes itself outwards.

Because the cambium is only active in spring and summer, there is a definite pattern of wood formation within it, which we can see as an *annual ring* when we cut across a woody stem. In spring, it forms open wood that enables sap to flow rapidly upwards; in summer it forms denser wood to help support the tree; and in autumn and winter it rests. The contrast between the lighter, paler springwood, which is always *inside* the related heavier, darker, summerwood of the same year, forms the visible ring. By counting these rings, we can at once tell the age of any branch at the point where it is cut across. Likewise, if we fell a tree, and count the rings *on its stump*, we can say how many years have passed since it first began to grow.

The fact that the cambium spreads through every branch and twig means that the tree can grow with every part of its structure in proper balance. As the trunk thickens, so do the branches, in a proper proportion, and this is the secret of the inherent strength of the tree's crown.

So long as the cambium layer is present and undamaged, it continues

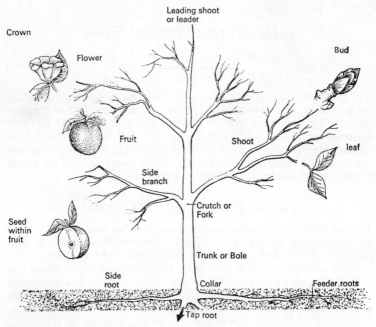

FIGURE 1. Main parts of a tree.

to produce fresh tissues. But if it is harmed in any way, its own renewal is a slow and uncertain business. This makes it important, in the practical handling of young trees, to avoid any damage to it. If it is removed all round a stem, that stem or trunk invariably dies from that point upwards. A lesser wound is healed, but only very slowly, from around its edges.

WOOD

The true wood that is formed, in one annual layer after another, inside the cambium, has a complex structure of cells. In the life of the tree it has three main functions, all important in planting practice.

First, it supports the crown and holds it firm against the wind. The strength required to do this at any point is provided by the varying activity of the cambium, which forms limbs of different thickness. Except for small twigs holding little wood, it is rare to find a *healthy* branch or stem that has broken under the forces of wind or weight.

Second, the wood carries upwards the whole supply of water needed by the tree's crown. In summer, when the leaves are actively transpiring moisture into the air, this flow is rapid. In winter, when the trees are

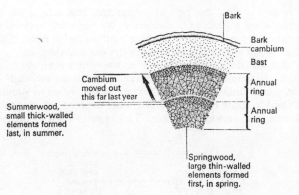

FIGURE 2. Annual rings. Each year the cambium lays down a layer of pale, thin-walled tissues in spriug and a layer of dark thick-walled tissues in summer. These two layers together form one annual ring. The process pushes the main wood cambium, a thin layer between wood and bast, outwards. Bark is formed by a separate bark cambium,

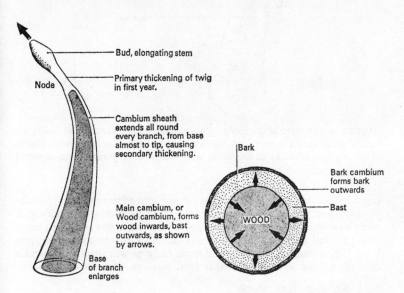

FIGURE 3. The marvellous cambium sheath that extends round every branch and large root, causing secondary thickening to cope with increasing strains, as the tree grows. It forms wood inwards and a thin bast layer outwards. The smaller bark cambium forms fresh bark.

either leafless or, in the case of evergreens, less active, the root-sap within the wood is practically stationary. We can safely move trees only during the colder months, from October until the end of April. Otherwise both their wood and their softer tissues dry out and they die.

The idea that the sap "goes down" in the winter is an old fallacy that dies hard. In actual fact, the sap stays up but stops moving! Timber felled in winter holds just as much water as that felled in summer.

The third function of the wood is to store the food reserves needed for growth from one season to another. This is well shown by the American

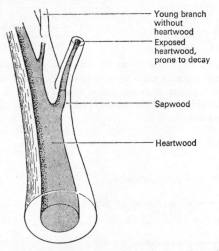

FIGURE 4. All wood is originally sapwood. As a tree or branch gets older, the central wood ceases to carry sap, turns darker and becomes heartwood. Heartwood is prone to decay in the living tree, but is more durable than sapwood when it becomes felled timber.

sugar maple, and to a lesser degree by our own sycamore (*Acer pseudoplatanus*) and birch. In these trees the ascending root-sap, in spring, is so rich in sugar that it tastes sweet and can be made into syrup or candy. The practical importance of all this is that a stout-stemmed young tree has a better chance of survival and rapid early growth than has a slender one; the sturdy stem holds bigger food reserves, and also more water.

SAPWOOD AND HEARTWOOD

All wood carries sap during its early years, but as the years go by and the stems grow thicker, the wood at the heart of the tree is no longer needed for this purpose. It is then gradually withdrawn from active life, and undergoes chemical and physical changes which can be seen, in most timbers, by a change of colour from light brown to darker brown. Naturally, heartwood is found only in the *stouter* trunks and branches, but a grand old oak will contain far more heartwood than sapwood.

Heartwood is usually sealed off from the air, and hidden from view, by layers of sapwood and bark. But if it is exposed—for example by the breakage or the pruning of a large limb—it is very *vulnerable* to fungal decay. In fact, in a hollow tree it is the heartwood that has vanished; the sapwood is still present and living.

Curiously, after a healthy tree has been felled, the heartwood of many kinds of tree, though by no means all, becomes very *resistant* to decay. The phrase "hearts of oak" reminds us how well and how long oak heartwood lasted in wooden warships.

The term *heartwood* should not be confused with *hardwood* which is a comprehensive name for the wood of any *broadleaved* tree, whether it be physically hard or soft. Its opposite is *softwood* which covers all the wood of any *coniferous* tree, including both hard and soft examples!

BAST AND BARK

Outside the cambium, and covering the whole surface of every stem of a woody plant, there are two layers of tissue that have quite different functions.

Immediately outside the cambium comes the bast, a thin layer of conductive tissue that carries leaf-sap *downwards* from the crown to the roots. This tissue is renewed and extended by the growth of the cambium cells, which produce bast *outwards*, just as they form wood on the inner side. But bast never becomes very thick, since the downward flow of leaf-sap, though essential for the life of the roots, is never large in volume.

The bark, which lies outside the bast, is a protective tissue. It consists of cells with corky walls that stop the water within the stem from escaping into the air. It also shields the bast and cambium from hot sun, chance knocks and bruises, and the sharp teeth of browsing animals. As the stem grows stouter, more bark is needed, and this is provided by a special growth layer, called the *bark cambium*, between the bast and the bark. At the same time the bark becomes thicker, and therefore more useful as a protective layer. It develops patterns that vary from one kind of tree to another, and are a useful help in identification.

In all work with trees, it is important that the three outer layers of the woody stems, namely the bark, the bast, and the cambium, should be treated with respect and harmed as little as possible.

BUDS AND SHOOTS

The upward and outward growth of tree stems is made by shoots that start life as buds. Buds are of three main kinds—those that develop into leaves, those that form flowers—and later seeds, and those that give

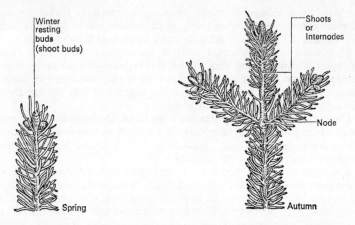

FIGURE 5. Shoot buds normally produce shoots during spring and summer and end with 'winter resting buds' formed in autumn. Each bud-cluster is called a *node*. The piece of shoot between two nodes is an *internode*; its length indicates vigour of growth each year.

shoots. Each bud holds a growing point protected by leaf-like scales. In an extending shoot, the young cells formed just behind this growing point expand steadily, so moving it forward; but this process is short-lived, and all increase in shoot growth stops with the cool days of autumn. Therefore you can see, on the young shoots of most trees, a clear pattern of *internodes* of annual shoot growth, between the *nodes* that mark each winter's resting spell. On broadleaved trees this pattern becomes indistinct after a few years, but on the coniferous trees it remains clear for far longer, and can often be used to judge the tree's age.

If the stem of a broadleaved tree is pruned, it readily forms new buds and new shoots, which renew growth near the cut surface. But only a few coniferous trees can do this; if an old pine tree, for example, is topped, it dies because it cannot form fresh buds, shoots, and leaves.

As a tree grows taller and its crown expands, the lower side shoots become overshaded, die and eventually drop off. The scars they leave are healed over by an outgrowth of cambium, called *callus* tissue, from the surrounding stem surface. Callus also strives to cover all accidental or pruning wounds, but it does not always succeed.

LEAVES

The leaves that the shoots bear hold the vital tissues that give the tree all its growth substance and energy. The essential chemical in this process is called *chlorophyll*, meaning "leaf-green". It is always green

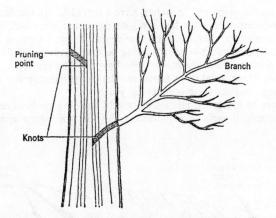

FIGURE 6. Knots are branches buried by outward growth of tree trunks, so they run across the grain of the timber. On *left*, a branch has been pruned flush with the trunk, and future healing will hide the knot end.

in colour, though in certain "freak" trees such as the copper beech or the blue cedar, the underlying green may be hidden by a superficial shade. Chlorophyll "fixes" the small amount of carbon dioxide in the air, in such a way that it forms carbohydrates. These food substances are carried to every part of the tree by the leaf-sap stream which runs through the bast. They are used in part to build up plant tissues, and in part—through oxidation with the oxygen of the air—to provide energy.

Leaves have three vital needs. One is air, and another is water. Some of the water is required to help form the carbohydrates, but far more is transpired into the air and so lost. The third need is sunlight, which provides the energy for the key process called *photosynthesis*, or "building up by means of light", which gives the carbohydrates.

Different trees vary markedly in the intensity of light they need, and this can be important in their care. Some, such as beech, are termed *shade-bearers*, because they can thrive under moderate shade from other trees, but they themselves cast so deep a shade that nothing else will grow beneath them. This gave rise to the old, mistaken belief, that plants will not grow below the "drip" of beech. It is not dripping water—quite harmless—that checks growth on the beechwood floor, but darkness!

At the other extreme come the *light-demanders*, such as birch and pine, which must have full sunlight at all times. These, however, cast so light a shade that other trees, shrubs or flowering plants will often thrive beneath them—a useful point to remember for the garden.

In general, shade-bearers make good hedges but poor overhead screens. Light-demanders, on the other hand, are useless as hedges because their shoots cannot thrive when close-packed.

Leaves, unlike stems and branches, have a short life. In the deciduous, or summer-green, trees they last for a single season, then fade and fall. In an evergreen tree, they live for a few years only, and there is a steady —though seldom noticed—leaf-fall going on each autumn. Fallen leaves carry with them much of the mineral food supplied by the roots, and leaf mould is therefore a valuable fertiliser. In the garden or the wood it costs nothing, and the dose is repeated yearly.

The leaves of evergreen trees are actively building up food nearly all the year round, though growth occurs only in the warm spring and summer.

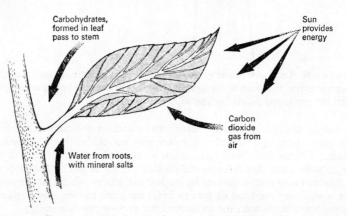

Carbohydrates, formed in leaf pass to stem

Sun provides energy

Carbon dioxide gas from air

Water from roots, with mineral salts

FIGURE 7. Every green leaf uses the energy of sunlight to cause carbon dioxide gas, always present in the air, to combine with water from the roots. The resulting carbohydrates are fed into the stem to provide both new plant tissues and energy for growth. Leaves only thrive in sunlight.

ROOTS

Underground, out of sight, the other half of the tree, its root system, continues growth and life all through the year, rapidly in spring and summer, but at a lesser pace through the winter months. It is important, when you plant a tree in autumn, to realise that its roots will start growth at once, though its shoots remain stationary until the spring.

The major roots, which develop from thinner members, last for the lifetime of the tree, and become stouter just as the branches do. They spread out in a network that is remarkably shallow, running only a few feet below the surface of the ground, but having occasional deeper *sinkers*. Often, though not always, there is a tap root below the tree's trunk.

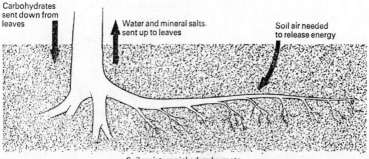

Carbohydrates
sent down from
leaves

Water and mineral salts.
sent up to leaves

Soil air needed
to release energy

Soil moisture picked up by roots.

FIGURE 8. Roots obtain energy by 'burning-up' carbohydrates provided by the leaves, using air already present in the soil. They absorb moisture and mineral salts from the soil and send them up to the leaves. Roots cannot grow in waterlogged soil.

These main roots bear multitudes of lesser roots which, like the leaves in the tree's crown, have only a short life. Each separate rootlet explores a patch of soil, extracts mineral food from it, and then withers away. Despite this, the tree as a whole always has a great number of rootlets, which supply it with all the water it needs for life. When a tree has to be transplanted, it is of great importance for it to have a compact and bushy root-system, so that it can readily take up an adequate water supply soon after being moved. Nurserymen ensure this by frequent transplanting.

FLOWERS AND FRUIT

Most trees, except for a few odd kinds found only in cultivation, bear flowers once they are old enough to do so. In some kinds, these flowers follow the common pattern of garden plants. They have protective sepals, petals to attract pollinating insects, nectaries to reward these insects for their visits, stamens that shed pollen, and pistils wherein the seeds develop.

But many trees are wind-pollinated, and where this is so it is usual for the male stamens to be borne in separate flowers, apart from the female pistils. The clusters of all-male, or all-female, flowers that result are called *catkins*. Since the catkins do not have to attract insects, they lack petals and nectaries, and have no pleasant scent.

Most people notice the male catkins, which are fairly large and become conspicuous when they shed clouds of yellow pollen in late spring. But the female catkins are smaller, and attract little attention until they develop, during late summer, into ripening fruits. Male catkins, and the stamens in flowers that have organs of both sexes, are short-lived;

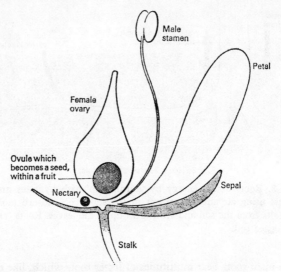

FIGURE 9. Typical flower. Sepals protect flower when in bud, petals attract insects and nectaries provide nectar to reward them. Insects carry pollen from male stamens to female ovary. Fertilised ovule within ovary develops into a seed. Many trees are wind-pollinated and bear separate male and female flowers which lack petals and nectaries.

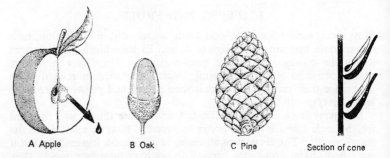

FIGURE 10. Tree fruits and seeds vary greatly. A, the familiar apple is a fruit that holds several seeds, or pips. B, the oak bears a single-seeded fruit, called an acorn. C, a pine cone holds many small winged seeds beneath its scales, typically two per scale.

after shedding their pollen they fade and fall away. Female flowers remain on the tree until their fruit is ripe, which takes only a few weeks in some kinds, but a few months for others, and as long as two or three years in a few conifers.

A *fruit* is the product of a single flower, and it may hold one, two, or many *seeds*. Both the seeds and the fruits of trees vary widely from one kind to another, from tiny grains that are wind-borne, as in the poplars, to the large *nuts* of the chestnut or the fleshy *pome* of the apple. In nature, they are dispersed in various ways, by the wind, by seed-eating squirrels, or by fruit-eating birds. They start life after a resting period that may be only a few days, a few months, or as much as two years. Under cultivation, each kind has to be stored and handled by its own particular method. For this reason, the raising of trees from seed is a task for an expert nurseryman who gives full time to it; amateurs are only likely to succeed with the easiest kinds.

THE LIFE CYCLE

Now that we have looked at the different parts of a growing tree, we can follow its sequence of growth and development. Taking a beech as an example, it starts life from a nut, which is technically a single seed, that fell from a tree one autumn. This nut lies on the moist soil through the winter, never drying out, and escapes being eaten by a wood mouse or a wood pigeon. The warmth of spring starts its life processes, and it draws in more water, swelling a little as it does so. Next it sends out a little root which starts sideways at one end of the nut, then turns downwards and penetrates the soil. Just behind its growing tip, the root bears root-hairs which draw in moisture and mineral food from the earth. This is the start of a root system that will extend for many yards all round the tree's base, exploring an ever-growing volume of soil.

Once root-hold is established, the shoot starts to develop in an odd way. As it grows longer, it bends at right angles, raising the nut itself above the surface of the soil. Two *seed-leaves*, or cotyledons, within the nut, then expand and crack the brown husk, which falls away. Once they are exposed to daylight, the seed-leaves develop chlorophyll, turn green, and begin the essential work of fixing carbon dioxide from the air.

All this happens within a space of four weeks, during which time the beech seedling has drawn its energy from the food reserves stored in the fleshy seed-leaves—a gift from its mother tree. From now on it will be independent. Its own roots will give it water and mineral salts; its own leaves will provide substance and energy. Incidentally, the seed-leaves of beech are broad and blunt, looking quite unlike the true leaves that succeed them. This is a common feature in most trees, and some also have curious *juvenile* leaves that are different to both seed-leaves and their *adult* foliage. All broadleaved trees have two seed-leaves, but conifers have from two to twenty, depending on species.

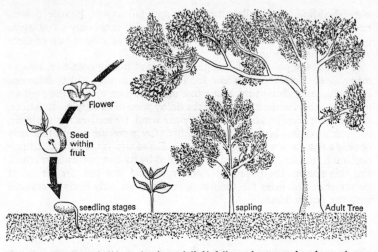

FIGURE 11. A tree's life cycle. A seed (*left*) falls to the ground and germinates as a seedling. This grows into a sapling and eventually becomes an adult tree, which bears flowers. After pollination, the flowers ripen seeds, and these renew the cycle.

Once established, the beech seedling starts to grow from a *shoot bud* set between its two seed-leaves. The shoot that arises bears typical beech leaves, oval and pointed, which begin to nourish the tree. When autumn comes, the shoot may be about three inches tall, and the root below ground will be about that length also. Before it stops growth, the shoot forms a resting bud at the tip of its shoot, while a cambium has already come into being all round its stem. As the weather grows colder, the leaves transfer their movable food reserves into the stems, and then fade, eventually to fall. Root growth slows down too, and the little tree rests through its first winter.

Next spring, as soon as the general temperature rises to about 45° Fahrenheit (6° Centigrade) root growth recommences. Shoot growth soon follows. The brown bud scales fall away from both leaf buds and shoot buds. Green leaves emerge and expand to start afresh the process of carbon fixation. A main *leading shoot* grows upright from the central resting bud, while *side shoots* give rise to twigs on either side. At the same time the cambium, below the bark all round the main stem, starts to produce the first annual ring of wood tissue, so making the stem stout enough to bear both its own increasing weight and the growing volume of sap that it has to carry. Bast and bark tissues, outside the cambium, grow thicker in proportion also. These processes go on steadily until the autumn.

The tree is now launched upon an annual rhythm of growth that may continue for two hundred years or more. There is no set limit either to its size or to its age. It may reach one hundred and twenty feet tall with a crown stretching thirty feet from its base, in all directions, and an even greater root-spread. But eventually its vigour of growth will slacken. It will cease to grow taller, and the outward spread of its branches will be offset by lost twigs. Only its trunk will continue to grow slowly stouter year by year, for the cambium never fails to work

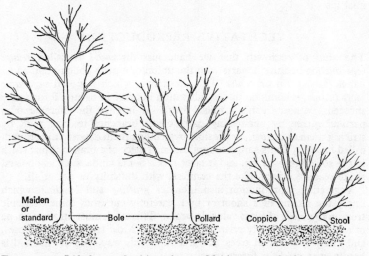

FIGURE 12. Life forms of cultivated trees. Maiden or standard has never been lopped. Pollard is repeatedly lopped about six feet up to give repeated crops of small poles, out of reach of cattle. Coppice is repeatedly lopped at ground level, also for pole crops.

whilst the tree lives. The trunk may become as much as twenty feet round at breast height.

Eventually, some accident brings about the decline and death of every tree. The commonest cause is the chance breakage of a branch which leaves an open wound, exposing heartwood. Those fungi that cause decay colonise this exposed wood by means of airborne spores. Slowly the fine threads of these lowly plants spread through the tree's trunk, causing rot and weakness. Eventually the weakened stem—now only a shell of sapwood and bark, collapses during a gale, and the tree's life is ended.

Some trees bear flowers and seed when only a few years old, and continue to do so throughout life. But a beech normally waits until it is about thirty years old, and even after that it only gives a heavy seed crop, or *mast*, every four or five years. These seed crops are so heavy that—through the sheer numbers involved, many nuts escape being eaten by pigeons, pheasants, rooks, mice, squirrels, and all the other birds and beasts that love to feed on them. During the course of its long life the beech tree will therefore give rise to many hundreds of seedlings, but only a few will advance to the sapling stage, and only one or two can eventually fill the place of the "mother" tree in the tall community of the forest. The rest will die through overshading, crowding out, or other mishaps.

VEGETATIVE REPRODUCTION

The kind of regrowth that we have just discussed is called *sexual reproduction* because it starts with the union of a male pollen grain and a female seed grain or *ovule*. The alternative, which is called *vegetative reproduction*, is common under cultivation but rare in nature, for it rarely succeeds without man's artificial help. It implies the increase of a particular tree by persuading parts of its branches to take root, by striking them as *cuttings*, or possibly by bending them down to the ground, called *layering*. In its simplest application, a piece of a branch is just stuck in the soil, right way up, and it takes root. Some kinds, such as poplars, strike readily; others, like the conifers, with difficulty or not at all.

Vegetative reproduction also includes *grafting* and *budding*, which imply the setting of a shoot or bud, carefully cut from some desirable tree, on to a *stock* of a less valuable strain. This stock must, in all cases, be of a kind that is closely related to the scion. Most fruit trees and roses, and many ornamental trees, are grafted in this way, but the method is hardly ever used for forest trees.

The great advantage of all kinds of vegetative reproduction is that every fresh tree is exactly like the original parent. The stock forms a single *clone* or *cultivar*, and nowadays it may even be patented! In contrast, sexual reproduction always results in a varied progeny, since the hereditary elements of male and female parents are combined in different ways in each individual offspring. This is as true of trees as it is of children.

Though certain trees are easy to grow from cuttings, others need special skills and equipment. Grafting is an art that can only be perfected by practice. With both modes of increase, it is necessary to own, or have access to, a parent stock of the specially fine strain of tree. In practice therefore most planters buy rooted cuttings, or established grafted trees, from professional nurserymen, who make it their business to select and maintain good foundation stocks.

Whether trees are raised from seed or otherwise, they are always prepared for planting as well-established, well-rooted individuals. Their size and age, and hence their cost, varies a great deal, as will be discussed later. Planters are rarely concerned with the earliest stages of tree growth, which call for an exacting knowledge of each different kind. Instead they deal with their charges after they have left their "nursery" stage behind them. At this time of life most sorts have a great deal in common. They are all alike growing through the period of adolescence to their grander mature state. This greatly simplifies their care.

2. Space and Time

FOLLOWING our basic theme that a tree is a growth organism, we must look next at its needs for space over an approximate span of time. Architects have been known to specify a tree of an exactly predesigned size and shape, to set off the lines of a new building, the tree to be brought into being immediately and retained at the same size for as long as the building lasts! With modern techniques the tree-tender can get somewhere near this, at high cost. But the common experience of most of us is that trees start too small and end up too big. We have to plot their progress against a time-span of many years.

Allied to the need for space comes the question of light. There are two sides to this. Leaves need light, and by the same token they cast shade. Every branch that occupies space makes its demands, and also affects its surroundings, to different degrees as it grows larger and older. Altogether, the problems of the planter are: first, how best he can fill the space and the light supply, at his disposal, in the shortest workable time, and second, how he can control growth later on, within these fixed requirements.

Prospective tree-planters are in practice presented with a site already limited in extent. It may be a garden, a new park, a roadside strip, or land for a plantation. Their aim will be to establish, within a reasonable time, attractive specimen trees, screens, or timber crops. The site will seldom be an entirely clear one. There will be obstructions or restrictions, seen or unseen, that limit the tree's living room to a surprising degree. Some of these will apply even in the broad open spaces of a new woodland or forest.

PLANS

The first step is to measure the land available and then to plot the proposed planting on a simple plan. The *constraints* on planting, that is the restrictions of all kinds, physical or legal, should first be marked in. Only then can one see what land is left for expanding trees.

Near buildings and roads this planning must be done with accuracy, to close limits. A foot either way can make a critical difference. Elsewhere there is little advantage in a strictly measured survey, since no tree will grow to, or remain at, any precise size. For practical purposes the following map-scales are recommended.

For small gardens: A plan based on a simple survey, using a tape measure, at a scale of *one inch to five feet*.

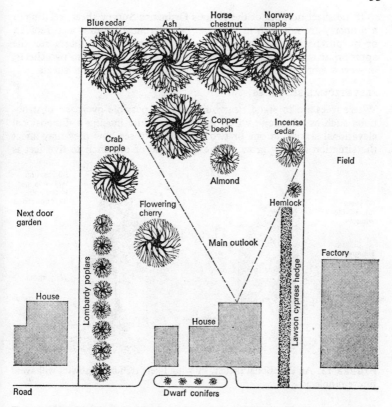

FIGURE 13. Planting plan for a garden, 100 yards deep. Conifers are shaded. Shelterbelt of Lombardy poplars (*left*) also serves as screen to next-door garden. Dense tall hedge of Lawson cypress (*right*) hides factory. Small flowering trees in middle distance. Tall forest trees beyond give woodland atmosphere.

For large gardens: A plan based on tape measurement, or possibly pacing on foot, at a scale of *one inch to ten feet*.

For parklands: The appropriate Ordnance Survey sheet on the scale of *twenty-five inches to one mile* is the best and cheapest basis. In some urban areas, Ordnance Survey sheets on a scale of *fifty inches to one mile* are available, and are naturally better, though more costly.

For plantations and farm shelterbelts: The appropriate Ordnance Survey sheet on the scale of *six inches to one mile*. This scale is accepted by the Forestry Commission for all its planting grant schemes, and also, where they apply, for felling licences.

If the sheet number of the various Ordnance Survey sheets relating to a property are not known, they can be ascertained from a map retailer, or by purchasing the Ordnance Survey County Index sheets for the appropriate scales. Some lands will, of course, extend on to two sheets, or—even more awkwardly—lie at the meeting point of four sheets.

ELEVATIONAL SKETCHES

Where trees are to stand near buildings, or possible overhead obstructions such as telephone wires, it is worth while making a dimensional elevational sketch, in one or two directions, to see how they may affect the situation as they grow. A vertical scale of one inch to five feet is

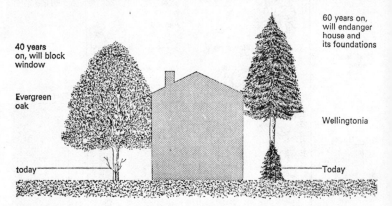

FIGURE 14. An elevational sketch, showing likely trends of growth, will avoid future problems.

appropriate, unless very tall structures are involved, when one inch to ten feet might be used. The likely outline of the trees at several stages of growth can easily be sketched in.

PERSPECTIVE VIEWS

The difference between an elevational sketch and a perspective view is that the former is drawn to a common scale and shows exact dimensions, whereas *perspective* drawing implies a change of scale as objects recede into the distance. Though only an artist can produce a perfect result, anybody can make a rough sketch that will guide a planting scheme. Imagination must of course be used to suggest the likely future outlines of crowns and branches, in relation to their surroundings. The choice of viewpoint matters a great deal. Usually it will be a window or a terrace from which the owner will most often look out over his garden or park. In a public park, it might be a restaurant or similar spot where the public will congregate.

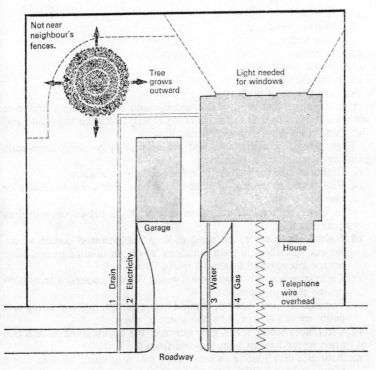

FIGURE 15. In a small garden constraints severely limit the sites for large trees. Allow for five services at front, light for windows and clearance from fences. Allow also for growth of tree.

CONSTRAINTS ON TREE PLANTING

Before deciding what we can plant and where to put it, it is advisable to examine, and to plot on plans and sketches, all the restrictive features on and around the site. These may include:

Overhead

1. Telegraph wires and electric power cables.
2. Aircraft approach paths, near aerodromes.
3. Crowns of neighbouring trees, which are to be retained.

Arising from ground level

4. Buildings.
5. Fences, hedges and walls.
6. Stems of neighbouring trees.
7. Posts and poles to carry wires, lights, or signs.

Below ground

8. Drains or sewers.
9. Water mains.
10. Gas mains.
11. Electric power cables.
12. Telephone cables.
13. Foundations of buildings.

It is fortunate that most of the underground obstructions to tree root spread are usually set at the front of a property, between the house and the road. This leaves back gardens clear.

There are other constraints that are only likely to affect large-scale planting in woodlands, such as:

14. Rights of way for walkers or riders, and forest roads.
15. Fire belts, to be left unplanted, for example, along roadsides or railways.

Five other constraints are often met with in urban or suburban situations, namely:

16. Sight lines—that is, the need to keep unobstructed certain views, for example-those at road junctions, where an ill-sited hedge, bush or tree trunk could become a traffic hazard.
17. Light supply to windows, which would become useless, if trees grew up too close to them.
18. Patterns of light spread, around street lamps, so that roads and paths are not obscured by the shade of trees.
19. Clearances beside roads, etc.; normally the centre point of each tree must be set back at least two feet from the kerb.
20. Attitudes of adjoining owners. As a rule neighbours seldom object to tree branches growing out across their fences, but circumstances may cause them, reasonably or unreasonably, to raise objections. A neighbour with a greenhouse might fairly object to the planting of a dense screen of evergreen Lawson cypress just to the south of it.

Once all these restrictions on the ground available for actual planting have been marked on the plan, and where necessary on an elevational sketch, the remaining free space will be much diminished. But it is better to face the facts at the outset, rather than have to remove, or severely prune, a badly-sited tree later.

It will be seen that certain of the constraints are fairly obvious ones— for example nobody would think of planting a tree, whose trunk must expand as it grows, hard up against a fence or building, or directly in front of a window. Others, such as overhead wires or the need to leave sight lines clear, are only too easily overlooked by people handling small planting stock. Two of the underground restrictions, which can prove very costly if ignored, call for detailed discussion.

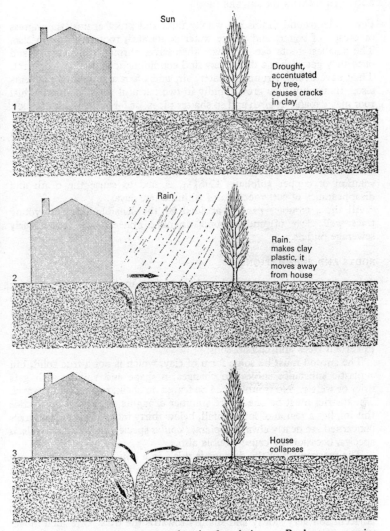

Sun

Drought,
accentuated
by tree,
causes cracks
in clay

Rain

Rain.
makes clay
plastic, it
moves away
from house

House
collapses

FIGURE 16. How tree roots can undermine foundations. 1. Poplar tree, growing on clay soil, transpires water rapidly in drought and accentuates natural cracking of soil. 2. After rain, clay swells and closes cracks, but weight of building causes movement of clay and foundations away from house. 3. Repetition of these slight movements breaks foundations, and house collapses.

ROOTS IN DRAINS OR SEWERS

Few underground drains are wholly tight and proof against the ingress or escape of water, and where water penetrates, roots seek to go also. The smallest roots can insinuate themselves through tiny cracks, and once they get within a drain they find conditions ideal for development. They have at hand running water, air, and often a supply of nutrients also. Inevitably they grow rapidly in two harmful ways. An individual root may expand in girth and so shatter pipes, or force them out of place. Or a mass of rootlets may develop until it blocks the drain.

Often no trouble is suspected until a drain ceases to function. Then a deep dig reveals extensive and expensive damage that must be put right without delay. If a pipe is simply obstructed, but not otherwise damaged, it is worth while trying to clear the blockage by poisoning. A strong solution of copper sulphate, $CuSO_4$, is said to cause the death and disappearance of soft root tissues within a few days.

All these troubles can be avoided by the sensible siting of young trees well clear of underground drainage systems, and particularly sewerage outlets.

ROOTS AND FOUNDATIONS

A large tree set close to a wall is obviously apt to disturb it as the trunk and main roots grow, but the danger of sheer physical upset is limited to a range of a few feet. Another form of danger, far less obvious but equally serious, can arise from large trees at a distance of many feet from a building. This risk of foundation disturbance is, fortunately, limited to certain trees and certain soils.

The subsoil must be some form of clay, which is not a true solid, but a plastic substance subject to changes in shape and volume as it gets drier or wetter. No trouble need be feared on chalk, rock, sand or gravel. The district must be one where summer droughts occur, and in practice this implies a region of low rainfall, below thirty inches a year. The trees concerned are nearly always poplars, *Populus* species, though elms, *Ulmus* species, occasionally cause trouble also.

The mechanism of the damage is this. In a hot dry summer clay soils lose water, shrink, crack, and move. Shrinkage is increased, and given a directional trend, wherever a large tree is actively transpiring water from a large crown of foliage. If such a tree stands to one side of a building, the weight of the walls tends to move the building's foundations and adjacent soil very slowly and slightly towards the tree. One such movement matters little, but repeated movements, over the years, result in the failure of the surrounding earth to support the foundations. These are then pushed sideways from beneath the walls, and the whole building starts to collapse.

Such damage can be avoided if no poplar tree is ever planted within sixty feet of any building on a clay soil. Most cases of damage have occurred in London or Essex, where clay occurs commonly in a region of low rainfall, with high summer temperatures that increase transpiration of moisture.

SPACING THE TREES

Having considered all possible constraints, and plotted the free ground on the plan, you have next to decide how far apart trees should be set. In small-scale work individuals will be plotted singly, but where a large expanse is to be planted up, the specification will be for a certain area at a certain spacing, needing so many plants. Likewise, for a long shelter-belt, the plan will show so many foot-run of belt, with trees spaced so many feet apart, to give the total of plants required.

The many considerations that govern, in theory, the distances at which trees should be spaced, have been resolved, in practice, to simple rules. These will not apply everywhere, but planters should always ask themselves whether there are real reasons for departing from them.

FOREST SPACINGS

The commonest spacing for trees to be raised as timber is five feet apart each way. There is nothing magic about this particular figure, except that it comes close to the 1.5 metre spacing that is usual in many countries with a metric system of measurement.

Experience has shown that if trees are spaced more closely, costs rise out of proportion to any advantage gained. For example, if spacing is reduced by only one foot, to a four-four distance, then the costs of plants and planting go up by 57%. The only gains are quicker weed suppression, smaller gaps where a few trees fail, and a greater number of surviving trees from which the forester can select the best specimens, for his final timber crop later on.

Conversely, if trees are spaced farther apart, the costs of plants and planting fall sharply, but weed suppression is slow and therefore the plantation must be weeded for a further year or more; gaps where only a single tree has failed are so wide that they leave a serious hole in the crop, with a loss of timber production; the choice of good trees for the final timber stand is much reduced.

Spacings of six feet apart are, however, used for quick-starting conifers such as Douglas fir and Japanese larch in districts where they are known to do well and to suppress weed growth early. A few exceptional timber trees—poplars, willows, and elms, are spaced much farther apart, averaging twenty feet in each direction.

The following table of the number of trees needed per acre at various spacings, and the related growing space per tree, may prove a useful guide.

FOREST SPACINGS

Distance between trees in feet	Growing space per tree in square feet	Number of trees needed per acre
3	9	4840
4	16	2722
4½	20¼	2151
5	25	1742
5½	30¼	1440
6	36	1220
7	49	889
8	64	680
9	81	537
10	100	435
12	144	302
15	225	193
18	324	134
20	400	109
24	576	75
26	676	64
30	900	48
40	1600	27
50	2500	17
60	3600	12

This table shows that the growing space allotted to each tree rises very rapidly, with quite a small increase in spacing. Conversely, the number of trees needed for each piece of ground falls.

SHELTERBELT SPACINGS

These resemble forest spacings, except that the trees in alternate rows are "staggered". This implies that the trees of each row stand opposite gaps between the trees of two adjacent rows. The obvious advantage here is that the wind finds it harder to blow through "blocked" pathways than through continuous gaps between parallel rows of trees. The staggered rows need just as many trees per acre, as do normal rows.

A useful improvement is to space shelterbelt trees on the *equilateral triangular* system, which puts every tree at the same distance from the six trees nearest to it. Each tree can be regarded as one corner of a group of equal-sided triangles, repeated indefinitely. To achieve this, it is only necessary to "stagger" the trees as before, and to reduce the distance *between rows* to seven-eighths of the distance *between trees* along

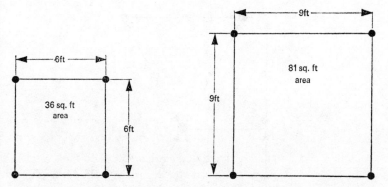

FIGURE 17. Spacing 'on the square'. Trees set six feet apart need thirty-six square feet each; 1,210 trees go to one acre. An increase of spacing by half, to nine feet apart, will more than double area per tree, at eighty-one square feet, and cut number needed to 536 trees per acre.

a row. For example, where the *between-tree* distance is eight feet, the *between-row* distance should be seven feet. See Figure 18, p.42.

This arrangement naturally crowds more trees on to a given area of ground; the number required is that for the *between-tree* distance in the table above, multiplied by 1.15. For example, triangular spacing at eight feet needs $680 \times 1.15 = 782$ trees per acre.

ORCHARD SPACINGS

The following spacings are usual for fruit trees. They are given here mainly as a guide to the amount of space that should be allowed for ornamental trees of comparable size.

	Feet apart	Square feet per tree	Trees per acre
Standards:			
apples or cherries	30ft	900	48
Large bushes:			
apples, pears, or plums	20ft	400	109
Small bushes:			
apples	10ft	100	435
Cordons:			
apples	7ft × 2½ft	17½	2,500

ROADSIDE AND AVENUE SPACINGS

As a general rule, it is inadvisable to set roadside trees closer than thirty

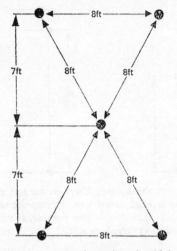

FIGURE 18. Triangular or staggered spacing should be used for hedges or shelterbelts. If trees are eight feet apart along rows, and rows seven feet apart, each tree will stand eight feet away from all its nearest neighbours.

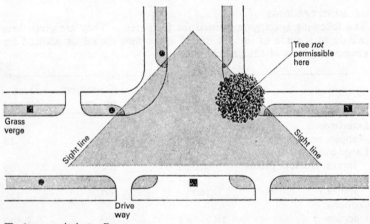

■ = Lamp standard   ● = Tree

FIGURE 19. Roadside planting plan. Trees must not obstruct sight lines of car drivers, nor the light from street lamps, nor driveways. They must stand one foot clear of kerbs, even when full grown.

feet apart, in any direction. Under the Highways Act, 1835, no tree may be planted within fifteen feet of the centre of any highway; this of course gives a tree-to-tree minimum of thirty feet, across the carriage-way. No tree should be set within twenty feet of any road junction; this leaves sight lines clear.

The spacing scheme for an avenue calls for a nice exercise of skill in judging perspective effects over the years, as the trees grow taller. The figures will depend on the length of the avenue, its width, and whether single or double rows of trees line each side. Altogether it is a task for a skilled landscape architect.

HEDGING SPACINGS

These are very much closer than those used for other kinds of tree growth, since the object is to form a dense screen as soon as possible. Distances between trees range from six to twelve inches, with nine inches as an average figure for hawthorn. At a nine inch spacing, four plants go to the yard, eighty-eight to the chain, and 7,240 to the mile. If a double row is used, a satisfactory spacing is one foot along the rows, with six inches between the rows, the trees being "staggered".

HOW FAST DO TREES GROW?

Foresters are often asked a simple question to which there can be no general answer: "How fast will this tree grow?"

Taking height as the most critical measure, one can say that a living tree may—at the one extreme—make no growth at all. It can even lose height through the breakage of its leading shoot. At the other extreme—a young fast-growing poplar on a very good site—it may shoot up by six feet in a single growing season. To give a very broad picture, one can say that most healthy trees, in most parts of the British Isles, grow about one or two feet taller each year for their first sixty years. Height growth then slows off and eventually ceases. Leading exceptions to this rule will be mentioned when the principal kinds are described.

Fast growth may be an advantage—or otherwise. The forester welcomes it, for it means a quick return on his capital investment. The gardener may well prefer slow-growing trees that take a lifetime to fill up his available, and limited, space. Both sorts of tree exist, and can be chosen in advance to suit the need.

OUTWARD GROWTH OF BRANCHES

Whether the outward spread of a tree's crown keeps pace with its upward growth in height, depends partly on management. By keeping trees closely crowded together, the forester can restrict crown spread to a surprising degree. In an unthinned plantation of spruce, trees sixty feet tall may stand only ten feet apart, with individual branches only five feet long. In contrast, open-grown broadleaved trees expand their crowns steadily, claiming more space and more light, and casting a broader shade.

Again we have the question: "How fast?" Few figures are available for open-grown trees, but there are many records of the growth of heavily thinned forest plantations. These clearly show that, under woodland conditions, the outward spread of a tree's branches is very much slower than the upward advance of its trunk. The actual branches will be longer than the figures that follow suggest, because they grow at an acute angle (upwards or downwards) to the trunk; but the *horizontal* spread of the crown is close to that stated.

During the period of a tree's active upward growth, say the first seventy years, to a height of some one hundred feet, crown spread is slow—it may be only one tenth of height growth, on each side, making one fifth overall. This means that a tree fifty feet tall will have an outward branch radius of only five feet, making ten feet across the crown. When it has reached one hundred feet, the branch radius will be only ten feet, giving a span of twenty feet overall.

After this, height growth slackens off, but the outward spread of the crown continues, for perhaps another fifty years. The result may be a tree with a branch radius of one sixth of its height, and an overall span of one third of that height. For example, an oak 120 years old and 120 feet tall may have a branch radius of twenty feet, and a span across the branch tips of forty feet.

It is possible for trees to live and grow in woodlands with much smaller crowns than this, but their trunks are then drawn up and thin, and of lower value as timber.

So much for forest-grown trees. In a garden, park or hedgerow, where the trees are open-grown, we will not find any such simple rules that apply to all trees.

SPACING OPEN-GROWN CONIFERS

Most conifers will not depart a great deal from the general rule that total sideways crown spread is about 20% of height during vigorous youth, increasing to 33% as each tree ages. Only a few conifers, such as the Cedar of Lebanon, *Cedrus libani*, and the stone pine, *Pinus pinea*, commonly develop broader crowns than this. Narrower crowns are only found in exceptional *columnar* or *fastigiate* varieties of the cypresses and kindred trees, such as the Lawson cypress, *Chamaecyparis lawsoniana*.

But if conifers are left to stand at the spacings indicated by these ratios —that is, if the distance between trees in youth is only one fifth of their height, their lower branches will die through overshading, just as they do in the forest. So, in order to keep the trunks fully *furnished* with side branches, almost down to ground level, wider spacings must be used. In such cases, the distance between trees should never be less than one third of their general height. If closer spacing has been done, thinning out should follow as that height increases.

SPACING OPEN-GROWN BROADLEAVED TREES

With the broadleaved trees, so much variation in crown shape and development can occur, that no simple rules for spacing can be laid down. Likely crown spread is only predictable for the *fastigiate* varieties, such as Lombardy poplar, *Populus nigra* variety *italica*, which always have narrow crowns. All other broadleaved trees respond to their surroundings, and to the treatment they receive.

Sycamore and beech, for example, follow the general rules for crown spread when grown in woodland, but spread out much farther when open-grown. In fact, for many years in middle age they appear to favour sideways spread at the expense of height. As soon as they form a crown at all, it is likely to maintain a spread of 40% of their height, or thereabouts.

Lopping, though risky with conifers, is a feasible means of governing the branch spread of broadleaved trees. If the top of the trunk is removed, height growth is naturally checked, while competition between the side branches, which now receive more nourishment from the roots, is stimulated. Many of our broadest-crowned trees will be found, on examination, to be *pollards*. This means that they were topped, many years ago, to yield small poles or firewood. The cluster of side shoots that followed have each forced one another outwards, in their struggle for light, to give a structure that is wide out of all proportion to its height.

Conversely, skilful pruning of side branches may be aimed at checking crown spread, by removing strong side branches. But this is far from easy to achieve, for fresh growth always aims towards a light supply. Frequent pruning is needed for success.

As a working rule, one should allow for the sideways spread of open-grown broadleaved trees being about 40% of height growth. Outward growth towards any direction will thus be about 20% of height growth.

ROOT SPREAD

Another common question often put to foresters is this: "How far do a tree's roots grow outwards?" Those who ask it seem to think that trees are designed in a drawing office and made in a factory, to a set of fixed rules!

Very few investigators have been industrious enough to dig up the whole root systems of forest trees. All we can say in reply is this: "At least as far as crown spread, often several times that."

If the crown is narrow, as in a plantation, root spread will be as much as ten times greater. Roots of individual trees explore the soil for many yards in all directions, criss-crossing with similar exploring roots from other trees. The same happens in an orchard or a garden; no tree confines its roots to its own immediate neighbourhood, if a good supply of water or nutrients lies beyond. It is seldom possible to say that any particular point is positively out of reach of a full-grown tree's roots, under a distance of one hundred yards.

The height of the tree can also be used as a rough-and-ready guide. While a tree's shoots have been going upwards to a height of, say, eighty feet, there is no good reason for believing that its roots may not have spread out sideways at least as far in the same time. That gives a circular zone of eighty feet radius, or 160 feet across.

Depth of rooting is also variable, but to nothing like the same degree. Tree roots are surprisingly shallow. An oak one hundred feet tall may have a tap root that strikes down for only ten feet; all its other main roots will probably be within five feet of the surface. The next chapter will show why this is so.

RANDOM OR REGULAR LAYOUTS?

People who plant timber crops, hedges, or shelterbelts naturally prefer simple regular spacings. Not only are they easier to create on the ground, but they make every later task—weeding, pruning and thinning out—easier to perform. Such regularity is often the last thing that is wanted in garden or parkland planning, for there relief is desired against the straight-line patterns that govern our workaday lives. An infinite range of variation is available, by using differing patterns of placing trees, various spacings at different points, changes in kinds used, and range of life-forms and colours.

Finally, every scheme must be adapted to its own particular site. Even if the surrounding houses are built to a mass-produced plan, each essay in tree planting should be a creation on its own.

3. Soils and Fertilisers

TREE roots make four demands on the soil. Three of these, for support for the trunk, for a constant supply of water, and for mineral nutrients, are obvious enough. The fourth, for air to breathe, is often overlooked, though equally important. Roots can only live in a well-aerated soil. If the ground becomes waterlogged they perish and the tree dies, though occasional brief floods do no harm. In some soils there is a water-table, or level below which free water is usually found. Roots can go down to this, and tap it, but they cannot make use of the waterlogged soil below. This restricts their feeding zone, and may lessen the ability of the soil to support the trunk. Deep drainage can often improve matters.

A tree's root system is rather different from that of a garden plant, or from that of a field crop such as wheat or potatoes. The demands it makes are therefore met in rather different ways. It has a large and permanent framework of perennial main roots which explores a large area of ground, going deeper than the roots of farm crops. These main roots bear shorter-lived side roots that tap every layer of soil, within their reach, that is likely to yield food or moisture.

In a forest, where there is a regular annual leaf fall, many of these feeder roots run only just below the surface. There they recapture the mineral food that falls in the leaves, from the tree's crown; fallen leaves become first leaf-litter and then leaf-mould. Their minerals are fed back into the trunk and crown, forming a nutrient cycle of plant-food that is repeated many times in the tree's lifetime. This explains why the timber grower rarely needs to manure his crop, whereas a corn grower has to do so annually.

Though a tree is far larger than a farm crop plant, it can tap a greater volume of soil over a longer period. This, combined with the nutrient cycle just described, means that a tree's needs are usually met, over its long life-span, by any good garden or farm soil. People who plant trees on land that was formerly used for agriculture, therefore, rarely need to add fertilisers to ensure good growth. Things are not so straightforward in towns and cities, where planting sites may consist largely of rubble, or spoil from some mine or factory.

Foresters who are replanting old woodlands seldom need to add fertilisers. An adequate reserve of mineral food is usually available from the old crop in several forms—decaying branches, or wood ash from fires used to destroy old brushwood, fallen leaves, and decaying roots within the soil. In contrast, people who start new woodlands on fresh ground

—that is, *afforestation* in contrast to replanting—often have to deal with a difficult soil.

The very fact that land is available for afforestation usually means that it is too poor for continued farming use. This in turn implies that the soil is very poor in nutrients, or hard to work because of its physical condition, or has both these drawbacks. It is therefore helpful to look at the various extreme soil types which tree planters may have to tackle. "Ordinary" soil gives them few problems.

Soils are nowadays classified in broad groups according to their pattern of formation. All soils arise from the weathering of parent rocks. They vary according to their underlying bedrock, and also according to the degree of drainage and the character of the vegetation they support.

The main rock formations of the British Isles are shown on geological maps; but the largest scale readily available, the ten miles to one inch Geological Survey of Great Britain, does not give the full detail needed for tree planting. Local variations only appear on one inch to the mile sheets. Unfortunately that is not the end of the story, for soils derived from a single bedrock vary so much that a separate survey is needed. This Soil Survey of Great Britain is still in progress, and soil maps are only available for certain districts. Where soil is a critical feature—which happily is seldom the case—an expert should be brought in.

SOILS

LOAMS AND BROWN FOREST SOILS

Traditional textbooks on farming and gardening always refer to *loams* of various types. A loam is a well-drained, easily worked soil containing varying proportions of relatively coarse-grained sand, fine-grained clay, and *humus*, or organic matter formed by the decay of ploughed-in, or dug in, plant residues from farm or garden crops. It has come into being through centuries of cultivation with the spade or the plough, and has usually been enriched with farmyard manure or artificial fertilisers. The starting point for many of these loams was a group of natural soils known as Brown Earths or Brown Forest Soils. These were formed from the original bedrock under a natural tree cover. They are well-drained and therefore well aerated. The tree planter who gets a good loam for his work is simply restoring to the land the kind of crop that originally brought this soil into being, and established its fertility. He is unlikely therefore to meet many problems.

Many of our parks were first formed by wealthy landowners on the best soils of their estates. Hedgerows also run between the most fertile fields of each country parish. The value of sites for new houses is far greater than the value of the same land for farming; this means that many new gardens stand on first-class agricultural land—land that carried thriving broadleaved forest before the Anglo-Saxon settlers cleared it over a thousand years ago.

Old woodland is not always such a good proposition for new tree planting, because the very fact that it has been left as woodland often means that it was found to have little value for cultivation. The ground was either too steep, too poorly drained, or too poor. This explains why trees in parks often grow more vigorously than those in neighbouring woodlands—the park was chosen for its good soil, the wood was left under trees because its soil was not worth tilling.

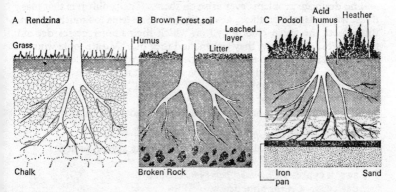

FIGURE 20. Three common forest soils. Rendzina (*left*) found below grass of chalk downs, has narrow dark, humus layer, with unaltered white chalk below. In a Brown Forest Soil (*centre*) the humus shades off gradually through fertile well-rooted loam into broken rock. The infertile Podsol (*right*) forms typically under heather on sandy subsoil. Below the dark humus comes a pale Leached Layer, poor in plant foods; below this a red-black Iron Pan checks drainage and aeration and shuts off roots from sandy subsoil below. Ploughing breaks pan and mixes soil layers.

SOILS ON CHALK AND LIMESTONE

Nearly all soils contain a proportion of the element calcium, which is essential for tree growth, and in practice it is hardly ever necessary, when growing trees, to apply lime to the land. Many limestones are impure ones, containing other rocks besides those made up of calcium carbonate, and the soils derived from these give little trouble to the forester. But there are two important rock formations which need special care.

Both are exceptions to the general rule that geological maps give little practical guidance. One is the chalk, which is always mapped in green; it covers a large proportion of south and east England, all of it lying to the south-east of a line linking Flamborough Head in Yorkshire with Lyme Regis in Dorset. The North Downs, the South Downs, and the Downs of Hampshire, Berkshire, and Wiltshire are all chalk hills, and so are the Chiltern Hills and the Wolds of 'Lincolnshire and Yorkshire. The surface soils on chalk downs may, however, be lime-free in some localities.

The other difficult pure limestone rock is the Carboniferous Limestone, which has a scattered distribution farther to the north and west, mainly near coalfields. This is mapped in pale blue.

Both Chalk and Carboniferous Limestone rocks are pervious to water, and no drainage problems ever arise on them. The problem is that many trees, when planted on them, absorb into their systems too much calcium; this upsets the green chlorophyll on which their life processes depend; their leaves turn yellow, they sicken, and they die. Most people who live on Chalk know that it is quite impossible to grow rhododendrons and allied shrubs on such soils. It is also very difficult to grow most conifers to any respectable size; any conifer will start well, and people who only want dwarf speciments need have no worries. But the *only* common conifers which remain happy to maturity are those listed below:

Conifers that thrive on Chalk and Limestone
   Austrian and Corsican pines, *Pinus nigra* in its several varieties
   Western red cedar, *Thuja plicata*
   Lawson cypress, *Chamaecyparis lawsoniana*
- Atlas cedar, *Cedrus atlantica*
   Larches, *Larix* species
   Broadleaved trees show a far greater tolerance of pure limestone rocks, probably because—like the larches—they shed their lime-rich leaves annually Beech is particularly vigorous, and is in fact the leading timber producer on most limestone formations.

CLAYS

Clay soils are inherently fertile but not very pervious to water. Yet they are seldom watertight, and moisture moves through them slowly through small gaps, such as those left where old roots have decayed. Provided drainage is good, they carry satisfactory timber crops.

Where drainage is poor, three adverse things happen. First, since roots need air, they do not go down into the waterlogged zone below the effective drainage level. This means that trees are undernourished, for only the top layers of the ground are being explored. Second, as these top layers easily dry out, the trees may actually suffer from drought in a hot dry spell, although ample water lies just below, where the trees cannot reach it. Third, because of the shallow rooting depth, the trees are apt to blow over in gales, through failure of roothold; this is most likely to happen when the ground is wet and the clay is plastic. The remedy is thorough and deep drainage, discussed later.

PEATS

Some organic matter, that is litter or humus derived from the decay of leaves, stems and roots, is found in every soil, and it contributes to drainage, aeration, and fertility. Peat soils are those in which the whole structure is built up of decayed plant remains, sometimes to a depth of several feet. Special treatment is needed to enable such ground to carry timber crops. First it must be ploughed and drained, and then—at planting time—phosphatic manures must be added. Only the larger forestry enterprises are likely to tackle this difficult soil type, and they will naturally draw on the fund of specialised local knowledge held by Government forestry departments.

SANDS

Dunes of pure blown sand have been stabilised and afforested by a few large estates and also by the Forestry Commission. The usual technique is to cover the sand with brushwood. This checks drifting until the new tree crop, usually of pine, has established itself and is able to shield the soil below. Brushwood and tree foliage check the wind that would otherwise carry away the sand. Impure sands, such as those of the Greensand formation, support most timber crops without the need for fertilising or special measures to keep them stable.

PODSOLS

These are an important group of soils found in poor heathy country. Their structure, which is clearly seen where a cutting is made through them, consists of a series of layers, variously coloured, like a sandwich-cake. Below the brown leaf litter there is a pale-coloured *leached* zone, from which all the nutrient minerals have been removed by water trickling downwards. Below this comes the *deposition* layer, in which dark-coloured black, brown, or rust-red minerals are deposited; this forms a hard layer called a *pan*, which resists the passage of water, air, and roots. Below this again comes the unaltered parent material of the soil—commonly a sand, clay or gravel.

The whole structure of a podsol is unfavourable to plant growth—which explains why such soils are so often left under heather, instead of being farmed. No trees will thrive on them until this layered structure has been broken up by ploughing, and young trees often need phosphatic fertilisers also.

SLAG HEAPS AND RUBBLE

Foresters are occasionally asked to plant trees on the dumps of waste material arising from mining or manufacturing operations. These "soils" are very difficult propositions, for several reasons. They have no normal soil structure, and their chemical composition is quite abnormal. The heaps have steep slopes, and their surfaces are not stable. Running water may cause serious erosion until some kind of plant cover develops —a slow process. Changes in the physical and chemical character of the dumps may go on for many years, and some may even catch fire! Although it is possible to grow trees to screen such dumps, and possibly to yield timber also, it is a task for the expert.

Ordinary builders' rubble and the spoil from excavations for house-building, etc., causes little difficulty. One common result is that *two* soil layers develop. One is the original soil at its original level; the other is superimposed on it. Tree roots soon exploit both.

BANKS

Along roadsides, tree planting is often done on the sides of cuttings and embankments made by the engineers when constructing the roadway. If the work has been skilfully done, the surface will be at, or less than, the natural *angle-of-repose* for the material concerned. This means that it is unlikely to slip downhill to any troublesome degree, though some soil erosion may occur before the surface gets grassed over.

In a cutting, the subsoil is exposed on the bank face, and the normal surface-soil structure is lacking. Cultivation and manuring are therefore desirable when planting is done. On an embankment, subsoil will again predominate, though some good top soil may have been dumped also. So similar steps should be taken. Once trees are established their network of roots binds the soil, and further erosion or slipping is checked.

CHANGES IN SOIL LEVEL AROUND STANDING TREES

At the collar of a tree, where the trunk joins the roots, a radical change takes place in a tree's structure and mode of life. A change of soil level amounting to more than a few inches can be fatal to a standing tree. If a cutting or embankment has to be made, and the tree is too large to be moved, one or other of the following steps should be taken:

1. Where a cutting is made, a pillar of earth must be left for at least three feet around the tree's base, firmly supported by a stout masonry or concrete wall, having good foundations.

2. Where the level of surrounding ground is to be raised, forming an embankment, a "well" must be formed. A circular retaining wall should be built within this "well", to hold back the ground on all sides. On all but the most porous soils, a drain must be provided to prevent the "well" becoming a water hole.

Work of this kind is costly, so one should consider carefully whether it is essential to retain the tree. With modern tree-moving plant it could possibly be lowered or raised, as the surroundings required. Or it might be felled and a young replacement set up in its stead.

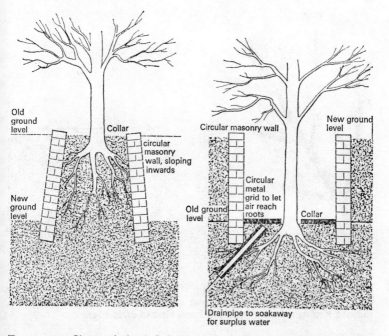

FIGURE 21. Changes in level. *Left*, where ground is *lowered*, tree is left on an earth pillar, held up by a masonry wall. *Right*, where ground is *raised*, tree is left in a 'well', surrounded by a sunk wall, with provision for drainage and aeration of roots. Tree's collar must remain at original level, in each case.

MEASURES FOR SOIL IMPROVEMENT

DRAINAGE

This is the soil improvement measure that has the widest application in practice. It is sometimes achieved by a partial ploughing of the ground, sometimes by dug drains, and sometimes by a combination of the two. Rising wages have made draining with hand tools a very costly job. Machines are used more and more, and can be hired from contractors at fair rates. The plough, where it will go, is cheaper than any alternative machine.

Drains near trees should preferably be open ones, that is, ditches. Pipe or "tile" drains set below the soil are liable to be clogged or at least disturbed by tree roots, but they have to be accepted in some circumstances, for example around sports grounds.

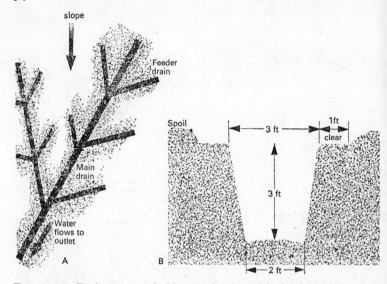

FIGURE 22. Drainage: A, typical layout of main and feeder drains in herring-bone patterns to catch water moving down slope. B, typical cross-section, showing sloping sides and spoil piled well clear of drain edge.

Spacing and siting will vary with the lie of the land, and so will depth and width. *One cannot overdrain.* In our moist climate trees thrive on the most porous soils, and all that drainage can do is to create a like movement of water and air on the less porous ones.

The following figures show *average* dimensions, and distances apart, for drains used in forest practice:

Main drains
   300 feet apart, or set in bottoms of natural valleys
   4½ feet deep
   4½ feet wide at top
   3 feet wide at bottom
Feeder drains
   60 feet apart
   3 feet deep
   3 feet wide at top
   2 feet wide at bottom

It will be seen that the top of a drain is always wider than the bottom giving a cross-section that is technically a *trapezium*. Sloping sides are absolutely essential. Vertical sides invariably crumble under the action of frost and moving moisture, fall in and block the watercourse.

The amount of fall in the bed of the drain is rarely critical. Provided the outlet is clear, water will run. Sudden changes in the degree of fall, and sudden turns in the path of the drain, should be avoided, as they lead to scouring. Scouring can in turn lead to the collapse of drain sides and the blockage of the channel.

In some situations it will be found, on careful examination, that the waterlogging of the land arises from a hidden spring, or a series of small springs such as often lie at the foot of a bank. One drain carefully sited

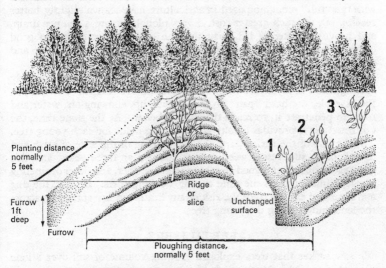

FIGURE 23. Forest ploughing is usually partial, with deep furrows cut every five feet. Trees are normally planted five feet apart on the 'furrow side'. *Right*, three alternative planting positions: 1, Furrow Bottom, used on dry soils; 2, Furrow Side; 3, Ridge Top.

to pick up such spring water will do more good than a whole network that only collects some of it by chance.

Feeder drains should never run straight up and down hill. They should go at an angle to the slope, so that they intercept water flowing downhill through the soil.

Trees should obviously be planted clear of drains—at least five feet back from the drain centre.

PLOUGHING

The ploughing of land before tree planting has become a routine measure on most bare land that is to be afforested for the first time. All the development in Britain was carried out by the Forestry Commission, but many large estates and forestry contractors have now followed its lead. It is a highly technical operation that calls for powerful equipment— crawler tractors pulling giant ploughs—designed and adjusted for the soil concerned. Expert advice should be sought for each site before it is done. Here we can only consider how this cheap and commercially successful method of soil improvement works.

Forest ploughing is done in strips corresponding to the distance between planting rows. The usual distance apart is five feet. Experiments with the "full" ploughing used in agriculture have shown slightly better results, but at much greater cost. Every plough furrow is an open drain, and provided water is led away through a few larger drains to good outlets, ploughed land cannot become waterlogged. So good aeration and an adequate rooting depth are assured for the whole crop.

Close to each tree, where it will go through the critical stage of early rooting, the soil layers are ripped through and overturned. In a podsol, for example, the hard "pan" layer is broken up, allowing air, water and roots to penetrate it, to reach the subsoil below. At the same time, the upturned earth provides a cultivated planting point for each young tree. The digging of the furrow, and the overturning of the slice of earth and turf from it, suppresses weed growth for two or three years, and this gives each young tree a good start over grass, heather, and other competing plants, whilst at the same time cutting weeding costs. Finally, the dug and upturned earth lessens the risk of any heathland fire spreading across the land and burning the young trees.

FERTILISERS

We saw earlier that trees exploit a growing volume of soil over a long span of years, and return much of the nutrients they gain to that soil, when their leaves fall or their branchwood and roots decay. In any plantation, which is thinned at intervals, the surviving trees have less competition from their neighbours after each thinning has been made, while further nutrients are released as the roots and branchwood of the removed trees decay.

In practice fertilisers are only applied to trees in a few particular circumstances that make them worth while, notably:

1. The establishment of forest crops on very poor heaths, peat bogs, etc., where experience and chemical analysis have shown notable shortages of key elements.

2. Establishment of ornamental trees on poor sites, such as spoil banks.

3. Occasionally, to promote better growth in established ornamental trees showing signs of decline.

4. On occasion, for fruit trees in orchards.

5. In forest nurseries, where repeated crops of young trees are raised annually on the same land, as discussed under "Propagation" in Chapter 6, page 85.

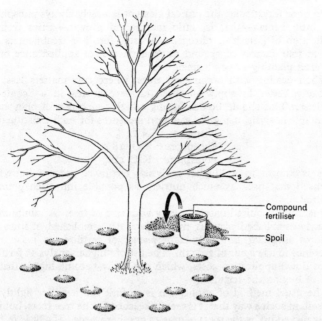

FIGURE 24. Fertilising a mature tree. Holes are dug about five feet apart under the tree's crown. Compound fertiliser is applied and the spoil replaced.

Essential Elements

Though many chemical elements are needed, in greater or lesser amounts, for plant growth, only three are usually in such short supply that it becomes worth while to add them in fertilisers. These are:

Phosphorus (Chemical symbol P)
Potassium (Chemical symbol K)
Nitrogen   (Chemical symbol N)

CHEMICAL FERTILISERS

These are manufactured substances made to fixed formulae, which guarantee a set amount of each element in each pound or ton of fertiliser. The same element may be made up in various compounds, but the quantity present is always known. It must, by law, be declared by the seller. Chemical fertilisers are easily obtained from large companies; they are easy and clean to handle, and their costs of transportation and distribution are relatively low.

They may be applied as "straight" fertilisers that add a single element, or as "complete" fertilisers, already mixed, which add a known proportion of each of the three main nutrients needed.

On poor forest soils, the critical element is nearly always phosphorus, and little benefit—that is, little increase in growth—arises from the application of potash or nitrogen. A usual fertiliser treatment is from two to four ounces of ground mineral phosphate applied once only—just after planting—to each small tree.

When dealing with ornamental trees, where cost matters less, it is probably better to apply all three major elements in a "complete" fertiliser. This should be one having a high proportion of phosphorus. A suitable analysis, using the standard measures for each constituent, is:

$$\text{Nitrogen:} \quad \text{N } 12\%$$
$$\text{Phosphorus: } P_2O_5 \text{ } 18\%$$
$$\text{Potassium:} \quad K_2O \text{ } 12\%$$

This is known as a "higher-analysis" fertiliser, because ingredients are used that pack as much nutrient as possible into each pound of material.

Quantities required naturally vary with size of tree. A minimum for a newly-established plant is two *ounces*. An established, mature tree, requires as much as twenty-eight *pounds* of fertiliser to make much difference to its vigour of growth. The use of "higher-analysis" fertilisers keeps down application costs, which can easily become higher than the cost of buying the fertiliser.

The usual method of application is to fork the fertiliser lightly into the soil, in such a way that it is readily reached by the tree roots, but is not easily picked up by the roots of grasses or other weeds. If a little fertiliser is applied at planting time, it is fairly easy to work it in to a patch of soil that bears few or no weeds. In contrast, the large quantities needed for mature trees have to be applied in small doses, in holes dug at suitable intervals throughout the tree's known rooting zone. Normally this is done below the crown of foliage, in doses of eight ounces or so at each point. A useful rule-of-thumb prescribes one pound of fertiliser for each inch of a tree's girth.

ORGANIC MANURES

These consist of animal dung or plant waste. Their composition is very variable, and they never contain more than a small percentage of the essential elements. They are bulky and heavy, and most hold much water; further they are awkward to handle, and often dirty and smelly.

Despite these drawbacks, organic fertilisers hold a definite, though a small, place in tree-growing, because they supply humus to the soil, and this humus is a natural soil conditioner and rooting medium in which tree roots are well adapted to thrive. The quantity of nitrogen in farmyard manure, for example, is only about 1% but it is released slowly and is taken up by the roots when it is needed, whereas the nitrogen in chemical fertilisers is more soluble and is liable to be leached out of the soil before much has been picked up by the roots.

Spent hops, a by-product of the beer trade, which is sold cheaply by brewery firms, is a very good organic manure for trees of all ages. Its physical structure is satisfactory, it is weed-free, and it is rich in phosphorus. It is widely used in forest nurseries, and makes a good mulch to apply to newly-planted trees. Hop *manure*, which consists of spent hops enriched with artificial fertilisers, is better still, and is the handiest kind of manure for the small-scale tree grower to apply. It is widely marketed and obtainable from most nurserymen.

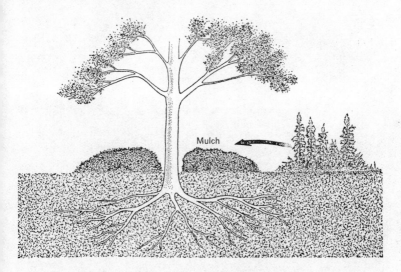

FIGURE 25. Mulching. Grass and weeds (*right*) are cut and piled around recently planted trees as a mulch. This checks weeds near tree and provides cool moist rooting conditions, ensuring survival through droughts.

MULCHING

On any soil, including rich ones that do not call for cultivation, drainage or manuring, the operation called mulching is a worthwhile aid to newly-planted trees. It is not followed in forest practice—except occasionally as part of the weeding work—because of its cost. Where ornamental trees are being grown it is fully justified. A mulch consists of a layer of organic matter spread over the surface of the soil. Straw and leaf mould make good mulches, but recently-cut grass, which is always on hand when a crop is weeded, is equally suitable. During the first summer or two after planting, the cut grass and weeds should be heaped in a shallow pile round the base of each tree. Just how this helps growth is uncertain; it checks weed growth, keeps the surface of the ground cool and moist, and supplies some nutrients as it breaks down. It certainly proves a very effective aid to establishment and healthy early growth, at low cost.

Finally, let us go back to our opening paragraph and recall that tree roots must always have air, and therefore a freely-drained soil. Except on the poorest land, failures through "poor soil" are far more likely to be due to bad drainage than to any lack of mineral nutrients.

4. Climate, Wind and Shelter

CLIMATE, like soil, is one of the hard facts that the planter must accept and come to terms with, before he puts in his trees. But his ability to alter wind and weather is even less than his power to improve the ground. The climates of western Europe and North America are particularly trying to perennial woody plants that must live through scores of years to reach maturity. In that time they are sure to encounter great extremes of heat and cold, drought and rainfall, and exceptional gales that threaten to lift them from the land. The meteorologist's maps commonly show averages, which are only the broadest of guides to anyone raising a long-term crop. What matters to the forester are the *extremes*, which are much harder to ascertain. *Average* rainfall and *average* temperature never harmed any tree, nor did an *average* wind ever blow one down!

This chapter will therefore be concerned with the problems that arise from the extremes of climatic variation—frost, drought, and high wind speeds; and also with two major kinds of impurities in the air—smoke and fumes, and sea-salt. No planting site is immune from one or another of these drawbacks. Each should be assessed before planting, and sensible steps should be taken—by a good layout and a sound choice of species—to minimise future damage.

CLIMATE

EXTREME WINTER COLD

What are the features of the West European climate that make extremes so important? The British Isles, and the Scandinavian and French peninsulas, project westwards from the main European continent, across the course of the warm Gulf Stream. So long as the prevailing south-west winds blow, they bring a climate that is remarkably warm, if rather wet, in winter. Whilst our more inland Continental neighbours to the east get frost and snow, we enjoy, or endure, rain and mist. For countries so far north, we get a mild, or "open" winter. In the British Isles foresters can continue to transplant trees from October right through to April, with only an occasional break for hard frost, whereas the German forester cannot move anything until the ground thaws in late spring.

If, however, the winds change, northerly or easterly gales may sweep across the western islands and peninsulas within a few hours, bringing with them arctic conditions that recall Siberia or the summits of the

Alps. Very severe cold, such as occurred in the winter of 1962 to 1963, kills off half-hardy trees such as the Australian *Eucalyptus* species and the Monterey cypress, *Cupressus macrocarpa*, from southern California. Only along a *very* narrow western coastal zone can you be sure of getting such trees, which are essentially sub-tropical, to survive. People who live in the favoured districts naturally like to raise rare and exotic palms, eucalyptus, and dracaenas, but anybody who tries to raise them elsewhere is simply inviting expensive disappointment. So we must define the regions where success is likely.

Zones suitable for sub-tropical trees
> The coasts of Scotland and the Western Isles, from western Sutherland south to the Solway Firth.
> The coasts of Ireland, Wales and the Isle of Man.
> The English coasts from the Solway Firth to the Dee, and from the Severn round Cornwall as far east as Worthing.
> The Isle of Wight, the Scilly Isles, and the Channel Isles.
> The Atlantic coast of France, as far east as the Seine.

Zones utterly unsuitable for sub-tropical trees
> The eastern Scottish and English coasts from Caithness south to Kent and East Sussex.
> All coasts of Continental Europe, north and east of the Seine.
> All inland districts in Ireland, Britain or north-west Continental Europe.

THE SPRING FROST PROBLEM

In countries with a "Continental" climate, which include those of the main European mainland, most of northern Asia, and all North America except the far west, there is a steady and predictable march of temperature as the year advances. In winter the ground and the air freeze. In spring, the ground thaws, warmer winds blow, and trees open their tender buds, and expand their delicate shoots, secure from risk of freezing.

Under the "Maritime" climate of the British Isles and north-west Europe, however, warm spring days influenced by south-west winds from the Gulf Stream occur early and unpredictably. They encourage shoot growth. If—as usually happens every year, easterly winds, or even still clear nights, follow, even if only on a few occasions, the tender shoots are suddenly exposed to freezing temperatures. Spring frosts, as they are called, strike at night. Though they may last for only a few hours on one night of an otherwise warm April or May, they can do considerable harm to trees.

Naturally, trees that have come from Continental climates, and particularly those from eastern North America, suffer most. But native kinds such as beech and ash, and even the Sitka spruce from western North America, can receive severe setbacks. The appearance of the young shoots of susceptible trees, after a really hard spring frost, is startling.

FIGURE 26. Only a narrow zone along the western and southern shores of Britain is suitable for sub-tropical trees.

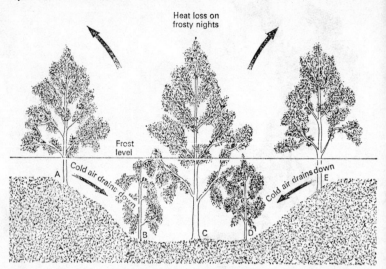

FIGURE 27. A frost hollow. On still cloudless nights, loss of radiant heat to outer space causes freezing, intensified by downward drainage of heavy cold air. Trees (a) and (e), outside hollow, do not suffer. Trees (b) and (d) have shoots and foliage killed, and are crippled. Leading shoot of tree (c) has grown out of hollow; only the lower branches are frosted.

They are cut right back as though burnt, and appear shrivelled, with black, brown, or grey foliage that never recovers. Nevertheless, the trees as a whole are seldom killed. After a pause, they put out a second crop of shoots which makes a small amount of growth that year—perhaps half of the normal quota.

The remedies? One is to avoid planting trees known to be spring-frost-tender in "frost hollows", where still air collects on cloudless frosty nights. To put it another way, only trees known to be hardy—such as most pines, birches, sycamores, poplars and willows, should be put in such places.

The second remedy is to keep as much side-shelter and overhead shelter as possible. Most of the harm arises when the heat from the surface of the soil radiates out, towards a cloudless sky, on a still night. Quite a light overhead cover of birch foliage, or the side-screen of a tall hedge, shelterbelt, or building, will hold back enough warmth to prevent lethal freezing temperatures being reached.

THE SPRING DROUGHT PROBLEM

Despite a lot of silly proverbs about February fill-dyke, March winds, and April showers, spring in north-west Europe is *dry*. Only Ireland and the western coastal mountains of Britain can be sure of enough rain at that time of year to make the transplanting of trees a simple and trouble-free operation. Elsewhere, long spells of rainless weather, accompanied by dry easterly winds, can be confidently expected year after year. Lack of soil moisture, coupled with these drying winds when shoot growth starts, proves fatal to millions of newly planted trees every year. It is the planter's worst risk.

One remedy is autumn planting. If the trees can be got in by the end of October, or even mid-November, their roots will make enough growth in the still-warm soil to give a good anchorage against midwinter winds and frosts, and losses will be low.

But due in part to human procrastination and in part to a belief that trees are safer in a nursery for the worst of the winter, most planting is done in the spring. The one effective precaution against drought loss after spring planting is this: *firm the soil*. After the tree is in, stamp on the surrounding earth brutally, as though you wished to crush the tender roots. You *won't* crush them. Instead you will give that firm contact that is essential to ensure early uptake of scarce soil moisture, by the root-hairs.

A handy precaution is to test the firmness of each plant's roots by a gentle tug. If the plant moves, it is too loose to live through a drought. Pull it right out and replant it more firmly.

In the face of this drought menace, it is futile to put in any young trees that are not, in simple terms, *well-rooted*. To get the essential bushy root system, the nurseryman transplants his stock at considerable cost, or at least *undercuts* the roots. In some favoured climates, it is possible to plant forests with seedling trees, without the cost of transplanting, but not here. Likewise, natural seedlings from the woods seldom survive replanting, simply because they lack the necessary bunch of bushy roots.

To be drought-proof, a young tree must have ample bushy roots, a short shoot, and a stout stem.

WINDS AND GALES

Winds govern the work of the tree tender in many ways. South-westerly winds bring warmth and rain and are generally favourable to growth. North-easterly ones bring frost, snow, and drought, which hinder the development of his charges. Gales seldom harm young trees, but as trees grow taller and larger, they present an increasing resistance to that violent movement of air, or air current, that we call a gale. The wind-force is then so great that, if the ground is soft and the roothold shallow —as commonly occurs on a waterlogged clay, the whole tree may be overthrown and hurled to the ground. Occasionally—though far more rarely—a whole tree trunk, or several large branches, may be shattered.

Damage would be far more frequent but for a curious scientific fact, discovered as recently as 1963 by Alistair Fraser of the Forestry Commission's research team. When a gale strikes a free-standing tree, the tree bends its branches into a tighter bundle, so that it presents a much reduced surface to the wind. The harder the wind blows, the narrower the tree's crown becomes. Watch out for this when next you see a birch or a pine swept by a fierce gale; the effect is quite visible to the acute observer, although it was only discovered by mounting young trees in a giant wind tunnel, used by aircraft designers.

Because they extend so far out into the Atlantic Ocean, the British Isles suffer worse, and more frequent, gales than any other part of western Europe or America. Trees considered wind-resistant in other lands, such as Douglas fir in British Columbia or Norway spruce in central Europe, suffer severe wind damage in Britain and Ireland. The worst-hit districts are—as one might expect—Northern Ireland and North-West Scotland. Everywhere, wind-force and gale damage increases as one goes up the hills, and gets farther from the physical shelter of ridges or mountain masses. Likewise, damage is far worse near the coasts than it is inland.

What steps can be taken to lessen wind damage? The most important one is good drainage at the outset, and the effective maintenance of drains throughout the life of the tree or the timber crop.

After this comes the adequate, *and regular*, thinning out of plantations, whenever it is needed. Many windblows in the past occurred in stands of trees that were, by modern standards, underthinned; or else, even more frequently, in stands that had been given a sudden, overdue, thinning just before a gale struck. Open-grown trees, and trees exposed to constant wind pressure in shelterbelts, suffer least in storms, because they have developed both crowns and root systems strong enough to meet the forces involved. "Irregular" stands such as those tended under shelterwood methods, with mixed ages, kinds and sizes of trees also suffer little.

Another common-sense measure is the removal, or at least the severe pruning, of all old trees that show any sign of disease or decay. Many reports of windbreak are found to arise from the mistaken retention of trees that had already become dangerous.

There will always remain the exceptional gale, with wind speeds exceeding 100 miles per hour, that will cause havoc despite every care. Foresters can console themselves with the thought that this only occurs, in any one place, about once every hundred years, and that few trees ever blow down until they are big enough to yield marketable timber!

Growers of tall specimen trees are often distressed to see that their leading shoots, on which further height growth depends, have been blown away by a spring gale. New leaders may arise—only to suffer the same fate whilst they are still soft and young. Nothing can be done about this. We have to accept the fact that, in windswept islands and coastal districts, few trees are ever going to exceed one hundred and fifty feet in height. The three hundred-foot redwoods found in California grow in a far less windy climate.

IMPURITIES IN THE AIR

THE SMOKE PROBLEM

Earlier on we saw that a tree's leaves are *breathing* organisms that absorb carbon dioxide from the air; they require also a constant supply of oxygen, and they also give out water vapour. They do this through fine pores in their surfaces, and any soot or other solid matter deposited on the leaf surface checks the flow of air, and reduces growth.

Next, leaves need sunlight to give them the energy needed to turn the carbon dioxide into solid substances. Any coating of soot or other solids restricts the energy available for this purpose.

Further, the burning of coal, oil, gas or even wood, releases into the air small but significant quantities of the gas, sulphur dioxide, SO_2. This is carried into the leaves along with the rest of the air, and there it unites with water to form sulphurous acid, H_2SO_3, which is actively poisonous to plant tissues. As a side issue, it is also poisonous to fungi, and checks some leaf diseases, but on the whole it does serious harm.

Modern ways of using fuel more efficiently, and the creation of smoke-less zones, have lessened damage to trees caused by:

1. blocking of breathing pores by soot and solids.
2. darkening of leaf surfaces by soot and solids.

But the third adverse factor:

3. poisoning by sulphur dioxide, remains unchanged, since few fuel-users can effectively take steps to stop this unseen gas escaping. It is found in the exhaust fumes of cars and lorries, as well as in those from gas, coal, oil and wood fires.

The best defence against smoke and fume damage is provided by the trees themselves. Deciduous trees—which means most broadleaved ones and also the larches amongst the common conifers, shed their leaves each autumn, and so get rid of tissues that have become clogged and coated with soot, and partially poisoned by sulphur dioxide. The next year they start with a fresh set of foliage.

Evergreens, in contrast, make each leaf do several years work, and only renew a proportion of their foliage each spring. They are thus at a great disadvantage in all smoky, or fume-polluted, zones. Evergreens include all common conifers, other than larch, and a few hardy broadleaved trees, such as the holm oak, *Quercus ilex*.

The tree planter must accept this state of affairs. He cannot, with success, grow evergreens in the heart of cities, nor close to any factory, power station, or gas works that regularly sends forth smoke, dust, or fumes.

How close? There can be no general answer here. Everything depends on local circumstances, and it cannot be taken for granted that these will remain the same throughout the lifetime of a tree. Things may improve or get worse. Ever since 1940 there has been a progressive lessening of the amount of soot carried in the air of our large cities, though the amount of sulphur dioxide has, unfortunately, increased. The millions of domestic chimneys no longer send up, all day long, their former smutty plumes of half-burnt soft coal. But where large power stations and industrial plants have been built, air pollution has inevitably got worse.

On the whole, the suburban gardener now has far less to worry about to-day, but anyone whose task it is to plant trees near factories or power plants must take more careful steps to avoid smoke-susceptible kinds. For him, evergreens are out!

It is generally true that the western or south-western side of a city suffers less than the north or east side, as prevailing winds carry more smoke towards the north-east. But it is unwise to assume that winds will *never* blow the other way!

THE SALT PROBLEM

The British Isles and the peninsulas of western Europe have exceptionally long coastlines in relation to their area. Many districts in which tree-planting is carried out are very exposed to the open sea, and to the winds that blow from it. A wind of any speed blowing over an ocean picks up minute particles of sea-salt and carries them with it for a matter of miles before they eventually fall back to the sea surface, or land-surface, or are deposited on some solid obstacle—such as a ship's superstructure or a seaside tree.

On the very edge of the sea the soil itself becomes impregnated with salt and only a few plants specially adapted to such soils can thrive. The sea-buckthorn bush, *Hippophaë rhamnoides*, and the tamarisks, *Tamarix* species, are about the only woody plants that can grow there.

Farther inland, damage is done solely by the continued deposition of salt on the delicate surface of young shoots and leaves. The effect is a physical one. The salt, as it dries in the sun, draws out the water from the green tissues, causing them to shrivel up and turn brown. The salt-killed foliage has a burnt appearance, as though scorched by fire or nipped by frost.

If rain falls while the salt is being deposited, or soon afterwards, the salt is washed away and does no harm. But if bright sunshine, or drying winds, follow the salt storm, the brine-spray is soon concentrated to a dangerous degree.

On the landward side of each tree or shrub, where least salt falls, fairly normal growth is made. But on the seaward side the branches can only elongate very slowly, whenever replacement shoots make some headway before being themselves cut back by the next salt-storm. The result is the one-sided growth typical of sea-side trees. They appear to be bent inland by the force of the gale. The main cause, however, is not strong air currents, but rather the salt that they bring with them.

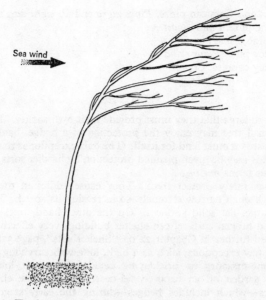

Sea wind

FIGURE 28. Tree's crown deformed by salt-bearing winds, blowing off the sea.

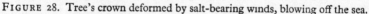

The distance inland to which trees are affected depends on their exposure, due to local topography. In broad terms, severe damage extends for a mile inland along *any* coast. Where the land rises from the sea, obvious damage goes five miles inland. Exceptional storms do minor harm to ridge top trees up to forty miles from the sea. Shelterbelts and hedges suffer most. The inner trees of a plantation receive little salt and escape harm until their shoots rise above the level of the salt-crippled outer rows.

The tree-growers defence is to plant salt-resistant trees. These are few in number, and it is hard to say *why* they are immune from salt-damage. The fact is, they *are*.

Salt-resistant broadleaved trees and shrubs
    All elms, *Ulmus* genus
    Evergreen holm oak, *Quercus ilex*—but not other oaks
    Tamarisks, *Tamarix* species
    Sea-buckthorn, *Hippophaë rhamnoides*
    Escallonia species

Salt-resistant conifers
    Sitka spruce, *Picea sitchensis*
    Lodgepole pine, *Pinus contorta*

Austrian and Corsican pines, *Pinus nigra* and *P. nigra var. maritima*
Maritime pine, *Pinus pinaster*
Stone pine, *Pinus pinea*
Monterey pine, *Pinus radiata*
Monterey cypress, *Cupressus macrocarpa*

SHELTER

Trees are so large that they must provide their own shelter. In its early years a small tree may enjoy the protection of a hedge, bank, or wall, but afterwards it must fend for itself. The only exception is that the more tender kinds may be given planned protection by hardier sorts, a method the forester terms *nursing*.

Buildings rarely protect trees. They cause eddies in the wind, or funnel it through narrow channels, so increasing its speed. This is due to their large, flat solid surfaces. On the other hand, trees—having a diffuse and broken surface, can shelter buildings very effectively. This is discussed further in Chapter 22 on "Shelterbelts", page 314.

With a few exceptions, such as a high, long wall surviving from days when stone-masonry or bricklaying could be done at low cost, or a sunken garden on an exposed sea-coast, trees will be sheltered by *other* trees—which includes hedges—during the early stages of their growth.

Tree shelter is basically of two sorts, though intermediate forms occur. These are *side shelter*—which can be on one side or possibly on two or even three sides, and *overhead shelter*. Each has its merits and disadvantages.

SIDE SHELTER

Advantages
Quickly established
Gives protection on the side, or sides, where it is most needed. Good shield against wind, and against airborne salt or soot

Disadvantages
Causes "sideways" growth towards the light, and hence a lop-sided tree

OVERHEAD SHELTER

Advantages
Gives good protection against:
Spring frosts
Drought, caused by hot sun or drying winds

Disadvantages
Slow to establish, unless use can be made of existing trees
Only suitable for sheltering shade-bearing trees; light-demanders cannot stand overhead shade

SHELTER STRATEGY

Whatever form of shelter is used, it is unlikely to be needed for the whole life of the protected trees. Most young plants benefit from some shelter in youth, but its continuance may cause spindly or one-side growth through lack of light. One workable plan is to establish shade-bearers such as beech or hemlock (*Tsuga* species) under the semi-shade of old birch trees. Once the youngsters have reached head-height, six feet or so, the birch *nurses* should be removed, preferably in stages.

Likewise, an old hedge that has been used to help establish light-demanders, like pines or oaks, may be cut out once they begin to overtop it.

Existing shelter should always be considered as a possible advantage on any planting site. It is nearly always wrong to "clear" a site prior to tree planting, unless it has to be ploughed by machinery. Mutual protection is a great help towards all tree growth.

STEM CRACKS DUE TO CLIMATIC EXTREMES

Occasionally the trunks of mature, established trees are damaged by climatic calamities. These are rare, and in practice little can be done except to leave healing to nature. The trimming of the rough edges of the crack, followed by coating with a wound dressing, as mentioned in

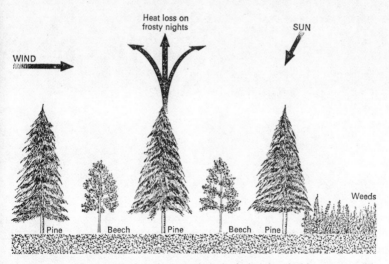

FIGURE 29. Nursing beech, a slow-starting, shade-bearing deciduous tree, with alternate rows of Scots pine, a hardy, light-demanding evergreen. The pines shield the beeches from strong drying winds and hot sun, and check radiant heat loss on frosty nights. They also suppress weeds.

Chapter 8, p. 119 on pruning, will help healing and keep out the fungi that cause decay. It should be done as soon as possible after the damage is seen.

Lightning is the commonest cause of stem cracks. It is more frequent on rough-barked trees than on smooth-barked ones—simply because smooth bark gets wet quicker and so may carry an electric discharge that would otherwise go through—and shatter—the actual wood of the trunk.

Drought crack occurs occasionally on fast-growing young trees standing on shallow soils that cannot—in a dry summer—supply water as fast as the tree needs it. Silver firs, *Abies* species, are the commonest sufferers, but only a small percentage in any plantation ever show cracks.

Frost crack occurs, though rarely, on trees exposed to extremely cold weather, in open situations.

Both drought crack and frost crack happen because the outer sap-wood shrinks more than the inner heartwood. Lightning cracks arise through the sudden generation of intense heat, which turns sap to steam and so splits the stem.

5. Trees and the Law

THE ownership of trees carries certain obligations, as well as privileges. Hence it is advisable to know the several points at which the law affects an owner or planter of trees and timber crops. This chapter relates mainly to Great Britain, but similar legal provisions apply in many other countries too.

The Common Law Affecting Trees

LEGAL OWNERSHIP OF TREES

In law, timber and timber-like trees are regarded as a permanent asset attached to the land, rather than an annual crop that is easily separated from it. In the absence of any precise written agreement to the contrary, they belong to the freeholder. A tenant, whether he be a farmer or the occupier of a suburban house and garden, cannot legally fell any trees on his property, or even lop them, without his landlord's consent.

Conversely, it is the landowner, and not the tenant, who must accept responsibility for any infringements of the law relating to trees, and for any damage that may result from tree growth. For example, if a tree should fall and injure a neighbour's property, it is the landowner, and not the tenant, who must pay compensation.

It follows from this that no tenant should take any major action regarding trees on his holding, without first obtaining the approval of his landlord. There has been much learned debate as to what constitutes "timber and timber-like trees" in this respect. In practice, flowering shrubs, small ornamental trees, and even fruit trees—provided they do not form part of a commercial orchard—are regarded as a tenant's property; he may plant, tend, or remove them as he wishes. But if a tenant plants timber trees, the landowner will claim possession of them when the tenancy ends; and the landlord need not, in the absence of prior agreement, pay any compensation. Only the landowner can authorise the felling of timber trees, and the proceeds from the sale of the timber belong to the landowner, not to the tenant.

Landowners should, in their own interests, make regular inspections of all the trees they own on land leased to others, at intervals of a few years or so. This enables them to decide which trees are due for harvesting as timber, as well as to spot any potentially dangerous trees before they are likely to fall.

TREES ALONG BOUNDARIES

Many trees grow along the boundaries of fields or of parks or gardens. Most of these trees grow, or grew originally, in hedgerows, and so they belong to whoever owns the boundary hedge or fence. In Scotland a boundary structure can be owned by two adjoining landowners, but in England and Wales it can—in law—only have one owner; it is often important to discover who this is.

The traditional method of planting a hedge in England is, first, to dig a ditch on the very edge of the property that is to be enclosed. This ditch may, or may not, be needed for drainage, but in any event it provides the earth for a bank that is always built on the property of the man who is enclosing the land concerned. The hedge, and any trees involved, are planted on the top of the earth bank.

It follows from this, that wherever a ditch-and-bank boundary can be found or traced, the landowner on the "bank" side owns the bank, the hedge, the trees, and even the land in which the ditch runs. The landowner on the "ditch" side cannot own either hedge or trees, nor can he be held liable for any harm that the trees may do. It is important to remember this, because the actual legal boundary is often lost sight of as development occurs; a fence built "inside" the hedge does not affect the ownership of the trees.

SPREADING BRANCHES AND SPREADING ROOTS

As trees grow, they often "trespass" across boundary lines, both above ground with their branches and below ground by means of their roots. This can give rise to disputes between neighbours which have often ended in the courts of civil law.

Taking the branches first, an owner of a tree growing near his boundary fence is under no obligation to prevent its branches spreading over that fence. In exceptional circumstances his neighbour might secure a court order obliging the tree owner to prune the branches back, on the grounds that they were creating a nuisance or becoming dangerous to his property, but otherwise the owner need take no action.

The usual remedy for the man who dislikes the branches of his neighbour's trees encroaching over his fence, is simply to prune them back himself, at the point where they cross his legal boundary. He is entitled to do this without prior notice to the tree's owner, though naturally most people would give such notice in the interests of friendly relations.

Curiously, the man who lops such branches off his neighbour's trees—or picks the apples off intruding branches—does not become the owner of his "spoils". In law, both branches and fruit are regarded as the

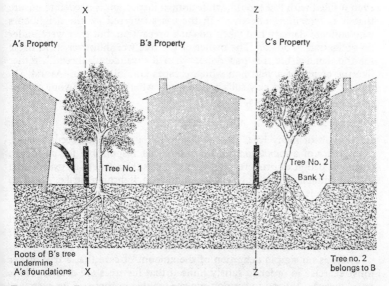

FIGURE 30. Boundary problems. Tree No. 1 belongs to B, but A may cut back its branches, or its roots, where they cross the boundary at x-x; B will still own the severed material. If the roots damage A's house, B is liable as his tree's roots have 'trespassed'. Tree No. 2 also belongs to B, although it lies outside his wall at z-z. He owns the bank and ditch all the way to y. He should fell this tree before it falls on C's house.

product of the tree-planter's enterprise, and the "fruit of his soil". The neighbour must, therefore, offer any such lopped branches or picked apples to the owner of the tree, on the other side of the fence; but the tree planter is not obliged to accept the fruit, nor to dispose of the branches.

Trespass by roots can—exceptionally—prove a more serious matter for both parties. Where poplars, or elms, are growing on clay soils in districts of low rainfall, their roots may adversely affect the stability of walls, and indeed of whole buildings. Unfortunate owners of poplar trees have, on occasion, found themselves liable to pay heavy compensation to their neighbours for such damage done by wandering roots— damage which had taken many years to become critical, and which had not been anticipated by either party.

Anyone is entitled to prevent the roots of a neighbour's tree from entering his property; he can do so by digging a trench along his boundary. But this is rarely done, because such a trench is unsightly, even if filled with leaf mould; while annual inspection is needed to ensure that it is remaining effective. In the cases referred to, the neighbours who suffered damage had taken no such precaution, but they were under no obligation to do so. The owner of the tree was, however, held liable for the damage his tree had done, when it "wandered abroad", rather like the owner of a wild lion which escapes and kills sheep. Moral: Do not grow poplars on clay soils near houses, whether they be your own or your neighbours' houses.

LIABILITY FOR DAMAGE BY FALLING TREES

As a result of many legal cases, the general situation has become clear. The owner of a *sound and healthy* tree is not responsible for any harm it may do people or property, if it should fall as the result of an exceptional gale or similar remarkable event—such as a lightning strike. Such a catastrophe is treated in law as an "Act of God."

By contrast, if it can be shown that, prior to the event, the tree was already so weakened by decay, disease, or damage, that its downfall could have been anticipated by a prudent owner, then that owner must accept full liability for all the harm that has been done.

There is no simple definition of the amount of care that a tree owner must exercise in order to satisfy himself that his trees are sound. He is not, however, obliged to employ experts for this purpose. The examination of the trees need only be a visual one; an owner is not obliged to look for hidden sources of weakness, but he ignores any obvious and outwardly apparent sign of decay at his peril.

A dead tree, for example, is an obvious danger to passers-by, for sooner or later it is sure to fall. It shows its weakness to the world at large. Leaning trees, and particularly those that lean across a highway, are another bad risk. Other sources of danger are discussed in Chapter 9, under Insect Attack and Diseases. No owner is obliged to lop trees at regular intervals; in fact, as explained in that chapter, lopping increases the risk of early decay, since it allows the entry of wood-rotting fungi. See page 150.

POISONOUS TREES

Among commonly grown trees, only the yew is regarded as dangerously poisonous to man and beast. There have been several legal cases in which the owner of cattle, poisoned through eating yew foliage, has claimed compensation from the owner of a tree or hedge. Livestock often ignore living yews, to which they have access, or else, if they do nibble them, suffer no harm. But clipped foliage also attracts them, and this seems to be particularly toxic. The legal position is that the owner of the tree is not liable for damages if the livestock have trespassed on to his land to eat the foliage; but if he has—for example—thrown yew clippings over his hedge on to his neighbour's field, then he must accept liability for the consequences.

PUBLIC CONTROL OF TREE GROWING

TREE PRESERVATION ORDERS

The most important legal means of public control of growing trees is the Tree Preservation Order. Such Orders are made under the Town and Country Planning Acts, 1947 to 1968, the similar Town and Country Planning Acts for Scotland, or the Civic Amenities Act, 1967. They are made by a Local Planning Authority, and have to be confirmed by a Minister. When it is proposed to make a Tree Preservation Order, the owner of the land must be advised; he is entitled to object to it, and if he suffers financially he is entitled to claim compensation. Orders can be made for any woodland, group of trees, or even individual trees whose appearance affects the amenities of a district, and they are binding on all later owners. Woods which are already included in the Dedication, Approved Woodlands, or Small Woods Planting Grant Schemes of the Forestry Commission (page 332) are, however, exempt from Tree Preservation Orders.

Once an Order has been made, the owner of the trees is obliged to manage them in accordance with its terms. These may be very wide. They can control the felling and even the lopping of trees, and may also require the replanting of the ground, with approved kinds of tree, after any felling has been done.

No Tree Preservation Order, however, can stop "the cutting down, topping or lopping of trees which are dying or dead or have become dangerous, or the cutting down, topping, or lopping of any trees in compliance with any obligation imposed by or under any Act of Parliament or so far as may be necessary for the prevention or abatement of a nuisance." But under the Civil Amenities Act, 1967, Section 13, the owner is obliged to replace any tree, (other than a woodland tree) which has been removed because it was dying, dead, or dangerous.

When such an Order is likely to be made, the best course for a landowner is to discuss its probable terms, in advance, with representatives of the Local Planning Authority. This may well enable him to ensure that they do not restrict his proper management of the trees or woods to an irksome degree. He will not, for example, wish to postpone the felling of all his trees until they become dead or dangerous; he will rather wish to harvest them while their timber is sound and valuable, and to re-invest some of the proceeds by replanting successors. A well-drafted Order will allow for sound management on such lines.

FELLING LICENCES

While Tree Preservation Orders can be made for small areas of ground, or even for a single tree, *Felling Licences* can only apply to a substantial volume of timber. Trees in gardens, graveyards, orchards and parks are entirely exempt from Felling Licences, and so are trees in London. No licence is need for felling small coppice or underwood, nor for any tree less than three inches thick at five feet above ground, nor for any "thinning" less than four inches thick at the same height. Dangerous trees, trees causing a nuisance, and trees that must be felled under Acts of Parliament, are likewise exempt.

In brief, only trees of large or medium size, intended for use as timber, require a Felling Licence, and even here there are exemptions for small amounts. Any landowner may fell 825 cubic feet of timber (hoppus measure) in any one quarter of the year, though he may only dispose of 150 cubic feet within that period. Owners who wish to fell or sell larger amounts must apply to the Forestry Commission for a Felling Licence.

Powers to control felling are held by the Commission under the Forestry Act, 1967. Their object is to secure the orderly harvesting of timber as it matures, and the maintenance within Great Britain of a reasonable reserve of growing timber. Permission is normally granted for all thinning and felling carried out in accordance with Plans of Operations approved by the Commission, for the thinning-out of other woods where that is good forest practice, and for the felling of mature timber.

As a condition of granting a Felling Licence, the Commission is empowered to insist on the replanting of the cleared land, where that appears to be desirable in the national interest. Such "Replanting Conditions" are frequently imposed.

COMPULSORY FELLING AND DESTRUCTION OF DISEASED TREES

Under the Destructive Insects Act of 1877, and related legislation, local government authorities may take powers to require the compulsory fellings of trees afflicted by specified pests or diseases. So far such powers have been taken for only three dangerous diseases: Dutch elm disease over most of midland and southern England; Watermark disease of cricket-bat willow in Essex and neighbouring counties; and Fire-blight attacking fruit trees and related ornamentals of the family Rosaceae, over most of the country.

TREES NEAR HIGHWAYS, RAILWAYS, RIVERS AND OVERHEAD WIRES

A number of public bodies have special legal powers to control trees growing near rights-of-way or other public services.

Where trees or bushes grow over a highway, or even a footpath, so as to hinder or prevent the public from passing freely along it, the Local Authority can take action to abate this nuisance, and can recover the cost from the owner of the trees concerned. If trees blow down across a highway, the Local Authority can—and often does—act at once to get the obstruction removed. It is not obliged to give the owner notice of intended action, but it is permitted, if it so chooses, to charge him for doing the work.

Under the Highways Acts 1835 and 1959 (Section 134) and the Public

Health Act, 1925, a Local Authority can oblige an owner to fell, prune or lop trees, bushes, or overgrown hedges, that are endangering, or even just *obstructing*, passers-by along any highway. These powers extend to trees that are obstructing the light from street lamps, or the sight of car drivers.

It is illegal to plant trees within fifteen feet of the centre of any highway; and a Local Authority can require the owners of any tree that is already growing in such a position to remove it forthwith. If a new opening, such as a roadway running into a forest, is to be made on to a highway, the permission of the Highway Authority is required. And if timber harvesting results in "extraordinary traffic" beyond that customary in the district, which damages the roads, those concerned may have to contribute to the cost of repairs.

In practice, the pruning of tree branches that obstruct a highway is often carried out, from special tree-pruning buses, by the transport authority that runs the local bus services, since double-decker buses are the first vehicles to be affected. But along by-roads where such tall vehicles do not regularly travel, the owner of trees is not obliged to prune the branches back, just in case a high van or bus may one day come along.

Under the Regulation of Railways Act, 1868, any tree standing near to a railway which shall be in danger of falling on a railway so as to obstruct the traffic, may, on complaint of the railway authority, be removed or otherwise dealt with by order of two Justices; but compensation must be paid to its owner.

Catchment Area Boards, and other authorities concerned with rivers, usually have powers to remove trees, and limit their planting, along river banks in their particular districts. The object of this is to leave the way clear for drainage machinery.

Special regulations also apply to land near airports and flying stations, where trees in the line of flight would cause risks of accidents.

The Electricity Supply Act, 1926, and the Electricity Act, 1947, empower electricity supply authorities to require the lopping or felling of trees that obstruct or interfere with any electric line, above or below ground. But electricity authorities must pay the costs involved, and compensate the owner for loss of use of his ground. A high-tension cable often puts a belt of land fifty feet wide out of use for timber production, in perpetuity. The authorities are, therefore, obliged to pay a continuing annual compensation charge to the owner.

The Telegraph (Construction) Act, 1908, gives the Postmaster-General powers to lop trees overhanging roads, or otherwise interfering with telegraph lines.

Finally we have the public bodies that operate water mains, gas mains, and even oil pipe-lines, all of whom have special powers to require that their service routes are not obstructed by trees or tree roots.

FINANCIAL HELP

After this recital of the possible legal restriction that can affect tree owners, let us have a look at the financial aid to which they are, in certain circumstances, entitled. There are no schemes of assistance for the planting of trees for ornamental purposes, nor for work on a scale so small that it is unlikely to result in the substantial production of timber. But a landowner who plants at least one acre of timber trees in any one year can apply to the Forestry Commission for an appropriate grant.

For "Small Woods," the current (1971) planting grant is £23·175 per acre; three quarters of this is paid in the year of planting, and the balance five years later, provided the trees have been satisfactorily tended for that time. For larger areas of woodland, Plans of Operations governing their ordered management, for ten years ahead, are required, before similar grants can be claimed. If the woods are formally "Dedicated," then an annual Management Grant is payable in addition.

Farmers who plant shelterbelts, with the prior approval of the Ministry of Agriculture or the Scottish Department of Agriculture, are entitled to claim grants, under Farm Improvement Schemes, which meet a substantial proportion of the cost, normally 25%. Alternatively, under Hill Land Improvement Schemes, 50% of the costs may be met on Hill Land used for raising cattle or sheep.

Finally, because of the long-term investment involved, timber-growing enterprises receive special treatment from the Inland Revenue. The provisions, which are set out in Appendix IV, page 332, cover Income Tax, Capital Gains Tax, Selective Employment Tax, and Estate Duty. On the whole, they place the woodland owner in a satisfactory position, especially as he can, within limits, elect to pay his taxes by the methods that he considers most favourable to himself.

6. Propagation or Purchase?

ONE of the first things a tree planter must decide is whether he will buy his planting stock or raise it himself. Unless he is working on a large scale, and over a long spell of years, the correct decision, on purely economic grounds, will always be: Buy!

Should a planter have a particular interest in young trees and their propagation, then he will get great satisfaction from overcoming the many technical difficulties, and from being able to say, later on: "I grew it myself, all the way from seed." But he is unlikely to challenge the professional nurseryman in cost, speed, or the quality of his planting stock. Large concerns, employing many gardeners, park-keepers or foresters, always delegate the nursery side to a few specialists. They have found that small and scattered nurseries do not pay their way.

Why is this? A combination of technical and economic factors favours the full-time professional nurseryman. He must choose his land carefully, finding a light, workable, yet fertile soil in a district of moderate rainfall. He must ensure that suitable labour is at hand, and likely to remain so for many years to come. Then he must find the capital for a fairly lengthy investment in a highly-valued growing stock. He cannot sell his output after only one year's growth, as a farmer can do; he must keep it for two, three, four or many years, costing money all the time, before it is ready for sale. Next he must assemble specialised tools and machinery for handling seed and small trees in large numbers. Then he must comb the world for satisfactory, reliable supplies of seeds and foundation stock plants, guaranteed true to name. None of this effort will prove worth while unless he can also find the special skills needed to handle land, capital, labour, machinery and plants. Finally he must build up a steady market, in other words a large body of people who have tried his trees and find that they grow to their full satisfaction.

The cost of all this, in time, money and long-term professional care, is of course reflected in the prices that the buyer pays for his young trees. But he still gets a bargain! He can order, within limits, *what* he wants, *when* he wants it. He pays only for those trees that have grown to the size and standard he requires, leaving the nurseryman to carry the costs of the "culls" or failures.

Whether the reader decides to buy his trees "ready-made" or to grow them himself, he will wish to know how the work is done. Only if he knows this can he specify just what he needs, and place his orders at the right time.

Basically, there are two ways of increasing trees: by seed, or by "vegetative" means. Vegetative propagation includes all methods that involve the division of already-growing plant material, including the taking and striking of *cuttings*, the taking and grafting of *grafts* or *buds*, the *layering* of branches—that is inducing a branch to strike root in the soil itself, so that it can later part company from its parent tree, and the raising of root-shoots or *suckers*.

A fundamental difference separates these two basic methods. Plants grown from seed are normally the offspring of two different parent trees. Therefore, like a human family, they show individual variation. Except in the rare case of identical twins, two parents never produce precisely similar offspring; each "child" has its own character. This is due to the marvellous mechanism of hereditary variation whereby each new original cell picks up, in different proportions, the characters of its parents, grandparents, and remoter ancestors.

In contrast, trees raised by vegetative reproduction—cuttings, grafts, and so on—are always exactly the same as their parent tree. You can carry this process on repeatedly—no change will ever occur except by some freakish mischance. Generation after generation will remain the same. Once a "line" of vegetatively reproduced plants has been established, described, and recognised, it is called a "clone" or a "cultivar", and it may even be patented. This is further discussed in Chapter 12, on Classification, page 177.

Vegetative propagation has the clear advantage that, when once a desirable strain of tree has been found, the growers can reproduce "carbon copies" of it indefinitely, without risk of variation. Its disadvantage is that, for many trees, the work of striking cuttings, or making successful grafts, is very difficult and uncertain, leading to high costs for planting stock. These initial costs are—with a few exceptions such as poplars and willows—too high for a timber grower to bear. As a general rule, we find that trees for forest planting, hedges, and shelterbelt work are grown from seed, whereas ornamental trees and fruit trees, and in particular the choicer varieties of them, are increased by cuttings or grafts.

RAISING TREES FROM SEED

If you set out to raise trees from seed you may either purchase the seed from one of the few specialist seedsmen who stock it, or else collect your own. Taking purchase first, the prices may appear high, but for all the small-seeded kinds a small quantity goes a long way.

In Britain, all seed of *timber* trees must be tested before sale, and the purchaser must be advised of the potential percentage germination; but no minimum percentage is laid down. No tests are required for the seed of *ornamental* trees; buyers acquire it at their own risk.

A very full account of traditional ways of raising forest trees from seed is given by John Aldhous in Forestry Commission Bulletin No. 43 *Nursery Practice* (see p. 337).

There are no quarantine regulations governing the importation of tree *seed* into the British Isles, though living plants, including trees, are subject to quarantine and some kinds are virtually prohibited. Certain other countries, such as the United States of America, apply quarantine rules to tree seed, and it can only be imported under permit.

SEED SOURCES

If you decide to collect your own seed, you must first find a suitable supply. If, on the other hand, you are buying seed, the seedsman will have done this for you. Seed firms have long experience and wide international contacts. They are always planning ahead, and are far more likely to be on the track of good sources than is an independent operator who has only his own nursery needs in view.

Several problems vex the tree seed supplier, which rarely trouble the man who deals only with farm crops or garden flower seeds. An obvious one springs from the fact that trees bear seed high up, out of reach from the ground. Only a few kinds—such as oak and beech, have seeds so large that it is worth while to collect them after they have fallen to the forest floor. One acceptable solution is to wait until good trees are due to be felled, to organise their felling so that it coincides with the time of year when seeds are ripening, and to collect from the fallen branches at ground level; but of course only one seed-crop can be then obtained from trees that have taken, perhaps, one hundred years to grow.

Another method is to send collectors up into the tree tops. This calls for special equipment to ensure safety, such as the "tree bicycle" for climbing trunks, and possibly a scrambling net to enable men to reach outer branches. With such aids, repeated crops can be gathered, year after year, from selected parent trees. Tree bicycles and nets are regularly used by the Forestry Commission, but only a large concern is likely to have such equipment and the skilled men needed to use it.

An *unacceptable* solution is to gather seed from stunted trees that have failed to grow to the proper size. Such seed is more than likely to give a second generation of stunted trees! Unscrupulous seed merchants have of course used such methods in the past, as some sorts of seed can be cheaply harvested by peasant labour from low scrub; but, where timber trees are concerned, no reputable seedsman will knowingly handle such poor stuff.

A major problem peculiar to trees is that good seed crops are irregular. In some years all the oaks or pines over a wide region will yield ample seed, but in other years the crop may fail entirely. Storage does not always solve this problem; some tree seeds can be stored for several years, others for only one year—or not at all.

Tree seeds vary greatly in size and substance. Methods devised for each kind must be used to collect them, extract them from cones or fleshy fruits, and keep them in good condition until they are needed for sowing. They ripen at different times of year; in fact there is not a month in the year during which one sort or another is not due for collection. Foresters must therefore make a detailed study of each kind before they start operations, and they must do this at least a year before they need to sow the seed.

CONIFERS FROM SEED Plate 20b, p. 253.

All the common coniferous timber trees bear small, dry seeds below the scales of their cones. Newly ripened cones are collected at a time of year to suit each kind (see table page 88), just before the scales have become

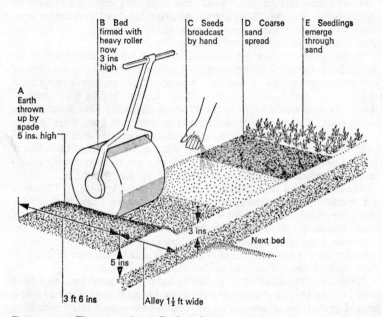

B Bed firmed with heavy roller now 3 ins high

C Seeds broadcast by hand

D Coarse sand spread

E Seedlings emerge through sand

A Earth thrown up by spade 5 ins. high

3 ins
Next bed
5 ins
3 ft 6 ins   Alley 1½ ft wide

FIGURE 31. Five stages in seedbed work.

dry and have started to open. The cones are then heated gently—for example over hot water pipes, in a well ventilated place, using temperatures around 140° F. As they dry, the scales open and the seeds fall out. Next the mixture of cones and seeds is shaken over wire mesh sieves, or tumbled in a wire mesh drum, to separate the seeds—which fall through the wire mesh—from the cones. Most seeds bear wings, which are rubbed off by hand or by a de-winging machine.

The extracted seeds, which look rather like grains of wheat, differ markedly in size, according to species. Most can be stored dry—but not *too* dry—for several years; the silver firs, *Abies* species, are a notable exception. Ideal storage conditions are provided by polythene bags, set

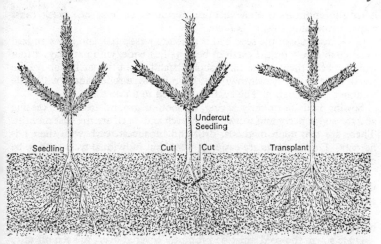

FIGURE 32. Two-year-old larch trees, grown by three methods. The seedling has the tallest shoots and the thinnest root system and is unsuitable for forest planting. The undercut seedling has shorter shoots and some bushy roots formed where its first roots were cut, so can be used. The transplant has short stout shoots and a bushy root system and is much the best.

within sealed tins, maintained at temperatures just above freezing, say 35° F. For this, a refrigerated seed store is required; if that is not available, the best substitute is a cool cellar.

Conifer seed is usually despatched to the grower in polythene bags, which help to preserve its correct moisture content, or in paper packets. On receipt it should be kept in a cool place away from dry heat; central heating will harm it. Some foresters soak the seed for a day or two before sowing it. They then dust the damp seed with powdered red lead, to stop the grains sticking together and to poison any mice that may attack it. Neither process is essential; once the seed has been sown in damp earth, it soon picks up all the water it needs, while hungry mice and birds ignore red lead! Stratification in moist sand (see page 89) is, however, beneficial for lodgepole pine, Douglas fir and silver firs.

Seed beds for conifers must be thoroughly prepared in advance. The soil must be well cultivated and weed-free. Fertility is best assured by the addition and thorough working-in of weed-free manures. The best are *spent hops* from a brewery, at 500 pounds per 100 square yards, or commercial *hop manure* at 250 pounds per 100 square yards. Unless hop manure (which contains added elements) is used, the commercial chemical fertiliser known as *granular potassic superphosphate* should be applied at the rate of 12 pounds per 100 square yards of seed bed.

After the application of a chemical fertiliser, at least one week must elapse before any sowing is done.

Good drainage of the seed bed is absolutely essential, and it is standard practice to throw up the earth in beds $3\frac{1}{2}$ feet wide, with pathways 1 foot wide between them. The earth should stand about five inches above the level of the path when thrown up. Firm it with a roller, and it will settle to about three inches. The surface is raked to a fine tilth.

Sowing is done in early spring, as soon as ground frosts are ceasing and the soil is becoming workable. March and April are the best months. There are two main methods, drill and broadcast, each with their adherents. Drill sowings are easier to weed, but individual trees tend to be crowded.

In *drill* sowing, a shallow notch is made in the surface of the soil, using the edge of a board, or a roller with slats nailed across it. Seed is sprinkled along this, at a calculated rate, by hand.

In *broadcast* sowing, the seed is scattered over the whole surface, again by hand and at a predetermined rate.

Once sown, the seed must be promptly covered over, to keep off mice and birds and to provide the right moisture conditions for germination. Sharp sand or fine grit are far better than soil, as they allow more seedlings to come through. They should be white or pale-coloured and free from lime; a depth of one-sixth to one-eighth of an inch is usual.

On a small scale all weeding can be done by hand, provided it is always attended to promptly and thoroughly. Large-scale commercial growers cut costs by applying "pre-emergence" weed-killers, which kill most weed seedlings, just before the tree seedlings emerge from the soil. A typical treatment is *vaporising oil* (such as *Shellspark* or *Esso Green Oil*), at the rate of 10 pints per 100 square yards of seed bed, applied by a pressure sprayer.

Because weeds grow so much faster than seedling trees, weeding must never be neglected. It must be repeated at intervals of two or three weeks in summer, or one month or so at other times of year, for as long as the little trees stand in the seed bed. Other treatments that are sometimes, though not always, applied, are:

1. Shading against bright sun, with lath shelter carried on wires six inches above ground level.

2. Protection against mice and birds, using fine-mesh (quarter-inch) wire netting.

3. Spray irrigation.

During the first growing season, the seedlings benefit greatly by top dressings of a nitrogenous fertiliser. Four pounds of sulphate of ammonia, per 100 square yards of seed bed, should be applied in June; a similar dressing should follow in August.

Conifers usually remain in the seed beds for *two* growing seasons, during which time they grow from four to fifteen inches high. Larches and pines sometimes grow so fast that they are ready to be moved after only one season. Slower starters, such as *Abies* silver firs, may need three years.

Once the seedlings have grown large enough, they are lifted from the ground during their resting season, between October and the end of April, and either transplanted to another nursery bed, or sold to other growers. Lifting is done with a garden fork or a mechanical, tractor-drawn lifter, and the little trees are then counted, bundled, and sorted out; "culls', or sub-standard trees are thrown away. Bundles of seedlings must be stored with their roots in trenches dug in the soil, or else polythene bags, to stop drying out.

Seedlings are sold by age, as one-year, two-year, or three-year, and also by height, as measured to the tip of the topmost bud. Their sturdiness—that is the stoutness or circumference of the stem at ground level, is often a better indication of quality. Seedlings are relatively cheap, a representative price in 1970 for two-year old Scots pine, six inches high, being only £5 per thousand, equivalent to 1¼d. (half a new penny) per tree.

Conifer seedlings, however, are unsuitable for planting, either in garden or forest. They are not big enough to compete with weed growth, nor are their root systems able to pick up moisture fast enough for a quick and sure start. They are therefore "grown-on" in the nursery as *transplants*, as described later on.

The table on page 88 gives months for seed collection, *average* numbers of seeds contained in each pound, the density for sowing, and the likely yield from seed of average germinative capacity, in a good season, for the commoner coniferous timber trees.

BROADLEAVED TREES FROM SEED

Unlike the conifers, the broadleaved trees produce seeds of great variety in size and character. Each kind must be gathered at a particular time of year (examples in following table). It must then be separated, if necessary, from its husk or berry; then stored under controlled conditions, and finally given individual treatment in the seed bed. To detail all this would take a book of its own. Here we can only give working procedures, for a few common broadleaved trees that bear easily-handled dry seeds. March and April are the usual months for sowing broadleaved seeds; exact dates may depend on their stage of development during storage.

Large Nuts

Hard dry seeds that fall free from their fruits are technically called *nuts*. These include the acorns of the oaks, *Quercus* species; beech nuts, *Fagus*; sweet chestnuts, *Castanea*; horse chestnuts, *Aesculus*; walnuts, *Juglans*; hazel nuts, *Corylus*; and sycamore and maple seeds, *Acer*. Seedlings of nearly all the species in these groups can be raised as follows: Gather the nuts as they ripen, from the tree or from the ground beneath it. Reject all the unsound or unfilled nuts. Store the remainder in a cool and slightly moist spot, protected from mice, until the spring. Sow in a seed bed,

CONIFER SEEDLINGS

Months for Seed Collection, Seed Data, Sowing Prescriptions, and Likely Yields of Conifer Seedlings

| Species (yd/lb) | Normal month of collection | Normal seed qualities | | Normal sowing area sq. yd./lb. (broadcast) | One-year seedlings Likely Yield per lb. of seed (Thousands) |
		No. pure seed per lb. (Thousands)	Germina-tion per-centage		
Scots pine	January	75	90	55	33
Corsican pine	January	32	80	40	12
Lodgepole pine	January	135	90	100	60
European larch	November	75	30	25	10
Japanese larch	September	115	40	60	22
Hybrid larch	September	110	30	35	16
Douglas fir	September	40	80	30	16
Norway spruce	October	65	80	35	25
Sitka spruce	September	190	90	95	80
Grand fir	Aug/Sept	23	25	7	3
Noble fir	Aug/Sept	15	25	4	2
Western hemlock	September	290	60	70	80
Western red cedar	September	400	60	100	80
Lawson cypress	September	210	50	70	30

prepared as for conifers, about early April. Cover with ordinary soil to a depth equal to that of the seed. Sowing densities are given in the table below.

The larger seeds will produce seedlings large enough for transplanting after *one* season's growth. Small ones will need two seasons.

BROADLEAVED SEEDLINGS

Months for Seed Collection, Seed Data and Sowing Prescriptions for the Production of Hardwood Seedlings

Species	Normal month of collection	No. pure seed per lb. (Thousands)	Normal sowing area broadcast (sq. yd/lb.)	One-year seedlings likely yield per lb. of seed (Thousands)
Oak	*October*	0.13	1	50
Beech	*October*	2.0	4	1,000
Sycamore	*Sept/Oct*	6.0	8	3,000
Ash	*October*	6.0	12	3,000
Birch	*Aug/Sept*	250	30	50,000
Sweet Chestnut	*October*	0.11	0.6	50
Gean (Wild Cherry)	*July/Aug*	2.5	5	500

OTHER COMMON BROADLEAVED TREES

Ash seeds, *Fraxinus*, and hornbeam nuts (*Carpinus*) are treated as set out above, but they must be stored for *eighteen months* in an intimate mixture with an equal volume of damp sand. This is done in a pit or —for small quantities—a plant pot sunk in a garden bed. This process is called *stratification*

The small seeds of birch, *Betula*, should be treated in the same way, but for *six months only*. All stratified seed should be sown just before it sprouts, and this calls for frequent inspections as spring comes in.

The seeds found within juicy fruits and berries are, in general, extracted from their pulp as far as is practicable, and then stratified for either four or eighteen months, according to species. Hawthorn, *Crataegus*, used for hedging, needs eighteen months; cherries of the genus *Cerasus*, and plums of the genus *Prunus*, require—as a rule—only four months.

TRANSPLANTS

The object of transplanting is to produce a tree better fitted to survive and grow, in forest or garden, than a *seedling* that has only just been lifted from its seed bed. A *transplant* must be taller and sturdier than a seedling, and—*most important*—have a large amount of root in relation to its shoot. This last feature enables it to take up water relatively quickly, and lose it relatively slowly.

An alternative to transplanting is *undercutting* or *root-pruning*. This means that the seedlings are left in the seed bed, but have their roots cut through with a sharp spade, or else with a cutter-bar pulled by a tractor. This is cheap, but means that the trees cannot be given more individual growing space, or be moved from one nursery to another, or be graded for quality. Transplanting is therefore the general rule—*once*

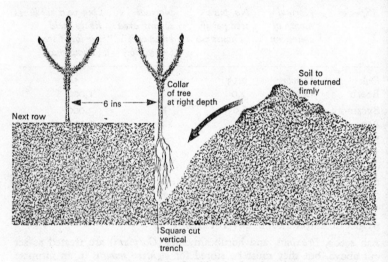

FIGURE 33. Transplanting details. Seedling is placed upright at correct depth against vertical side of trench. In large-scale practice seedling will be held in a board, at correct distance of two inches or so from its neighbours.

for forest or hedgerow trees, and *once*, *twice*, or *thrice* for larger trees to be planted for ornamental purposes.

Transplanting is always done during the resting season, when the tree's water demands are lowest. It can be done at any time from early October to late April, provided the ground is free from frost. The ground used must be fertile and reasonably level. It must be ploughed or dug over well in advance, and then harrowed or raked to give an even surface; this cultivation checks weeds also. During the process of transplanting the ground is inevitably compacted again by men or machines, but it is also re-dug or re-ploughed, so restoring its previous good tilth.

For practical reasons, trees are always transplanted in the nursery along straight lines, and the work is therefore often called *lining-out*.

Distances between lines, and between plants within a line, naturally depend on the size to which the trees are likely to be grown before their *next* move. Plate 22, p. 277, shows the whole process.

For ease of work and economy, seedling trees are set against the sides of a trench rather than in separate holes. In the simplest method, *hand lining-out*, a length of stout string, called a *nursery line*, is stretched across the bed in the desired position. A sharp garden spade is then used to cut a trench, to the desired depth of six inches or so, along the string. The worker makes the far side of the trench vertical and draws the disturbed soil towards him in a rough pile. Having completed the trench, he takes a bundle of seedlings and places each one in turn in the trench, at the tree's correct, original, depth in the soil, and at the desired distance apart; the distance is usually judged by eye. Each little tree is temporarily held in place by a clod of wet earth. Once the whole row is done, the worker takes his spade again and throws back the rough earth, so as to fill the trench and hold all the trees firmly in place. Then, using the back of his spade, he compresses the surface and flattens it out.

He then repeats the process for the next line of trees, starting by cutting the next trench in the soft earth that he has just thrown up.

Because hand work is tedious, dirty, and slow, nurserymen who work on a large scale have speeded it up and cheapened it by bringing in machines. Most of these are basically tractor-drawn ploughs which do the hard work of cutting the trench and filling it in again. In one "pass" over the ground, they fill in one trench and cut the next one. The seedling trees are placed in long boards called *lining-out boards*, each being set at its right depth and distance apart, fixed by a spacing bar on the board. This enables one worker to put out about sixty seedlings at one time. The machine works so fast that a gang of workers is needed to keep the operation supplied with seedlings; one machine deals with at least 50,000 young trees each day. Machines are therefore only a practical proposition in large nurseries that handle millions of trees each year.

Machines on the cabbage-planter principle, in which the worker places each plant into a groove on a wheel of the machine, which then transfers it to a groove that the machine cuts in the soil, are widely used in America. But they can only operate when weather and soil conditions are just right, and so they have little application in the more variable climate of western Europe.

Average distances for transplanting young trees, for numbers of growing seasons—are given in the table on page 92, which also shows acceptable sizes. Plate 22, p. 277, illustrates operations.

The after-care of the transplanted trees, for the year or two in which they grow-on in the transplant lines, consists mainly of weed-control. This can be done entirely by hand, but it is now common practice to apply a weed-killer called *Simazine*, a week or two after lining-out, to keep down costs. The standard rate is only $1\frac{1}{2}$ ounces of the commercial powder, applied as a spray in 1 gallon of water, to 100 square yards of

TRANSPLANTS
Recommended Distances between Plants

No. of growing seasons	Expected average height when lifted from lines	Spacing in inches at lining-out	No. of plants per 100 sq. yds.
One	Less than 9 inches	$1\frac{1}{2} \times 8$	10,800
Two	9 to 18 inches	2×8	8,100
Three	Over 18 inches	3×8	5,400

transplant bed. Half this rate is applied to larches, while poplars and ash *cannot* safely be sprayed. Simazine must *never* be used on freshly-sown seed beds, for it operates by killing the newly-germinated seedlings of weeds—or trees! Applied at the stated rate, it does no permanent harm to the soil.

Transplants are often given a single dressing of a nitrogenous manure, such as *Nitrochalk* at 4 pounds per 100 square yards, during their first summer.

After one season—or two or three seasons where larger trees are required—of growth, the transplants are lifted from the nursery and dispatched, either for sale or for planting in the forest.

LARGE TRANSPLANTS

Repeated transplanting is necessary for the raising of satisfactory large transplants for garden or landscape use. Such trees should not be allowed to remain for more than two years in one spot. Every two years they have to be lifted and replanted in a fresh situation where they get new soil and more growing space. This is *essential* for all conifers, but broad-leaved trees will often survive their later replantings if they are left standing for three years, or even more.

Frequent movement costs money, which may or may not be recovered by subsequent sales; so one finds that repeated transplanting tends to be neglected by the less efficient nursery firms. A good firm is ready to guarantee the number of times that a tree has been transplanted; it keeps careful records to that effect.

Side-root pruning is often resorted to when a nursery cannot afford the money, or the space, for repeated transplanting. This involves the cutting through of side roots with the spade, so obliging the tree to replace them with clusters of small bushy roots that resemble those developed after transplanting. It works reasonably well with broadleaved trees, less so with conifers. The drawback is that root-pruned trees get neither fresh soil nor more space to extend their branches. They therefore tend to be spindly, and they cannot match properly transplanted specimens for appearance, or for early growth after planting out.

VERY LARGE TRANSPLANTS

Side-root pruning is, however, the only way of preparing very large transplants, those exceeding twelve feet in height, for their next move from nursery to forest. Such trees are grown at least six feet apart. Two years, or at least two growing seasons, before they are moved, a broken ring of trenches about one foot deep is cut round each tree, a yard from its base. There are usually three trenches, and their total length equals half the circumference of the ground around the tree. These trenches are filled with leaf mould. This process severs the long side roots and forces the tree to send out clusters of short bushy roots to tap the moisture and nutrients in the leaf mould. This means that, when the tree is transplanted two seasons later, it has enough root-surface to supply the essential water throughout its first critical summer. One year later, the same process is repeated on the rest of the ground around the tree, so causing it to develop bushy roots all round.

VEGETATIVE PROPAGATION

Increasing trees by vegetative means—that is, the division of an existing tree as cuttings, grafts, layers, or suckers—calls for a high degree of skill. On a commercial scale it is best left to the trade nurseryman who employs professional propagators. But every tree grower should know how it is done, for it affects later care and tending.

The first essential is a sound foundation stock, known to be true to name, of the desired clone or cultivar. This foundation stock must itself be maintained by suitable means of propagation, since it will be constantly drawn upon to supply cuttings, or *scions* for grafting. Nurserymen build up their foundation stocks by purchase from other established firms, by selecting desirable trees from a general group, or by deliberate breeding.

CUTTINGS

The shoots of certain trees, if cut off at the right age and time of year, and set upright in moist, well-drained soil, will take root and establish themselves as separate individuals. Certain trees "take" very readily, others with difficulty, and some not at all. Because the degree of care needed varies so much, and because conditions must often be closely controlled, propagation by cutting is usually left to the trade nurseryman.

Most poplars and willows, however, root so readily that anyone can strike their cuttings with good hopes of success. Cut off a six-inch length of well ripened branchwood, from $\frac{1}{4}$ to $\frac{1}{2}$ inch in diameter, during the resting season. Make sure that it carries at least one live bud near its tip. Insert it in well-dug earth, leaving only the bud and a short length of twig showing, and firm up the soil around it. Next spring the buried twig will take root, and send up a thin shoot from the bud. After one

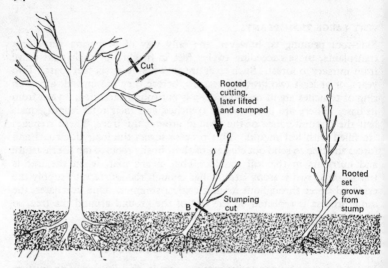

FIGURE 34. Propagating poplars. Cutting from selected parent grows in one year into a rooted cutting. This is lifted and stumped. Basal bud (b) then grows into a straight rooted set, fit for planting out in the woods; sets often grow six feet tall in one year.

season's growth, the "rooted cutting", as it is now called, should be dug up, and the shoot cut back to a basal bud. The resulting "rooted stump" is then replanted in a fertile nursery bed about six inches from its nearest neighbour. During the next growing season it will send up a very vigorous shoot from the basal bud, for it is now well equipped with roots. A sturdy stem at least four feet high will result, which is indeed rapid growth for only two seasons. This is called a "rooted set", and it in turn is dug up, during the winter resting season, and moved to its final position in garden, field, or forest.

Many broadleaved trees that root less readily need a specially equipped propagating frame. Such frames are also used for those few conifers that readily take root—mainly cypresses of the genera *Cupressus* and *Chamaecyparis*, red cedars and white cedars of the genus *Thuja*, and the Taxodineae group that includes the *Sequoias* and *Cryptomerias*.

In order to get "difficult" species to take root, the propagator uses one or more of the following techniques:

1. A special *rooting medium*, in place of ordinary soil. For example, a mixture of vermiculite and peat.

2. *Soil warming*, usually provided by low-tension electric current running through wires embedded in the soil, and controlled by a thermostat.

3. *Mist*, provided by a supply of water, activated by electrical units that are controlled by atmospheric humidity sensors.

4. *Auxins*, that is synthetic plant hormones, such as indole-butyric acid, which promote rooting. The cuttings are dipped into a carefully prepared auxin powder or solution prior to rooting.

A propagating frame with all the requisite equipment is an expensive capital item. It is made to pay its way by crowding into it successive batches of cuttings. Once these have rooted, they are transferred to ordinary cold frames, and later on, when larger and more fully rooted, they are moved out to open nursery beds for growing to a "usable" size.

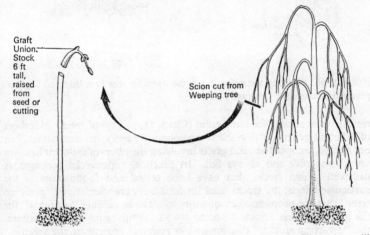

Graft Union. Stock 6 ft tall, raised from seed or cutting

Scion cut from Weeping tree

FIGURE 35. High-grafting a weeping tree, e.g. beech or ash. The scion will perpetuate the downward trend of its race.

GRAFTING Plate 20a, p. 253.

The origin of the art of grafting, whereby a shoot, or *scion*, cut from a desirable kind of tree, is made to grow upon a root, or *stock*, of a commoner kind, is lost in antiquity. The Romans certainly practised it, and it was kept alive by monastic gardeners throughout the Middle Ages. To-day it is a most important process commercially, being used for virtually all fruit trees and roses, and for many ornamental trees also. No grafter claims 100% success, and it is recognised that some trees are far harder to graft than others. But professional propagators become highly skilled, and achieve 90% success with the easier sorts.

In all grafting it is a firm rule that stock and scion must belong to closely related trees, in order to be *compatible* with one another. Different varieties or cultivars of one *species* are mutually compatible, and so are

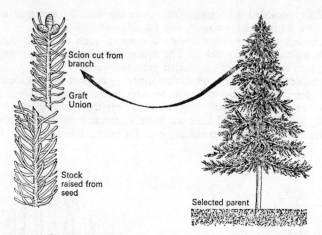

FIGURE 36. Grafting a conifer, a process used for tree breeding and for perpetuating decorative cultivars.

most species within the same *genus* (Chap. 12, p. 177) of trees. Members of different genera, within the same botanical *family*, are sometimes, but not always, compatible. But grafts involving members of different families are *incompatible* and always fail. In practice, commercial propagators use well-known stocks that have been tested and found suitable for particular scions; the stocks used for fruit trees are themselves "pedigree trees" that are propagated in quantity to serve as reliable "supports" for the grafted scions. Some selected stocks favour rapid growth; others, the "dwarfing stocks," discourage too vigorous growth by the scion.

All grafting depends on the principle that similar plant tissues, of closely-related plants, will carry on their functions if brought into close contact, and maintained there, in the living state. Thus, in a typical tree graft, both stock and scion include *wood* at the centre, a *cambium layer* outside this, a *bast* layer outside the cambium, and finally an outer cover of *bark*. If the stock and the scion are of the same diameter, as in a *saddle graft*, (wherein the scion becomes a straight extension of the stock) the two sets of four different tissues will all meet closely enough for each to join up with its partner all round. This will only happen if final preparation of both stock and scion is done just before the graft is made, so that there is no time for tissues to dry out. Once the graft has been made, it must be firmly bound with tape so that the two "halves" are held together whilst healing proceeds, and promptly sealed with wax to exclude air.

Conifers, and some broadleaved trees whose tissues hold resins, gums, or latex, are hard to graft because these natural wound-healing substances ooze out, cover the cut surfaces, and prevent a union between the adjacent related tissues. This difficulty is overcome by using small, young shoots

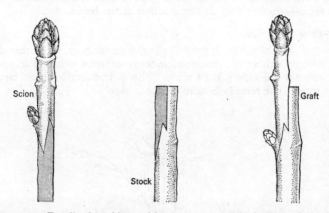

FIGURE 37. Detail of grafting; whip or tongue method. The scion, which must carry one or more buds, is trimmed to fit into a sloping cut on the stock. The two are then bound tightly together and the joint is sealed with wax.

or buds that hold little resin or gum, which implies intricate work needing extra care and skill. In practice, only the choicer conifers are ever grafted for general use; the high rate of failure raises the cost for common sorts too far.

The physical shapes of the two living stems that are to be brought into contact is a matter of practical convenience. The diameters of stock and scion must be similar, but need not always be exactly the same. In a *whip graft* the stock is cut across on the slant; the scion is shaped in the corresponding way so that the two sets of tissues meet when the two members are brought together. In a *side graft*, or a *bud graft*, a section of the bark, bast and superficial wood is cut off from one side only of the stock. A similar superficial section, which must always include a bud, is cut from one side only of the scion's stem. This is bound on to the cut side of the stock.

Grafting is done during the resting season, usually in spring just before growth is due to recommence. The skilled grafter works quickly, cutting each stock and scion only a matter of seconds before he brings them into contact. The union is promptly made firm with plastic tape and sealed with wax. A few weeks later it is possible to tell whether the graft has succeeded. If the scion bud starts growth, all is well. Once it is well-established, and in all events not later than the end of the next growing season, all competing shoots from the stock must be pruned back. This obliges the stock to direct all its sap into the new, grafted, scion shoot.

Here are some major points about grafted trees that concern all who tend them—whether they do any grafting themselves or not.

Root-shoots or Suckers

Since the roots of the stock are still alive, there is always a risk that they may send up a shoot of a common, undesirable strain of tree in competition with the valuable grafted scion. This is frequent in roses, rare in other trees. The remedy is simple—cut it back!

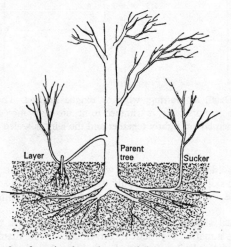

FIGURE 38. Left, a *layer* is a branch pegged down and persuaded to take root. Right, *sucker* or *root-shoot* arising from mature tree, e.g. elm.

Differences in Diameter

Two strains of tree often differ markedly in their rate of diameter growth, even under identical conditions of situation and nourishment. It is quite usual to find that a stock becomes, after some years of growth, markedly thicker than the scion; there is a sudden contraction at the union. Occasionally it is the scion that grows thicker, giving the stem a top-heavy look; this is less welcome as it gives a point of weakness, but in practice it can rarely be foreseen or prevented.

Graft Unions

However perfect the union between the other tissues may be, the bark of one tree never unites precisely with that of another. The actual point of any graft union can therefore always be seen on the tree trunk. On some trees it is close to the ground, and on others—as in most weeping trees and standard fruit trees, about six feet up. Very occasionally, this union proves to be a point of physical weakness, and a stout stem may actually break at the union, after many years of healthy growth. This can be serious if it happens to a large tree, growing near a building.

SUCKERS OR ROOT-SHOOTS

Certain trees that do not strike readily as cuttings can easily be increased by suckers. The English field elm, *Ulmus procera*, is a common example, and along the hedgerows it increases naturally this way. These trees have shallow roots that send up, at intervals, upright shoots which develop into trees. If the parent tree is cut down, sucker growth becomes very vigorous, as all the tree's root system then nourishes the root-shoots. All you need to do to increase a suckering tree is to cut through the surface roots all round a selected sucker, and then transplant the newly-isolated shoot, complete with a fair-sized cluster of roots. Root-shoots cannot, of course, be used to increase grafted kinds, but they are a good way of increasing root-stocks for future grafting.

LAYERING

This consists in bending down a side-shoot of a tree to ground level, pegging it and covering the bend with soil. After one growing season, the bent shoot—if it will layer at all—will be found to have put forth roots. It can then be separated from its parent tree by simply cutting through the stem on that side. A layer is usually given a further season to establish itself fully, and is then transplanted. Some garden shrubs, such as the golden bell, or *Forsythia*, and the brambles of the *Rubus* genus, layer their side branches without any attention; in fact they spread through the garden so fast by this means that it becomes a nuisance.

COSTS AND PRICES

From the foregoing account of propagation methods, it will be clear that the cost of raising a tree fit for planting can vary enormously—literally from a few pence to a few pounds. In commercial nursery practice three main grades are recognised; prices relate to 1970, and are quoted for comparison only.

Trees for Forest Planting

Usually transplants raised from seedlings, which in turn have been raised from seed. Around £15 per *thousand*, equivalent to 1½ new pence per tree.

Trees for Hedging, Screens etc.

Larger transplants, sold at about £6 per *hundred*, equivalent to 6 new pence per tree.

Specimen Trees

Sold singly, within a height range of two feet to ten feet. Anything from £0.5 to £5 per tree.

Large specimens needing special equipment for transport

Ten to fifty feet tall. £3 to £12 each, *before* movement; £6 to £60 after transplanting at new site.

IMPORTED TREES

The importation of trees from other countries is often undertaken to meet shortages in home supplies. But from the planter's point of view, the shorter and quicker the journey from nursery to planting point the better. No matter how fast the transport, the crossing of a frontier, with the usual formalities for customs and quarantine inspection, causes unwelcome delays which in practice tend to be cumulative. A saving in cost, for a particular quality, must be quite substantial to offset this risk.

Certain countries, and in particular the United Kingdom and the U.S.A., operate strict quarantine rules that limit the importation of living trees.

The British Isles—including the whole of Ireland, the Channel Isles, and the Isle of Man, forms a single quarantine zone, and any kind of tree may be freely moved *within* those limits. Certain well-known forest trees can only be imported into this zone under special licence, and so far as the conifers are concerned, licences are only granted exceptionally when small numbers of trees are needed for scientific purposes. The main regulations covering this are the United Kingdom Statutory Instrument Nos. 1426 and 2121 of 1965, which give full details. The main trees affected are these:

Broadleaved Trees

Oaks (*Quercus*), sweet chestnuts (*Castanea*), and poplars (*Populus*), from all countries; elms (*Ulmus*) from non-European countries.

Conifers

Pines (*Pinus*), larches (*Larix*), spruces (*Picea*), silver firs (*Abies*), hemlocks (*Tsuga*), Douglas firs (*Pseudotsuga*), Californian redwoods (*Sequoia*), white cedars and red cedars (*Thuja*) from all countries.

The purpose of these controls is to exclude insect pests and fungal diseases that could cause serious economic loss to timber production.

PROVENANCE AND CERTIFIED STOCKS

In timber-growing, it is important to use a carefully chosen strain of forest tree. The true origin of each stock is called its *provenance*; for example, if a stock of Sitka spruce comes from South Alaska, then South

Alaska remains its provenance, no matter where it is raised. A second generation of the same stock would still have that provenance, even if raised from seed harvested, say, in Scotland.

Certified stocks of seed, seedlings, or transplants, are derived from selected parent trees or stands.

Under *The Forest Reproductive Material Regulations 1973*, seed, plants, and cuttings of fourteen timber trees may only be marketed in Britain if they have been certified by the Forestry Commission (address p. 326). These trees are: European silver fir, European larch, Japanese larch, Norway spruce, Sitka spruce, Austrian and Corsican pine, Scots pine, Weymouth pine, Douglas fir, beech, sessile oak, pedunculate oak, red oak and poplar.

All other species, and all purely ornamental trees and shrubs are free of such controls.

7. Planting and Establishment

THE critical stage in all planting is on the transfer of the living trees from their parent nursery to their final position. Far more trees fail through lack of due care at this time than through poor planting after arrival.

ADVANCE PLANNING AND ORDERING

Most planters have a clear idea of the amount of work they propose to do during any given season, several months before it begins. They can therefore draw up a schedule of the kinds and sizes of tree that they will need, with provisional dates for receipt and planting.

Each planting season runs from 1st October to 30th April in the year following—except for larches which should always be planted by 31st March. Under the fickle climate of the British Isles and western Europe, the season is sure to be interrupted, in nine years out of ten, by at least one spell of frost which makes the soil rock-hard. It is quite impossible to predict the date or length of these hard spells. They may fall at any time between 1st December and 31st March. They may last a few days, or exceptionally, as in 1963, for over two months. Hard frost is much more likely to occur frequently, and to last a long time, on the *eastern* side of Britain than on the *western* side. Distance north or south makes no odds here—Kent gets far more hard frost than Argyll. In practice the British planter thinks in terms of two planting spells—an autumn one from October to December, and a spring one during March and April.

In contrast, planters in Scandinavia, in northern Europe east of western France, and in North America, anticipate a single long spell of frozen soil from mid-December to early March. All their planting is crowded into a few weeks of March and April.

Trees planted in autumn do not remain completely dormant during the cold winter months. Whenever the soil is warm enough, their roots grow, making that intimate contact with the soil that is essential for successful shoot growth next spring. On the whole, therefore, autumn planting is to be preferred for all fully hardy trees.

The planting of half-hardy trees, suitable only for the western coastal zone (see Chapter 4, p. 62) is best delayed until spring.

With these points in mind, the planter should decide when he wants his stock delivered, and instruct his nurseryman accordingly, as far ahead as he can. But all delivery dates must be *provisional* and subject to weather conditions both at the nursery and the planting site. Adjustments are often needed at short notice, and are best made by telephone.

INSPECTION AND SAMPLING

Every reputable nurseryman is ready, and indeed happy, to show his prospective purchasers samples of his stocks. The ideal way to decide what you want is to visit the nursery, preferably by appointment, during the summer growing season. Where specimen trees are concerned, many firms will reserve individuals chosen by their customers, for later delivery. Small forest trees, needed in larger quantities, can be verified by the provision of labelled sample trees; the buyer should preserve these carefully so that they can be compared with the actual stocks delivered later. You cannot say "Not up to sample!" unless a sample *still* exists!

Even the largest nursery firm cannot grow, at any one time, all the sizes, ages, and kinds of trees that its customers may demand. It is therefore a common practice for firms to make good their own shortages by buying-in, from other growers, stocks that are surplus to the other growers' own order books. This is naturally done at trade prices. Some firms, however, prefer to refer inquirers to the actual growers of the stocks.

There are also occasional seasons when stocks of a desired kind and size of tree are simply not available anywhere in the country, or even obtainable by importing. The intending planter has then two alternatives —postponement until a year later, or the substitution of some alternative kind.

LIFTING, TRANSPORT, AND CARE BEFORE PLANTING

These three aspects of tree handling must be taken together—the success of each depends on the others. Three principles govern the combined operation:

1. The shorter the period between lifting and final planting the better; all the time roots are out of the ground there is risk of water loss.

2. Cold—even frost—does no harm to hardy trees; if anything, it helps to hold the water within their tissues.

3. Heat, and any form of drying such as an east wind, are very harmful; they encourage water loss.

When you see the roots of trees wrapped in sacking during transport, it has *not* been done to keep them warm; its object is to hold soil against the roots so that they do not dry out.

SMALL TREES FOR FOREST PLANTING

The use of polythene bags, described later, is always advisable, but first we will look at the traditional methods, without this aid.

Small forest trees up to three feet in height, and including both seedlings and transplants, are moved in bundles, without soil. They are lifted from the nursery bed by using a fork, which is less liable to cut their roots than is a spade, or else with a mechanical lifter. They are then counted, culled, and bundled; these jobs should be done on a bench in a shed to shield the exposed roots from drying winds.

Counting is done in units of 100, or 50 for the larger descriptions of plants. Culling consists in throwing out any obviously inferior specimens —those that are dead, diseased, stunted, or show a number of weak, branchy upright shoots instead of a single strong leader. In a good batch of plants, the proportion of culls will not exceed 10%. The bundles are tied with binder twine—not too tightly as that would damage the bark.

Unless immediate transport is available, the bundles are next *heeled-in*. *Heeling* comes from the old Norse word *hylle* meaning to shelter or protect,

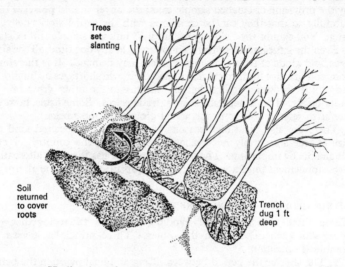

Trees
set
slanting

Soil
returned
to cover
roots

Trench
dug 1 ft
deep

FIGURE 39. Heeling-in, to keep tree roots safely moist pending planting. Roots are lightly buried in a shallow trench.

and the roots are in fact protected by burying them in a trench cut in soft moist earth, leaving the shoots projecting above ground.

During transport the young plants are always stacked with the same object of keeping the roots moist. Stacks of bundles must have roots inwards, shoots outwards. With evergreens, air must always be allowed to circulate round foliage; if evergreen trees are tightly stacked, for more than twenty-four hours, they heat up just as a damp haystack would do, and all the inner trees are killed.

Lorries or vans are the usual means of transport, since they can ensure through delivery from nursery to planting point. If rail is used, it should be passenger train—trees are living material. Where seas must be crossed, air transport has a clear advantage over ship, in that the trees are aboard for only a few hours and are not exposed, for a long spell, to the drying

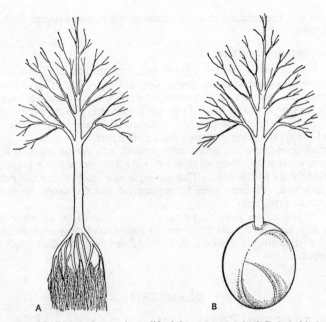

FIGURE 40. Ball-rooted tree; A, as lifted from nursery bed; B, baled in hessian for transport.

effects of a hot cargo hold. It is false economy to save transport costs for live trees.

On arrival at their destination the young trees should be promptly off-loaded and again *heeled-in*. If the ground is frozen, they can be stacked in piles with the roots of each bundle inwards, shoots outwards, until the ground thaws.

Polythene Bags

Polythene is impervious to both water and water vapour, and polythene bags are therefore widely and wisely used for the transport and storage of trees. The usual size and specification for a returnable bag, which can be used for several journeys is: 18 inches by 20 inches, 500 gauge.

Alternatively, a cheaper bag of lighter-gauge polythene can be used for a single journey, on a "throw-away" basis.

Trees in their dormant winter state can be stored in polythene bags for a matter of several weeks, but there is one important precaution that must be observed. *Trees in polythene bags must always be shaded.* If they are left in the sun, the polythene acts like a greenhouse, and in the absence of ventilation, and with no cooling by the evaporation of water, the trees heat-up to a temperature that kills them outright; this happens within a few hours.

TRANSPORTING SPECIMEN TREES

Trees between three feet and ten feet in height are handled individually. Each tree is dug out with the spade, complete with a ball of earth around its roots. The root ball is then wrapped in a sheet of sacking or hessian, which is secured with twine. If the stem is slender, a stout rod of round wood, such as a hazel stake, should be included in the bundle to lessen the risk of the stem getting damaged during transport.

Broadleaved trees are occasionally moved without an earth ball, to save transport costs. Instead, their roots are enclosed within a polythene bag tied firmly to the stem. This saving is not really worth the risk of loss involved. Conifers over three feet tall should never be moved without an earth ball.

On arrival at the planting point, the trees should be set with their roots in a trench, or else be stored in a cool shed away from artificial heat. At this stage the root ball, or polythene bag, should be left undisturbed.

PLANTING

SMALL FOREST TREES Plate 21, p. 276.

On the forest scale, small trees are planted by very quick, cheap and simple methods that appear, at first sight, too crude to succeed. Nevertheless, given good plants and some care, the forester gets a 90% success, which is adequate for his purpose. One man can plant from 500 to 1000 trees in one day. Quick methods are acceptable for small trees because they have not yet formed permanent roots; their main root system develops only after planting.

Much forest land nowadays is ploughed before planting. Ploughing is possible only on land that is free from tree stumps, hard rock, or large boulders, and which does not slope too steeply. Over much of the poor heathland, moorland and peat bog that is available for afforestation, it makes an enormous improvement to early growth for three reasons:

1. By cultivating the soil, it makes all its layers quickly available to tree roots, so ensuring an early supply of nutrients.

2. Since ploughing is done on a "partial" basis, with furrows at or about five feet apart, it provides, cheaply and effectively, an ideal network of open drains.

3. It checks the competition of weeds with the young trees for two or three years.

A further important advantage is that, by smothering heather or grass near the trees, and exposing earth in the bare furrows, it lessens fire risk —always serious on moorlands—for several years.

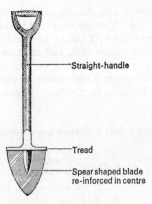

Straight-handle

Tread

Spear shaped blade
re-inforced in centre

FIGURE 41. Notching spade of the Schlich pattern for notch planting.

Forest ploughing can only be effectively done by specially large and strong ploughs pulled by powerful crawler tractors. The type of plough and the pattern of the work depends on local terrain and soil. In Britain, the techniques have been developed by Forestry Commission experts, and anyone unfamiliar with ploughing should seek the advice of the Commission before starting work.

Coming now to the actual planting, one-man working is the rule. In order to have both hands free, the planter carries his stock of young trees in a bag slung from his shoulders. Planting bags of stout waterproof fabric are on sale, but a sack will serve for a small quantity.

An ordinary garden spade is a satisfactory planting tool, but foresters with a large number of trees to plant prefer a *notching spade*. The usual pattern is that invented by a great German forester, Professor Sir William Schlich; his "Schlich" spade has a straight shank and a pointed blade. On stony ground a mattock is used instead.

Spacing between planting rows is done by setting up sighting rods at the end of each row. The planter then uses the handle of his tool to measure distances along the row. On ploughed land the furrows serve as guides. Spacing distances have already been discussed in Chapter 2, page 39.

NOTCH PLANTING

In its simplest form the notch is just a slit cut into the ground, into which the tree's roots are inserted. In practice, two notches are made, at right angles to each other, in the shape of a letter L or a letter T. The spade is first thrust into the soil to cut one "arm" of the letter. Then it is used to cut the second arm. Next it is levered sideways, whilst still in the ground, and this raises a wedge of earth and so opens a hole to take the tree's roots.

These roots are slipped into the gap, and the tree is drawn up to its original depth in the soil. The spade is next withdrawn, and the wedge of earth falls back into place, holding the roots firmly. The ground around the tree is now stamped firm, and the planter moves on.

On ploughed land, the notch is usually cut through the disturbed earth half-way up the "slice" thrown up by the plough. In very dry places the notch may be made in the furrow bottom instead.

TURF PLANTING

Spruce trees, which are planted in very large numbers in the forest, will

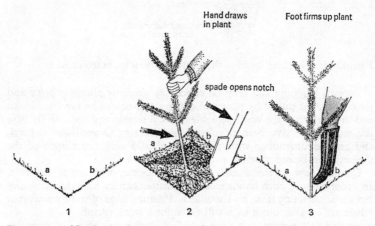

FIGURE 42. Notch planting. 1, two vertical notches, *a* and *b*, are first cut to meet at a right angle. 2, spade, inserted along line *b*, holds notch open, while hand draws plant into gap. 3, foot firms up plant, which is fixed upright where the two notches meet.

only start growth quickly if their roots are set at a very shallow depth. One easy way to achieve this is to cut out a "square" of turf or peaty soil, about one foot square, and to turn it upside down at the desired planting point; turf squares are best cut some weeks ahead of planting, to give them time to settle down.

At planting time a notch is cut, with the spade, through one side of the turf, running as far as the middle. The tree is then drawn through this notch, and the turf is raised, so that the roots can be spread out just beneath the turf; they then lie between *two* turf layers—one on the ground surface, and the other inverted so as to face it. The weight of the turf holds the tree firm until its flat roots have gained a good anchorage. As the meeting point of two opposed turfs always remains damp, failures are rare.

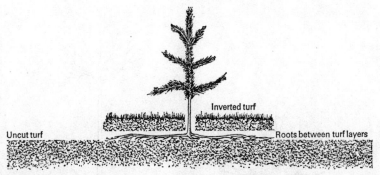

FIGURE 43. Turf planting. Tree roots are drawn between inverted turf and uncut turf layers. Inverted turf may be cut by spade or by plough.

On ploughed land, the upturned "slice" of turfy or peaty soil thrown up by the ploughshare is treated as a continuous "turf" and the trees are planted through it at five-foot intervals.

PIT PLANTING

This is the usual way of planting small numbers of small forest trees in gardens, as hedges or screens, or in the smaller woodlands. It is no longer

FIGURE 44. Pit planting. 1, hole is dug large enough to take all roots, and plant is held with its collar at original ground level. 2, soil is returned and tree firmed with foot.

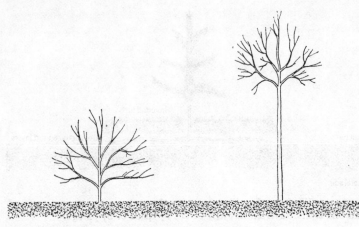

FIGURE 45. Bush (*left*) and standard tree (*right*).

used in large-scale forest planting because of high labour costs; since it takes about five times longer to put in each tree than does notch planting. For quick, sound work, two men, or a man and a boy, are needed.

The turf or leaf litter covering the planting point is first cut away, with the spade, over an area about eighteen inches square. The exposed soil is then dug out to a depth equal to that of the tree's roots, from nine inches to one foot, and is piled at the side of the pit.

One operator now holds the tree at the centre of the pit, with the roots well spread out, at the same depth as the tree previously grew in the nursery.

The other operator, using his spade, returns the earth to the pit, making sure that it is well broken up and spread both above and below the roots. Leaf litter is best mixed in with the soil; but a turf cover should be set on the surface, being turned upside down to check regrowth of grass.

All the disturbed earth, and turf if present, is then stamped firmly around the newly planted tree. *This is most important.* Failures in pit planting nearly always arise from insufficient firming-up; roots can only draw water from soil pressing tightly against them.

Mulching

Successful establishment after pit planting is greatly aided by piling a mulch of mown grass or weeds, or indeed any plant material, around the base of the young tree. This mulch should extend about nine inches from the stem in all directions. Initially it may be from four to six inches high, since it soon settles down.

In small-scale work, enough mulching material can usually be found reasonably near. On a larger scale, the weed growth cut back at the first summer weeding provides ample mulching stuff; as a rule one such dressing will suffice.

The mulch works in two main ways: it holds moisture close to the tree's roots, and it checks immediately competing weed growth. It also provides some nutrients and keeps the soil cool. Turf-planted trees are—automatically—given such a mulch; while in practice notch-planted trees are seldom mulched. But anyone who goes in for pit planting amid grass or woodland weed growth will find that the cost of this extra step is amply repaid by a better percentage of success, and quicker early growth.

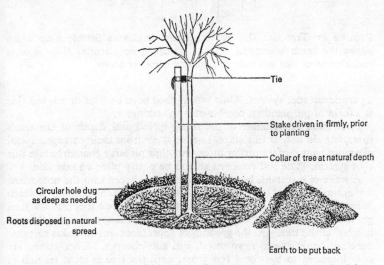

Tie

Stake driven in firmly, prior to planting

Collar of tree at natural depth

Circular hole dug as deep as needed

Roots disposed in natural spread

Earth to be put back

FIGURE 46. Planting a standard tree. A circular hole is dug and a stake driven in. After tree has been set at correct depth its roots are spread out and soil is returned and firmed up. The tie must not be tightened till tree is firm.

Manuring Small Forest Trees

On poor moorland or heathland soils, fertilisers are applied at the time of planting. The usual treatment is two to four ounces of ground mineral phosphate per tree, or its equivalent in some other form of phosphatic manure. This fertiliser, in the form of a fine powder, is simply sprinkled around the base of the newly-planted tree.

PLANTING SPECIMEN TREES

The planting of trees that are to stand as individuals calls for more care, and a quite different technique, than does the planting of small forest trees. Specimens are more valuable, and they have already developed

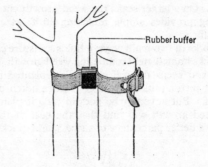

FIGURE 47. Tree tie. This buckle pattern employs a flexible strap which allows the trunk to expand without strangling or scarring. Note separate encirclement of tree and stake and adjustable rubber buffer.

a permanent root system. Only one method need be considered, and this is a form of pit planting, combined with staking.

First make an estimate of the likely spread and depth of the tree's roots, but do not, at this stage, remove them from their package. Next, clear away any surface turf or litter, and dig a pit large enough to take this root system. The soil removed should be neatly piled on one side.

A stake of a suitable length should now be driven into the untouched soil at the bottom of the pit, within an inch or two of the position in which the tree is to stand. This stake should go at least one foot into the firm ground; this means that it must be about two feet longer than the "staked height" of the tree. On the grounds of appearance, round stakes carrying bark are preferable to sawn wood, and also cheaper. Since stakes are only intended to last for a few years, until the tree is stout enough to stand on its own, it is not necessary to use a durable timber, nor to treat

PLATE I   *Trees for places*

Above left A monkey puzzle strikes a bizarre note in a landscaped garden. Branches sweeping down to ground level are only seen where there is all-round exposure to light and complete protection from browsing animals.

Above left Swamp cypress, a deciduous conifer from the southern states of America, is the only temperate-zone tree that thrives with its roots in water. This specimen in a pond in Kew Gardens shows the buttresses that give support on soft, marshy ground.

Below The great yew in Selborne churchyard, Hampshire, immortalised by Gilbert White.

The association of yews with churchyards dates back to the Christian mission-aries who preached in their shade, before churches were built. The Selborne tree, already a giant in the eighteenth century, may thus date back to heathen Saxon times.

the stake with a preservative. A pointed length of sweet chestnut, about $1\frac{1}{2}$ inches in diameter, is satisfactory and cheap; and it has some natural durability in its slender heartwood.

Several patent makes of ties for securing tree stems to stakes are on the market. The main requirements are that they should be strong, easily tied, adjustable to allow for distance, diameter of stake and diameter of tree, and fairly flexible. Alternatively, strong twine may be used; if so, the tying knot or loop around the stake should be distinct from that around the stem, and a small amount of movement should be possible between the two. Twine, rubber, and most plastics are sufficiently soft to hold strong-barked stems without injury; stems with thin bark may be shielded by a strip of sacking below the tie. Never use wire, or any form of metal, in a tree-tie; as the stem expands wire is sure to dig in and cause a dangerous wound.

Any fertilisers that are to be applied should now be added. Organic manures, such as spent hops, hop manure, leaf mould, or farmyard manure, should be spread over the base of the pit. Chemical fertilisers are better mixed in with the soil that is to be returned, as this prevents immediate close contact of concentrated chemicals with tree roots.

When all is ready, the tree is taken from its package, and the actual planting is done by two men. One holds the stem upright so that the previous level of the soil against it coincides with the level of the ground at its new station. The other spreads out the roots evenly over the ground. Then he fills in the soft earth that has been removed from the pit. When it has all been returned, the new earth level is likely to be higher than that of the surrounding ground. The loose earth is next stamped down with the feet until the original level is restored, as far as is possible. This firming-up plays a large part in ensuring the success of the job. Finally, when the stem is unlikely to be moved again, the tie is used to hold the stem firmly to the stake; and the surface, only, of the soil is roughened with the rake for appearance sake.

When dealing with fairly small and valuable shrubs, it is best not to disturb the earth ball, or even the packing that surrounds it. A covering of hessian or sacking soon rots away in damp earth, and such methods

PLATE 2 *Branch form in conifers*

Above left Serbian spruce, native to a small mountain zone near Sarajevo, has a notably narrow crown, upswept branches and hanging twigs.
Above right European larch, from the high Alps, bears sturdy, downward-trending branches; it sheds its needles in winter.
Below left Lawson cypress, from British Columbian foothills, bears frond-like foliage at the tips of slender branches. Many trees have forked stems like this one, which is a major drawback for timber production, though not for scenic effect.
Below right Deodar cedar, from the Indian Himalayas, bears evergreen needles on gently sloping branches, which always droop at their tips.

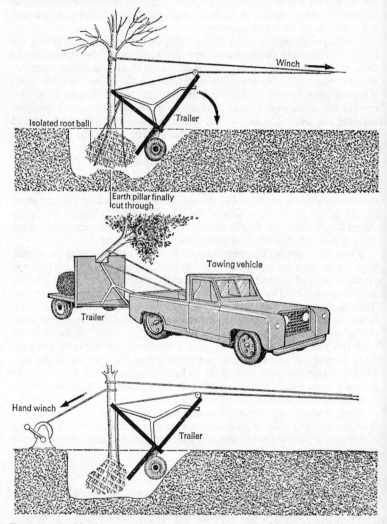

FIGURE 48. Moving a semi-mature tree. A, the tree, with root ball isolated all round, is drawn on to trailer by a winch on the towing vehicle. B, the tree can now be transported any distance by road, with root ball—bound in hessian—intact. C, at the new site, the tree is lowered into a prepared hole, then drawn upright and staked.

FIGURE 49. Types of label. A, to hang on branch or tree guard. B, to stand in ground. Made from aluminium or plastic.

reduce the chances of loss to the minimum. A few "difficult" trees, such as Maritime pine, Monterey pine, and Monterey cypress, are sometimes planted direct from pots; the earth-ball is loosened by a sharp tap on the pot, and inserted into a suitably shaped hole.

TRANSPLANTING VERY LARGE TREES

The movement of really big trees, from ten to fifty feet in height, has a curious history. Around the year 1800, huge horse-drawn carriages, with winches attached, were quite often used to move large trees when noblemen laid out their parks, regardless of cost. The practice then lapsed until about 1960 when tractor-drawn machinery was imported from America to do the same work at acceptable present-day costs. Because special plant is needed, the work is only done by a few contracting firms who are experts at it. Their charges are (in 1970) around £1.25 for every foot in height of each tree. Only broadleaved trees can be moved with real prospects of success; conifers are very chancy.

Before a big tree is moved, it must be prepared—preferably two years ahead—by digging short trenches around its base equal in total to half the circumference; these trenches are then filled with leaf mould to encourage bushy roots to form. Next year the severance of the side roots is completed by cutting similar trenches round the remainder of the tree's base.

During the following resting season, the whole root-ball below the tree is dug out by machinery. The tree is then winched over, using special plant, so that it is gradually tilted to a horizontal position on a wheeled trailer. This lifts the heavy root-ball clear of the ground, and it is carefully supported and protected with sacking. Once mounted on wheels, the tree may be towed for any distance to its new station. There, a hole is dug to receive it, corresponding to the size of the root-ball.

The tree's root-ball is then carefully lowered into the hole, and its trunk is drawn to an upright position with suitable tackle. During its first few years the tree is held firmly upright with guy-ropes, but after that root-growth and soil pressure make it fully stable and safe.

These "instant trees", as they are sometimes called, are mostly in demand on new housing schemes, or close to important new buildings.

LABELLING

The temporary label that arrives with each tree should always be left attached until a permanent label has been put in place. The type of label to use depends on personal choice, but it is surprising how difficult and expensive it is to produce a pleasing and easily readable label that will last as long as a tree. Most materials suffer from the weather, or the atmosphere, or attract marauders, either human or animal. Machines for engraving or embossing durable materials are naturally expensive, while anything written or painted is sure to fade or be rubbed off.

One cheap and durable type of label is the aluminium strip that can be embossed on one of the machines found on railway stations. Another, more colourful pattern is the "Dymo" embossed plastic type, which is cheap in itself but needs an embossing machine costing about £15. The Forestry Commission uses an engraved laminated plastic, of sandwich construction, in which dark lettering shows up through a white surface, but this calls for an engraving machine to form the letters. Kew Gardens prefers white lettering showing up through black, which makes the labels less conspicuous but harder to find.

Labels are best attached to stems by a loose tie of galvanised, or plastic-covered wire. As trees and shrubs grow outwards, it is necessary, from time to time, to move labels to some fresh position so that they are not hidden by foliage.

WEEDING

Weeding is seldom needed for specimen trees, since they are already large enough to stand clear of all competing growth. The digging-over of soil, close to their roots is more likely to do harm than good, since it is difficult to avoid root damage. There is no great advantage in keeping the adjacent soil completely free of weeds or grass. In practice the simplest method of controlling competition is to maintain a mulch of cut grass or leaf litter around the base of the stem, for a few years after planting.

Small forest trees normally need weeding, to a degree that depends on the surrounding vegetation, but it is never necessary, and it can be harmful, to maintain bare soil around their roots. Trees planted on ploughed peaty ground, or heather moorland, may need little weeding, or possibly none at all, because they can keep their growing shoots clear of the surrounding grass or heather, which has already been checked by the ploughing.

On most kinds of ground, however, small forest trees need one or two

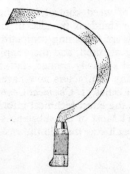

FIGURE 50. Reap hook, a sickle-shaped tool used for most forest weeding.

weedings during their first summer, and an annual weeding during the next summer or two, in order to prevent them becoming smothered by surrounding plants. The main object is to keep the tree's main stem, and leading shoot, free from all risk of being pressed down by the surrounding grass, heather, bracken, fern, or other wild plant growth when that dies down each autumn. Temporary shading during the summer causes the young trees only a slight setback. It is the crushing of a soft and tender shoot, which may be intensified by snowfall, that can cause the fatal damage.

Weeding usually begins in June, when the surrounding growth has become tall, and continues until the end of September. If two weedings are needed, they should be done at an interval of about two months. The usual tool is called the reap-hook; it has a sickle-shaped blade (without teeth on it) and is made in both right-handed and left-handed patterns. Each weeder should also carry a stick, which serves two purposes. It is used to clear the weed growth to one side of each tree, so that the tree itself is not damaged when the weeds are cut. It is also used as a "distance piece", to measure the distance, along the rows, between the trees. This is necessary because the trees are often hidden below overgrowing weeds, and cannot be found without a search.

It is seldom necessary to clear *all* the weed growth. All that must be done is the freeing of the trees along the rows. The cut weed growth is usually left where it falls; when dealing with a small number of trees it is worth while to pile it as a mulch around the base of each one.

Many suggestions have been made for the use of machines in place of a cutting tool, for weeding forest trees. Any machine must be quite small, since it has to work along a space between trees that is, in practice, never more than three feet, after allowance has been made for side branches. No really practical machine that can cope with rough ground, stumps, rocks, and slopes, has yet been devised. At present, this line of approach must be considered experimental.

Chemical methods of weed control have been developed in recent years and are now the standard practice in large forest nurseries. In young plantations they are becoming competitive with hand tool work, even though the chemicals used, and their application, are fairly costly. Special equipment, and specially trained staff, are needed for their safe and cheap use, but many contractors now have the necessary expertise. Forestry Commission Leaflet 51, *Chemical Control of Weeds in the Forest* (H.M.S.O. 20p.) gives the latest technical information.

Mistakes are murder! Most of the substances used, if misapplied, kill the crop trees just as readily as they do the weeds.

REPLACEMENT OF FAILURES

No matter what care is used, a proportion of planted trees is sure to fail. In forest planting it is usual to tolerate up to 10% of failure; provided the gaps are evenly spread over the crop, they will not seriously upset its future progress or timber yield. If there are more failures than this, or if they form groups, the losses must be made good during the following planting season. This operation is usually called "beating up", from the Anglo-Saxon word *betan*, meaning to mend or repair.

It is not worth while to beat up a crop *after* the season following planting. Small trees put into a crop only two years after planting hardly ever catch up, and are simply smothered by their neighbours.

In hedgerows, screens, and shelterbelts, gaps are more serious. They should be filled up for anything up to five years after planting. If necessary, larger trees—naturally costing more—should be used to ensure that the additions keep pace with those trees that were planted first.

Failures among specimen or roadside trees inevitably attract attention. In any planting scheme, an allowance should be made, and funds should be reserved, for their replacement during the first year or two after the planting is done.

TREES IN CONTAINERS

A recent development has been the marketing of trees in waterproof fibre containers, usually from garden centres with car parks adjacent to nurseries. The purchaser can choose his specimens ready packed, each with its own root ball and supply of soil. Though the weight for transport is heavy, this method simplifies transport and virtually eliminates losses. All that is needed is to dig a hole of appropriate size, strip off the container just before planting, and firm up the ground around the root ball.

8. Pruning

ANY healthy and vigorous tree, left to itself, strives to fill the available space within reach by growing upwards and outwards. By so doing, it gains the greatest possible amount of sunlight, which it needs for life and growth. It also outgrows, and overcomes by shading out, weeds and other trees, including those of its own kind. Growth to maximum size is part of a tree's natural struggle for existence. Only the taller and larger specimens are likely to flower, bear fruits and seeds, and so propagate their kind.

Under cultivation, this natural process is aided, but also controlled, by spacing at planting time, weeding during the first few years, thinning out as the tree crowns expand, and by pruning in a variety of ways.

The main types of pruning that concern the tree grower are these:
1. The pruning away of dead or dying side branches that have served their purpose, which is sometimes called *dead-pruning*. This is a regular practice with conifers growing in plantations, but is unusual elsewhere (See "Pruning Conifers" below).
2. The pruning or lopping of live and vigorous street or specimen trees, to control their growth within available space. This *live-pruning* is frequently done to broadleaved trees, but seldom to conifers.
3. *Orchard pruning*, to promote the production of flowers and fruit in fruit trees.
4. *Side-shoot pruning* of poplars and willows to provide a knot-free bottom length of timber.

All pruning aims to control the natural pattern of growth, so we will consider this presently before detailing practical methods to apply.

WOUNDING AND HEALING

All pruning involves cutting through the full range of tissue that make up every branch—that is: bark, bast, cambium and true wood. Even in the smallest branch, sapwood is exposed by any pruning cut; in the larger branches heartwood is exposed also. From the tree's point of view, every pruning cut is a wound that must be healed.

Pruned trees always try to heal over every wound made by a cutting tool, but they do not always succeed. Their mechanism for healing cuts acts very slowly. Their scar tissue, which is called *callus*, can only grow out from the living, undamaged cambium, and after a branch has been cut off cambium tissue is only present around the circular edge of the cut. The callus grows out over the surface of the wound at the rate of perhaps one sixth of an inch a year; thus a wound only one inch

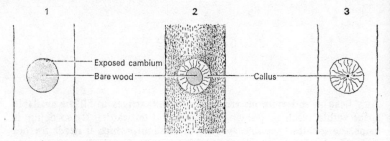

FIGURE 51. Natural healing of a pruning scar. 1, exposed bare wood surrounded by exposed cambium layer. 2, three years later, callus produced by cambium is healing over scar. 3, six years after pruning, callus ring has closed, healing is complete.

across, healing from all sides, needs three years for the callus to meet in the centre. Until the wound is fully healed over, there is always a risk that a fungal disease may gain entry to the exposed wood, as described in Chapter 9, page 148, and ultimately cause the death of the tree.

This risk of unsuccessful healing need not be exaggerated. It is slight in the following circumstances:

a. The *dead-pruning* of side branches of conifers (see 1 above); here the wounds are protected by the natural resins of the tree, which ooze out and cover the cut.

b. The *live-pruning* of *small* branches of broadleaved trees (as in (2), (3), and (4), above).

In these cases it is unusual for any protective steps to be taken.

But risk of unsuccessful healing, and therefore of fungal decay, is serious as soon as *large* live branches are cut away, as may arise under (2) and (3) above, i.e. lopping and orchard pruning.

As a practical working rule, all live pruning wounds over half-an-inch in diameter should be promptly coated with a wound dressing. The purpose of this is simply to protect the exposed surface from invasion by fungal diseases until the callus tissue, arising from the surrounding cambium, has had time to heal the cut. The material used must be waterproof, flexible, lasting, harmless to plant tissues, and unsuitable for colonisation by fungi. Bituminous dressings answer best, and the brand most widely marketed and successfully applied in Britain is that called "Arbrex". Alternatively, ordinary lead paint, of the undercoat type, gives a reasonable protection.

PRUNING CONIFERS

A typical coniferous tree shows the simplest pattern of growth. Its main upright shoot becomes a *leader*, which grows vertically upwards to the ultimate limit of the tree's height. At intervals along the upright stem that results, side branches grow outwards. Often these are in *whorls*, from about six inches to three feet apart, corresponding to each annual stage of upward growth; by counting these whorls, it is possible to make a fair estimate of the tree's age.

Those side branches that are nearest to the foot of the tree are naturally the oldest, and so they are normally the longest and stoutest. The result is the beautiful, symmetrical, pyramidal shape that is seen, all too rarely, when a conifer has been allowed to grow unpruned on a clear open space such as a lawn. Such a tree is described as being perfectly *furnished* with side branches. As a rule, the very youngest whorls of side branches have vanished; they have been overshaded by stronger branches higher up, but these branches now sweep down almost to ground level.

Many events may lead to a disturbance of this ideal pattern. There are few gardens in which space can be spared for the full sweep of branches at ground level, so as the tree grows larger the lower branches are usually pruned away. If the leading shoot or bud is damaged, two or more side shoots may grow up to take its place, giving a *double leader*, or *fork*. This fault can be corrected, if it is seen in time and happens at a height within reach, by pruning away all but one of the competing shoots.

In woodlands, the lower branches of conifers gradually die, and slowly disappear, through overshading by more vigorous branches that grow higher up and all around them, on their own stem or the stems of neighbouring trees. The *canopy* formed by the *crowns* of the trees restricts the amount of light reaching the leaves lower down. When these leaves can no longer function, they are no longer renewed when they fall, and the branches that bear them are discarded. This is sometimes called *natural pruning*.

All the time that living side branches are growing outwards, at the rate of a few inches—or a few feet—each year, the trunk of the tree is also slowly expanding outwards, but only at the rate of a fraction of an inch—say one tenth to half an inch—each year. Nevertheless, it is steadily growing over the base of each branch, and whenever any side branch dies and falls off, or is pruned away, its base remains embedded in the stem wood. This branch base is called a *knot*. Sound knots are not a serious fault in timber, though decayed ones, or large and numerous ones, lower its value. *Knot-free* or *clear* timber is formed after side branches have disappeared, and then only in the outer layers of the lower part of a tree's trunk; the centre of any tree is always knotty. Consequently knot-free timber is scarce and expensive, and it is reserved for special uses, such as uprights of wooden ladders.

BRASHING CONIFERS Plate 4b, p. 149.

The lower side branches of coniferous trees, growing in plantations, have usually become overshaded, and so have died, by the time the crop is about fifteen years old. They may take another fifteen years to disappear, and in the meantime they get in the way of the orderly working of the crop. So it is a common forestry practice to prune them away, up to a height of six feet, in the operation known as *brashing*.

The best tool for this task is a curved pruning saw mounted on a two-foot handle, so that *both* hands can be used. Its teeth are pointed in such a way that it cuts only on the "pull" stroke, and it can be used all day, even by women, without unduly tiring the operator. Like all saws, it must be regularly sharpened and its teeth must be regularly re-set. It must also be cleaned from resin at intervals, and oiled to ensure smooth working. Billhooks are sometimes used instead, but unless a worker is highly skilled he leaves rough branch stubs that are slow to heal, and he also wounds the bark of the main trunk.

Brashing justifies its cost in several ways:

1. It enables the forester and his staff to move freely through the wood to mark, fell, trim, and remove those trees that are to be cut out, in stages, as thinnings.

2. It removes side branches that must, in any event, be trimmed away from poles or logs before they can be sold.

3. It returns to the soil those nutrients that would otherwise remain locked up in the dead branches for many years; at the same time the fallen branches form a mulch on the forest floor, a mulch that retains water and checks soil erosion.

4. By removing a network of inflammable material between the ground and the canopy of the trees, it lessens fire risk; it also makes all parts of the plantation accessible if a fire should occur.

HIGH PRUNING CONIFERS Plate 4, a and c, p. 129

As a conifer crop grows taller, other branches higher up also become overshaded and die. By removing these also, it is possible to promote, and in fact to guarantee, the production of knot-free wood in the outer zones of a substantial length of tree trunk. Unfortunately, the costs of pruning rise very steeply as soon as work has to be done higher up. A man with a long-handled pruning saw can reach up to twenty feet, without using a ladder; but once ladders are needed costs become prohibitive. As there is no promise that a higher price will in fact be obtained, many years later on, for the knot-free or clear wood that results, little high pruning has been done so far.

PRUNING BROADLEAVED TREES

The growth patterns of broadleaved trees are far more variable, and less predictable, than are those of conifers. The buds from which their shoots spring are not so regularly disposed, and broadleaved trees are also well equipped with what the botanist calls *adventitious buds*. These structures, though not visible to the naked eye, are very important for pruning and maintenance. No matter how or where you prune or lop a broadleaved tree, new shoots will spring out around the base of the cut and start to form a fresh cluster of branches. The only, infrequent, exceptions to this rule concern very large and old trees, which gradually lose their power of quick recovery from injury.

The readiness with which broadleaved trees will send forth fresh sprouts was formerly used by foresters and farmers who wished to grow repeated crops of small poles. If they chopped their trees at ground level, the resulting pole crop was called *coppice*, from the French verb *couper*, to cut. If they lopped the trees six feet above ground, so that cattle could not reach the fresh shoots, the trees were called *pollards*, from another French word *poil*, meaning "head". Many coppices, or copses, and pollarded trees can still be seen throughout the countryside, but these methods are only used locally to-day; for example, sweet chestnut is coppiced in Kent, and willows are sometimes pollarded in the English Midlands. But pollards arising through drastic lopping of ornamental trees are very common, and not particularly beautiful!

Broadleaved trees, when grown in plantations, follow the same patterns of branch growth and decline, as do the conifers. Their lower branches gradually die and fall away as their supply of light diminishes. In broadleaved woods, however, self-pruning is the rule; neither the low pruning or *brashing*, nor the high pruning, that we considered for the conifers, are commonly done in forest practice. So for the broadleaves we are mainly concerned with the *live pruning* of extending leaders and branches, and not with *dead pruning*, or the removal of side branches that have served their purpose.

Broadleaved trees have an altogether more variable pattern of branching than do the conifers. Their side branches spread out in all directions, and often change direction as they go. They frequently become as vigorous as the leading shoot, which becomes hard to trace amidst a maze of curving branches and lesser twigs. The result is the wonderful rounded crown formed by many fine garden and hedgerow trees, which makes very good use of all available sunlight. Such open-grown trees grow fast; both trunk and crown expand rapidly.

Wherever space allows, this glorious, natural crown of branches and foliage is best left alone. It is a mistake to suppose that pruning or lopping is needed for the benefit of the tree. Every cut carries with it some risk of the entry of decay, and a healthy tree is well able to maintain its proper balanced strength and weight distribution, and to shed unwanted small branches as they become overshaded, without a pruner's help. Pruning and lopping should be regarded as exceptional measures made necessary by restrictions on the growth of the tree. The commonest restriction is, of course, lack of space—both physically and in its effects; there may, for example, be room for a tree's crown to expand, but such expansion may be inadmissible because it would obstruct light.

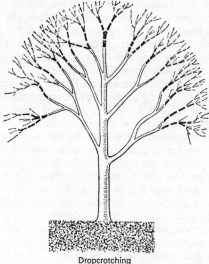

Dropcrotching
Branches removed shown by dotted lines

FIGURE 52. Drop-crotching holds the crown within set limits without spoiling appearance. Every few years the upper and outer branches—only—are shortened.

Patterns of Broadleaved Tree Pruning

Before describing details of methods, we must look first at the basic patterns that can be followed, where a free choice is allowed. Often the present tender of established trees has little choice, since a pattern has already been established by his predecessors. Change from one pattern to another is so difficult that one can usually rule it out. The old proverb:

> As the twig is bent,
> So grows the tree

applies with particular force here.

DROP-CROTCHING

Drop-crotching is the technical term for the lightest and least unsightly method of pruning, which best preserves the natural appearance of a broadleaved tree's crown. For the successful application of this method, it is essential to start it before the tree has grown beyond its intended maximum size, and while its branches are still fairly young and fine.

The principle of the method is that the lower branches, and the main trunk, are touched as little as possible. Instead, the upper growths are cut back to a level below that regarded as the desirable maximum. Likewise side shoots are trimmed back to points well within the limit of desirable outward branch spread.

The reaction of the pruned tree is to send forth a fresh crop of irregular shoots, of natural appearance, which gradually refill the space above and around them. Once the limits are again reached, the *drop-crotching* is repeated. This implies a regular pruning cycle, which may be a matter of four to five years. Provided a reasonable amount of light always reaches the lower branches, they will continue to grow healthily and to bear green leaves. This healthy lower foliage, and the general irregular appearance of the tree's crown, maintains the beauty of street and park trees, without the sudden ugliness that is forced upon the public gaze by more drastic methods.

Though many cuts must be made, they are small ones and therefore

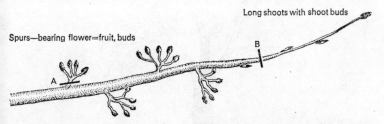

FIGURE 53. Pruning a spur-bearing fruit tree, e.g. apple. Spurs which bear flower buds and therefore fruit may be thinned out, as at A, but must never be wholly removed. Pruning of long shoots, as at B, controls growth.

cheap, and since heartwood is only occasionally exposed, risk of fungal disease is low.

ORCHARD PRUNING

Though this is not a book on fruit production, we must look at *orchard* methods because they are sometimes the best to follow for flowering trees or shrubs, and particularly for crab-apples and ornamental cherries.

The fruit grower has two main objects—to maintain a well-shaped crown, at a workable size, and to secure repeated annual "crops" of flower-buds, which alone can produce flowers and fruits. He is of course ready to spend a lot of money on pruning, and to do it annually.

To maintain crown shape, you must select likely *framework* shoots and branches, which will grow in the desired directions. Shapes vary in detail, but a common pattern is a circle of framework shoots radiating outwards and upwards from the central trunk, like the spokes of a wheel or the framework of a wicker basket. Light must always be allowed in towards the heart of the crown, since only those branches that get ample sunlight will bear flowers and fruit. Left to itself, the tree would soon fill the hollow of the "basket" by sending out shoots across and over it; each separate branch is also liable to encroach on its neighbour's growing space, by sending out side shoots. At each main pruning, therefore, any shoots that would cross the path of framework branches, or overshade them, are cut back or cut off. As soon as the framework reaches its desired size, it is stopped by the regular cutting back of shoots that strive to grow out beyond this.

Most fruit trees bear their flowers on short *spur* shoots that arise at intervals along the framework branches. It is essential to respect these, by leaving them untouched, unless they become unduly numerous or

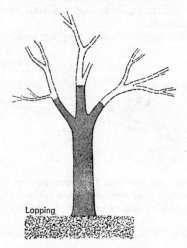

Lopping

FIGURE 54. Lopping inevitably leaves an unsightly trunk and limbs. Avoid this treatment wherever possible.

crowded, when they may be thinned out. These spurs do not extend growth, but continue to bear flower-buds for many years. So long as the framework is regularly and thoroughly pruned, most of the tree's nutrients go into these spurs, and so help to form fruit. But if the pruning of a young and vigorous tree is neglected, then after a season or so all its efforts are put into expanding its crown, and fruit production then ceases for several years.

Plums and a few other fruit trees are "tip bearers". They do not bear their flowers on side spurs, but on young shoots formed in the previous season near the tips of their branches. So it is essential to allow ample growth near the outer and upper surfaces of the crown. In practice this is done by keeping pruning down to the minimum needed to maintain a reasonable size and a good shape.

LOPPING AND TOPPING

The common alternative to drop-crotching, or to orchard pruning, is the *lopping* of side branches and the *topping* of the main trunk, which is seen far too often, and always with unsightly results. Sometimes, because of past neglect, it is the only possible course.

Briefly, a tree that has grown far beyond the desirable limits of height and spread is "cut down to size" by the removal of stout branches and a portion of its sturdy upper trunk, at points well within or below the allowable size-limit. This is costly, because large cuts must be made at awkward positions far above the ground. It is also risky, because the large exposed cut surfaces are difficult to treat effectively with preservative dressings. Worst of all, it is unsightly because the trees look like dead stumps for two or three years after lopping. Their regrowth takes the form of clusters of weak young shoots arising from many points all round the edges of the cut, like the hair of a golliwog. Only gradually do the weakest of these shoots die, leaving the stronger ones to assume a less unnatural appearance. The "lopped" look is never entirely lost, no matter how long the tree may stand.

The one point in favour of lopping and topping is that it need only be done at intervals of many years. Ten years is quite likely to elapse before another lopping is needed, whilst there are many instances of trees needing no further attention for twenty years. Also, there are circumstances in which it is the only alternative to felling. For example, an

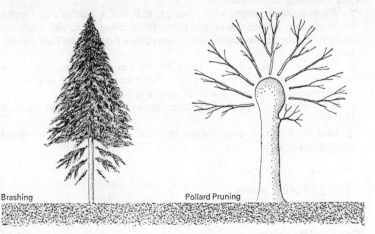

Brashing Pollard Pruning

FIGURE 55. Brashing (*left*) means the cutting away of lower, dead branches from young conifers. Pollard pruning (*right*) involves the cutting back of twigs to a single bole every few years; acceptable in confined spaces, but only applicable to broadleaved trees.

airport or electricity supply authority may have legal powers to limit established trees to a certain height or spread of branches; the owner must conform to these limits, or else remove his trees entirely.

POLLARD PRUNING

In *pollard pruning*, trees are first cut back to one or more points at which the growth of *stout* branches is to be permanently held. Clusters of pollard shoots spring out from these branch terminals, and are allowed to grow for two or three seasons. They are then cut right back to the terminals. Next year a fresh shoot crop arises, and so the process continues indefinitely.

The method has some merits. It is simple and can be continued by semi-skilled labour, whilst there are never any large branches to dispose of, only twigs. Its great disadvantage is that every three years or so the pollarded trees are reduced to bare poles which develop, during the following season, only as far as "poles-with-whiskers". Only for one or two summers in each pruning cycle do they remotely resemble natural trees. However, it is a plan often seen in towns and cities, and it works after a fashion with poplars, planes, and limes.

SIDE-SHOOT PRUNING Plate 4d, p. 129

Side-shoot pruning or *shrouding* consists simply of removing the small side shoots or *laterals* that spring out from the trunks of most broadleaved trees, so as to gain a branch-free lower stem. It is an essential operation in the following circumstances:

1. When growing poplars for veneers, that is for matches or veneer baskets, since side shoots on the lower butts cause knots and spoil the timber. Poplars have side shoots removed to a height of at least twenty feet.

2. For cricket-bat willows grown for cricket bats, since knots are considered a defect in the bat clefts. Willows are pruned to a height of fourteen feet. Likewise ash for sports goods.

3. Roadside trees, where side branches would obscure the view of traffic.

4. Park and garden trees, wherever unobstructed space is needed around the trunks.

PLATE 3 *Conifer crowns*

Above The graceful symmetrical crown of an open-grown cedar of Lebanon, with great branches evenly balanced to resist the weight of winter snow and the forces of fierce gales.

Below Stone pine, from the Mediterranean, has a crown that spreads outwards to intercept maximum sunshine. This top-heavy look explains its alternative name of umbrella pine. Its large edible seeds, used in confectionery, are the pine kernels of commerce.

5. High-grafted trees, or standards, where the side shoots arise from the stock, and not the grafted scion.

Lateral pruning is best done by the simple process of disbudding. All buds or small shoots that appear in spring are simply cut off flush with the bark, using a sharp knife. The cuts are so small that no antiseptic treatment is needed. Provided the tree is being allowed to grow a good-sized crown higher up, side growth on the lower trunk is unlikely to be vigorous; as the bark matures, side growth usually ceases altogether.

Pruning Tools and Methods

SIMPLE-EDGED BLADES

Pruning *can* be done by simple-edged tools such as knives, chisels, and bill-hooks, but all these require a high degree of skill. With the exception of a knife for disbudding, they cannot be commended to people who only undertake pruning occasionally.

Pruning knives were once widely used for fruit trees and ornamental shrubs, but have now been replaced by secateurs. Knives are needed, however, for removing buds, or weak side shoots, in lateral pruning. Pruning chisels, which can be mounted on long handles if necessary, are also effective for weak side shoots on broadleaved trees, but need much skill for brashing or pruning conifers. The bill-hook, unless handled expertly, can cause rough snags on branch bases and bark wounds elsewhere. But it is sometimes the only practical tool on branches too stout for shears, yet too weak for the saw.

SECATEURS, SHEARS AND TREE-PRUNERS

These tools, which all belong to the scissors family and embody two opposed edged blades, are fully satisfactory on all branches up to half-an-inch thick. Long-handled tree-pruners, operated by a lever at the base of the handle, enable the operator to reach many high branches, otherwise out of reach, from the ground or a suitable platform.

PLATE 4   *Pruning*

Above left A magnificent stand of Corsican pine in the New Forest, which needed no pruning. The trees suppressed each other's side branches by mutual shade, leaving clean stems with 'clear' timber, knot-free except at the centre.
Above right Lawson cypress plantation after brashing, also called low-pruning. Access has been made easier and fire risk reduced, but only the lowest six-foot length of timber will be knot-free.
Below left High-pruning a Douglas fir plantation to stop further knot formation over the lowest twenty-foot length of each stem. Clear timber, expected to command high prices, will be the result.
Below right It was essential to prune this ash plantation, since no knots are accepted in its final product—hockey sticks.

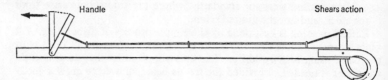

FIGURE 56. Long-handled tree pruner. Movement of handle at foot closes shears at top.

SAWS

Three distinct types of saw are commonly used in tree-pruning:

1. One-handed pruning saws, which can be carried up into the crown where necessary.
2. Two-handed pruning or brashing saws, used only at, or near, ground level, mainly for brashing conifers.
3. Bow-saws, with replaceable blades, which are very handy and can be used with one hand or with two; they are easily "parked" in the crown of a tree by slipping the bow-shaped handle over a short stout branch.

Carpenters' saws, whatever their type, are of no use for tree-pruning. They have insufficient "set" to their teeth, and this causes them to jam in the narrow *kerf*, or cut, that they produce.

All tree-pruning saws must have a high degree of *set*, and this must be maintained at intervals by using a saw-setting tool. This set enables them to work through both green and dry wood, at most of the awkward angles that will be encountered on living branches.

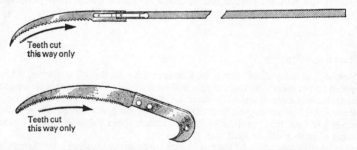

FIGURE 57. *Above*, two-handed pruning saw. *Below*, one-handed saw.

See also figures 64 & 65, pages 155 & 157, for other pruning tools.

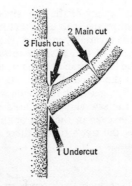

FIGURE 58. Removing a large side branch: sequence of cuts. 1, undercut to prevent splitting of bark. 2, main cut to sever branch. 3, flush cut to leave good healing surface.

OTHER ITEMS

A hand-axe or hatchet should always be available for tackling awkward limbs. Though it will seldom be used in the actual pruning, it may be needed, for example, to help free an accidentally jammed saw.

A rope, of half-inch diameter, for securing and lowering cumbersome branches, is frequently useful, and a lighter hand-line, for hauling up tools, is often handy.

A first-aid outfit should always be kept at hand, and tree wound paint should always be available.

The special equipment needed for felling, the lopping and topping of large trees, and for tree surgery, is described in Chapter 10, page 154.

Pruning Cuts

Any cut larger than that for the simple severance of a small branch, under half-an-inch in diameter, demands a special technique, which is easily learnt.

FLUSH CUTTING

First, all cuts to remove branches over half-an-inch in diameter *must be made flush with the larger branch, or tree trunk, that bears them.* Never, never, leave such a cut even as little as half-an-inch out from the branch base. It must be made or trimmed flush every time.

All healing starts from the cambium ring round the edge of a cut, and it will only proceed effectively from the cambium of a *living* branch or trunk. A stub dies, and healing stops; it's as simple as that!

But worse follows. A stub fails not only to heal itself; it physically obstructs the possible healing of the gap, since the cambium around its base cannot grow through the stub until that has decayed and gone.

As the stub dies, it is invariably invaded by the fungi that cause decay. These, in nine cases out of ten, advance inwards down the rotten stub to the heartwood of the larger branch or main stem. This ruins the timber and eventually causes the downfall and death of the whole tree.

Since it is very hard to get truly flush cuts with any simple edged tool, such as a bill-hook, the saw should be used wherever possible. Minor scarring of the bark, or even of the bast or the wood at the base of the branch, matters little; the tree's tissues there are alive and will quickly heal such surface wounds.

AVOIDING SPLITS

Any branch over half-an-inch thick tends to split as it is cut through. This happens because most of the wood, bast, and bark tissues involved are individually very strong and flexible, although when taken together they build up a rigid limb. At a certain stage in the progress of the cut, rigidity is lost. The branch then swings over on a flexible "hinge", and its weight, now otherwise unsupported, tears a long, ugly strip from the larger stem that formerly carried it. Such a wound is both unsightly and dangerous, since it provides a large expanse of naked tissues well suited to invasion by the fungi that cause decay, and ill-adapted to quick healing from the sides.

Splitting should be anticipated with *every* pruning cut involving a green, living branch over half-an-inch thick, and steps taken against it. Since the most flexible tissues lie in the sapwood, bast and bark on the outer surface of the branch, and since the physical forces that cause splitting are most effective there, it can be checked by the simple precaution of making a shallow cut *all round* the branch that is to be removed, *before* the main cut is begun.

This all-round cutting is tedious when many branches have to be removed, and in practice it is usually sufficient to make an *undercut* prior to the main cut. The depth of this undercut will naturally depend on the size of the branch, but as a rough guide it should extend to *one quarter* of its thickness. It should also extend, on the surface but to a lesser depth, to one half of the branch's circumference; otherwise splitting of the cut sides may occur.

The drill, then, is simple. First make a shallow all-round cut through all the surface tissues, or else a deeper undercut extended on both sides to involve the lower half of the branch's circumference. Then make the main cut from above.

With large and heavy branches, further measures may be needed. One is to secure the branch by ropes to some point higher up in the tree's crown, in such a way that its weight will not immediately cause it to swing over as it becomes almost severed and so non-rigid. Another method is to remove it in sections, so that the weight of its basal section, and the turning "moment" that actually causes splitting, are reduced to the minimum before the final flush cut is made.

All exposed flush surfaces, and any wounds due to inadvertent splitting, must be coated with a tree wound paint as soon as possible. A delay of only half an hour or so is enough to allow the entry of fungal spores. So antiseptic treatment should come first, ahead of the tidying up of the branchwood.

9. Safeguarding Trees against Damage, Insects and Disease

ANYONE who cares for trees knows that, over their long life-span, they are exposed to many perils. The fact that so many survive to reach a large size and a considerable age is, however, proof that trees can fight off many kinds of attack, and heal damaged tissues surprisingly well.

The steps that foresters and gardeners can take to safeguard trees are very limited. In timber growing, cost is a major consideration for it is easy to spend more on treating an ailing tree than its timber can ever be worth. But even where—as with favourite ornamental trees—there is no limit to the money available, there are common-sense limits on what can be carried out in terms of space and time. Seedlings, and small trees recently planted, are so small that they are easily treated with sprays, but a grown tree fifty feet high, with a crown thirty feet across, is a very different proposition. It is not only big, but it is getting bigger every year, and the problem will increase as time goes on.

Further, since trees last so long, protective spraying must be repeated yearly. This year's treatment does no good at all to *next year's* shoots and leaves. The fruit-grower recognises this and sprays annually to a regular schedule; he can do so because he prunes his trees to keep them within bounds, and markets a valuable yearly crop. The man who tends timber trees or garden trees is not so happily placed. On occasion he may resort to tree surgery, described in the following chapter, but only on the understanding that a single operation will show good results over many years.

In practice, the main defence of the grower against most of the perils that can beset his trees consists in choosing the right kind for each particular site. This is combined, of course, with the avoidance of species or varieties that are known to carry a high risk of damage from insects or fungal diseases. Mistakes with trees take many years to put right, and often they are not immediately evident. For example, a gardener who plants eucalyptus trees, away from the West coast, may find that all is going well for several seasons; then an exceptional winter may kill every tree outright, and it will take many years for the gaps they leave to be filled in by other, hardier trees. Hence it is worth taking a lot of trouble to avoid starting off on wrong lines, and the weaknesses of particular trees are given detailed attention in Part II of this book.

CAUSES OF DECLINE AND DEATH

When a tree ceases to "do well" it is seldom easy, even for a skilled tree pathologist, to say at once what has caused the trouble. Often two or three causes have worked together, and therefore he must, like a human doctor, make general inquiries about the tree's surroundings and previous life. Once a tree is dead, it looks equally brown and withered whatever the cause may have been; diagnosis by a post-mortem examination alone is difficult. *Die-back*, which is the withering of shoots and branches, may result from several ailments.

Possible causes of harm to trees can be analysed in various ingenious ways, but from the practical point of view there are five types:

1. Faults inherent in the site—usually present at the time of planting.
2. Physical damage occurring later.
3. Grazing, gnawing and browsing by beasts and birds.
4. Attacks by insects and related small animals.
5. Diseases caused by fungi, bacteria or viruses.

1. Faults Inherent in the Site

The factors that govern tree growth in any particular soil or situation have been described in Chapters 2 to 4, which dealt with growing space, soils, climate, and exposure to wind or smoke and fumes. But even if sound decisions were taken at planting time, it is advisable to review the site once more when any falling-off in growth occurs. Conditions may have changed as the years rolled by. For example, though drainage may have been satisfactory earlier on, a later drain blockage may have led to the waterlogging of the soil, with consequent die-back.

On poor soils, trees that were given a start with fertilisers may slow down after a few years and lapse into a state of slow growth, or even no growth at all, which is called "check". The remedy is simple—another dose of fertiliser!

2. Physical Damage Occurring after Planting

This takes many forms. Let us look at the extremes of weather first.

FROST

In the discussion of climate in Chapter 4, it was made clear that only truly frost-hardy trees are worth planting in northern Europe or North America, except for a few favoured zones near the coasts. These frost-hardy trees resist the lowest extremes of *winter* cold, yet some of them still suffer damage from *spring* frosts. See pages 61 to 64.

The young, quickly-growing shoots of several sorts of common trees are quite frost-tender. When they first expand in spring, a few hours of freezing temperature on a still night will kill them outright. This damage, which only becomes evident a few days later, is quite alarming. The tender shoots wither and turn brown, and the whole outer surface of the tree looks as though it had been scorched by fire.

Spring frost damage is easily identified, partly by the weather at the time when it occurs, and partly by its pattern on the tree. It is more serious on the *lower* branches than it is higher up, for the coldest freezing air sinks to the lowest point. It is also far worse on branches exposed to the open sky, which lose heat readily, than it is on branches protected by an overhead screen, or even a side screen, of other trees or hedges. On evergreen trees it is easily known because the previous year's leaves remain undamaged.

Although frost damage looks alarming, the tree itself repairs it by sending forth a second crop of young shoots later in the spring, when the nights are warmer. A badly frosted tree suffers a check in growth for that particular year, but it is very seldom killed.

A few trees, including oak, beech and ash among the broadleaves, and Sitka spruce of the conifers, are notably susceptible to spring frosts; others, including birch, pines and poplars, rarely show damage. As a protective measure, tender trees can be planted under a light overhead screen of hardier ones. It is inadvisable to plant tender trees in hollows, where cold air collects on still nights, unless some overhead shelter can be given. But spring frost-tender trees need not be ruled out completely anywhere. Frosts may check them in youth, but will not delay their upward growth indefinitely. Once their leading shoots get above the critical frosty zone near ground level, their progress becomes normal.

DROUGHT

Damage through the drying out of a tree's tissues, because it cannot draw enough water from the soil, is only common among newly-planted trees during their first summer. If planting has been done well, as described in Chapter 7, page 106, losses will be light.

Drought damage in newly-planted trees is easily known because the upper and outer shoots and leaves wither first. Lower branches and inner leaves, buds and shoots often remain green and may resume healthy growth in time to save the tree's life. If recently planted trees look withered and brown above, they need not immediately be abandoned as a dead loss. Such wilting and withering is occasionally seen with some sorts, including beech, Scots pine and Douglas fir, that later make a good recovery. So an assessment of losses can only be made at the end of the first summer.

To check whether a withered tree is still alive, scratch its bark with your finger nail. Green bast below indicates life, but brown bast shows dead tissue. Broadleaved trees can sometimes be saved by cutting back the main stem, with a sharp knife, as far as the first bud on the still-green tissue. But once die-back has gone as far as the collar of the tree, at ground level, it can be written off.

Another useful test of "life" in a drought-stricken tree is to give it a gentle tug. So long as its roots grip the soil and resist the pull, it is alive and may survive. If it comes out without resistance, it is dead.

Established trees rarely die of drought, though such losses can occur if the water-table of a lowland soil is suddenly lowered by artificial drainage. During very hot dry summers a few trees, such as silver firs, may develop drought-cracks in their stems; but these are not fatal, and only a small proportion of a crop is ever affected.

WIND

When discussing climate in Chapter 4, we saw that high winds can harm trees in several ways, as by uprooting them, breaking their stems, or simply moulding the shape of their crowns, in a streamlined pattern pointing out of the prevailing wind direction. Nobody can stop the wind blowing, nor prevent it from "shaping" trees by its persistent pressure. But there are two steps that should form part of regular tree care.

One is the maintenance of good drainage, so that the roots gain and keep a firm and deep hold on well-aerated soil. The other is regular thinning, outlined in Chapter 11, page 170. If trees are continually given space to expand their crowns, they expand their trunks also, and this results in a well-balanced structure that is proof against all but the worst of gales. This applies, of course, mainly to trees grown in plantations. Open-grown trees, which have no need of thinning, usually prove surprisingly wind-firm, despite (or because of) their exposure on all sides.

LIGHTNING

Tall trees, which stand for many years as projections above the general level of the land, are occasionally struck by lightning. It is unusual for them to be shattered, but a fairly common form of obvious damage is the *lightning crack*. This can be seen as a long continuous crack in the bark and outer wood of the tree, sometimes straight and sometimes spiral, running down from the crown to ground level. It is caused by the sudden expansion of sap, which has been turned to steam by the heat of the lightning's passage.

Lightning does not always kill the tree, and the crack may heal over and cause no serious loss of strength. But some strikes prove fatal, and the tree withers and dies within a matter of weeks, or maybe a couple of years. No steps can be taken to prevent lightning strike on trees; nor can much be done after it has occurred. The tree either survives, or dies and must be felled.

It is a matter of common observation that rough-barked trees, such as oak, suffer more frequently, or at least more obviously, than do smooth-barked ones such as beech. This is probably due to the continuous film of water—a naturally good conductor of electricity, which develops outside the bark of a beech during a rainstorm; no such film can form on the rougher-barked oak.

WOUNDS AND BLOWS

Wounds caused by physical impact vary greatly in size and seriousness, from small cuts to the shattering of a stout trunk. A tree's ability to heal them also varies with its size and age, and with the kind of tree concerned. Young broadleaved trees show tremendous powers of recovery and their young shoots can rebuild a shattered wreck into a shapely tree. Old conifers, on the other hand, die only too easily after any major damage.

Most trees will strive to heal any surface cut that *does not completely encircle a stem or branch*. The application of simple tree surgery, discussed in the next chapter, is usually all that is needed to obtain a sure, though slow, recovery.

If, however, a deep wound *completely* encircles a tree trunk, the whole stem from that point upwards is sure to die. The only hope of saving it lies in a "bridge graft" to carry living tissues across the gap in the outer bast and bark, and this is only attempted with valuable fruit trees or ornamental ones. Note the word "completely". Quite a minor link across the wound, such as a strip of undamaged bark and bast covering one sixth of the tree's circumference, is enough to give a fair chance of survival. If this "life-line" is preserved, all the rough edges of the wound trimmed, and the bare wood coated with a wound dressing, the broken tissues may heal and eventually knit together all round the tree. But it is a slow business and several years will be needed to restore the tree to its full vigour.

A circular, or nearly circular, wound of this kind is usually the result of vandalism, but it can also arise through the careless use of wire rope, wrapped round a tree during timber felling or haulage work. If a tree must be used as a holdfast, its bark should always be protected with boards placed against it, so as to spread the pressure of the rope.

Blows that harm tree trunks are usually caused by moving tractors or motor lorries, etc., by carelessly-handled tools, or by thrown or rolling stones. As a rule a patch of bark is ripped off, leaving a jagged edge of bark around bare wood. Sometimes the bark is unbroken, but damage is done to the tender cambium tissues below it, and an ugly open wound appears when the bark scales off later.

The first step in treating an impact wound is to shape its broken edge to a smooth outline, using a strong sharp knife. It is then coated with a wound dressing, such as "Arbrex", and left to heal itself.

The carving of initials and true-lovers' hearts in the bark of trees rarely causes real harm. The result is unsightly, and even the lovers may eventually regret their enterprise, but the tree is equal to the occasion and soon heals over such shallow wounds. They may remain visible for years, but are trivial and only bark-deep.

INGROWN METAL

A tree trunk should never be used as a fence post, to support wires. Nor should wire railings ever be set hard up against a tree trunk. As a tree trunk expands, it grows around any metal object, which eventually becomes hidden, partly or wholly, within it. Nails and spikes driven into the side of a tree are particularly apt to disappear; they are not pushed out, but are overgrown by the expanding surface tissues.

Curiously, ingrown metal rarely harms a tree. But it sets a major problem for the sawmiller who buys hedgerow timber. If his saw strikes iron embedded in a tree trunk, it will be severely damaged and maybe shattered, causing grave risk to the men at work in his mill. This risk is so great that many sawmillers test hedgerow logs with magnetic metal-detectors before they put them on the saw-bench.

FIRE

The risk of forest fire is serious wherever trees are planted on a large scale amid vegetation that becomes dead and dry, at any season of the year. Those who raise trees in gardens or parks, along roadsides, or in woods or on wastelands where a layer of dead dry foliage never covers the ground, have little to fear.

The green foliage of most living trees is too moist to burn—holly is a rare exception, for its leaves are coated with an inflammable wax. Even the stem of a coniferous tree is too moist, during the tree's life, to burn readily.

When trees "burn" in a forest fire, it is hardly ever a *living* tree trunk that forms the main fuel, though it is the scorching of living bast and cambium that kills the tree. The actual main fuels are:

a. *Dead tree tissues*, such as the lower branches of conifers, their twigs, and the old withered needles that have fallen from them. A simple and practical way to keep such fuels away from the living upper trunk and foliage is to *brash* the lowest six feet of a conifer stem, as explained in the previous chapter.

b. *Surrounding vegetation*, such as living gorse or living heather, or dead bracken or grass. Gorse and heather will burn at any time of the year, but bracken and grass are only inflammable when the dead dry tissues of the previous summer form a mat on the ground surface; this makes fire risk highest in late spring, when the weather is usually driest and fresh green growth has not yet begun. Complete removal of surrounding vegetation is too costly for the forester to contemplate, but he can suppress it, and keep fire risk low for several years, by ploughing the ground before planting.

There is no space here for an account of the many methods that foresters employ to lessen fire risk, detect fires, and combat them when they break out. But mention must be made of *fire scorch*, a form of damage found wherever fires occur anywhere near trees. It is commonest, and most troublesome, where people light picnic fires or bonfires. Flame need not touch a tree to cause a wound—heat is enough. The scorch occurs below the bark, through damage to the delicate cambium, and only becomes evident weeks later, through the drying of a patch of bark, often accompanied by resin flow. The best treatment is to remove the bark, and then treat all the scorched surface as though it were an open wound.

Fires should never be lit on the floor of a conifer plantation, no matter how safe conditions may seem. Such a fire scorches soil and roots, and the latter are then invaded by a serious fungus called *Rhizina undulata*. This spreads from tree to tree and causes a whole group to die outright in a neat circle around the original site of the fire. If a fire is needed, it should be lit on a hard road well clear of tree roots.

3. Grazing, Gnawing and Browsing by Beasts and Birds

GRAZING

Grown trees are rarely harmed by large animals or birds, but young trees are very vulnerable. Any animal that eats grass as its main food eats a tree's tender growing shoots just as readily. There is no reason why it shouldn't! The grass restores itself by sending up fresh leaves and shoots from its mat of turf, but a small tree cannot do this. It is killed outright, and the grower must face the cost, and loss of time, involved in its replacement. The grass-eaters range in size from field voles through rabbits and hares to sheep, goats, cattle, horses, and wild deer.

GNAWING

No bird or beast can make use of wood as a food, and the bark that protects it is also unpalatable and indigestible. But between the bark and the wood lies the soft green bast tissue which can make a satisfactory food for a hungry beast that cannot find anything else. The gnawing of bark occurs locally and at particular seasons only, and certain animals prefer particular trees. Rabbits gnaw the bark at the foot of beeches, grey squirrels attack sycamores and other broadleaved trees at points on the stem that they can easily reach by sitting on a side branch, red squirrels go for pine bark, and horses—if shut up in a paddock with insufficient food, bite the bark of elm and also—rather appropriately, that of horse chestnut.

BROWSING

Browsing consists of biting back young soft shoots and leaves at heights above grass level. Any beast that eats grass, and is tall enough to reach a tree's upper foliage, will browse. Trees in parks where deer, sheep, or horses are kept seldom have any branches sweeping down below a height of six feet or so. This is called the *browsing level*, and any

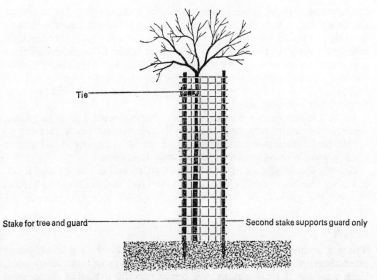

Tie

Stake for tree and guard

Second stake supports guard only

FIGURE 59. Welded mesh wire guard for standard tree, supported by two stakes.

shoot that tries to grow below it is promptly bitten back by the animals.

Another form of browsing is caused by blackgame or black grouse, *Tetrao tetrix*, a large bird which likes to pluck tender young shoots of pines with its sharp beak and to eat them whole. It seldom attacks other conifers and the widely planted Sitka spruce is almost immune. To-day the black grouse is only found in Scotland and, very locally, in Wales and northern England. It is protected by the Game Laws, but its numbers are easily restricted to a level at which little economic harm is done, by shooting in the open season.

Similar damage is done by its larger relative, the capercailzie, *Tetrao urogallus*, found only in Scotland.

TREE GUARDS

The protection of individual trees by guards is a sensible practice in parks where grazing and browsing animals are kept, or in open spaces and along roadsides where the public have access. It is too costly for consideration in timber plantations. At one time stout structures of oak or iron, built to last indefinitely, were employed, but these are too expensive for general use to-day. In practice, there is a choice of three materials, galvanised woven wire, galvanised wire netting, and light timber.

Galvanised woven wire, which resembles sheep-netting but is stouter and less flexible, lasts longer than wire netting and gives better resistance to farm stock and human injury. Owing to its wide gaps it offers little protection against rabbits, but in practice it is mainly used around trees that already have woody bark and so are unlikely to be attacked by small rodents. Galvanised wire netting is cheaper, but more flexible and less lasting. If of a sufficiently fine gauge, $1\frac{1}{4}$ inch or less, it will keep out rabbits, but not field voles.

Light timber guards consist of four stakes linked by cross pieces, spaced close enouth to stop animals thrusting their heads through to nibble bark. Unless a naturally durable wood is employed, all timber used in guards should receive preservative treatment.

Guards should always be attached to a stake, and not to the tree itself. If a large tree has to be shielded, two or even four stakes should be used to support the guard, the tree itself being staked independently in the centre.

FENCES

There are three main types of fence that are used to protect young plantations of trees; namely stock-proof, rabbit-proof, and deer-proof. Each type has it local variations according to the nature of the ground and the animals to be kept out. The materials used in all three are galvanised wire (plain or barbed) and galvanised wire netting where needed, supported on stakes of durable wood. Oak heartwood makes good stakes and straining posts, and needs no preservative treatment. Sweet chestnut and yew are also naturally durable, but stakes and posts of all other timbers require treatment with creosote, or a similar strong preservative, to give them a satisfactory service life in contact with the soil; so treated, stakes will last for forty years.

Forest fences owe their strength to *strained* wires. Straining posts of suitable size must be set at every corner in the fence line, at sharp changes of slope, and at intervals of 100 yards on long straight stretches. Struts, of a strong and durable wood, must be set on each side of each post, to keep it firm when strain is applied. The wires are set at suitable intervals of height. Number 8 gauge, galvanised smooth steel wire is the kind usually employed. Special wire-strainers are used to get it tight, and once this has been achieved it is fixed by staples to the lighter intermediate stakes that complete the fence.

Stock-proof fences, designed to resist sheep, cattle, and horses, need straining posts seven feet long and six inches square, or seven inches in minimum diameter if round posts are used instead. The strainers are sunk about $2\frac{1}{2}$ feet in the ground, leaving an effective height of $4\frac{1}{2}$ feet. Intermediate stakes, which are spaced 6 to 9 feet apart, must be $5\frac{1}{2}$ feet long; they are driven into the ground to a depth of one foot, leaving $4\frac{1}{2}$ feet projecting. Square stakes must have a 3-inch side; alternatively, cleft oak stakes, having a 4-inch face, may be used. Seven galvanised wires, spaced

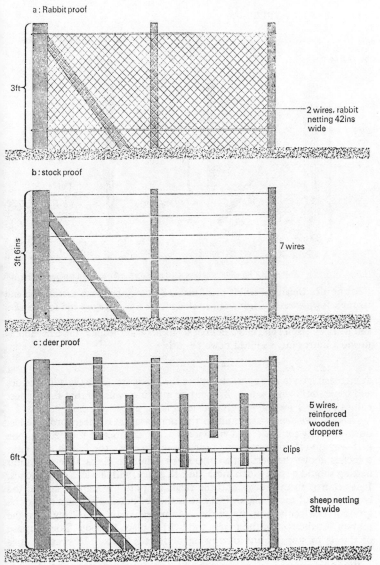

a : Rabbit proof

3ft

2 wires, rabbit netting 42ins wide

b : stock proof

3ft 6ins

7 wires

c : deer proof

5 wires, reinforced wooden droppers

clips

6ft

sheep netting 3ft wide

FIGURE 60. Three types of fences. a, rabbit-proof, two strained wires, wire-netting 42 inches wide, 36 inches high, six inches out at foot. b, stock-proof, seven strained wires at increasing vertical intervals, three inches to seven inches, giving three feet six inches of height. c, deer-proof. Six feet high with three feet of sheep netting at foot, five strained wires above. Wires must be linked by wooden droppers or deer will force their way through.

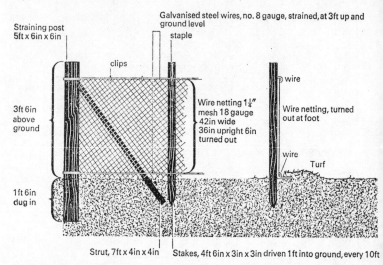

Galvanised steel wires, no. 8 gauge, strained, at 3ft up and ground level

Straining post
5ft x 6in x 6in

staple

clips

3ft 6in above ground

wire

Wire netting 1¼″ mesh 18 gauge 42in wide 36in upright 6in turned out

Wire netting, turned out at foot

wire

Turf

1ft 6in dug in

Strut, 7ft x 4in x 4in   Stakes, 4ft 6in x 3in x 3in driven 1ft into ground, every 10ft

FIGURE 61. Details of rabbit-proof fence. Straining posts are first dug in and strutted. Two wires are next strained along fence line, near top and foot. Stakes are driven in every ten feet. Wire-netting, 42 inches wide, is secured to posts and wires by staples and clips. Bottom six inches is turned out 'towards rabbits' to check burrowing, and held down by turfs.

at increasing distances apart, complete the fence; the lowest is 4 inches up, and others follow at 5, 6, 7, 8, 9 and 10 inch intervals, so that the highest comes about 4 feet above ground level.

Rabbit-proof fences are built in the same way as a sheep-proof fence, but need only four wires. One wire is set at the foot of the netting, one half-way up (18 ins.), and one near the top (3 feet); the fourth wire runs 9 inches above the netting, to give extra height to check sheep. Rabbit netting should be of 1¼ inch mesh, and 18 gauge, with a width of 42 inches. It is secured to the stakes and the straining posts by staples, and to the wires by small metal clips. Only 36 inches of netting projects above the ground; the remaining six inches is turned outwards—"towards the rabbits" at the foot of the fence, and held in place by sods. The purpose of this is to stop rabbits burrowing under the fence. In practice it is *not* necessary to *bury* the bottom strip; turning outwards is better.

Where there are no livestock to be kept out, a lighter and cheaper rabbit-proof fence, with stakes ten feet apart and two strained wires, at top and foot of netting, will suffice. Rabbit fencing will not check hares, which jump higher; if hares are too numerous, they must be kept in check by shooting.

Deer-proof fences. Deer of any kind can leap over any fence less than six feet high, and deer fences are therefore elaborate and costly structures. Where only a few deer are present, it is not worth while to build fences, and to-day they are only seen around parks, or in the Scottish Highlands where the numerous wild red deer threaten timber plantations along the glen sides. Upright stakes, 8 feet long and 6 inches in top diameter, must be spaced not more than 24 feet apart; eleven wires are needed, spaced not more than six inches apart; and small wooden uprights, called *droppers*, must be added to stop a deer forcing the wires apart.

GENERAL POINTS ON FENCING

No fence is effective unless it is regularly patrolled and repaired as necessary. All gates and stiles must be proof against wandering animals also. The rabbits, or deer, that it is desired to exclude must of course be driven out, or exterminated, before the fence line is completed and the trees are put in. A watch must be kept for strays that may find their way back, for as many years as is necessary.

It is always cheaper to fence in a *large* area, of any given shape, than a small one. A square fence 4 chains long, costing £5 a chain or £20 in all, encloses only one square chain, that is one-tenth of an acre, at a unit cost of £200 *per acre*. But a similar square fence 40 chains long encloses 10 acres for £200 at a unit cost of only £20 *per acre*. (1 chain = 66 feet. 10 square chains = 1 acre.)

CONTROLLING HARMFUL WILD BEASTS AND BIRDS

Whether fences are put up or not, some measure of control has usually to be exercised against wild creatures that harm trees. The shot-gun is used against rabbits, hares, grey squirrels, blackgame and capercailzie, and on occasion against deer also, though the rifle is essential for the larger kinds of deer. Traps are used to control rabbits and grey squirrels, and in certain circumstances rabbits may be killed by fumigating their burrows with lethal "Cymag" gas.

No simple and economical method is known for reducing the numbers of field voles, which occasionally multiply to great numbers and destroy newly-planted trees. But here nature eventually provides a balance, in the shape of short-eared owls, weasels and foxes, which also increase in numbers and eventually keep down the rodents.

4. *Insect Attack*

Several hundred kinds of insects and related small animals attack forest and ornamental trees, and no part of any tree is completely immune from insect attack. Despite this ever-present risk, it is the exception, rather than the rule, for tree-growers to take special measures to safeguard trees from insects. These steps are confined to particular trees or to special circumstances, such as the seedling stages in the nursery. As a rule, insect attack, even where it develops to plague proportions, only weakens

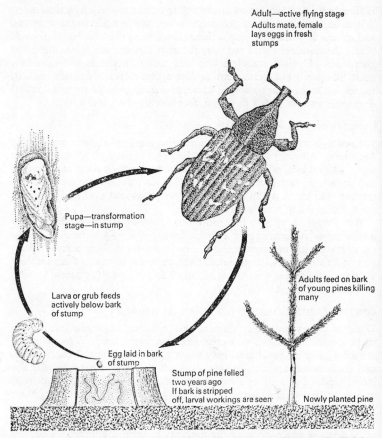

Adult—active flying stage
Adults mate, female lays eggs in fresh stumps

Pupa—transformation stage—in stump

Adults feed on bark of young pines killing many

Larva or grub feeds actively below bark of stump

Egg laid in bark of stump

Stump of pine felled two years ago If bark is stripped off, larval workings are seen

Newly planted pine

FIGURE 62. Life cycle of a typical harmful forest insect—Pine weevil, *Hylobius abietis*. Egg, laid below bark of newly felled pine, hatches into larva. Larva feeds, grows and pupates in stump, doing no economic harm. Adults emerge and feed on bark of newly planted pines—killing large numbers. Cycle is repeated on further stumps and young trees or pine branches, perpetuating damage.

a tree for a few seasons, or disfigures it temporarily. Trees are seldom killed outright by insects alone.

One reason for this happy state of affairs lies in the many adverse factors that limit insect activity. Insects are very sensitive to small changes of temperature or humidity, and most sorts can only feed on a narrow range of host plants. All have many enemies, in the shape of insect-eating beasts and birds, and other insects that attack them externally or live as parasites within their tissues. An increase of insects to plague proportions can only happen when the season is just right, and the plague ends when conditions change, or the enemies of the insect concerned increase in numbers also.

A typical insect has four life stages, as follows:

1. Larva, commonly called a grub or worm, which is an active feeding stage.

2. A pupa, a resting stage during which metamorphosis from larva to adult takes place.

3. An adult, in which the insect reveals its characteristic form, flies around actively, and mates. Adults of most species usually feed, though only for a brief period.

4. An egg, laid by the female adult after mating, from which the larva hatches out to recommence the cycle of life.

Damage to trees may be done by either the larva or the adult insect. At all stages of its life the insect itself is vulnerable to attack, but especially so in its immobile egg and pupal stages.

Not all insects go through this full life cycle. Certain aphids that damage trees increase by eggs laid by females, which simply hatch out into a further generation of females. No male insect, nor any intermediate stage of life, has yet been discovered for these creatures; they include the common felted beech coccus, *Cryptococcus fagi*, which causes fluffy white patches on the bark of beech.

Only one tree that could otherwise be widely grown in Britain has been eliminated solely through insect attack. This is the European silver fir, *Abies alba*, which suffers so severely from the silver fir aphid, *Adelges nordmannianae*, that it is no longer planted. Instead we use giant silver fir, *Abies grandis*, from western North America, which looks very much like the European kind, but proves immune from this aphid's attacks.

A related insect, *Adelges strobi*, plays a part in preventing the successful growth in Britain of the North American Weymouth pine, *Pinus strobus*, though that tree also suffers from the serious blister-rust disease. A third aphid, *A. cooleyi*, often produces masses of white fluffy specks on the foliage of Douglas fir, but does not weaken it seriously. A fourth kind, *Elatobium abietinum*, can on occasion eat all the recently-formed needles on Sitka spruce; but though it checks growth for a year or two, it rarely kills any tree.

On the whole, insect attack is more disfiguring than dangerous. It is rarely progressive, and if trees survive for a season they usually recover completely.

In the woods, active steps are sometimes taken to check the pine weevil, *Hylobius abietis*, a fair-sized black beetle, half-an-inch long, with a long snout and yellow bands across its wing-cases. Its larvae feed harmlessly in pine stumps, but the adult beetles gnaw the bark of young conifer shoots, including the stems of newly-planted trees. If young conifers are planted where pines were felled a couple of years earlier, they attract adult weevils that have bred in the stumps of the previous crop. The hungry weevils eat so much bark that many young conifers are killed outright, and the whole plantation may prove a failure. The remedy is to dip the young conifers in an insecticide—a specially formulated emulsion of D.D.T.—before planting them amidst the stumps of freshly-felled pines. Any weevil that bites the bark of the young trees is then automatically poisoned and killed.

The little pine beetle, *Tomicus piniperda*, a tiny black creature without any snout, may also need control measures. In summer, its larvae feed below the bark of recently felled conifer poles and logs, and when the adults emerge a few weeks later, these adults feed greedily on the shoots of standing conifers round about. The remedy is to bark all felled poles, or remove them from the forest, within six weeks of all summer fellings. In this way, the pest never has time to complete its life cycle in the forest, so it cannot increase in numbers.

The elm disease, caused by the fungus *Ceratocystis ulmi*, is carried from tree to tree by the elm bark beetle, *Scolytus scolytus*. This can be checked by injecting an insecticide into the tree's sap stream, but the process must be repeated yearly, and so proves expensive in relation to the risks involved. Luckily, some strains of elm are immune to this disease and only these should be used for future planting.

Exposed dead wood, forming part of still living trees, is sometimes attacked by the larvae, or "wood-worms", of small beetles that live by boring into dead wood. This may cause alarm, since people fear that the adult beetles may fly into houses and start similar damage in structural woodwork or furniture. This *can* happen, though infestation is far more likely to arise through insects flying in from other houses nearby. If precautions are thought necessary, the simplest step is to treat infested dead wood in the tree with creosote, which is poisonous to all wood-boring insects.

On the whole, those insects that attack trees are more alarming than harmful. The Forestry Commission, for example, has half a million acres under pine trees, exposed to constant risk of insect attack. Yet on only two or three occasions has it had to take full-scale measures against a leaf-feeding insect, and then at only two of its many forests. This involved the spraying, from low-flying aeroplanes, of D.D.T. insecticides to kill the caterpillars of the pine looper moth, *Bupalus piniarius*, which is normally considered a scarce insect.

Obviously, each tree grower will keep an eye always open for signs of serious insect attack, but only rarely will he have to seek the advice of professional entomologists regarding insect control.

5. Diseases

Where trees are concerned, *disease* nearly always means attack by a group

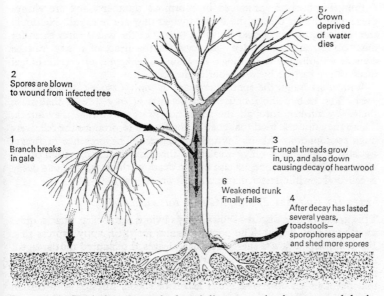

FIGURE 63. Typical progress of a fungal disease, causing heart rot and death.

of lowly plants known as fungi. A few diseases are caused—as in man and animals—by bacteria or by viruses, but as a rule the causative organism is usually a fungus—that is, another plant.

Fungi differ from the higher, green, plants in having no chlorophyll or green colouring matter, in their tissues. Those kinds that concern us here get all their energy for life by breaking down the tissues of higher plants. If the fungus attacks living tissues, it is called a *parasite*, or more simply, a *disease*. If it attacks dead tissues, then it is called a *saprophyte*, or a *decay*. This distinction is useful in the classroom but of little value in the forest. Some fungi can work in both ways at the same time. The commonest form of trouble in a living tree is the decay of "dead" heart-wood within a living tree, causing its downfall and death through the gradual destruction of support.

Fungi have complex life histories, and their full life story can only be investigated properly by a plant pathologist, or *mycologist*, as a student of fungi is called, who has microscopes and a specially equipped laboratory available. In fact, laboratory techniques are often needed even to identify a fungus. Fungi spread from tree to tree by means of spores, so small as to be quite invisible to the naked eye, which are produced by quite large and obvious structures called *sporophores*. Mushrooms, toadstools, and the brackets or "conks" that appear on the sides of stricken trees, are examples of sporophores.

Fungal spores are produced in enormous numbers, and are always present in the air during the seasons when they are released. Naturally they are most frequent near decaying trees, but the winds carry them for many miles, and no garden—not even in the heart of a city, can be considered immune from fungal invasion. The spores of certain fungal diseases are carried by wood-boring insects.

With most fungi, the sporophores are the only tissues that are readily seen. The rest of the fungus tissue consists of tiny threads that make their way unseen through the substance of the tree that they attack. There they find the food that enables the fungus to produce the relatively huge sporophore, with its myriads of spores. The presence of fungal threads, or *hyphae*, is only revealed by the decay or discoloration of the attacked plant substance, or else by the death of the tree. Serious decay is called *rot*, while lesser damage is known as *stain*.

EXTERNAL DISEASES: *Blights, Mildews, Rusts and Cankers*

This group of tree diseases shows fairly obvious signs of its attacks quite soon after they begin. The popular names for them aptly express this. *Blight* implies surface tissues, particularly leaves, discoloured and damaged. *Mildew* refers to the white, floury surface mass of small sporophores produced by certain small fungi. *Rust* records the reddish-brown colour that develops on otherwise green leaves or shoots infested with certain other fungi. *Canker* describes ugly open wounds on young shoots and branches, which may be caused by a fungus or a bacterium.

Most of the fungi and allied organisms that cause these external attacks on trees are *specific* to one particular kind of tree, and often indeed to particular strains of that sort of tree. For example, the bacterial canker of poplar is serious on certain *cultivars* (Chap. 12, p. 179) only; the simplest way to defeat it is to plant cultivars that have been found resistant to it.

Elm disease, caused by the fungus *Ceratocystis ulmi*, readily attacks and kills the Dutch elm, *Ulmus hollandica* variety *belgica*, but proves a minor trouble on most other species and varieties of elm. Chestnut blight, *Endothia parasitica*, which is practically harmless on its original host tree, the Chinese chestnut, in China, proved a deadly disease when accidentally introduced to North America and to the American chestnut; on the European chestnut, *Castanea sativa*, it has proved only locally serious so far; luckily, it has not yet reached Britain.

The best preventive measure against serious external diseases is, therefore, the choice of a species or strain of tree that is known to resist them—or one which, at the least, has not shown any particular susceptibility to them. The use of sprays is, in practice, confined to small trees still in the nursery, where a large number can readily be treated at low cost, during a particularly susceptible stage of their life.

INTERNAL DISEASES: *Rot and Decay*

The fungi that cause decay in a tree's woody tissues, inside the cambium, are the most serious from the grower's point of view. They feed upon heartwood, sapwood, or both, and do not emerge from the interior of the tree until they are ready to produce sporophores and shed spores. Some kinds attack only a small group of trees, but others grow readily on trees of any kind.

A feature common to the fungi of this group is that they cannot gain entry to a tree's interior wood through the healthy growing tissues that normally surround it. The four-fold barrier of bark, bark cambium, bast and wood cambium, that protects every living stem and twig, resists their entry. As soon, however, as bare wood, and especially bare heartwood, is exposed, an entry point is provided for their spores. Wounds that expose bare wood commonly arise, in nature, through the breakage of a side bough by high wind, or perhaps the death of a stout branch through over-shading. Man often causes similar wounds by his pruning or lopping, or by accidental impacts with tools or vehicles.

Once its protective outer sheath of living tissue is pierced, at any point, a tree is in peril. Spores germinate on the exposed wood, and fungal hyphae grow steadily, though slowly, right through the heart of the tree, down to the trunk, towards the roots, and upwards to enter other branches. By degrees the whole inner core of the tree is reduced to rotten wood, useless for support and worthless to the timber merchant. Only when decay is far advanced, and it is fast becoming too late to save the tree, does the fungus bear sporophores. These consist of toadstools or brackets, sometimes at the foot of the tree, sometimes higher up. They bear countless tiny spores that carry infection to other trees.

The extensive decay, and the invasion of the tree's outer tissues by the fungus when it bears the sporophores, usually causes the whole tree to look sickly; branches are often killed outright. At this stage the owners of the tree, who have overlooked the wound through which the fungus gained entry—and often the sporophores also, call in an expert. But it is too late! Only too often a consultant hears the S.O.S. call: "Something is wrong with my tree. Its leaves are withering, and mushrooms are growing out at its foot. Please come and put it right."

Occasionally, where only part of a tree is affected, it can be saved by tree surgery. As a rule, it must come down.

The worst feature of internal decay is that it *is* internal. The outer bark of the tree remains healthy and intact at every point save the small side wound where the trouble began. The bast and outer sapwood have carried on its life processes, and the cambium has increased its size, through all the years when the fungus was insidiously working away at its heart. Only when the trunk has been weakened to the point when it can no longer be safely left standing, does the fungus reveal its presence.

Though cure is seldom possible, prevention is simple. Pruning cuts should be made skilfully, (see Chapter 8, p. 131). Exposed wood surfaces should be promptly treated with antiseptic wound dressings such as "Arbrex". Wounds caused by wind-breakage or similar damage should be trimmed up, and their exposed surfaces painted over with a wound dressing. If only one or two branches are found to be affected by a fungus, they should be pruned right back to the main stem, and the whole cut surface dressed as a wound.

Once healing callus tissue has closed completely over a break in the tree's outer bark, the tree is safe from fungal invasion, but not before that.

Any inspection of standing trees, to see if they are sound and healthy, should include particular attention to the stubs of pruned or broken branches, to check whether heart-rotting fungi have gained entry.

Fomes annosus is the scientific name for the fungus that causes the white pocket rot of many kinds of conifers. It is particularly serious because, besides spreading through the air by means of spores, it also spreads underground through roots, passing from an infested tree to a healthy one by growing from one root to another where roots touch or cross. When conifers are removed during thinning, the exposed stumps of those trees that are removed provide ideal points of entry for the spores of *Fomes*. This fungus then spreads underground and, within a year or two, kills many of the surrounding trees that the forester wishes to retain.

The control of *Fomes* is simple. As a thinning is made, the stumps of those trees that are removed are painted with a fungicide. This may either be creosote, or a strong solution of a chemical called sodium nitrite. The fungicide simply stops the entry of *Fomes*, and the cut stump eventually rots away through the action of other, less dangerous, fungi.

The honey fungus, *Armillaria mellea*, merits notice because it is common, conspicuous, and attacks a great variety of trees in a peculiar way. It starts life in the stumps of old hardwood trees, and then spreads to other trees nearby, by means of relatively large strands of hyphae, grouped together to form "black bootlaces" or "shoestrings". These fungal strands grow up beneath the bark of attacked trees and, by feeding on soft outer tissues, kill the tree outright. The fungus then bears clusters of toadstool-shaped sporophores at the tree's foot. The colour and scent of these toadstools recall honey, but while the fungus is quite harmless, it is not particularly good to eat!

In the woods, the forester usually takes the risk of honey fungus attack just as it comes. He knows that if he plants, say, Douglas fir on felled woodland still holding many oak stumps, a proportion of his firs will die; but the resulting loss will be far less than the cost of removing the stumps. Those who plant ornamental grounds or orchards, however, must take the risk more seriously, since their trees, as individuals, are more valuable. Land that holds many hardwood stumps should be avoided. If it must be used, then the stumps should be extracted first, before any choice trees are planted.

10. Tree Felling, Tree Surgery, and Stump Removal

THIS chapter is concerned with the heavier work that has to be done, on occasion, to trees and their stumps. Because special skill, experience, and equipment have to be used, these jobs are generally given to contractors who make them their main livelihood. But all who own trees will wish to know how these tasks are carried out, what is physically possible, and how costs of different operations compare.

In the woods, timber trees are regularly felled at very low costs which leave a fair profit to the tree-growers, the fellers, and the timber merchants who buy the logs. But as soon as tree-felling, lopping, tree surgery, or stump removal have to be carried out in towns or suburban gardens, work becomes far more expensive. The value of any timber contained in an urban ornamental tree is usually far less than the cost of bringing it down and hauling it away. If a tree is decayed or defective it may be quite worthless, and money must be spent on destroying it as well as on bringing it down safely.

The reasons for these differences between profit and loss—between a tree that is an asset and one that is a liability, are fairly simple. In the woods the trees are grown well clear from obstacles that might restrict their free fall. They are felled at a carefully chosen stage when each will show its best profit, related to the progress of the crop as a whole. They are sold in substantial numbers, all at one time, which makes it worth while for a timber merchant to bring in skilled men and tackle, and to look for profitable uses for their timber when he resells it. In short, everything is arranged for a large-scale commercial operation to be carried out to its profitable conclusion.

In contrast, if the same timber merchant is asked to remove a number of ornamental trees from a park or large garden, he can rarely see his way to covering his costs, even if he is given the resulting timber free of charge. First, he is handling a small "parcel" of material, not worth much in total; but he must bring in much the same equipment as he needs on a bigger job. Some of the trees will have been marked for removal because they are unsound, diseased or dangerous—and so unlikely to yield marketable timber. Others may stand very close to buildings or overhead wires—indeed that may be the main reason for their removal, so he must use special tackle and work slowly to avoid damage to valuable surrounding structures. Finally, once the tree is down, he cannot here haul heavy trunks or branches in large sections over rough woodlands,

fields, or farm tracks; instead he must manœuvre them carefully, often
in short lengths, around flower beds, lawns, and over physically weak
paths to the public road.

Further, in the forest it is quite exceptional for any work to be done
by men working "off the ground". But the care of garden trees often
requires men to work in the treetops, where their output falls to a fraction
of what they can do at ground level. Safety precautions must be followed
with particular care, and all workers must be heavily insured against
possible accidents. Hence far higher costs result.

EQUIPMENT

AXES

A strong two-handed felling axe with a head of about five pounds weight
is essential. A hatchet is also needed. A file and an axe-sharpening stone
are required for maintaining a keen edge.

A word here about axe-strokes. Basically there are two kinds. A
vertical or near-vertical stroke is made to cut one side of a wedge-shaped
chunk of wood from the trunk. This is followed by a horizontal stroke
that cuts the other side of the wedge and so frees a large chip.

SAWS

Three distinct types of saw are used in tree felling:

1. A bow-saw, with a detachable and replaceable blade, for felling and
limbing small trees. A thirty-inch model, costing about £2, is convenient.

2. The two-man cross-cut, or felling saw, with adjustable and detachable handles. A usual size is four feet, costing around £6.

3. Power saws, with replaceable cutting chains. These vary greatly in
size, weight, cost, and performance. A usual one-man model has a
blade two feet long, weighs twenty-two pounds and costs around £60.
A two-man model may weigh fifty pounds, have a blade four feet long
and cost £100.

Except for the one-man power saw, which can be manipulated so as
to fell trees thicker than the length of its blade, no saw can tackle any
tree trunk that is not substantially *thinner* than the saw's blade length.
Work on very large trees, therefore, involves an extra long two-man saw,
or a good deal of axe-work, or both these measures.

Wear on saws is heavy, and they need constant maintenance. They must
be re-sharpened, re-set, cleaned and oiled, and replaceable blades or cutting
chains must be renewed at suitable intervals. Sharpening files, a saw set,
and an oil can, are needed on every felling job.

WEDGES AND SLEDGE-HAMMERS

Big timber cannot be safely felled without the aid of strong wedges to hold open the saw-kerf and tilt the tree in the desired direction. Wedges are usually of steel or special alloy, and are supplied in sets consisting of three wedges, in graded sizes. A sledge-hammer is needed to drive them home, a customary weight for the head being six pounds.

SMALL HAND TOOLS

Every felling gang needs a bill-hook for clearing brushwood, a hand-axe

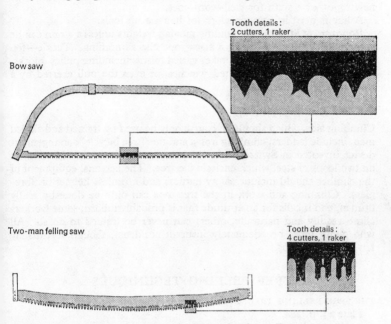

FIGURE 64. Bow saw for cutting small limbs, (*above*). Two-man felling saw (*below*); note four cutting teeth followed by one raker (*left*), to clear sawdust.

or hatchet for tackling the smaller branches, and at least one sharp knife. A hammer is handy, and a first-aid kit must always be available.

ROPES AND LINES

Tree fellers, working at ground level, use ropes as little as possible, but they are essential in tree-top work and on many occasions when trees have to be felled or shifted clear of obstacles. Ropes may be measured by their circumference or by their diameter, so it is important to know which! It is helpful to know the breaking strains of the usual sizes of manila rope, which are:

Diameter	Approximate equivalent circumference	Breaking strain
½ inch	1½ inches	2,240 lbs.
¾ inch	2 inches	4,500 lbs.
1 inch	3 inches	8,000 lbs.

The weight or strain that can *safely* be put on any rope is much less than this; it should not be more than a quarter of the stated figure for new ropes, or a sixth for well-worn ones.

A line is need in tree-top work for hauling up tools.

Ropes are of little help in guiding moving weights unless a strain can be continually exerted on them; a slack rope checks nothing. Tackle—too complex for description here, takes varied forms, including pulley-blocks, hand winches, tractor-mounted winches, or even the pull exerted by a tractor itself.

CLIMBING AIDS

Climbing aids, which should of course only be used by trained and skilled men, include ladders, climbing irons, and the "tree bicycle", an ingenious device invented in Switzerland, which supports the weight of a climber on two loops of steel which encircle the tree. The personal equipment of the climber should include safety harness and a rimless helmet of fibre-glass. Climbing and work in the tree-tops can only be done by really fit men, and it calls for an aptitude that is probably inborn; some workers climb readily and naturally, others can never be trained to do so. All who climb must be adequately insured; accidents, though fortunately few, can be serious.

TREE FELLING TECHNIQUES

THE FREE-FALLING TREE: *Felling with Axe, Saw and Wedge*
  Plate 23, p. 284.

All methods of tree-felling are based on what happens when a tree, that is free to fall in any direction, is brought down by removing support at its base, without any aids elsewhere to guide it. The direction and timing of its fall are then controlled only by the skill of one or two men working at its foot.

In a typical job, the stages are:

1. The fellers look at the tree and its surroundings, and decide in which direction it should come down—for example, well clear of neighbouring trees. The side towards which it will fall is known as the *face*, while the opposite side is called the *back*.

2. Using the axe, the fellers chop away the swelling that is usually found at the foot of any tree, together with any spurs or side roots projecting outwards above ground level. This is known as *rounding up*, and it brings the outline of the tree's base to a circular shape.

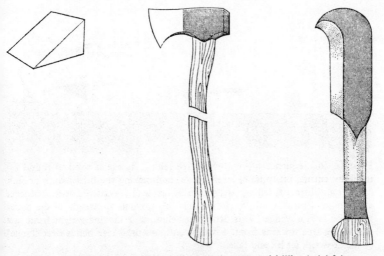

FIGURE 65. Felling wedge (*left*), felling axe (*centre*) and billhook (*right*).

3. Still using the axe, the fellers make an *undercut*, on the side towards which they wish the tree to fall. This undercut has a flat base and a sloping "roof" and it extends for about one third of the thickness of the tree. The gap that results is called the *sink*, or—because of its shape— the *birdsmouth*. The tree is now unsupported on its "face" side, but it does not yet lean that way. It is still kept up by the remaining two-thirds of its wood at the *back*, and it remains vertical.

4. The fellers now take their two-man felling saw, and start to cut through the remaining two-thirds of the wood from the *back* of the tree. They start the cut about one inch higher than the base of the *sink* at the other side. They continue sawing until the tree falls or the saw jams in the cut. As a rule the saw jams, because, as support is removed at the *back* of the tree, the tree's weight presses down and grips the saw blade.

5. The fellers then insert one or more metal wedges into the saw-cut or *kerf* behind the saw, and drive this wedge (or wedges) firmly into the gap, with a sledge-hammer. This does three things. It lifts the weight of the tree off the saw, so that the saw is free to move again, and felling can proceed. It also tilts the tree towards its *face*, so that it is forced to fall in that direction. Finally, it puts the fibres at the base of the tree under tension, and makes them easier to cut.

6. Sawing now proceeds, and if the saw should jam again, the wedges are driven farther in, tilting the tree still farther. Eventually a stage is reached when the tree is supported only by a thin *hinge* of uncut wood. Because it is leaning slightly, this hinge is insufficient to support its weight. The tree then starts to fall, and the hinge bends as it does so.

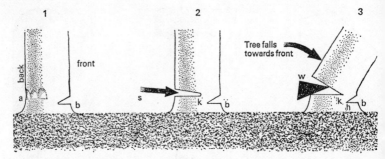

FIGURE 66. Sequence of cuts when tree felling. 1, axe is used to round up trunk by cutting off spurs or swellings (a) and making the birdsmouth or sink (b) at *front* of tree. 2, felling saw, shown by arrow (s), is entered at *back* of tree, above base of birdsmouth, to cut the kerf (k). 3, when the weight of the trunk traps the saw, a wedge (w) is driven in behind it, removing weight from saw and tilting tree towards front. Sawing continues until tree bends over 'hinge' of uncut wood, (at h), and falls.

7. At this point the fellers, who have been warned of the tree's impending fall by the creaking of the hinge, lift their saw clear of the falling tree, through the gap that is rapidly opening at the back, and stand clear to avoid any risk of accident.

The tree falls, with its base still held in place by the hinge, until it strikes the ground. At that moment, the shock of the impact breaks the hinge, and the tree lies clear of any link with the stump.

At the final moment of impact, a thin strip of wood is torn out of the stump at the bottom of the hinge. This is called the *sloven*, and it remains attached to the tree trunk until it is sawn off to tidy things up.

FELLING SMALL TREES

Simpler methods can be applied to small trees, under one foot thick at the butt, because of their lower weight. The axe may be used for the whole of the felling; but the resulting tapered end lowers the value of the resulting log, since a square-cut end is needed, as a rule, for each marketable length of timber.

Alternatively, the axe may be used only for the rounding-up, and the rest of the cutting be done with a bow-saw. If no undercut is made, the whole log has a square-cut end, which is an advantage for certain uses.

Another method is to use a light one-man power saw, either after the axe-work has been done, or throughout.

POWER SAW FELLING

Power saws are now widely used in place of hand bow-saws and hand cross-cut saws, and also, to a growing extent, instead of axes for rounding-up or making the undercut. Thus, instead of the undercut being gradually chipped out with the axe, stroke by stroke, it is cut out as a wedge in two passes of the power saw. But in all power saw work the same principles and basic methods apply, as for hand-tool felling. Support must be removed on the *face* side of the tree first; then the main cut must be made from the back, with wedges when necessary to keep open the kerf, until the tree actually falls.

DIFFICULT TREES

Problems arise whenever trees that are to be felled show any substantial degree of lean; when they have a larger amount of weight—such as heavy branches—on one particular side; when they must be brought down in one particular direction to avoid hitting buildings, walls, overhead wires, or similar obstacles; and when they fail to fall freely and so

Motor

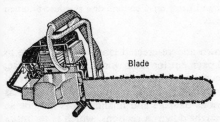

Blade

Details of chain

FIGURE 67. Power saw or chain saw.

lodge or hang-up in other trees. Many of these problems can only be overcome by skilled tree-fellers who have the requisite experience and equipment needed. It would be misleading to suggest simple solutions to them here, but a few hints may help where only minor complications are likely to arise.

Leaning trees, and trees with an undue proportion of weight on one side, can be brought down *in that direction only*, without special tackle. Particular care is needed, as it is not easy to judge when they will actually start to fall. If it is essential to fell them in any other direction, that is against or across their natural lean or distribution of weight, expert assistance and special tackle are needed. It is wrong to suppose that a simple rope, secured to a holdfast, will guide the fall of a leaning tree; such a "dead" rope is useless, as it slackens the moment the tree starts to fall. The rope must be "live", that is, kept constantly under the pull provided by a winch, a pulley-block system or possibly a tractor, to keep it taut and under strain throughout.

Obstacles that restrict tree felling are of two kinds—fixed and movable. Movable obstacles include telephone wires and overhead power lines,

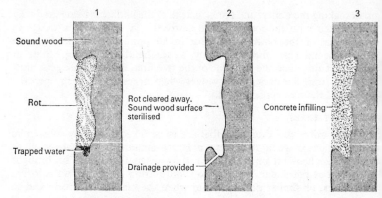

FIGURE 68. How a tree surgeon repairs a cavity: sections through a trunk at three stages. Rot is cleared away, drainage is provided for trapped water, and all surfaces are sterilised with wound dressing. Concrete or a sawdust-bitumen mix is then used to fill in the cavity.

which can usually be taken down and re-erected later, on due notice to the authorities concerned, and payment for their work. Fences, likewise, can be taken down and re-erected after the felling has been done, and portable buildings can be moved. With immovable obstacles, such as fixed buildings, the risk of serious damage and financial loss may be so great that the tree must be brought down in sections, which is far more costly than felling it in one piece.

TREE SURGERY

Tree surgery is the imaginative name given to operations intended to prolong the life of ornamental trees that are threatened with a premature death through damage or decay. It is always expensive, and any job except the simplest will cost more than the replacement of an ailing and ageing tree, using a young, healthy specimen with a far longer life-span ahead of it. No amount of surgery can make a tree immortal, but skilful work on a suitable subject will prolong its life by a substantial spell of years, perhaps twenty, perhaps fifty—possibly more.

The first step to take, whenever tree surgery appears a possibility, is to decide whether it is really worth while. The pleasure that an owner, or a group of people, may derive from maintaining a well-loved tree in a favourite situation may well justify it. Or the preservation of a well-sited specimen may add materially to the market value of a house. Alternatively, it may be found that the cost far outweighs the value that those concerned place upon the amenities provided by the tree; in that event the best course is to remove it and replace it with a younger one that will, within a few years, acquire a beauty and attractiveness of its own.

Tree Preservation Orders do not affect the issue much here. If a tree needs surgery, then it is usually becoming dangerous and can be felled despite any such Order, though its replacement may be obligatory. (See Chapter 5, page 76).

Trees, like human patients, differ markedly in their suitability for surgical operations. So much depends on the nature and extent of the damage, the tree's age and vigour, and its physical surroundings. The kind of tree concerned is also important. Oaks have a reputation for growing and surviving well after treatment; elms, on the other hand, often prove disappointing, and die despite every care; other trees fall somewhere between these extremes.

No prudent tree surgeon is going to guarantee the success of his treatment, but from his experience he can usually say whether it is likely to be worth while. In Britain and America there are now associations of tree surgeons whose members undertake to observe professional standards. They will not undertake doubtful work without advising their clients that the risk of failure is high.

For all but the simplest of jobs, a professional tree surgeon should be engaged, but the tree owner will wish to know how the surgeon works and the purpose of each step. He deals with the repair of physical injuries, and with the weakness due to disease, progressive decay or insect attack of *woody* tissues. Only exceptionally can he take any effective steps against diseases of *non-woody* tissues, such as leaves, or against the insects that attack the softer parts of the tree.

A tree surgeon's operations take two forms. One is the restoration of physical strength to the tree's trunk and branches. The other is the removal of weakened wood damaged by fungi or insects, and the prevention of further decay by antiseptic measures. The two are naturally done at the same time, and in fact often combined.

SURFACE WOUNDS

The simplest surgery, which is often within the scope of an amateur, consists in treating surface wounds due to such causes as collisions by traffic, or the breaking-off of a branch in a high wind. The rough surfaces of exposed wood are carefully cut smooth with a saw. Then the edges are trimmed with a sharp knife so that the adjoining cambium gets a fair start for its vital work of growing out over the cut and forming *callus* tissue. Finally the whole exposed surface is coated with a bituminous wound paint such as "Arbrex". The sooner all this is done, after the wound occurs, the better; any delay increases the chance that a fungal disease, causing decay, may gain entry to the wood through its exposed surface.

CAVITIES

Cavities in trunks and branches arise through the neglect of open wounds. Fungi which have entered through such wounds spread through the wood, feed on it, and cause its gradual decay and disappearance. As the wood goes, the stem is weakened, until the point is reached where breakage threatens. Fortunately, cavities form mainly in the heartwood, and the sapwood around it is seldom affected. As the tree puts on a fresh layer of sapwood each year, it can regain much of its physical strength, provided the decay that causes the cavity can be stopped. Further, if the cavity can be filled with some suitable strong material, some of the lost strength may be immediately restored.

The tree surgeon first removes all decayed and damaged wood from the cavity, which is much easier said than done! Next, he treats the sound wood, which is now exposed all round the cavity's surface, with an antiseptic, such as creosote, to check any re-invasion by the fungi that cause decay, or by wood-boring insects. Then he fills in the cavity as firmly as possible with a material that is inert and harmless in itself, but has similar physical characteristics to wood. This material must be both strong and flexible, and in practice a compound of wood-based material or sawdust, mixed with bitumen, is found to answer best. Concrete is less suitable as it is brittle and never makes firm contact with the tree's wood, though it is in fact often used. Finally the surface of the filling is smoothed off and coated with wound paint. Callus tissue will then slowly seal the edges, and may indeed grow out over the whole of the repaired surface.

If the cavity cannot readily be filled, its inner surface is simply coated with bituminous wound paint. Provision must also be made for any water, that can reach the cavity, to drain away.

BRACING, CABLING AND STAKING

One possible cause of a tree's premature death is the splitting-off of large branches under their own weight. Where this threatens, but has not yet actually happened, it is possible to prevent it by giving the threatened branches artificial support. This can be done only by linking them to the tree's main trunk, or to other suitably disposed branches, by strong metal links. Rigid iron rods do not allow the necessary play to the flexible branches, while chains are heavy and unsightly. The modern practice is to use woven steel wire ropes secured at both ends by special holdfasts, designed so as not to damage the tree. Rigging is a task for the expert. As the strength of wire rope is about six times that of manila rope of similar size, quite thin rope will serve, so it is not unsightly.

It is not a practical proposition to try to hold up, by guy ropes or rigid supports, any *large* tree that would otherwise fall. But small specimen trees, up to fifteen feet in height, can often be successfully restored to an upright position, after a windblow or an accidental down-

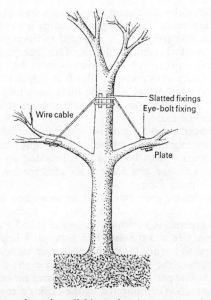

FIGURE 69. Heavy branches, liable to break away, can be strengthened by bracing to a sturdy trunk, using wire cables. Fixings must not damage the expanding limbs.

fall, by suitable staking, aided perhaps by guy ropes. For such methods to succeed it is essential that at least one main root be left undisturbed in the soil, and for the tree to be young, healthy and vigorous, so that it soon re-establishes a physically sound root-hold, and no longer needs artificial support.

STUMP REMOVAL

Stumps present various problems to the owners of land on which trees have been cut down. They have no value, and can be both difficult and costly to remove. In the forest or along the hedgerow the answer is simple; stumps are *not* removed, and as and when replanting is done, the young trees are simply planted in the gaps between the stumps. The slight risk arising from the fact that stumps can, in certain circumstances, prove to be sources of fungal diseases or insect pests, is accepted. The resultant loss of trees, or cost of preventive measures, matters far less than the cost of getting out the stumps.

Elsewhere, removal is often needed, but the owner of the land should always ask himself whether it is really worth the trouble or expense.

In ordinary garden soil a large stump may vanish through natural causes in a matter of a few years. How long will stumps last if left untouched?

Only three common trees can be regarded as having *durable stumps*. These are oak, sweet chestnut, and yew. Oak stumps surviving from fellings made in the 1914-1918 war—that is over fifty years ago, can still be found in many of our woods. But it is only the heartwood core of the stump that endures; all the side roots have long since decayed and all grip on the ground has gone; such ancient stumps are easily unearthed and moved aside.

The stumps of nearly all other trees rot away rapidly once life has ceased. A small poplar, for example, may have decayed right through after only three years, and even a stout beech will be breaking up five years after felling. Conditions around ground level are ideal for invasion and rapid growth by wood-rotting fungi.

Assuming that a stump must be shifted, let us see how it is constructed before we tackle it. The *collar* of any tree, that is the point where its trunk leaves the ground, is obviously the stoutest and strongest part of its whole structure. It withstands forces that—in a large tree—can be of the order of ten to twenty tons, whenever a strong wind blows. Because of the changes in the direction of the grain of the wood, where the roots join the stem, it is particularly hard to cut with axe or saw. Further, the use of cutting tools is complicated by the earth nearby.

A direct attack on a stump is therefore the most difficult way to remove it. It is easier in practice—though at first sight it may look tedious and difficult, to attack its support and anchorage in the soil. This means using digging tools as well as cutting tools.

Below ground, the roots of a tree fan out very much like the fingers of a hand, rapidly becoming smaller as they go. It is this network of support that must be exposed and cut through. Only rarely is the *tap root*, the one that goes vertically downwards from the trunk, of remarkable size and strength, though it is of course always the hardest root to get at for cutting. Many tall trees, growing on shallow or ill-drained soils, develop no substantial tap root at all.

A very handy tool for uprooting a large tree is the "two-bill" or axe-bladed mattock. This has one blade shaped like a hoe, for digging, and the other one shaped like an axe, for cutting through roots. Alternatively, the digging can be done with a spade and a pick-axe or pick-bladed mattock, and the cutting of the roots with a felling axe. Avoid, if possible, using a good new axe; it is sure to suffer damage, and an older, part-worn tool is adequate. A surprisingly large hole must be excavated in order to get at the buried roots, with freedom to wield cutting tools against them.

LEVERING AND WINCHING

When tackling small trees, it is often helpful to leave a length of the lower stem uncut when the tree is felled. This basal three feet or so can then be used as a lever to force over the stump and so speed its removal.

The same principle may be used for larger trees, provided a stout mechanical winch is available. If the rope for hauling out the tree is attached at a point several feet up a tree trunk, a terrific turning movement can be exerted on the base of the tree, far exceeding the "straight pull" of the winch. If the tree is winched over with all its length intact, then the weight of its crown exerts a further turning force as soon as it is tilted from the vertical. Very big trees can thus be uprooted without undue difficulty, when once the earth has been dug clear of their base, and their main side roots have been severed.

Two main kinds of winches are in use. One is mounted on a tractor, usually a machine used for timber haulage, which has its own holdfast in the form of a metal bar that is lowered until it digs into the ground. The other is the hand-powered winch which is anchored to a fixed hold-fast, such as the base of a stout tree, or even a group of pickets. Because of the "built-in mechanical advantage" of a tree-pulling winch, one man can exert enough force to uproot all but the stoutest of trees.

Winches can of course be used to pull out stumps *after* the whole trunk of a tree has been removed down to ground level. But this calls for greater force, and it is far less easy to get a good grip on a stump than it is on a standing trunk.

BULLDOZERS, EXPLOSIVES, AND STUMP-GOBBLERS

Where heavy earth-moving equipment is being used, as for example on a building site, stumps are easily shifted by brute force. A bulldozer blade mounted on a powerful crawler tractor will shift practically any stump it encounters. Bulldozing combined with powered winching, using the leverage of the tree's stem, will uproot *any* tree.

Another method that can prove very effective for small roadside trees is to bring along a powerful mobile crane which simply lifts the whole tree, roots and all, out of the ground.

Explosives can only be used well away from buildings, because of the risk of damage to people or property, particularly glass windows. Special safety precautions must be followed and legal requirements met, so it is all an expert's job. The usual method is to set a *lifting charge* below the stump; this forces it clear of the ground, but does not shatter it.

A machine called a "Stump Gobbler" is used in America, and occasionally in Europe, to destroy stumps physically by cutting them away from above, using a system of rapidly revolving toothed chains. In effect the stump is chewed into little bits. Such machines, being expensive and having only one purpose, are usually operated by contractors.

CHEMICAL MEASURES FOR POISONING OR BURNING-UP STUMPS

In these days of scientific wizardry, many people hope to find some chemical that will make stumps decay and disappear completely. But wood resists all common chemicals, even strong acids and alkalis. For this very reason, it is used for benches in chemical laboratories, because

it remains unharmed by substances that would quickly eat away metal
There are only four ways to destroy a stump, and all are slow. It can be
rubbed or cut away into chips or shavings. It can be broken down, very
slowly, by fungal attack. It can be broken down, still more slowly
through insect attack. The fourth method is burning, but this too is
a slow one because when a stump is felled it is saturated with water
Water may account for half its weight, and so long as it remains alive
and in contact with the ground, a stump will stay wet and so remain
practically impossible to burn.

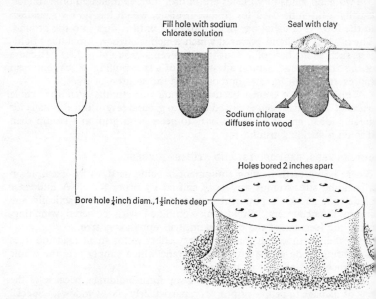

FIGURE 70. Poisoning a tree stump to check sprouting. Holes are bored with
auger or brace-and-bit, two inches apart, filled with concentrated sodium
chlorate solution and sealed with clay.

The only way to render a stump inflammable, without taking it out of
the ground and giving it time to dry, is to treat it with a chemical that
will both kill it and supply extra oxygen to its tissues, so that it is more
ready to smoulder. There are two common chemicals that will do this;
one is sodium chlorate, $NaClO_3$, and the other is potassium nitrate or
saltpetre, KNO_3; both are what the chemists call *oxidising agents*.

SODIUM CHLORATE TREATMENT

In practice, sodium chlorate is most often used. It is cheap and easily
obtained from chemists and nurserymen who sell it as a weedkiller. It is

often used to stop regrowth from tree stumps, even when there is no intention of burning them. It is sold as a white crystalline powder, usually in tins, and the only preparation it needs is dissolving in water; the minimum amount of water should be used, so as to make the strongest possible solution. It is not dangerously toxic to humans or animals, but it will kill all small green plants that it touches; it also makes fabrics highly inflammable, so you should be careful not to spill it on your clothing.

The stump is prepared for treatment by boring into it, on its flat top surface, a number of small, short holes. A brace-and-bit is the best tool for this; alternatively a drill or a gimlet will serve. These holes should be about one quarter-inch wide and one inch deep, and be spaced about one inch apart; they should be evenly spaced, with plenty in the living sapwood around the edge of the stump.

The strong solution of sodium chlorate is applied to the stump by pouring it into the holes, with the help of a small funnel. Each hole is then plugged or covered over with clay, to keep out the rain. The poison slowly spreads sideways from the holes, all through the stump, and kills the tissues, so that no sprouting occurs.

About six months after the poisoning has been done, the surface layers of the wood will become dry enough to smoulder. If a fire is now lit on top of the stump, it will slowly burn down into it and char its main mass, though side roots will remain unburnt.

Sodium chlorate can also be used to check the sucker shoots that spring up from the side roots of certain trees after they have been felled, particularly elms, plums, and the locust tree, *Robinia pseudoacacia*. Each shoot is cut back to ground level and a little of the strong solution of sodium chlorate is applied to its exposed surface, to poison the tissues. Care must be taken not to spill the chlorate on neighbouring grass or flowers; it will kill these, though it does no permanent harm to the soil.

However, the simplest way to check sucker shoots is simply to cut them back as they appear. If this is done repeatedly, the roots that bear them will soon die from lack of nourishment, and there will be no need to poison them, nor to dig them up.

11. Long-term Planning, Thinning and Maintenance

LONG-TERM PLANS

BECAUSE trees last so long, and appear to change rather slowly after their first youth is past, their long-term control is often neglected. Many planters plan for only one year ahead, which is far too short for trees that often stand for a century. See Plate 24, p. 285.

A farmer makes plans for a rotation of crops on his fields, running through several years ahead, even though each separate crop is sown and harvested within a single season. So a prudent tree grower must make plans for the land, as well as for the trees, for a reasonable future span of time. What does "reasonable" mean here?

A guide can be found in the Forestry Commission's *Plans of Operations*, which are drawn up by private estates that co-operate with the Commission in grant-aided schemes for woodland management. The woodland owner sets out his proposals, for planting, thinning, tree-felling, and other work in his woods, in fairly close detail, for five years ahead. He then adds, but only in outline, his plans for the succeeding five years, making ten years in all.

As the first five-year spell draws to its end, he reviews and revises his plans. *Details* are now worked in for the second five-year period, and an outline made for a *third* five-year spell. So everyone concerned with the woods know what the intentions are for an overall period of at least six years, and perhaps as much as ten years ahead. The system works on these lines far into the future.

Over time spans as short as five or ten years, important changes take place in any age-group of trees. Those recently planted will pass through their tricky early years and become independent, needing no further weeding. Middle-aged crops will need thinning out. Older trees may mature and become ripe for felling, or they may need inspection to ensure that they are remaining sound and healthy, and present no danger to passers-by. The felling of mature timber stands may free some ground that will need replanting. Drains, roads and fences may each be needing attention.

In a small garden every tree is always under its owner's eye and he will see at once what care is needed. But on an estate with a large number of park or roadside trees, a scheme for the annual inspection of a set proportion of them, say one fifth, is very desirable. In woodlands, intended for timber production, it is quite essential. The available funds and

CROSS-SECTION

5 years hence

Now

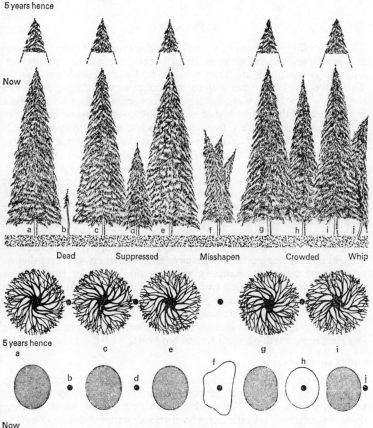

Dead   Suppressed   Misshapen   Crowded   Whip

5 years hence

Now
PLAN

FIGURE 71. Thinning a line of trees to secure even growth. The five trees a, c, e, g and i are desirable ones that will be retained to grow taller and larger. Five others will be cut out, i.e. b, dead, d, suppressed by neighbours; f, forked and misshapen, h, crowded by neighbours; i, too thin and whippy. In the lower diagram, the shaded trees are those allowed to remain.

labour can be spread over this five-year cycle, and sudden peaks of expense and rushes of work are avoided. The income that arises from thinnings or fellings is likewise evened-out over the several years involved.

THINNING

The most effective means of control over the growth of trees that stand in plantations, groups, or even lines, is their periodical thinning out. The poorer specimens are taken out, and sold where possible at a profit. This leaves the better ones with more room to expand their crowns, and so to grow to a larger size. Each gets more sunlight than before, and a bigger share of the nutrients that are available to the roots below ground.

In garden, park, street tree and landscape work, thinning is only practised occasionally. Instead, planters set their trees widely apart to keep down costs. Yet it can prove, in some circumstances, a useful means of improving appearances. When the Mall, in St. James's Park, London, was planted with a double avenue of plane trees about 1910, they were deliberately set close together to give well-defined screens as early as possible. Fifty years later, alternate trees were removed, leaving the survivors, now better spaced, room to achieve their full size and stately proportions.

In forests and shelterbelts there are, in principle, two schools of thought on thinning out, and perhaps as many variations on these themes as there are foresters! Basically, you can aim either for regularity or irregularity in the remaining crop. On either plan, the grade of thinning can be *heavy*, removing a high proportion of the crop, say 20% or, *light*, affecting only a small percentage, say 10%. The thinning *cycle*, or interval of years between thinnings, can be *short*, say only three years, or *long*, implying anything from five to ten years.

REGULAR THINNING

In regular thinnings a definite proportion of the growing stock of trees is taken out, by selecting the poorer specimens, as evenly spaced as possible, for removal. The marker walks through the wood selecting these, usually with an assistant who marks those trees due to come out with a dab of paint or a *blaze* cut with a billhook to expose white wood below grey bark. Dead, dying, and diseased trees are naturally chosen for removal, and so are trees with forked stems, misshapen and crooked trunks, and any *suppressed* trees that have fallen behind their neighbours in the struggle for survival. A few unduly vigorous, but badly shaped trees that are damaging well-shaped, less vigorous neighbours, may also be cut out. This leaves the better trees, of more uniform size and shape, well spaced out.

The first "thinnings" are naturally a rough lot of poles, worth very little to anyone. But when the forester takes out his second thinnings, a few years later, he is obliged to cut out many good straight poles in order to give the other trees more room. These later thinnings are of fairly even size, and they are readily sold for the many uses to which small timber can be put, such as fence stakes, pit props, small sawmill timber, or the raw material for the paper-pulp, hardboard, and chipboard industries.

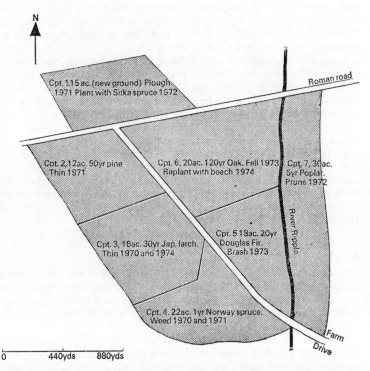

N

Cpt. 1. 15 ac. (new ground) Plough 1971 Plant with Sitka spruce 1972

Roman road

Cpt. 2, 12 ac. 50yr pine Thin 1971

Cpt. 6, 20 ac. 120yr Oak. Fell 1973 Replant with beech 1974

Cpt. 7, 30 ac. 5yr Poplar. Prune 1972

River Ripplo

Cpt. 3, 18 ac. 30yr Jap. larch. Thin 1970 and 1974

Cpt. 5 18 ac. 20yr Douglas Fir. Brash 1973

Cpt. 4. 22 ac. 1yr Norway spruce. Weed 1970 and 1971

Farm Drive

0   440yds   880yds

FIGURE 72. Sketch for a management plan. The wood is divided into seven compartments, by roads, rides or the river. Each is numbered and its area is stated, together with present crop and work proposed during five years 1970-1974 inclusive.

It is a fairly easy matter to judge the number of trees to take out in regular thinnings. "Forest Management Tables" are published by the Forestry Commission as Booklet No. 34 (H.M. Stationery Office, £1.60), to give guidance, for each kind of tree, at every likely age and rate of growth. But even without tables, a forester with experience can tell, by looking up from below, whether he is leaving the remaining trees enough room to expand their crowns without crowding too closely against their neighbours, during the few years that will elapse before he comes round again.

IRREGULAR THINNINGS

Irregular thinnings have very real attractions for people who wish to create or maintain a natural, or at least a pleasantly varied appearance to their woods. It is hard to make them successful financially because the very concept of irregularity means that trees of a variety of sizes, as well as different shapes, are removed from the wood at one time. The resulting "parcel" of poles is difficult for any merchant to work, prepare, or sell profitably, so he can offer only a low price.

Irregular thinnings are also difficult to mark, because there are no simple tables to follow, and no rules except the forester's judgment. Skill comes only with long experience. No tree can be removed, just because it is too small or too large. The marker must look at every tree, and also at all its neighbours, to decide whether it is likely to develop satisfactorily during the coming thinning cycle, or whether it should now be taken out. The outcome of repeated, skilled, irregular thinnings, is often beautiful. Trees of varied ages, sizes and perhaps varied species grow in harmony together, and their combined rate of timber production can be high. The method is well suited to woodlands where appearance counts for more than early profits; it is also essential in alpine forests, where land cannot be cleared of trees because of the avalanches and soil erosion that would ensue.

NATURAL REGENERATION

In nature, forests renew themselves without the aid of any tree-planting, by growth from the seeds that they shed in abundance season after season. Foresters can achieve much the same results through the skilful management of their thinning or tree felling, according to the kind of tree and the local conditions.

For example, if *irregular thinning* is carried the whole way, quite large trees will eventually be taken out, leaving gaps in which young seedling trees, arising from naturally-fallen seed, can find enough light and space to grow. This is called the *selection system* of forest management because control of the woods is maintained simply by selecting those trees that are to be removed. Nature fills the gaps, and if the forester is not satisfied with those trees that nature provides, he removes them, knowing that others will soon grow up to take their place.

In other systems of natural regeneration, part of the crop is removed, in groups or strips, and young trees are nursed up between a surround of older trees that supply abundant seed. Alternatively, occasional seed trees, or "mother trees" may be left unfelled over the whole area, until they have shed ample seed; or the forester may fell *all* the trees just after a heavy seed crop. But all these methods are limited in their application to particular trees in particular districts, under the care of foresters who have long experience of the techniques required.

CLEAR FELLING

As stands of trees *mature*, that is, reach the age and size when their timber can be sold at the highest profit, before any deterioration due to old age sets in, they are usually clear-felled and the land is replanted. The age for this *final crop* felling, as it is called, depends on the kind of tree and the prices ruling in the market for timber of various sizes. The forester also has his "Forest Management Tables" showing likely rates of timber production, to guide him; growth eventually slows down as the trees mature. The owner will also consider his own financial affairs, whether he wishes to turn his trees into cash or to keep them standing and still slowly increasing in value.

Tree felling is controlled in the several ways outlined in Chapter 5, page 72, on "Trees and the Law"—that is by Tree Preservation Orders, Felling Licences, or Plans of Operations approved by the Forestry Commission. In most circumstances, this control requires the replanting of the land within a reasonable space of time.

Under sound, long-term management, one crop of trees follows another, partly because of this control, but mainly because the owner wishes to see his woodlands devoted continuously to profitable timber production, which experience has shown to be a satisfactory investment. The age to which each crop of trees is allowed to grow is called its *rotation age*; it may vary from a short span of years to a long one. Cricket bat willows are harvested after twelve to fifteen years, poplars after twenty-five to thirty, fast-growing conifers from sixty to seventy years, Scots pine when eighty to one hundred years, and most hardwoods, including oak and beech, from one hundred to one hundred and twenty years, or even older.

Within any forest or woodland estate there are naturally many stands of trees of various sizes, which have been planted at different times, and often with different kinds of trees. These form units of management called *compartments*, and in the *working plan* or *plan of operations* that the forester prepares, each individual compartment is given is own particular schedule of work to be done.

In order that those in charge may see how closely the provisions of a plan are carried out, records of work done must be carefully maintained for many years. These are usually in tabular form, so that achievements can be readily compared with proposals. In this way a history of the tree-growing enterprise—whether it be a large forest or a collection of park trees, is steadily built up. This can prove of great value to all later planning and practice.

MARKETING TIMBER

Most woodland owners, other than those with very large estates, usually engage professional land agents or forestry consultants to market their timber. They do so because crops are only available for sale at intervals of many months, or even several years. An agent who is constantly engaged in the business is better able to judge the trend of prices, and to know the keener purchasers, than an owner who can only offer trees occasionally. He will, therfore, usually earn his fee and still produce a higher return than the owner himself could get.

The usual unit for the sale of timber in Britain is one of volume. The traditional hoppus foot, or "cubic foot quarter-girth measure" was succeeded in 1971 by the true cubic metre. Volume is now calculated from the length and mid-diameter of the useful section or sections, of each tree, measured according to accepted trade practices, and following the Metric Volume Ready Reckoner for Round Timber, published as Forestry Commission Booklet No. 26 by H.M. Stationery Office at 35p.

The prices that buyers will pay, at the same time and place, for one cubic metre of timber, vary enormously. They depend on the kind of tree and the size of log offered, and also on the ease with which the trees concerned can be cut down and hauled out.

A contract for the sale of standing timber is often a complicated document. If big trees are involved, the owner is likely to say what roads may be used to take them out, to fix time limits for removing them, and to make conditions for clearing up the ground after felling has been done.

The details of such transactions lie beyond the scope of a simple guide to the planting and care of trees and woods. But they should always be in the minds of the owners of growing timber. If marketing, like management, is considered as part of a long-term plan, and regular purchasers are encouraged, a steady income is much more likely to be realised, than if matters are only handled just when the need arises.

PART TWO

CHOOSING TREES

12. Nomenclature, Classification and Identification

ONE of the most puzzling things for the tree grower is the business of naming, classifying, and distinguishing the various kinds of trees that he tends. Three systems of naming will be found used, at one and the same time, in most trade catalogues—that is the common or vernacular name, such as "oak"; the Latin or scientific name, such as *Quercus petraea*, which is the sessile-flowered wild oak with stalkless acorns; and the modern cultivar name, given to varieties known only in cultivation, such as *Quercus petraea* 'Purpurea,' the purple-leaved sessile oak. There is in fact an *International Code of Nomenclature for Cultivated Plants*, including trees, to which the Royal Horticultural Society and other leading organisations have, since its issue in 1958, aimed to conform. Why is all this necessary?

COMMON NAMES

Most of us use common names for common trees and common timbers, but as soon as you start to bring in trees from abroad you encounter difficulties. The English species of oak are not found wild in America, so when an American speaks of "oak" he is thinking of similar trees but seldom of just the same kinds as those known in Europe. Then oak is known by other names in other languages—for example it is *Eiche* in German and *chêne* in French. Botanists, foresters, and nurserymen often find it easier to follow scientific names for trees, which mean the same throughout the world, than the vernacular names that vary from one country to another, especially when they read literature or trade catalogues from another country. Common names, moreover, are not very precise; for example a "mountain ash" resembles a common ash only in its leaf, and not in its flowers, fruits or timber. Finally, there are so many sorts of trees and shrubs in cultivation to-day that there are not really enough common names to go round.

SCIENTIFIC NAMES

THE GENUS

Botanists, faced with these problems, have devised a method of giving Latin names to trees, all of which they have carefully identified and described. This is called the Linnaean system after the great Swedish eighteenth-century naturalist Linnaeus, who gave Latin names to most animals and plants that he knew in his day. The basis of scientific nomenclature is the *genus* or kind of tree, and this is particularly important for tree growers. The generic name is always given first. It always carries a capital letter and is usually printed in italics. Trees belonging to the same genus are usually very much alike in leaf, bud structure, bud arrangement, flowers, fruits, timbers and even bark. A good knowledge of the commoner genera is the best starting point for identification.

THE SPECIES

Within this main grouping by genera, lesser differences appear. These are recognised by calling each clearly defined group a *species*, and giving it a specific name. Specific names are set in italics, with small initial letters, and always follow the generic name. Specific names were originally intended to describe the tree, or some feature of it; but most of them are in fact meaningless, or arose in such an obscure way that any search for a meaning is pointless! But each specific name indicates a clear difference of character, *within* the framework of the genus. For example, among the oaks, *Quercus robur*, the pedunculate oak, has *stalked* acorns, whereas *Quercus petraea*, the sessile oak, has *stalkless* acorns. *Q. ilex*, the holm oak, differs from both in having evergreen leaves.

THE VARIETY

Within the species again there may be *varieties*. These have a varietal name, set in italics with a small initial letter. The words used here are generally full of meaning, and it is worth while to master the simple Latin adjectives involved. For example, the varietal name of *Picea pungens glauca*, the blue Colorado spruce, shows quite plainly that its leaves have a bluish tinge, as the last word means "blue".

The "Latin" used for all these scientific names sometimes employs words actually known to the Romans, as with such common trees as *quercus*, oak; *fagus*, beech; and *fraxinus*, ash. But more often it is "botanists' Latin", since the Romans knew only a fraction of the trees we grow to-day.

No scientific name is complete without an "authority"—that is, the name of the botanist who described a specimen before giving it the stated name. Authorities are often abbreviated; for example, "L" stands for Linnaeus. In this book, the authorities are omitted from the general text, but will be found in the Index.

Scientific names are *intended* to stand unchanged for all time. But as knowledge advances botanists may decide to alter a specific or even a generic name. For example, the Douglas fir, which is here called *Pseudotsuga menziesii* (a specific name derived from Menzies, its dis-coverer), was known at different times in the past as *P. taxifolia* or as

P. douglasii. This makes it hard for people to follow the early records, for these superseded names are often the only ones found in old text-books and even in modern catalogues.

CULTIVAR NAMES

Many cultivated plants, and some trees such as apples and roses, have been cultivated for centuries, and much cross-breeding has taken place. To-day, it is almost impossible to assign many well-known strains to a particular species or variety. Nurserymen, farmers, and foresters have recently got over the difficulty by giving, to strains that are known only in cultivation, a *cultivar* name. This is set in ordinary Roman type, within single quotation marks, and carries a capital letter. *If* the species is known, it is included; for example, *Ilex aquifolium* 'Golden Queen' is a yellow-leaved cultivar of the native wild holly. But if the species can no longer be traced, only the generic name appears; for example *Prunus* 'Amanogawa' is a well-known Japanese cherry with an upright habit of growth. Cultivar names may be in any language; English, Japanese, and Latin are all equally acceptable.

Note that cultivar names are *alternatives* to varietal names, not additional to them.

CLASSIFICATION

PROVENANCES

There is a further aspect of tree classification that concerns the grower of timber trees, though it will seldom worry the gardener who raises ornamental specimens. This is the *provenance* or *original* home of the strain of trees that he is growing.

Certain trees grow wild over a large extent of the earth's surface, and during past ages local strains have developed which are well suited to each part of the tree's natural range, though they may prove less happy elsewhere. Outwardly, these different provenances look much alike, and the botanist is unable to tell one from another. But each behaves in its own way when grown as a timber tree, and in any one situation some prove more successful than others.

As an example, British foresters prefer to grow Sitka spruce with a provenance in British Columbia, which has a climate similar to that of the British west coast. Sitka spruce trees with a provenance in northern Alaska, much farther north, grow more slowly in Britain, probably because they are adapted to the longer summer days of the Arctic zone; those of Californian provenance also grow slowly in Britain, because they are accustomed to a warmer climate.

Provenance properties are passed on from one generation to another, so it is important in forestry to know where the foundation stock comes from. If Japanese larch seed is collected from mature trees growing in Scotland, its provenance may still be Mount Fuji. Prudent foresters therefore keep records of seed origin throughout the life of each crop.

CERTIFIED SEED AND PLANTING STOCK

In forestry, it is so important to know just where each stock of trees arose, that schemes for certifying planting material have been set up. The British scheme is operated by the Forest Seed Association. (See Appendix II, p. 326, for address). When each lot of seed is gathered or imported, it is given a reference number. The seedlings and the transplants that are raised from this seed lot also carry this number—so it goes all the way from seed store, through the nursery stages, to the plantations. It is just like the pedigree of a prize bull or the guarantee of a selected strain of wheat. The seedsmen and nurserymen who operate this scheme naturally charge a little more for their certified stocks, but the extra cost is a sound investment for the commercial timber grower.

CLASSIFYING TREES BY FAMILIES

After the botanists had placed the plants and trees they had described in genera, they made large groupings of similar genera which they called *families*. All the genera and species within one family have arisen from a common stock, and this natural relationship is shown in many ways. For example, trees of the *same* family can be grafted one upon another, whereas grafts between trees of *different* families always fail. The flowers within a particular family have a common resemblance, and so does the microscopic structure of the timber.

But it would be misleading to suggest that a knowledge of family characters will help the ordinary tree grower. There are only two very large families that concern him—the pine family or Pinaceae which includes most of the common conifers, and the rose family or Rosaceae, which includes apples, pears, plums, cherries, and rowan trees. Each of these families is so large and varied that, to make headway, you must learn to know the genera too. Many of the other families have only one

PLATE 5 *Oaks in winter*

Above Turner's oak, a hybrid between the native sessile oak and the Mediterranean evergreen holm oak (see Plate 13c, p. 212), never loses its leaves entirely. This vigorous specimen at Kew Gardens has formed its vast dome-shaped crown without treatment.
Below Pedunculate oak, *Quercus robur*, one of our two native kinds, develops a characteristic broad crown with contorted branch-ends, due to random arrangement of terminal buds. This Somerset hedgerow tree was lopped or pollarded about two centuries ago, to promote greater branch spread for firewood and tan-bark harvests.

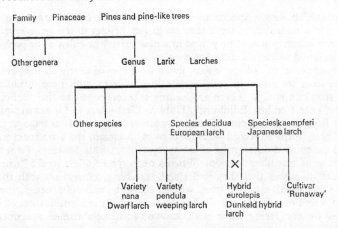

FIGURE 73. Terms used to classify and identify plants. A large plant family, Pinaceae or pine-like trees, holds many genera, including *Larix*, the larches. The *Larix* genus has several species, including *L. decidua*, European larch. This species has natural varieties, such as *pendula* or weeping larch. Cross-breeding with Japanese larch species *kaempferi* gives hybrid larch, x *Larix eurolepis*. The imaginary cultivar, *Larix* 'Runaway', is known to have Japanese larch as female parent; the male parent *might* be a hybrid larch. 'Runaway' will be increased by grafting.

or two genera of trees that are hardy in temperate lands; so it is easier to learn the generic characters than to study the more complex family ones.

IDENTIFICATION

The identification of particular trees is not covered here, for it needs a whole volume to itself. Readers should consult a standard, well-illustrated work (see Bibliography, p. 334). But it is worth our while to consider *how* trees are identified or proved true to name. When a botanist names and describes a new plant or tree he does it from an actual specimen, which is then carefully pressed and preserved as a "type specimen" in some great herbarium such as that of the Royal Botanic

PLATE 6

Above left Scots pine set at a landmark on open heathland in Sussex.
Above right American red oak makes a brilliant solitary parkland specimen.
Below Wellingtonias from California, used on the grand scale to frame a broad vista across the Sussex Weald.

Gardens at Kew. Specimens taken from other, similar trees can be compared with this to see if they do in fact belong to the same species, or whether they should be placed in a new variety or cultivar, or perhaps be assigned to quite a different species.

Besides these dead specimens, living examples of nearly all temperate-zone trees are grown in collections called *arboreta*, which are invaluable for scientific study. There are leading arboreta, open to the public, at Kew, near London, Edinburgh, Dublin, Westonbirt in Gloucestershire, and Bedgebury in Kent. Details appear in Appendix I on page 323.

Three forms of record—the herbarium specimen, the arboretum tree, and the printed description of the species, often with drawings, form the basis of all tree identification. When a nurseryman offers stocks "true to name" it means that they will stand searching comparison with these type specimens, arboreta trees, written accounts, and published pictures.

If a tree owner has any doubts, he can check the identification of his trees by comparing them with known, accurately named specimens. When planting records have been lost, comparison is the only certain way to name the tree concerned.

In theory, you should have every part of each tree available—leaf, flower, fruit, seed, bud, bark and wood. But in practice a great deal can be done with leafy shoots (*not* separate leaves), especially if *one other* feature is at hand. Shoots for identification are best gathered from a "middle-aged" branch, for the leaves on rapidly growing young shoots, or on very old ones, may be quite different from the tree's typical form.

Identification is a fascinating pursuit because trees are only *closely* alike if they belong to the same clone or cultivar; and even trees of the same cultivar will differ in vigour of growth, size of leaf, and so forth, according to soil and surroundings. When you are dealing with wild trees, or naturally variable cultivated ones that have been raised from seed, rather than from cuttings or grafts, you must expect considerable variation from both specimen and published account. Only the "type" tree chosen by the botanist fits the description exactly—and that tree will seldom be found alive to-day!

There is also considerable variation throughout the various shoots and branches of the *same tree*. This is more marked in the *sizes* of leaves, shoots and buds, though it also affects their *shapes*. So do not try to name a strange tree on the strength of one or two leaves only; examine it more generally to get a good idea of average size and form.

Certain trees show a definite progression from one type of foliage or leaf-pattern, called "juvenile" to another pattern, called "adult". This happens in most conifers, though with many the "growing-up" stage occurs when they are only one year old, and the juvenile form is only seen in the seed bed. In others, such as larch, every new "long shoot", throughout the life of the tree, has the "juvenile" pattern of foliage, with solitary needles; the "adult" needles, set in groups, only arise from "short shoots" on older twigs. Do not be surprised, therefore, if you find two kinds of leaf or shoot on the same tree! A good textbook will mention both, and their presence together will help identification.

The vigorous "coppice" shoots that spring up from the stump, after a broadleaved tree has been cut down, often bear huge leaves. Sometimes their shape is unusual; for example, a white poplar often has leaves of a simple outline on its coppice shoots, though the smaller leaves on a normal branch have five lobes.

Shape always counts for more than colour, which varies widely with the season of the year.

13. Growth Forms and Colour Variations

EACH *species* of tree has a *typical* form, which is that usually found wild in nature. Foresters usually grow this typical form for timber, and it is of course also widely used for ornamental planting. But gardeners often prefer something out of the ordinary run, sometimes for the simple reason that it *is* rare and strange, sometimes because its shape, size or colour happens to fit in well with their general scheme of landscape design.

In practice most of these exceptional trees and shrubs are increased by vegetative means, as individuals raised from seed cannot be relied on to come true to type. This means that they are *clones* or *cultivars*. But many are still listed in nurserymen's catalogues as *varieties*.

Variations from the normal pattern are of two main kinds—form and colour. These may occur separately or together. For example, the variety of Lawson cypress called "*Chamaecyparis lawsoniana* variety *aurea*" is golden, that called *erecta* is upright, and that called *erecta aurea* is both golden-foliaged *and* upright.

This addition of adjectives is cumbersome, and buyers often suspect that every addition of a name means a bit extra on the price! So for simplicity many varieties are given a cultivar name such as 'Fletcheri', which may not itself give any clue to the tree's appearance. Only a description in a text book or a trade catalogue can then tell you what to expect if you order the tree so named. In this instance it means a slow-growing, blue, juvenile-foliaged, pyramidal form of Lawson cypress first cultivated at Chertsey by a famous Victorian nurseryman named Fletcher.

GROWTH FORMS

A tree can vary from the typical form in four distinct ways, so:
1. It may grow exceptionally large.
2. It may remain exceptionally small.
3. Its branches may follow an exceptional pattern, for example by growing downwards instead of erect, as in weeping trees, creeping trees, and fastigiate kinds.
4. Its foliage may show unusual characters.

GIANT TREES

Taking the first kind of variation first, it is odd but true that races of trees which grow remarkably large or remarkably fast hold little attraction for the gardener, or even for the landscape planter. This is because such trees rapidly reach the "desirable" size and then prove troublesome to control, since they need constant hard pruning. An exception is the Lombardy poplar, *Populus nigra* variety *italica*, which has a very erect habit of growth and consequently a narrow crown needing no pruning; it quickly forms a high narrow pillar, while a row of such trees makes a quick screen.

Timber growers naturally prefer quick-growing trees. Fast-grown wood is acceptable for all the big bulk-consuming industries, and slow-grown stuff only has merit for a few specialised trades, such as ladder-making, which take relatively small quantities. However, most timber trees are raised from seed, and so far foresters have obtained quick growth through the choice of the correct *provenance* or the use of a *hybrid*. Choice of strain is only one of many factors that raises timber yields, when these are worked out on the basis of output from a certain area of land over a certain number of years; cultivation, the use of fertilisers, and the thinning methods applied, also affect the outcome and the ultimate profit.

Poplars and willows provide exceptions to this general rule. With both these trees, choice of a fast-growing *cultivar* is a critical matter. The favourite fast-growing willow is the cricket bat willow, *Salix alba* var. *coerulea*, a female strain which yields bat material after only twelve years growth. With poplars there is, in theory, a wide choice. In practice the following kinds are currently recommended by the Forestry Commission as being both disease-resistant and very fast-growing: *Populus* 'Berolinensis', *P.* 'Eugenei', *P.* 'Gelrica', *P.* 'Laevigata'. *P.* 'Robusta', *P.* 'Serotina', and the balsam poplar hybrid: *Populus tacamahaca* × *P. trichocarpa* 'No. 32'.

DWARF TREES

Here the possibilities are endless! Slow-growing trees, and strains that can be guaranteed not to exceed a set height, are always in demand for small gardens, rock-gardens, and even for pots! The "very dwarf" kinds, grown in rockeries, or as miniature trees in the Japanese fashion, are described in Chapter 21, page 307. There are many others that grow somewhat taller, reaching bush height, but never becoming tall trees.

The usual varietal names applied to these trees of gradual growth and low stature are:

Variety *nana* = dwarf
  „   *humilis* = low
  „   *minima* = small
  „   *pygmaea* = pygmy

WEEPING AND CREEPING TREES

Within the growing tissues of most tree stems there are special cells that govern the direction of growth. These cells persuade the new shoots to head towards the sunlight, and also upwards, away from the earth, which normally amounts to much the same thing!

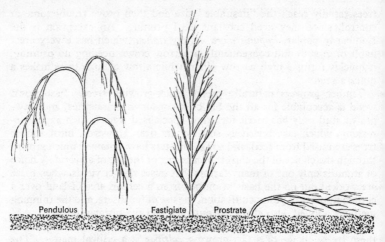

Pendulous · Fastigiate Prostrate

FIGURE 74. The main life-forms of exceptional decorative trees. In *pendulous* forms, all branches grow downwards; in *fastigiate* ones they grow upwards; in *prostrate* ones they are horizontal.

In the weeping and creeping trees, the stimulus to grow *away from* the earth is, in some strange way, reversed, and although the branches still seek the light, they grow downwards instead of upwards.

The well-known weeping willow, *Salix babylonica*, is one of the very few trees that are able to grow downwards or upwards, according to circumstances. It usually grows beside rivers, and after it has reached a fair height it directs its "water-side" branches towards the bright light reflected from the water surface, while its "inland" branches still grow upwards. Such a tree provides its own "standard" or upright stem, and needs no grafting.

By contrast, most other weeping "trees" are incapable of upward growth, and cannot form their own trunks. They exist only as grafted forms, and are increased by nurserymen who graft them on upright stems of some nearly related tree.

If they are persuaded to take root, as cuttings, they will then only grow sideways, which means that they spread over the ground as creeping trees.

The usual varietal name for weeping trees is *pendula*. That for creeping trees is *repens*. But as we have seen, the same kind can often be persuaded to follow either habit of growth. Both variations arise in nature as freaks. These have caught the eye of the ingenious nurseryman, and have been brought into cultivation by taking scions for grafting.

FASTIGIATE TREES

In a normal tree there is a clear division of growth direction, between the main trunk and the side branches. The trunk arises through the steady upward growth of a leading shoot, which always aims to remain vertical. The side branches are inclined outwards at various angles—upwards, level, or downwards according to the kind of tree.

If the bud at the tip of the leading shoot of a normal tree gets damaged —for example by insect attack, then two or more side buds may each aim to take the lead. This results in a "double leader", or even a "treble leader", and a forked trunk follows. A keen tree grower, if he sees this happening in time, will check it by pruning away one or more of the competing side shoots, leaving a single leader again.

Fastigiate trees are quite different from *forked* ones, and no amount of pruning will ever persuade them to mend their ways. For them, every side branch is a potential leader that can only grow upwards. So the whole tree comes to resemble a bundle of twigs, or a sweeping broom—which is in fact the Latin origin of the variety's name. The commonest term for these varieties is naturally *fastigiata* though some are called *columnaris*.

The best-known tree of this growth pattern is the Lombardy poplar, *Populus nigra* var. *italica*, so called because it is particularly common on the plains of the Po Valley in Lombardy, northern Italy. It is useful as a narrow screen or shelterbelt tree, but the countless knots in its trunk, arising from the multitude of side branches, make it useless as timber. See Plate 10, page 197.

FOLIAGE PATTERN VARIETIES

Individual leaves may show a hereditary variation from the shape that

Adult   Juvenile

FIGURE 75. *Left*, typical adult foliage of Lawson cypress, found on mature twigs; scale-leaves clasp and hide the twigs. *Right*, juvenile foliage of free-standing needles, found on seedlings and exceptional varieties.

is typical of a particular kind of tree, and this can prove very confusing to beginners in the art of tree identification. A common example is the fern-leaved beech, *Fagus sylvatica* var. *heterophylla*, in which every leaf is delicately lobed, instead of having a plain oval outline. The typical shape of bud and twig, together with the tree's smooth grey bark and the fact that this pretty freak is invariably grafted, all help to show that it *is* a beech and not some strange exotic tree. The varietal name *heterophylla* may however, be applied to other varieties of other trees that bear oddly-shaped leaves, for it simply means "odd-leaved".

Lobed leaves may be very finely divided along the lines of their main veins, and such strains are usually called *laciniata* or "cut-leaved". In some forms of the well-known Japanese maple, *Acer palmatum*, this leaf-division is carried to an extreme degree, which may be considered elegant or just absurd, according to taste. The variety *linearilobum*, meaning "linear-lobed-leaved", is an example.

Some trees that normally bear compound leaves, composed of many leaflets, have freak varieties in which every leaf remains entire and undivided. The simple-leaved ash, *Fraxinus excelsior* var. *monophylla*, is perhaps the commonest. Since the early leaves of all ash trees, in their seedling stage, are always simple and undivided, this *monophylla* variety can be considered a *juvenile* form. Although it becomes a tall tree, so far as its leaves are concerned it remains a "Peter Pan" tree that never grows up!

Juvenile foliage patterns are very common among conifers, and are important to growers because they are found on many of the most decorative kinds. Most genera of conifers have needles of two distinct sorts. One, the juvenile pattern, which is also considered the ancient ancestral type, is normally seen only on seedlings during their first year of growth, or else on young shoots at the tip of each branch. For example, pine seedlings have solitary needles, but all their later needles are in groups of two, three, or five. Lawson cypress has distinct, narrow, sharp-pointed needles in its seedling stage, but these are followed by broad, blunt needles pressed tightly against the twig in a pattern that resembles the frond of a fern. Juvenile-foliaged conifers keep the first simple, single, free-standing needles throughout their life, and never develop the *adult* foliage form. As might be expected, they rarely become tall trees; most remain short trees or much-branched bushes.

Two common ornamental junipers—the Virginian pencil cedar, *Juniperus virginiana*, and the Chinese juniper, *J. sinensis*, are peculiar in

PLATE 7

Open-grown sycamore in Scottish parkland. Note the clear 'browse-level' below which all foliage and branch growth is checked by grazing livestock. Introduced from France, sycamore is now naturalised throughout Britain.

having both adult and juvenile foliage intermixed on nearly every twig. This strange feature is found in the typical strain of each tree.

There is no common distinctive name for juvenile forms, but they are fairly easy to recognise as such. If their foliage is feathery in its general appearance, the variety concerned is often called *plumosum*; if the juvenile leaves stand out from the twigs in an angular fashion, then the terms *squarrosa* and *squarrosum* are frequently used; if the general effect resembles the foliage of a heath or heather plant, then the term *ericoides*, meaning "heath-like", may be applied.

This review of foliage forms could be extended quite indefinitely because nurserymen are always on the lookout for exceptional strains that merit a place in their collections and catalogues.

COLOUR VARIATIONS

We saw in the first chapter that the green colouring substance called chlorophyll is absolutely essential to the life processes of every tree. Therefore we may expect to find all our trees, during the summer-time at least, all uniformly green. Instead, we find that the green of tree foliage is one of the most variable and exciting of all the colours in nature. It may be pale or dark, bluish or yellowish. Its hue varies from one month to the next, and from one tree to another; in fact, even on a single tree, leaves of different shades of green can often be found at the same time, according to the amount of light each one receives. On evergreen trees and shrubs, the older leaves are often darker than those more recently formed.

None of these minor differences is enough to form a colour variety, which must have a clear and constant difference from the typical green of the common strain. In practice there are five major kinds of colour variety, and in each of these the natural green colour of the leaf is hidden or displaced in a different way.

VARIEGATED FORMS

In a variegated leaf the green chlorophyll is absent from *part only* of each leaf. If it were absent from the *whole* leaf, then the tree would die. The chlorophyll-free tissues may appear golden, in which case the name *aurea* may be given to the variety concerned. Or else they may appear

PLATE 8 *Birches*

Above Silver birch forms a graceful, though relatively short-lived, ornamental tree. Its drooping branches and airy foliage give only light shade, and many flowers and bulbs can thrive below them.

Below Wild Highland birches, too tortuous for use as timber, are valued for the shelter they give to sheep. Grasses growing in their light shade give sustenance, even below winter's snows.

white, in which case it is called *alba*; or they may look silvery, so giving rise to the name *argentea*.

The part affected may be the tip of each leaf, so justifying the varietal name *alba-spicata*, meaning white-tipped. Or the pale colour may be found all round the edges of each leaf, in which case it may be called, say, *aurea-marginata*, meaning golden-rimmed.

BLUE OR GLAUCOUS FORMS

In hot, dry, climates trees have difficulty, in summer, in restricting their loss of water to a tolerable level. Water vapour is always escaping from the breathing pores or *stomata* in every living tree's leaves, and during a hot dry summer the tree may not be able to replace this fast enough from its roots, set in a dry soil. Therefore many trees, particularly conifers, produce a layer of wax on the surface of their leaves or needles, which is waterproof and so lessens the rate of water loss. These waxy or resinous deposits look whitish, bluish, or bluish-grey according to the angle at which they reflect the sunlight.

Some of these trees thrive well when grown in much damper climates, where a hot dry summer is unusual, and as the blue foliage colour is hereditary, they look almost as striking in a moist British garden as they do in the deserts of California or Morocco. However, nurserymen naturally prefer to make sure that a truly-blue tree is supplied, and they have therefore picked out exceptionally bluish varieties which they propagate by grafting or by striking cuttings. The usual name for these is variety *glauca*.

Well-known examples are the blue Colorado spruce, *Picea pungens* var. *glauca*, and the blue Atlas cedar, *Cedrus atlantica* var. *glauca*. The Lawson cypress, *Chamaecyparis lawsoniana*, has many blue varieties in cultivation; *glauca* is again the common name for these, but it is more satisfactory to order a particular well-proven cultivar, such as 'Milford Blue Jacket'.

COPPER, RED AND PURPLE FORMS

In all colour varieties that have a reddish tinge, the green chlorophyll is present throughout each leaf, but it is masked by another pigment. The intensity of the red hue varies, but it is usually most marked in young leaves when they are just expanding, and in maturing leaves just before they begin their annual colour change in autumn. Most of the red-foliaged trees are deciduous broadleaved ones, that shed their leaves annually. The few conifers that have reddish foliage usually look most "bronzed" in winter.

By far the best-known of the red-foliaged trees is the copper beech, *Fagus sylvatica* var. *cuprea*, which arose as a natural "sport" in Germany in the eighteenth century. Other similar strains bear the varietal names *purpurea* and *atropunicea*. All these varieties grow more or less true from seed, but in practice they are usually grafted, and most copper beeches show clear graft unions.

Equally common to-day is the copper-leaved plum, *Prunus cerasifera* 'Pissardi', often referred to as *Prunus* 'Pissardi'. This forms an attractive brownish-foliaged street tree that bears brightly contrasting white flowers, and seldom grows large enough to require pruning. In the purple-leaved sycamores, such as *Acer pseudoplatanus* 'Spaethi', the unusual coloration is only obvious on the undersides of the leaves, so is seen best when they are stirred by a breeze. The purple oak, *Quercus petraea purpurea*, is an attractive colour variation of the common oak, with leaves that are bright red in spring, reddish-green in summer, and purplish-green in autumn. Most of the red oaks, however, are typical examples of their species, and not freak forms at all; the North American *Quercus borealis* is the commonest and most vigorous kind.

One of the few red-foliaged conifers is the variety *elegans* of the Japanese cedar, *Cryptomeria japonica*, which turns reddish-bronze every autumn, resuming a bluish-green shade in the spring. It is also remarkable in bearing juvenile foliage and in forming a shapeless bush rather than an erect tree.

WHITE-BACKED LEAVES

Another colour variation possible in foliage is the white, or pale-green shade of the reverse side of the leaf. The commonest example is the whitebeam, a tree whose Anglo-Saxon name aptly means "the white tree". This grows in very dry soils on the chalk downs of southern England, and every leaf has a thick coating of white hairs which help to lessen water-loss from its breathing pores. This clear, light, colour is very obvious when the buds break in spring, forming for a brief week or so goblet-shaped leaf clusters not unlike tulips; it is also seen in autumn when the brown leaves fall, each still backed by a white surface. But it is displayed most dramatically when a summer breeze stirs the foliage, a moment caught by the poet Meredith in the line:

"Flashing as in gusts the sudden-lighted whitebeam."

EVERGREEN AND SUB-EVERGREEN VARIETIES

A fifth kind of colour variation is a rather more fundamental one. Certain sorts of tree can be obtained in varieties that hold their leaves right through the winter, or even for several winters. The commonest is perhaps the Lucombe oak, *Quercus* 'Lucombeana', which is in origin a hybrid between the cork oak and the Turkey oak. Its foliage is always darker and more leathery than that of the common deciduous oaks, and of course it provides a mass of green foliage right through the winter.

Beeches, hornbeams, and the common oaks all have the peculiar habit of holding their faded leaves on their twigs all through the winter, but only on the lowest six feet or so of each stem. This provides a warm russet shade for a winter hedge, but cannot be employed otherwise as a decorative effect as the higher branches become bare.

The Right Use and Choice of Form and Colour Varieties

With such a wide range of possibilities at hand, the landscape planter may be tempted to overdo the use of the more exceptional shapes and shades of trees. But it is only in exceptional situations that a "peculiar" tree will fit the scene better than one of the common form and colour. Occasionally, in a botanic garden, you may come across half an acre or so devoted to a collection of rare, exceptional strains. The combined effect is disturbing, but scarcely attractive.

The unusual tree gains most effect from its contrast with the familiar kind. Victorian gardeners usually had the good sense to limit their planting of the copper beech to a single tree amid a group of normal green-foliaged ones. One purple-foliaged tree strikes an instant, unique effect; two would show that the feature is not so unusual, after all. It is the same with a tall pyramidal cypress—it is most effective beside a group of broader-crowned trees.

Do not, therefore, run through the nurseryman's catalogue ticking off all his rarities. Rather decide which few you can reasonably employ in well-chosen situations, flanked by more normal specimens. Collectors, of course, will ignore this sound advice, but then nobody can knock sense into collectors!

14. A Brief History of Arboriculture

THERE are two ways of looking at the care of trees and forests. One is to start with the natural wildwood and devise a plan to bring it under management so as to ensure a steady harvest of timber and also the regular replacement of the trees removed. This is a very important practice in all tropical forest lands, and also in those parts of Europe, Asia and North America where extensive natural woodlands remain. But in the British Isles, and also in the more closely settled regions of Europe and America, the original natural forests have gone. So the forester is obliged to start with the raising of young trees from seed or cuttings, then tend them in their youth, and next see to their establishment in plantations.

The science and craft of tending trees as individuals is called *arboriculture*, while the management of forests, whether they have grown naturally or have been formed artificially as plantations, is called *silviculture*. In practice every forester must be skilled in both.

Men have tended fruit trees and nut trees, as orchard crops, from the earliest historic times. But few people troubled to raise trees for timber or ornament until late in the Middle Ages, because there was little need to do so. Extensive natural woods remained uncleared, to provide all the wood and the scenery that a man could want. As most of the land lay open and unfenced, planted trees could not be protected against grazing cattle and sheep, and without such safeguards it was futile to try to raise plantations.

In William the Conqueror's day great stretches of natural woodlands, holding countless oaks, beeches, birches, ash and elm trees, still spread across the English lowlands. The Norman kings valued these mainly for sport, and placed them under harsh Forest Laws to preserve the deer. Their successors, however, gradually gave up their control of most of the Royal Forests, which passed into the ownership of great noblemen and lesser lords. By degrees the tree cover, unprotected by fencing, disappeared through timber felling, clearances for agriculture, and the pasturage of ever-growing flocks and herds.

COPPICES

In the fifteenth and sixteenth centuries, during the days of the Tudor sovereigns, a change took place in the management of the English countryside. The landowners were given legal powers to make permanent enclosures, for farming or for forestry. This led to a far more profitable use of the land, for all concerned, and the Enclosure Movement, as it is called, has continued right to the present day. A leading Act of Parliament authorising enclosures was passed by Edward IV in 1483, and a similar law was made by James IV of Scotland in 1504.

The first kind of woodland to be enclosed and brought under management on an extensive scale was the *coppice* of hazel bushes, hornbeams, sweet chestnuts, birches, or oaks that could be worked on a short *rotation* of years. This was done to obtain regular crops of small poles for fencing, firewood, and tanbark for the leather tanneries. Once every seven to ten years, each section of the coppice was cut in turn. A fresh crop of young shoots then sprang up from the stumps to provide fresh poles for the next harvest.

Soon the practice began of leaving selected young trees, called *standards*, to grow up to full size, to yield building timber. This resulted in the *coppice-with-standards* system.

This kind of forestry was very sound under the agricultural economics of the day, and it went on almost unchanged from the fifteenth century to the twentieth. Coppices can still be found in most parts of Britain, and also over much of France; but the return from firewood and poles is now very low, and most of the remaining coppices are maintained only as game coverts.

Some coppices were of natural origin; others were planted. The people who began to establish trees in this way were probably the monks whose abbeys owned large tracts of forest land. One of these, the Scot William Blair, who was cellarer to the Abbey of Coupar Angus in Perthshire, has left a record of tree raising at a remarkably early date, 1460 A.D. In the abbey grounds he tended seed beds of ash, birch and broom, and struck cuttings of willows. These were planted in the Forest of Ferter, around Blairgowrie on the fringe of the Highlands.

PARK TREES AND TIMBER PLANTATIONS

As the landowners began to feel more secure in their tenure of the land, they started to plant trees intended to stand for a century or more, to grow to full size and yield large timber, as well as to provide a fitting ornament to their new mansion houses. During the Middle Ages noblemen had lived in fortified castles, and they did not allow any trees to grow near the walls because trees might give cover to enemies who attacked them. But the invention of gunpowder, together with more powerful and stable central government, made all these grim buildings, with their bare surroundings, out of date. In their place, the richer landowners were able to build large unfortified mansions with wide windows, and to surround them with whatever garden or trees suited their fancy. Arboriculture, therefore, really began to flourish in Tudor times, during the days of the Reformation and the Renaissance. The reasons behind it were sound and economic, and related to new ways of managing the land.

The Tudor landowners employed men whom they called "gardeners" to raise the trees they needed. At this time the title of "forester" was reserved for men who looked after large expanses of woodland with particular regard to the wild game.

It was the "gardener" who raised the trees needed for the new parks, avenues, and plantations, and many of these men showed quite remarkable skill and wide knowledge for so early a time in history. No doubt they drew on the past experience of the monks who had raised trees for the coppices, as well as that of orchardists who grew choice fruit trees. The earliest English account of tree planting is found in John Fitzherbert's *Book of Husbandry*, published in 1523.

The leading authority on the planting of trees during the great extension of parks and gardens in Tudor and Stuart times is John Evelyn, who lived from 1620 to 1706. He is best known to history as a diarist and statesman who supported the Royalist cause in the Civil War. Evelyn was brought up on his family's estate at Wotton near Dorking in Surrey, on the edge of the well-wooded Weald, and eventually he inherited this property. He travelled widely and knew most of the leading landowners of his day, and he has left an account of great activity in their woods and parks. Many of the fine trees, avenues and plantations he describes were already full grown, and had clearly been planted in Elizabethan days. The enrichment of English woods with foreign trees had already started, and Evelyn took great pride in raising Italian cypresses from seed.

Evelyn recorded all he knew, in a quaint rambling style, in the classic work entitled: SILVA, *or a Discourse of Forest Trees, and the Propagation of Timber within His Majesty's Dominions*. This was published by the newly-formed Royal Society in 1664, and a copy was presented to King Charles II, who was a keen supporter of tree-planting, as well as a lover of the chase.

Charles did much to encourage tree-planting in the New Forest of Hampshire, and the Forest of Dean in Gloucestershire, which were the only extensive Royal Forests to survive from Norman times. One of the main objects of tree-planting in this period was to raise oak for wooden warships. Supplies from natural forests were dwindling, and Charles wisely looked ahead to future navies and their needs.

Many of the oaks he planted were in fact felled a hundred and forty years later to build ships for Nelson's fleets in the Napoleonic wars. Buckler's Hard on the Beaulieu River was the main centre of New Forest shipbuilding in Nelson's time. The great admiral himself, in his turn, visited the Forest of Dean to examine timber supplies and to urge the Commissioners of Woods and Forests to plant more oaks for the needs of future navies. Under such directives, the Royal Forests became storehouses of naval timber, but they were not extended in area; future development of arboriculture rested with the private estates.

EIGHTEENTH CENTURY EXPANSION

The eighteenth century was a golden age for landowners in Britain. As more and more land was enclosed and let to tenant farmers for money rents, the landowners' incomes rose and they were able to build them-selves substantial mansions in every fertile part of the country. They planned ahead with every assurance that wealth would always be there to support their gracious way of life. No great house was complete without its surrounding park, and its distant woods to hold game. Arboriculturists who knew how to raise the trees and plan the new land-scapes of lake, wood, and hill were in keen demand; the most famous was Lancelot "Capability" Brown, who planned many of the greater park-lands.

In 1776 one Alexander Hunter, an Edinburgh doctor who practised at York, and took a great interest in husbandry, published an expensive and elaborate illustrated edition of John Evelyn's *Silva*. Expenses of publication were met by an initial subscription from 700 landowners whose names were duly inscribed, and this shows the tremendous and widespread interest in tree growing at that time. The book is beautifully illustrated with engravings by John Miller, the leading botanical artist of the day. Its additional *Notes*, which are as copious as Evelyn's original text, were collected by Hunter from gardeners, foresters and botanists, and give an excellent idea of the state of arboriculture at the time. The Chelsea Physic Garden, then in the care of a famous gardener and botanist named Phillip Miller, was the source of much of Hunter's information, and he was also in touch with Linnaeus, the great Swedish botanist.

All the common trees and shrubs native to Europe and the eastern side of North America had by now been introduced to England. Most methods of propagation were in use—from seed to sucker-shoots, grafting, budding, and layering. Planting was in full swing on every great estate where poor lands, unsuited to agriculture, were being enclosed. A great army of labourers toiled to form woods, dig lakes, plant avenues, and even throw up hills, wherever ingenious planners thought the land-scape needed improvement.

Trees were planted, too, along the hawthorn hedgerows that were spreading in a green network across the old open fields. Under successive Enclosure Acts the landowners fenced in their better land and leased it to tenant farmers. Oaks, elms, and ash trees were planted at suitable intervals along these hedges, partly to give shelter, but mainly to yield timber, which remained the property of the main estate when it matured and was felled. Landscaping did not stop at the park walls, but embraced all the land within each owner's control.

PLATE 9   *Beechwood*

Native beechwoods, like this maturing stand on the Chilterns, grow vigorously on the chalk and limestone hills of southern England. Their marvellous mosaic of small oval leaves intercepts nearly all the sunlight. Few plants can thrive beneath them and, except in clearings, the forest floor lies bare.

NEW TREES FROM NEW WORLDS

The nineteenth century was a time of great botanical exploration and excitement. By the year 1800 nearly all the world's coastlines had been discovered and charted by Europeans, but few people had penetrated into the interior of great sub-continents such as China and the western side of North America. At first the botanists sent home only dried specimens of the new trees and shrubs that they discovered; but soon the horticultural societies in Europe sent out men with commissions to procure seeds too, in order that the new-found rarities could be introduced to European gardens.

A leading collector in North America was David Douglas, a Scottish botanist whose fame is preserved by the Douglas fir. He was active in Oregon and British Columbia around the year 1825, and sent home seeds of the noble fir, the grand fir, the Sitka spruce, and the Lodgepole pine. All these to-day are leading timber trees in British plantations.

Japan proved a rich source of new trees and shrubs, and also of methods of handling them; its climate is close enough to that of western Europe for most sorts to thrive in the West. From the forest of Mount Fuji came the Japanese larch, now a major timber tree, while gardens were enriched by many kinds of ornamental maples and flowering cherries, which Japanese gardeners had been perfecting for centuries. China provided the maidenhair tree and many attractive flowering shrubs, including the purple buddleia. The higher reaches of the Indian Himalayas gave us the deodar, the beautiful weeping spruce, and countless rhododendrons.

Little of value could be drawn from the southern hemisphere. Its forests lie too near the equator for their trees and shrubs to be fully at home in northern Europe or North America. Many trials were made with Australian eucalyptus trees, but with very limited success. Chile, however, gave us the bizarre monkey puzzle, and provided fuchsias for the shrubbery.

As these new introductions reached the nursery trade, they were

PLATE 10 *Poplars*

Above left Winter silhouette of black poplar, showing leaning trunk and haphazard branching. A typical outline, since poplars of many strains resemble giant branches stuck in the ground, rather than well-balanced trees.
Above right Grey poplar in summer foliage, beside a Norfolk river. Poplars are typically waterside trees and often develop slanting trunks bearing random branches.
Below left Lombardy poplars, a fastigiate race of the common black poplar in which very numerous side branches follow the upward trend of the trunk. Useless as timber, Lombardy poplars make fine upright screens and windbreaks, like these on the flat plain of Somerset.
Below right Avenue of white poplars, so-called from their pale bark, near Ashford in Kent.

catalogued by J. C. Loudon, the diligent author of the five-volume *Arboretum et Fruticetum Britannicum* (1841). By the middle of the century a fantastic choice of species and varieties was being maintained and propagated, to meet the ever-increasing demands for things new and strange.

These demands came largely from the newly-rich, who had profited from the Industrial Revolution. As the mines and factories spread, smoke palls grew ever wider and darker over the industrial towns where miners, foundrymen and mill workers were crowded together in grimy terraced dwellings. But no such hardships faced the successful merchant or manufacturer who could afford a country house and the staff to run it. His property might appear modest when compared with the impressive seats of greater landowners, yet he was able to follow, on a small scale, their general plan of landscape planting in his small park or large garden.

This new wealth, combined with the natural inclination of the newly-rich to live in the style of the older landowners, led to a great and long-sustained wave of ornamental tree planting. Capitalists and their gardeners vied with one another to collect and cultivate as many new and rare trees as possible. Commercial nurseries sprang up and expanded to meet the call for more and more curious trees and shrubs, from all the known temperate world.

To-day, in the 1970's, we are able to appreciate and enjoy the surviving great trees established in the heyday of Victorian planting. The Californian wellingtonia, for example, which was introduced in 1853, can now be seen, for the first time, as a centenarian around 130 feet tall. Like all good foresters, these people planted for a future they would never see. People tend to take their achievements for granted, forgetting how much effort and expense went into their creation.

These splendours of tree and parkland scenery cannot be frozen for ever, in their present prime and glory, by the simple imposition of Tree Preservation Orders. Harmful insects and the fungi of decay are not bound by such Orders, nor do the gales heed them! Trees are not timeless ancient monuments, but living beings with their own life rhythm that can only end, eventually, in downfall and decay. Much can be done, by skilful tree surgery, to prolong their lives. But the really progressive approach lies in further planting, for posterity to benefit.

TWENTIETH CENTURY DEVELOPMENTS

During the twentieth century there have been four notable trends in the ownership and management of woods and trees in the British Isles, and all seem likely to continue.

The first of these has been the establishment, in 1919, of a Forestry Commission for Great Britain, with parallel authorities in both Northern Ireland and Eire. The new forest authorities are concerned, almost exclusively, with the planning and planting of great expanses of land for timber production. By 1971 the Forestry Commission had 2 million acres under tree crops and was extending this great estate at a rate of 50,000 acres a year.

Secondly, there has been a great increase in the public ownership of parkland trees and small woodlands. Under changed social and economic conditions, a high proportion of large private houses, with their associated parklands and ornamental trees, have come into the possession of local authorities and the National Trusts. This movement, together with the growing practice of opening privately-owned parks and gardens to the public—either occasionally or throughout the year—has made fine trees far more accessible to everyone.

Thirdly, trees have won a firmer place than before along streets and highways, and in new schemes for town planning and landscape design. Road builders and architects have come to appreciate their merits as sources of shade and shelter, and their values for breaking up the monotony of an endless motorway or the hard edges of a modern building design.

Fourthly, the spread of home ownership and of the garden-city pattern of development, giving land to as many house-owners as possible, has greatly increased the numbers of people who can own and tend trees of their own, if only on a modest scale.

Despite these new trends, the larger private estates still have a very substantial share in trees and woods of all kinds, valued for timber production, game coverts, shelter and landscape ornament. Over sixty per cent of the county's woodlands are still in private ownership, and the landowners nowadays do forty per cent of all planting aimed at timber production, as well as much ornamental planting.

All this has led to a large increase in the number of people having an active interest in trees, and to the growth of new professions to look after each aspect of their care. The private estate foresters, with their associated nurserymen and timber merchants, have been supplemented by the Forestry Commission's professional forest staff, by the arboriculturists of the local authorities who own parklands, and by the landscape architects who design new roads and housing estates. Any private owner whose estate is too small to merit a forester, can nowadays find contractors for the planting of trees and timber crops, and advisers on the management of plantations and the sale of wood.

Economists can use their computers to calculate the country's timber resources and their rate of growth. But the full value of the other benefits that trees bring us defies calculation. Some of them find expression in the real estate market whenever a house surrounded by tall trees changes hands, at a price far greater than a treeless property, of the same class, could ever fetch. Yet we cannot set down, in cold prices, all that trees mean to us as a whole. The most we can say is that trees, and therefore the craft of tending them, which is arboriculture, make life more worth while.

The first public body to take an active part in the development of arboriculture was probably the Society of Apothecaries at its Chelsea Physic Garden, founded in 1673; for trees, like smaller plants, formerly played a large part in the physician's medicine box. Development now rests with the Royal Botanic Gardens at Kew and Edinburgh, the National Botanic Garden at Glasnevin near Dublin, the Royal Horticultural Society, the National Trusts and the national forest authorities. The Forestry Commission has notable collections of rare trees in its Westonbirt Arboretum in Gloucestershire, the National Pinetum at Bedgebury in Kent. Kew has recently taken over a fine arboretum at Wakehurst, near Ardingly in Sussex. At all these centres, practice in the handling of the living tree out of doors is linked to research in the laboratory, and to extensive libraries of tree science and lore. Leading arboreta are listed on page 323.

15. Tall Forest Broadleaved Trees

THE tall broadleaved trees that build up the great hardwood forests of Europe, Northern Asia and North America give us the grandest ornaments for landscape planting, and present the greatest challenge to the tree grower's skill. During the present century their importance as timber producers has greatly diminished, for metal, concrete and plastics have been found better for many of their traditional uses in building, furniture, and household goods. But there can be no substitute for their beauty of form, nor for their ever-changing pageant of colour throughout the year, from the tender emeralds of spring to the full rich greens of high summer and the glorious golds and russets of autumn.

Most of these broadleaves soar to heights that, in nature, enable them to overshadow all other kinds of wild plant life. One hundred feet may be taken as a fair average stature which they can achieve in good surroundings. Few will stop short of fifty feet and the real giants—limes and elms —will aim for 140 feet. With this height comes an equal vigour of crown spread. In the forest, the crown of each tree is restricted to some degree by its neighbours, but in the open no such restraints operate, and a handsome broad dome of foliage is the result. There is room enough for this in a great nobleman's park, or even along a hedgerow, but in an ordinary garden, or along a highway, it presents problems.

After the usual slow start, broadleaved trees grow rapidly. The forester, for reasons of economy, usually sets them out in his woods, spaced four or five feet apart, when they are only eighteen inches tall. He has then to weed them thoroughly for two or three years, and nurse them through their slow "thicket" stage. The gardener or landscape planter, on the other hand, usually starts with "standard" trees already ten feet tall, which have spent their first eight years or so in the nursery. Or he may go farther and obtain "instant trees" already twenty to forty feet high, for most broadleaves show great tolerance of transplanting. In either event, he is likely, in many situations, to have to resort to pruning fairly early, in order to keep the crowns of these large forest trees within reasonable bounds.

For the convenience of reference, the principal tall forest broadleaved trees have been arranged, in this chapter, in alphabetical order of genus.

SYCAMORE AND MAPLES, *Acer* species   Plates 7, 15a.

The common sycamore is in all respects a typical member of the maple group; it got its peculiar name through confusion with the "sycamore" of the Bible, when it was first introduced to Britain. It is native to

Europe, including northern France, and was probably brought to England by monastery gardeners in the Middle Ages. Nowadays it is firmly established as a wild tree that can seed itself only too readily in any wood or garden. Seed-strewing is its only fault; it bears a heavy seed crop regularly year after year, and if you have (as I do) a vigorous sycamore dominating your garden, you must be ready to weed out thousands of seedlings annually.

Sycamore grows vigorously and stands up to most of the adverse influences that check other trees. It is wind-firm and resists sea winds well; the northernmost wood in Britain is a sycamore plantation at the Castle of Mey in Caithness, right on the edge of the bleak North Atlantic. Sycamore stands up to town smoke and thrives on a wide range of soils, from chalk and limestone to clay and builder's rubble. It can recover well after lopping, though the great rounded dome of an untouched specimen is a far more rewarding sight than any pruned tree. The wood is valuable for furniture, and large old trees suitable for cutting into figured veneers occasionally fetch several hundred pounds apiece.

The flowers of sycamore, though elegant, are greenish yellow in colour, and as they appear just when the leaves do, they seldom attract attention. The autumn leaf-colour is a rather drab brown enlivened a little by the multitudes of winged dark brown seeds, set in opposite pairs.

Sycamore's scientific name is *Acer pseudoplatanus*, meaning the "false-plane maple". In Scotland both tree and timber are often known as "plane". The leaf is indeed plane-like, but you have only to look at the opposite placement of leaves or buds to tell that you are dealing with a maple.

Sycamore has few varieties. There are variegated-leaved forms that look more bizarre than beautiful. The purple sycamore, cultivar 'Purpureum', is a truly handsome tree of unusual colouring; the upper surface of its leaves is dark green, and the rich purple of the undersides provides an attractive contrast, particularly when the wind makes the foliage flutter.

Norway maple, though nearly related, has quite another range of attractions for the landscape planter. It is less vigorous, and so more desirable where less space is available. The spring tint of its foliage, a clear russet, ornaments the bare branches before most trees have leafed out, and its autumn colours are stronger and redder than those of other common trees. The flower clusters break forth in early spring, ahead of the leaves, and form upright tufts of gay greenish yellow. The scientific name of this tree is *Acer platanoides*, meaning, "plane-like maple", and it is very hardy, thriving both in Scandinavia and the central European mountains. It is too small to merit planting for timber, but deserves wider use as a garden, park or street tree. There are several copper-leaved, reddish, and purple cultivars, one of the best being 'Crimson King', which despite its name bears dark purple foliage.

American maples have seldom proved successful in Britain. The climate is so different that they lack vigour and fail to reproduce the vivid scarlet and orange colours of the North American fall. The only one commonly planted is the silver-leaf maple, *A. saccharinum* (also called *A. dasycarpum*), which has prettily lobed leaves, with white under-surfaces. This decorative tree should not be confused with the true sugar maple, *A. saccharum*, which grows in New England and eastern Canada, and is tapped for its sweet sap every spring, when the thaw comes and the buds break.

Japanese maples have become, in recent times, one of the most important and exciting features of both British and American gardens. Most of them are cultivars of *Acer palmatum*, though a few stem from *A. japonicum*. They have been developed by Japanese gardeners through centuries of selection, and they are always increased by grafting. Nearly all are dwarf trees or bushes, which will fill a small space without the need for constant pruning. Their autumn colours, in every shade from brown through yellow to scarlet and crimson, are almost unbelievably brilliant. They can be seen at their brightest in the marvellous Acer Glade, maintained by the Forestry Commission at its great Westonbirt Arboretum in Gloucestershire, where they reach their peak of brilliance in late October.

Linked to the colour variations there are many foliage forms, with leaves that may be more or less divided into fine lobes along the veins. Amid so diverse a group, everyone will have his favourite cultivar. My own choice is 'Osakuzuki', with fairly broad lobes, pale green leaves laced with crimson in summer, and the brightest vermilion tints when autumn comes.

The odd ash-leaved maple or *Acer negundo*, is curiously known in its American homeland as "box-elder". Varieties of this are widely planted in suburban gardens and even as street trees, with invariably untidy results. They form straggly, misshapen bushy trees which are supposed to have variegated leaves—green and white. In practice, some of the branches always *revert* to the dark green of the wild species, so you end up with an unevenly coloured tree, or perhaps a dull green one. Not recommended. Plate 15, p. 220.

HORSE CHESTNUTS, *Aesculus* species Plate 18c, p. 245.

The wonderful white horse chestnut gives us the grandest of all displays of blossom. It is the only tall forest tree, hardy in northern climes, that bears conspicuous flowers bold enough to match its size; all other trees of the first stature carry only catkins, or greenish-yellow blossoms scarcely seen against the surrounding foliage. Horse chestnut, by contrast, first opens a lustrous canopy of deep green leaves, each elegantly divided into leaflets like the fingers of a hand, and then sends forth a multitude of white flowers, ranked in brave spikes like candles lighting up a festival.

So grand a tree needs a broad space to expand its great crown, and it should be set at a distance from the main viewpoints so that it can be appreciated, in its whole outline, from afar. Otherwise its needs are few; it is at home on any reasonably favourable site having fertile soil and not suffering undue exposure. It always grows bolt upright, and blooms unfailingly year after year. It will even flower freely if cut back, within a few years of lopping. Cultivation is easy, for nuts sown in autumn, or stored under slightly moist conditions through the winter, sprout readily in spring. Horse chestnut grows quickly to a magnificent size and lives long.

This great tree has a few drawbacks. It cannot be safely used as a street tree, nor even along roadsides adjoining parks, because of the irresistible attraction that its large nuts, or "conkers", hold for small boys; they gather them as they fall, or throw sticks into the tree's crown to dislodge them, causing a serious traffic hazard. Its timber has no modern commercial use, and the tree is valueless for plantations.

The common white horse chestnut, *Aesculus hippocastanum*, comes from Asia Minor, where its nuts really were once used as a medicine for ailing horses, though normally no animal will touch them.

The red horse chestnut, *A.* 'Carnea', does not make so bold a tree, but its warm colour strikes a rich exotic note over its lustrous foliage. Because of differences in vigour and habit, the white and the red horse chestnut should not be mixed in any formal arrangement. Each may set off the other by contrast of form and colour, but the two will never grow in step.

TREE OF HEAVEN, *Ailanthus altissima*

No tree could ever live up to a name like this, but the *Ailanthus* makes an impressive specimen when planted along a roadside or in a park. It is a native of China and gained its odd name through confusion with similar "sky-smiting" trees that grow only in Indonesia. You may know it by its very large compound leaves, which are often a foot long over all and show a reddish tinge in midsummer. The bark is dark brown with pale fissures, and the trunk grows straight and erect. Each Tree of Heaven is either male or female, but males are rarely seen as their greenish

PLATE 11 *Pollards*

Above Pollarded hornbeam in a Hertfordshire hedgerow. Until a century ago this tree was lopped, at six feet above the ground, to obtain firewood and faggots. Cutting was done high up to keep the regrowth of sprouts out of the reach of browsing cattle. It was repeated every few years. Since lopping ceased, this tree has formed a splendid dome-shaped crown.

Below Pollarded white willows beside the River Brue in Somerset; one year after their last lopping. Their swollen heads record scores of such cuttings, at intervals of a few years; the cut stems are woven into hurdles, wattle fences or rough baskets.

flowers are foul-smelling and unattractive. Female trees are raised from root suckers; their flowers are greenish white and inconspicuous, but the autumn display of seed is bright and gay. Golden seeds and wings appear in clusters above the foliage, looking as though the whole tree had burst into blossom.

The Tree of Heaven is very resistant to town smoke, dust and fumes, and has therefore been freely planted in many cities. It is sometimes used, in parks or large gardens, as a foliage feature at bush height. A young tree is first established and is then cut down to a stump. Next spring it sends up vigorous coppice shoots that bear leaves of extraordinary size, two or even three feet long. These give an exotic appearance to a herbaceous border, suggesting some rare tropical plant, for each is composed of many leaflets and is tinged with crimson. In the autumn, the shoots are cut back and cleared away, and next spring the display is repeated.

ALDERS, *Alnus* species

The common alder, *Alnus glutinosa*, is seldom planted for landscape effect because it has no particular appeal. Nor is it grown for timber, since its only market to-day is as low-priced turnery poles. But it grows freely from self-sown seed in the only situation where it is really at home —the waterside. There it is worth preserving, or even planting, for its remarkable catkins and cones. In spring, the golden-brown male catkins, shaped like lambs' tails, add a note of colour before the deep green leaves open. In autumn, as the leaves fade and fall, the ripening female catkins become obvious as greenish-brown balls. After they have shed their seeds, which have little floats to aid their spread by water, these "cones" turn black and woody, and hang on the twigs for several years. Alder, which is raised from seed, is our only "cone-bearing" broadleaved tree. Along fast streams, its roots play a useful part in holding up the banks and checking soil erosion.

The grey alder, *Alnus incana*, is common in the Alps and the Scandinavian mountains, where its roots help to bind the gravel and sand of stream beds; but it has no ornamental merit. Italian alder, *A. cordata*, can prove a useful tree on difficult sites, such as embankments or chalk downs; it rapidly expands a pyramidal crown of glossy, deep-green heart-shaped leaves.

BIRCHES, *Betula* species Plate 8, p. 189.

The graceful white-barked birches are very desirable and rewarding trees,

PLATE 12

White willow beside a wide drain on a Kentish marsh. Willows are typical waterside trees, since their tiny seeds only sprout on damp, bare soil. When allowed to reach full size they make good windbreaks, and shade trees for sheep and cattle on open marshes. Their roots stabilise stream banks and check erosion.

especially for those who have little ground to spare. They grow fast, and in a few years provide well-proportioned trunks and crowns, without passing through any awkward stage of adolescence. The shade that they cast is the lightest of any timber tree, and this makes it possible to grow flowering plants directly beneath them; spring bulbs are a particularly happy choice. Birches tolerate almost any soil and make small demands on it. They are also very hardy and resist the wildest winds. Their only serious fault is their relatively short life and limited size. It is rare to find a birch living for more than sixty years or growing much taller than sixty feet.

The beauty of the birch is made up of several associated elements. Its young twigs are very fine and whip-like, dark brown in colour but covered with a purplish sheen. As the trunk and larger branches grow stouter they develop the striking white bark peculiar to these trees, a silvery shade that makes each birch trunk an arresting pillar of light in the garden or woodland scene. Later, the lower portions of the trunk may carry a more rugged bark, black in patches, that adds character by its contrasts. Each spring the waxy leaf-buds, as they open, exude an attractive aromatic scent. The leaves, bright olive green at first, soon expand to mid-green ovals or diamonds, dangling from slender stalks, and finally change to gold before they fall, to litter the lawn, in autumn. In spring, the male catkins, shaped like yellow lambs' tails, enliven the foliage, and in late summer the ripening female catkins repeat this pattern before they break up and shed their tiny wind-borne seeds.

Birches are usually raised from seed, and there are several kinds to choose from. Most cultivated strains are of the silver birch species, *Betula pendula*, which bears tiny bumps on its twigs. Despite its Latin name, its branches do not always droop. If a weeping strain is required from the nursery, this must be stressed when ordering. Many weeping birches are delightfully elegant trees; two reliable weeping cultivars of *B. pendula* are 'Tristis' and 'Youngii'. But the most delightful decorative kind is the Swedish Dalecarlian birch, variety *dalecarlica*, which has delicately divided leaves hanging from drooping twigs.

An alternative native species is the hairy birch, *B. pubescens*, which bears bark of a softer, chalk-white shade, and has hairy twigs.

The Canadian paper birch, *B. papyrifera*, has a white bark that peels away in strips; this is the kind used by the North American Indians to construct their amazingly light and strong birch-bark canoes. Birch bark is waterproof, and almost impervious to air also; the conspicuous dark marks on its surface are lenticels or breathing pores. The Manchurian birch, *B. ermanii*, is a vigorous ornamental kind with a creamy-white trunk contrasting with orange-brown branches.

The birches of Scandinavia and Canada have large, round trunks that yield excellent veneer for plywood. They are also used for furniture and household goods such as wooden spoons and platters. In Britain, birch rarely grows large and straight enough for this, and the only sale for its small, irregular logs is as firewood or turnery wood for making broom heads, tool handles, and the like. Therefore the forester seldom plants it, though he often makes good use of the overhead shelter provided by self-sown birch trees, when he is raising some more profitable crop.

HORNBEAMS, *Carpinus* species Plate 11a, p. 204.

The European hornbeam, *Carpinus betulus*, is used in landscape work mainly as a hedging shrub. Like the beech, which it resembles in many features, the hornbeam holds its faded leaves, up to "hedge height", right through the winter, but they are of a lighter brown and a softer texture than beech leaves, with more golden autumn tints. The hedge is equally firm and dense, and hornbeams prove very hardy.

Grown as a specimen tree, hornbeam shows an attractive trunk, quaintly furrowed or fluted, with veins of a brighter metallic grey enlivening its smooth grey bark. Its fruits are tiny nuts, each borne on a three-lobed wing, and the light-brown fruit clusters, hanging from the twigs, are a decorative feature in autumn. The name "hornbeam" means horny-wooded tree, but the farmer no longer needs yokes for oxen or dairymaids, nor the miller wooden cog-wheels, so hornbeam is never planted for timber to-day. It is raised from seed and may reach seventy feet tall.

SWEET CHESTNUT, *Castanea* species

This remarkable tree, *Castanea sativa*, was introduced to northern Europe by the Romans, who used its nuts to feed their legions, nearly 2000 years ago, and over its wide range it has many economic uses. Most of the chestnuts we eat come from warmer lands around the Mediterranean. North of the Alps the nut crop is low, though fertile seed is ripened in southern England and, if carefully stored in damp sand, yields seedlings next spring. In Italy the tough, naturally durable timber is used for building, furniture, and—after boiling and cutting into strips—for basket making. Waste wood yields tannin, used for tanning leather.

Sweet chestnut forms a magnificent tree in England also, but its trunk is so often marred by deep cracks called "shakes", that it is nowadays never planted for timber. In Kent and the neighbouring counties there are extensive coppice crops of sweet chestnut, which are raised by cutting young trees back to the stump, and then harvesting the clusters of poles that arise thereafter. The pole crop is cut every twelve years or so. Most of these poles are used for making the strong, durable and cheap cleft-pale fencing that is so useful in parks and gardens; each pole is cleft by hand into segments that are then linked together with galvanised wire, using a simple machine.

Sweet chestnut makes a magnificent specimen tree, with huge dark green glossy oval leaves. Its flower display in July is attractive, for golden catkins ornament the rich foliage in gay profusion, though they soon fall and litter a lawn. The spiny-husked nuts are quaint, but rarely well-filled, and they too provide a tidying-up task for the gardener. On the whole, a tree for the large park where ample space can be allowed and casual litter causes little concern. There are no exceptional ornamental varieties. The French cultivar 'Marron de Lyon' gives a heavy nut crop at an early age.

CATALPA, *Catalpa* species

The beautiful catalpa tree from the mid-western states of North America is also called the "Indian bean" because of the shape of its seed-pods, and the "trumpet flower" on account of its bell-shaped blossoms. The usual species cultivated is *C. bignonioides*, and this is hardy in the south-east of England but not in colder regions that get less summer sun. Catalpa makes a magnificent feature for anyone with only moderate space to spare, provided the planter is ready to wait several years for blossom to appear.

Catalpa bears an attractive pinkish-brown bark and large heart-shaped pale green leaves; these leaves are always grouped in threes, and this makes the tree very easy to identify. Its flowers, which open in July, are carried in clusters like those of the horse chestnut, but more open. Each separate blossom has a white bowl-shaped corolla of united petals, which are marked within by blotches of purple, gold and chocolate brown. The odd, slender, black seed-pods follow in autumn, and hang on the leafless boughs throughout the winter. Catalpa never grows into a large tree; its crown is low and spreads widely, and can be relied on to fill a broad space to only a moderate height.

BEECHES, *Fagus* species Plate 9, p. 196.

The European beech, *Fagus sylvatica*, is in Britain native only to southern England and south Wales, but it thrives well as a planted tree on most lowland ground anywhere in the British Isles. It is one of the few trees that is entirely at home on chalk and limestone soils, and on such land, where few conifers can thrive, it is the forester's most profitable timber tree. In woods, on the chalk downs, young beeches spring up readily from self-sown seed, and in cultivation the beech is easily raised from seed —provided good sound nuts can be obtained. Crops of well-filled and fertile nuts are only ripened every three or four years, and in practice the seed can only be stored through a single winter.

Beech is a good tree for screens and shelterbelts but its early growth is slow and it is often checked by frost and drought. So it is the usual practice to raise it in mixture with a coniferous "nurse" tree, such as Scots pine or European larch; the nurse provides early shelter and is removed when the beech is well established. Alternatively, natural birch may be retained as a screen.

In the garden beech is slow to develop, but later demands ample room and responds badly to control by pruning. After being lopped, it rarely reforms an elegant crown. Beech always casts a deep shade and nothing can be grown beneath a beechwood or even below a clump of beech trees; where side-light strikes in, however, bulbs and other spring flowers may thrive. Altogether, beech is an appropriate tree for a park or the grounds of a mansion, but too greedy of space and light for a small garden or roadside situation. The useful life-span of beech specimen trees can be set at two hundred years; after that they are very liable to be weakened by fungal attack. Heights between eighty and one hundred and twenty feet are often reached by mature beech trees.

The copper beech, *Fagus sylvatica* 'Cuprea' and similar reddish or purple foliaged forms, are usually increased by grafting. They show similar habits of growth to the typical race, but cast an even deeper shade and are less likely to grow very tall. A well grown copper beech provides the richest feast of colour found on any tree, for sunlight penetrating to different depths of the canopy is reflected in varied shades, from russet to dark purple, that alter as the wind stirs the leaves. The cultivar 'Purpurea' is more purplish in colour, and it has a weeping form, called 'Purpurea pendula'; 'Atropunicea' is the darkest kind.

The fern-leaved beech, variety *heterophylla*, is one of the few leaf-form sports of the common beech. Weeping birch, variety *pendula*, is a shapely tree that occupies relatively little room. It is the tallest of the weeping broadleaves, having the engaging habit of growing upwards for a few feet and then sending down a long cascade of pendulous branches, twigs and leaves. The best-known upright, columnar form is the Dawyck beech, variety *fastigiata*, which was found by a keen-eyed gardener growing naturally in a beech wood outside the gardens of Dawyck House, near Peebles in south Scotland.

ASH TREES, *Fraxinus* species Plate 4d, p. 129.

The European ash, *Fraxinus excelsior*, is grown for its timber though only on a small scale. High-grade wood, commanding a good price, is produced only on really fertile soil in districts with a hot summer climate. It is used for furniture and for the handles of hammers, axes, spades and similar tools, also for sports goods like oars and hockey sticks, because it is strong, tough and resists shock without splintering.

As a landscape tree, ash is frankly disappointing. It comes into leaf very late, seldom before May, and its leaves fall early in October. So for seven months of the year it shows only a framework of rather angular bare twigs and branches. Though it casts little shade, its surface roots are greedy feeders, and depress the growth of garden plants, crops, or grass beneath it. Ash is, however, windfirm and tolerant of lime-rich soils, and can provide some shelter to fields and livestock on limestone uplands where no other tree succeeds. It is also surprisingly tolerant of town smoke, and is perfectly hardy right to the far north of Britain.

Weeping ash, cultivar 'Pendula', is the most dependable and long-lived of all our weeping trees. Raised as a graft on a tall standard of common ash, it grows a few inches taller, and then turns downwards, repeating this process a few years later and so slowly adding height. With a little pruning and training it is easily persuaded to form a well-rounded "inverted pudding bowl". In many old country gardens a "doorway" has been cut in the drooping branchwork, and a seat set within to provide a shaded bower. Another attractive kind is the golden-bark ash, cultivar 'Aurea', which provides an unusual touch of bright colour right through the winter; its leaves turn an attractive yellow shade each autumn too. The single-leaved ash, variously known as 'Diversifolia', *heterophylla* or *monophylla*, is a freak race with simple oval leaves instead of compound ones; but most planters will prefer the intricate elegance of the normal feathery ash leaf.

WALNUTS, *Juglans* species

The common walnut, *Juglans regia*, makes an attractive and unusual decorative tree. You must be ready to wait until late May for its leaves to break, later than those of any other tree. They then form a lustrous-bronze crown that soon changes to a rich mid-green. Each compound leaf is highly aromatic, though its rich odour is hardly noticed until it is crushed. The bark is a soft silvery-grey shade, and is broken into an elaborate network of ribs and hollows. As the dome of branches and foliage matures it spreads out sideways in bold curves.

About ten years after planting a walnut tree starts to bear catkins—long drooping male ones and short, upright, flask-shaped female ones. Nuts ripen rapidly during the summer, passing first through the green-fleshed plum-like stage in which they are fit for pickling, and then reaching the hard-shelled state, filled with a delicious kernel. In northern lands the nut crop is uncertain. The beautiful wood fetches high prices, but only when the trunk has grown stout enough to yield decorative veneers. Both nuts and timber are best regarded as a random harvest that may or may not arrive. The tree itself is sure to gladden the eye.

The American black walnut, *J. nigra*, which has rougher leaves of darker green and a harder-shelled, less tasty nut, is occasionally grown as an ornamental specimen too.

TULIP TREE, *Liriodendron tulipifera*

The tulip tree does not live up to the magnificence that its name suggests. Its scientific name means "the lily tree that bears tulips" but it is in fact grown for the splendour of its foliage rather than for any display of flowers. The Americans call the tree "yellow poplar", because the wood has a yellowish tinge and the form of the grown tree recalls a poplar; while in the British timber trade the wood—used in pattern making, bears the odd name of "canary whitewood" because it is yellowish white.

Tulip tree comes from the eastern United States, where it reaches a height of one hundred and eighty feet in the broadleaved forests. It is hardy in the lowlands of western Europe, and grows vigorously to full timber size, though it is only planted as an ornamental specimen. Its sturdy upright trunk bears an open crown of light green leaves that have shiny surfaces and reflect the sunlight. Each separate leaf is shaped like the outline of a saddle, and has a broad notch, instead of a point, at its tip. The flowers, which open in June, resemble a water-lily rather than a tulip, but since they are greenish-white in colour they do not contrast with the foliage, and many people never notice them. They are followed, in autumn, by slender cone-shaped fruits, made up of the hard slender seeds from which the young trees can be raised.

If you are looking for an unusual tree, with exceptional grace of form and foliage that looks alive in the play of wind and sunshine, tulip might well be your first choice; but it needs ample space to display its splendour.

MULBERRIES, *Morus* species

Mulberries are a suitable choice for those who want a neat tree unlikely to become too large for a small plot or lawn, one which will grow happily for years with little attention. The commonest species is the black mulberry, *Morus nigra*, native to Persia; the white mulberry, *M. alba*, from China, and the North American red mulberry, *M. rubra*, are occasionally seen. All these trees bear a rounded crown of heart-shaped dark green leaves on a short trunk with pinkish-brown bark. In late summer they bear red fruit clusters that look very like raspberries but have a sharper taste. Few people take the trouble to gather all the mulberries that ripen; birds scatter many and the tidying up of the fallen fruit makes an extra task for the gardener.

Mulberries were introduced to Europe from the East in Classical times, in order to provide food for silkworms, which prefer their leaves to all other kinds. James I brought them from southern France to England, in the hopes of founding a home-grown silk industry, but that venture never prospered.

PLANES, *Platanus* species

For practical purposes only one plane need be considered. This is the glorious London plane, *Platanus* 'Hybrida', also called *P. acerifolia*, which arose about the year 1670 as the chance offspring of two introduced planes, namely the American plane, *P. occidentalis*, and the Oriental plane, *P. orientalis*, which comes from Asia Minor. Neither of the parents is happy or vigorous in northern Europe, but their offspring shows hybrid vigour to a marked degree. It is thought to have arisen in an Oxford garden, and since it seldom sets fertile seed, it is usually increased by cuttings. This results in a certain sameness in an avenue of planes, for all are likely to be, in origin, detached branches from a single parent. But to the town planner this has advantages; if he specifies a row of planes, he can be sure that they will all march in step, reaching an equal height and branch spread at the same time.

The commonly-grown clones of plane develop into magnificent and stately trees of great size, with a life-span of at least two hundred and fifty years. In fact we do not yet know their true limits of size and age. There is a tree one hundred and twenty-five feet tall at Carshalton in Surrey; another, planted about 1680 at the Bishop's Palace at Ely, is twenty-six feet round.

The bark on the robust trunks is a highly decorative feature, for as the trunk of a plane expands, the outer, brittle bark is shed in patches. Hence brown areas fall away, revealing pale yellow or green surfaces below, all in a gaily dappled pattern that recalls the play of sunlight. In a smoky city this bark-shedding is a great advantage, for the trunks of all trees have to breathe through bark pores that tend to become clogged with soot; in the plane that cannot happen.

Another merit of plane trees is their tolerance of pruning; they can be kept to a desired size by repeated loppings for an indefinite number of years, and suffer little harm thereby. "Miniature planes" have been held down to a set size in this way, for scores of years, in some London streets. But the true glory of this magnificent tree is only seen when it is allowed full scope to develop an immense crown.

The planes of Berkeley Square in London, which were planted about 1770, are among our oldest and grandest, but many other London squares, laid out in the eighteenth century, rival them closely. Paris, too, is rich in planes in squares and along boulevards. In the brighter, more southerly sun of Continental cities the summer shade of swinging plane leaves is especially welcome. Plane yields an excellent furniture timber, known as lacewood, but in Britain it is only planted as a decorative tree.

POPLARS, *Populus* species Plates 10, p. 197; 15b, p. 220.

The poplars are a group of trees that must be treated with particular care by the tree planter. They include some of our most desirable ornamental trees, but also others that can become a dangerous and expensive menace, ruining gardens and even wrecking houses!

Nearly all poplars are raised from cuttings, and you are more likely to grow a cultivar than a species. Most cultivars have arisen through the planned hybridisation of different species, and since poplars cross-

PLATE 13   *Avenues*

Above Cedars of Lebanon at Butleigh in Somerset. Bold landscape planning, using a broad-crowned evergreen conifer amply spaced to allow majestic development.

Centre Limes at Blair Castle in Perthshire, Scotland. Common lime, with its vigorous upward growth and pale green foliage, has long been the landscapist's first choice to line the narrower approach roads.

Below Holm oak at Holkham in Norfolk, chosen for its resistance to salt-laden winds near an exposed northern shoreline. An evergreen tree from the Mediterranean, holm oak sheds dense shade from interlocked crowns.

breed freely the number of hybrids is endless. So "hybrid poplar" means little or nothing without closer identification. Nor do the common terms "Canadian poplar" and "Italian poplar" help us much on their own; there are scores of different poplars in both countries.

Poplars are among the few trees that bear flowers of only one sex on each individual tree. Female poplars are unpopular with gardeners, because every summer they scatter clouds of tiny, fluffy seeds which litter paths, blow into houses, and stick to fresh paint. Therefore only a few nurserymen ever stock them, and unless you make a special search you are fairly sure to get a male tree; this will bear dangling caterpillar-shaped male catkins just before its leaves open in spring, but will never shed any seed.

Black poplars Plate 10a, c, p. 197.

Most of the commonly-grown poplars are hybrids of a group technically called "Black", after *Populus nigra*, a wild species occasionally found in English lowland hedgerows. There is nothing notably black about them; the name only means that their bark is dark grey rather than white, as in some other kinds. This is a numerous group which includes several kinds recommended by the Forestry Commission as timber-producers, as listed on page 185. The commonest is the Black Italian poplar, *Populus* 'Serotina', which is the hybrid offspring of *P. nigra* and the American *P. deltoides*. We can describe its vices and virtues as a fair representative of its group. It does, however, show one characteristic feature not found in other kinds. When its leaves open in late spring, they are a lovely warm copper colour.

Black Italian poplar is a tree for a man in a hurry—just the job if you want a quick and profitable crop of veneer wood for chip baskets or matches. In any fertile garden it quickly outstrips all other trees, growing from three to five feet taller each year. If you lop it back, its sprouts will shoot out again even faster than this.

Plantation-grown trees are fairly upright, but isolated specimens always develop a lean, away from the prevailing wind, which can only too easily cause their trunks to threaten neighbouring buildings or over-head wires. Felling, or even lopping, such poplars becomes a difficult and costly job. With street trees, the leaning habit seldom becomes a problem, for Black Italian poplars grown in such situations are nearly always lopped.

PLATE 14 *Lime tree*

Above A splendid open-grown common lime, in full summer foliage.
Below The same tree in winter, showing the marvellous tracery of tapering stems and finer twigs that support the leaves. A mansion is now revealed at the left, and the lime's dominating situation—as a hilltop centrepiece to the view from its windows—becomes clear.

They can stand up to repeated loppings, and they also show tolerance of town smoke.

Below ground, the roots of the Black Italian poplar grow at a pace to match the shoots above. They rapidly explore a large volume of soil in search of water. The wood of poplars has very large pores or vessels, and during a hot summer day its leaves draw upwards, through this open-pored wood, exceptionally large volumes of water. On many soils—such as chalk, sands or gravels, this need not cause any concern, for the soil does not "move" as the water is drawn out from it. But on a clay soil the action of poplar roots increases the tendency to shrinkage and drying out that is always present on any day during hot dry weather. Buildings exert pressure on clay, which moves, as it shrinks, *away* from the building. When winter rains swell the clay again, and close the cracks, it does not return, and this gradual removal of support from a building can eventually cause its downfall. Therefore, in any district with a clay soil and a warm dry summer, Black Italian poplars should be kept at least one hundred feet away from buildings. See Figure 16, page 37.

These considerations, fortunately, do not apply to that most desirable decorative tree, the Lombardy poplar, *Populus nigra* variety *italica*. This sends its slender column of foliage straight up, and its narrow crown makes such small demands for water that it seldom causes any serious harm to buildings. It can therefore be planted, without qualms, in quite restricted spaces close to houses, walls or pavements. It makes an ideal screen for a factory, a slag heap, or any other unpleasant feature that is better hidden from view. Because of its narrow shape, it is often planted too close to its neighbours; ten feet is not too much to leave, to allow good illumination of the leaves all round. As a landscape feature, grown on its own or in a small group of two or three, it can have tremendous impact, drawing the eye skywards and contrasting, by its tall plume-shaped outline, with all other rounded or pyramidal trees in sight.

Balsam poplars

Poplars of the balsam group are distinguished by the presence of a remarkably strong-scented gum on their winter buds, and when these buds open in spring they spread a wonderful fragrance all around them for a week or two. It is only fair to add that a few people find this scent distasteful. Certainly, it is so overpowering that a single balsam poplar is enough, even for a large garden. Otherwise they have no special merit to attract the planter; their foliage is a pleasing mid-green, but nothing more. The kind usually grown is the eastern balsam poplar, *Populus tacamahaca*, from New England. The western balsam poplar, *P. trichocarpa*, is rather more vigorous, particularly in the west of Britain.

The kind that should *never* be bought is the Ontario balsam poplar, now believed to be a hybrid, and usually sold—yes, unscrupulous nurserymen still sell it—under the cultivar name of *Populus* 'Candicans' It also masquerades as *P. × gileadensis*, under the mistaken belief that its sweet-scented bud-gum resembles the Biblical balm of Gilead! It is an extremely vigorous and fast-growing tree, with a root system to match. As soon as you lop it or fell it, it responds by sending up huge sucker shoots from its roots, all over your garden. Cut them back, and you get twice as many. Only the liberal application of an all-out weedkiller, such as sodium chlorate, will rid your land of this Hydra-headed pest, and this is sure to cause harm to choice plants or lawns also.

White and Grey Poplars Plate 10, b, d, p. 197.

The white poplar, *Populus alba*, is an uncommon native tree with a handsome white bark, and white undersides to its leaves. The grey poplar, *P. canescens*, now thought to be a hybrid between this and the related Aspen poplar, is a less strikingly white tree and grows more vigorously and to greater size—so you can take your choice—according to your preference, for bright colour or a large, quick-grown tree. Both kinds are liable to send up thickets of sucker shoots, and this makes them useful where rough and damp slopes, subject to landslips, have to be stabilised with some sort of tree cover. Their network of roots helps to bind loose ground. They have an amazing tolerance of salt winds, and so can be used right on the sea-coast. They also make fine avenue or specimen trees, providing pale columns that are more robust than those of silver birch and of a softer colour that strikes a less sharp contrast with other garden trees.

ASPEN Plate 15b, p. 220.

The Aspen poplar, *Populus tremula*, forms a fine timber tree in Scandinavia, where it is preferred over all other trees as a source of veneer for matches and match boxes. Although it is native to the British Isles, it rarely makes a good specimen with us, and it is most often seen as a clump of small trees and bushes arising from root suckers. Its main attraction lies in the incessant fluttering motion of its leaves, which are stirred by the least breeze and reflect the sunlight in a pretty rhythm as they sway.

Two Ornamental Poplars

The golden poplar, *Populus* 'Aurea', which is a yellow-leafed form of the hardy Black Italian kind, provides an unusual foliage colour and thrives in difficult situations, such as smoky towns. The Chinese giant-leaved poplar, *P. lasiocarpa*, lends an exotic touch to a garden by bearing enormous bright green leaves, a foot long by nine inches wide, with conspicuous red veins and leaf stalks.

Raising poplars

Aspen is grown from sucker shoots or else from seed—a difficult task since its tiny, hairy seeds live for only a few days and must be sown in fine damp soil as soon as they ripen in midsummer. The best way to raise the commoner poplars is to take cuttings of branchwood, about one foot long, and strike them in ordinary soil in spring. A high proportion take root, and in the following autumn these are lifted and *stumped*—that is, cut back to a basal bud, and then replanted. The basal bud then sends up a very strong and vigorous shoot that forms, within one or two seasons, a tree sturdy enough for forest or landscape planting.

When grown for timber, poplars are planted about twenty feet apart, either in lines along streams, roads or hedgerows, or else in a square arrangement on fertile, well-watered land. The basal branches are pruned off as the trunk expands, up to a height of twelve feet. This ensures that the valuable lower bole is free from small knots, which would lower the quality of the veneer wood cut from it. Poplar logs are usually peeled to provide thin sheets of pale veneer, which is made into matches, match boxes, or chip baskets. The trees are felled when they are about thirty years old and eighty feet high, with trunks at least four feet round.

OAKS, *Quercus* species Plates 5a, b, p. 180; 6 right, p. 181; 13c, p. 212.

Throughout most of Europe, including the British Isles, the commonest broadleaved tree is the so-called European or English oak. Foresters and timber merchants regard it as a single kind of tree, but botanists recognise two separate species, with a great number of intermediate forms that arise through natural cross-breeding. In one of these, the pedunculate oak, *Quercus robur*, the *acorns* are stalked, but the *leaves* are stalkless. In the other, the sessile oak, *Q. petraea*, the *acorns* grow directly upon the twigs, without slender stalks, but each *leaf* has a distinct stalk at the base. Stocks of oak grown for forest planting usually include a range of forms, but landscape planters usually prefer trees of the distinct species. There is little to choose between the two, except that the sessile oak tends to produce a clearer and straighter central trunk.

Oak yields a very strong and naturally durable timber, with an attractive grain. But it only shows a good profit to the timber merchant or grower when it has reached a large size, which implies an age of at least one hundred years. Therefore little oak is planted for timber to-day, because a quicker yield can be obtained from practically any other kind of tree. Oak, however, grows so readily from acorns along hedgerows and on waste land that it maintains its place in the lowland countryside. Because it *is* such a common tree, it is seldom planted on any scale in gardens or parks; indeed, most specimen oak trees seem to be planted to commemorate some special event, such as a royal visit! Yet the common oak is a very rewarding tree, hardy and long lived, wind-firm and tolerant of most soils, and sure to develop an intricate branching pattern that never lacks an individual character. Because of the clustered arrangement of the buds, found on no other tree, each separate oak tree grows in its own random pattern.

Oak is rarely a very tall tree, heights over eighty feet being exceptional. Its life-span is quite indefinite; many veterans have reached five hundred years. All the common oaks are easily raised from their seeds, the well-known acorns; but it is important to remember that acorns must be stored under cool moist conditions, and never exposed to drying heat. The sturdy seedlings need transplanting after one year of growth.

Turkey oak, *Quercus cerris*, proves valueless for timber when grown in western Europe, though the Turks make good use of it in its homeland. It can easily be recognised by the angular lobes of its long leaves, the long stipules that surround every bud, and the mossy hairs that clothe each acorn cup; a distinct bright orange colour can often be seen in the cracks of its bark. Turkey oak grows vigorously, and its rapid upward extension is achieved by a strong central trunk. It can be recommended for any situation where a very big broadleaved tree is needed as soon as possible, but not elsewhere, for it is hard to keep within bounds.

Several oaks, native to North America, bear reddish foliage. It is not a constant colour like that of the copper beech, but is seen first as a rose-red shade on the new leaves in spring, next as a crimson glow over dark green blades in midsummer, and finally as a rust-red or scarlet flame as the leaves fade in autumn. This seasonal march of colour makes the red oaks striking features, particularly when set, as they should be, against a background of normal mid-green foliage. The best-known of these handsome trees is the northern red oak, now called *Quercus borealis*, though formerly known as *Q. rubra*. Others are the scarlet oak, *Q. coccinea* and the pin oak, *Q. palustris*.

Purple oak is a cultivar of the European sessile oak, *Quercus petraea* 'Purpurea'. Its leaves are first reddish purple, and later green, flushed with shades of red. An apt tree for those who want a single exceptional feature in a small garden, but really more bizarre than attractive.

Evergreen oak, or holm oak, *Quercus ilex*, is a tree of major importance in landscape work, since it is our largest broadleaved evergreen. It resembles a huge holly tree—in fact the word "holm" is an old English name for holly—but its leaves are spineless and it bears small dark brown acorns instead of red berries. The bark is jet black and finely divided. Holm oak grows slowly, and rarely exceeds sixty feet in height, but it is very long lived. Though native to the warm Mediterranean zone, where most trees are evergreen, it is hardy throughout lowland Britain. A good tree for large seaside gardens, for it is absolutely resistant to salt winds. Its dark green foliage casts a deep shade the whole year round, so no plants can succeed beneath it, not even spring bulbs.

The evergreen cork oak, *Quercus suber*, is not hardy in Britain, and is seen only as a rare specimen in southern botanical collections. This is the tree that yields the cork for bottle stoppers. Cork bark is stripped from the trees at intervals in Spain and Portugal, and is renewed by natural regrowth.

Lucombe oak, *Quercus* 'Lucombeana', is one of several hybrid oaks that have arisen in cultivation. Its parents are the cork oak and the

Turkey oak, and it is named after an Exeter nurseryman, William Lu-combe, who discovered it in 1765. An exceptionally vigorous tree, it shows the unusual character of being semi-evergreen; it holds its dark green leaves well through the winter, but drops them in early spring. All these hybrid oaks are increased by grafting, using a common oak as the stock. Turner's oak, *Quercus* 'Turneri', has a similar appearance and habit of growth, but a different parentage; it was found in Turner's Nursery at Holloway Down in Essex in 1795, and probably arose through the natural crossing of the evergreen holm oak with the native deciduous pedunculate species.

ROBINIA, *Robinia pseudoacacia*

This magnificent decorative tree bears three common names. When the early settlers in North America found it, some of them, noticing its spines, called it the "acacia" after a spiny tree mentioned in the Bible, and it is also called "false acacia" because it is so obviously unlike the real thing! Others looked at its seed pods, holding seeds that nobody has ever found worth eating, and decided that it was the "locust" which nourished the Israelites in the wilderness! Robinia, the handiest name, recalls a French botanist, Jean Robin, who introduced it to Europe in 1601.

The trunk and stems of the robinia are always irregular and snaky in outline. This, together with the boldly-ribbed bark, adds to their beauty, but makes the tree useless for modern timber growing, although its heartwood is hard, strong and naturally durable. The foliage consists of airy masses of finely divided, feathery compound leaves, and the flowers are a real joy. Snow-white, they hang down in delicate clusters, and each has the shape of a sweet-pea blossom. They are followed in autumn by slender black seed-pods. The twigs bear little spines, always in pairs, but these are absent from the stouter limbs.

A robinia needs ample room to expand its glorious crown and display of June blossom. It is not a tree for a small garden, and it has a few drawbacks. Tidy park-keepers complain that it is "always dropping something"—faded flowers, bitty dead leaves, or spent seed-pods. It may also send up strong sucker roots at surprising distances from the parent tree, though it only does this vigorously after it has been felled or lopped.

Robinia has been used as a "tree of last resort" by landscapers who have to clothe slag heaps with some sort of greenery, where damage from vandals is rife. Once it is established, cutting back or wanton damage just causes it to throw up more sucker shoots, and as these are very spiny they deter invaders. It has been widely planted in France, as coppice for firewood.

A pink flowered form, the cultivar 'Decaisneana' is sometimes grown, but its colour is too pale to please everyone. Other exceptional kinds are the upright 'Pyramidalis', the weeping 'Pendula' and the golden-leaved 'Frisia'.

WILLOWS, *Salix* genus Plates 11b, p. 204; 12, p. 205.

The willows form a remarkably varied group of trees, bushes, and creeping woody plants. Many are drab and attract the attention of botanists, but of nobody else! A few are attractive ornamental trees or shrubs. Willow trees are nearly always wholly male or wholly female; it is very rare, though not quite unknown, for the same tree to bear both male and female catkins. The male catkins bear bright golden anthers in spring; the female catkins are more greenish and they eventually release tiny seeds, tufted with a fluff of white hairs, at about midsummer for most species. On the whole the male tree is the more attractive, and should be preferred where a choice is available. Willows are raised from cuttings, which strike very easily, and the sex of young trees is therefore usually known from the outset.

Weeping willows give us one of the finest of all arboreal landscape features—gleaming cascades of silvery green foliage falling in a graceful dome from gay orange-yellow branches. The typical weeping willow is *Salix babylonica*, which is native to Asiatic riversides from the Euphrates east to China; but many of the weeping willows in cultivation belong to the cultivar 'Tristis' of the European white willow, *Salix alba*. This is remarkable for being the very first tree to open its leaves in spring, when they appear as emerald points on its hanging twigs, and also one of the last trees to lose its leaves in autumn.

Many "weeping" trees are really freak branches that have the exceptional habit of growing downwards instead of upwards. Such false weepers can only be propagated by grafting, and they must be set on a stock of a normal tree in order to get the required height. But the weeping willows droop naturally, after first growing upwards, and they can therefore be raised from cuttings without the need for grafting. Willows seldom weep on an entirely symmetrical plan. One side of a tree often grows taller than the other, which gives to each individual its own peculiar character and charm. If a willow grows beside a lake or stream, it is sure to weep more strongly on the water side than on the landward side. This is a response to the strong reflected light that is thrown upwards from the water surface, as from a mirror.

Few gardeners who own a pond can resist planting a weeping willow beside it. This handsome tree also thrives well on an open lawn away from water; but it must have full and unobstructed light on all sides. Otherwise it starts to grow upwards on one side and the full beauty of the dome-shaped cascade of leaves is lost.

Cricket-bat willow, *Salix alba* variety *coerulea*, is usually grown for its timber, and thrives best on rich alluvial soil along watercourses in south and east England. There it is planted thirty feet apart, pruned up to a height of eight feet, and harvested for cricket-bat clefts when only twelve years old. As an ornamental tree it is even more valuable and can be allowed a much longer life-span. Cricket-bat willow is one of the few broadleaved trees to develop, without artificial training, a truly pyramidal crown. Its foliage has a pleasing and unusual shade of shining bluish-green. A tall row or plantation of cricket-bat willows will allow a lot of sunlight to penetrate to the ground beneath, which means that grass can be maintained in a healthy state all around them. They are quick-growing and altogether very desirable screen trees. Incidentally, they are nearly always female.

The typical race of white willow, *Salix alba*, forms a large tree with a rather untidy, wide-spreading crown. Its pale-green, shining foliage is particularly attractive in sunlight, when stirred by summer breezes, but it must be allowed ample room and is best sited as a distant feature in the view. It rarely grows erect, and it tends to fork low down. White willow is most often seen as a pollarded tree along the banks of the Thames and other lowland rivers. Few farmers lop their pollard trees to-day, and preservation of old pollards is difficult because their main trunks readily become rotten and eventually hollow.

Crack willow, *Salix fragilis*, forms a shapeless tree with a loose untidy crown. Its branches, as its name suggests, are apt to break, while its twigs, if pulled backwards, snap off with a sharp crack; the timber is brittle and useless. Not a desirable tree for planting, save in the rare instance when a patch of damp rough ground must be filled with some-thing that is both acceptable to the eye and virtually indestructible.

The corkscrew willow, *Salix matsudana* 'Tortuosa', is a freak form from Japan, in which every branch and twig is curiously twisted. This gives the whole tree a restless appearance, and there are few situations in which it looks really at home.

Willows coppice readily if cut down to ground level, and all the osiers or willow wands used in basketry are grown in this way. These shoots are cut when only one year old, and the crop is very exacting. On the commercial scale, basket willows are grown only in districts with a rich, alluvial soil, notably in the fenlands around Langport in Somerset. In the garden, this ease of coppicing can be employed to give highly decorative effects. Certain willows have brightly-tinted stems which add a strong note of colour on wintry days when flowers are lacking and evergreens look drab. The coloured-stem willows need little attention—

PLATE 15 *Trees out of place*

Above The strain of ash-leaved maple, also strangely called 'box elder' and botanically *Acer negundo* variety *variegatum*, that is grown in Britain, should be confined to the suburban garden, if planted at all. Its green leaves, blotched everywhere with faded cream, never blend with natural foliage. The wild American race, however, forms a magnificent deep green shade tree.

Below Aspen poplars always send up sucker shoots—ideal for maintaining the species on marshland, but a nuisance in any garden. Here they dominate a Norfolk hedgerow, but will never reach timber size.

just a hard cutting back, right to the stump, in autumn at intervals of three years or so; regrowth during the following summer restores their form and beauty. They make good bushes for odd corners, but they must have ample light.

Desirable varieties are *Salix daphnoides*, the violet willow, *S. alba* 'Vitellina', the golden willow, and *S. alba* 'Chermesina', which bears shoots of a brilliant orange-scarlet hue.

LIMES, *Tilia* species   Plates 13b, p. 212; 14, p. 213.

The common lime, *Tilia vulgaris*, holds a well-deserved place as a leading park and avenue tree. This is due to a happy combination of beauty, hardiness, vigour and adaptability. Its shape is satisfying to the eye, both in winter and in summer, and its foliage has a rewarding march of colour, from pale green through richer shades of darker greens to the pale gold of autumn. The greenish-yellow flower clusters enliven this around midsummer, and their leafy bracts, found on no other tree, add a note of fawny-brown as they mature in autumn. Lime grows fast and provides many of our tallest broadleaved trees; in fact the tallest known broadleaved tree in Britain is one that stands, very appropriately, in Great Limes Wood, Duncombe Park, near Helmsley in Yorkshire; it is 148 feet high.

Though often recorded as a species, the common lime is usually held to be a hybrid between two native kinds, the broadleaved lime, *Tilia platyphyllos* and the small-leaved lime, *T. cordata*. Both of these can be found as rare trees scattered through our few surviving natural woodlands. As its seed often proves infertile, common lime is increased by cuttings. It succeeds on a wide range of soils, but naturally thrives best in fertile

PLATE 16   *Flowers and fruit of outstanding small ornamental trees*

Above left Forsythia, introduced from China, displays abundant golden bells on bare twigs in March.

Above right Cornelian cherry, *Cornus mas*, from the Mediterranean, opens exquisite bright yellow blossoms on leafless twigs in February. Botanically a dogwood, it is called a 'cherry' because of its small juicy berries.

Centre left Eucalyptus gunnii, one of the hardiest species, though safe only in western districts, comes from Australian mountains. The blue-green foliage is evergreen, the quaint seed pods persist all the year round, and the dainty flowers open in June.

Centre right Chinese witch hazel, *Hamamelis mollis*, opens its gay tassels of yellow blossom in mid-winter, from December to February.

Below left Strawberry tree, *Arbutus unedo*, native to Killarney in south-west Ireland, bears evergreen foliage and carries strawberry-like fruits all round the year.

Below right The native spindle tree, *Euonymus europaeus*, bears bright pink fruits in autumn.

parklands. Lime tolerates pruning better than any other tree and it can also grow satisfactorily in the close neighbourhood of its fellows. This fits it well for screens and avenues, and in old-fashioned gardens it was often kept low and trained into pleached screens and arbours. "Pleaching" implies the intertwining of growing stems, so that those of adjacent trees are united. Clipped and lopped limes bear leafy twigs repeatedly, no matter how often they may be cut back; this is a great advantage where you need to maintain a leafy screen within a confined space.

Our commoner kinds of lime have one sad drawback. In summer their leaves are often attacked by aphids that secrete a sticky fluid known as "honey-dew". This is promptly attacked in turn by a fungus that turns it black, producing an unsightly substance called "sooty mould". Though the trouble is a minor one in most situations, it causes a cleaning problem wherever cars are parked beneath lime trees. None of the commoner sorts of lime, then, should be used as street trees. The hybrid *Tilia* 'Euchlora', which is not attacked by aphids, should be employed instead.

Two species of lime have attractive gleaming silver-white undersides to their leaves. One is the silver lime, *T. tomentosa*, of normal upright habit, and the other is the weeping white lime, *T. petiolaris*. The latter is to be preferred, since its foliage is livelier, moving with every stir of the breeze and displaying bright reflections with every turn of the leaf; it also bears richly-scented flowers.

Limes are never planted for timber to-day, though their wood has curious specialised uses, for example as piano keys, hat blocks, and in fine carving.

ELMS, *Ulmus* species   Plate 17, p. 244.

The elms pose many problems for those who plant or tend trees, and the whole group must be treated with particular caution. First, they are hard to identify; even the experts disagree as to how to tell the different sorts apart, so particular care must be taken over the purchase of stocks. Next, they have been threatened over many years by the serious elm disease caused by the fungus *Ceratocystis ulmi*, which has done grave harm in Holland and North America. Fortunately many individual elms growing in countries other than those two have proved resistant to this disease. Third, because they grow to exceptionally large sizes, and often arise along hedgerows, elms cause more boundary problems and hazards to property, than do any other trees. Finally, some kinds of elm are liable to shed branches, on still days in midsummer, without apparent cause or warning.

The grandest of the elms is the English field elm, *Ulmus procera*, a local race that has developed in the eastern counties, where it is grown as a hedgerow tree. This is the magnificent kind which figures in the landscapes of Constable. Its trunk forms a sturdy pillar reaching a great height, up to one hundred and forty feet, and it bears huge billowing clouds of foliage that reflect the midsummer sunlight from myriads of remarkably small leaves. This elm is raised from root suckers, since it rarely bears fertile seed. Mature trees are regularly harvested by farmers for their tough timber, which is widely used in furniture making, and their place in the hedgerow is usually taken by younger stems springing up from their roots. But the hedgerow is really the only safe place for this highly scenic tree. If used in a garden or a park, it brings with it a risk of windfall and branch shedding, and once it has been lopped it is exceedingly prone to develop butt rot and to become, by slow stages, a grave but unsuspected menace to passers-by. When fields have been developed for housing, huge field elms have often been left along hedges that have become garden boundaries; such trees can cause complications of maintenance that may become very costly. Disagreements arise between neighbours as to who owns the trees, and whether or when they should be lopped or felled. They decay so quickly under fungal attack that Tree Preservation Orders can rarely save them, and they are poor subjects for tree surgery.

The Huntingdon elm, *U. x hollandica* variety *vegeta*, is a similar kind, with a more drooping pattern of branch arrangement. There are several other regional races.

The faults of the common field elms can easily be avoided by planting the narrow-crowned kinds. One of these, the Jersey elm, *U. carpinifolia* variety *sarniensis*, comes from Guernsey and Jersey in the Channel Islands, while another, the Cornish elm, *U. carpinifolia* variety *cornubiensis* is native to south-west England. Both have light, small, side branches that never become a danger, and form slender pyramidal outlines. They can readily be pruned, and they make good trees for streets or avenues.

The wych or Scots elm, *U. glabra*, is quite a distinct tree, and as it does not bear suckers it is grown from its winged seeds; these must be sown just after they fall in midsummer, since they cannot be stored. The growth habit of the wych elm is attractive though unusual, for its sturdy bole soon divides into several ascending limbs that form a gracefully rounded crown. Because of its hardihood and resistance to town smoke, it has been widely used for park planting in cities that are difficult for trees, such as Edinburgh and Glasgow. A native tree, it is occasionally grown as timber, for its tough wood serves well for furniture and in boat building.

Weeping wych elm, *U. glabra* variety *pendula*, forms a very attractive feature, not too large for a garden. It is increased by grafting on an upright stock of the common race, and forms a shapely dome, with twigs going right down to ground level. Early in spring, before its leaves open, it bears clusters of purple catkins, and about midsummer its foliage is overlaid by masses of greenish-yellow winged seeds—so gay that they are often mistaken for true flowers.

16. Smaller Broadleaved Trees

MANY trees that never approach timber size play a useful part in the garden because of their compact habit of growth and pleasing foliage, flowers and fruit. They differ from shrubs, discussed later, in forming a single upright trunk or bole, rather than a group of much-divided woody stems. The following descriptions are arranged alphabetically, by the generic name of each group.

STRAWBERRY TREE, *Arbutus unedo* Plate 16e, p. 221

The strawberry tree is a very attractive evergreen, though hardy only in the south and west. It grows wild in Spain and Portugal, and like many evergreens it is adapted to a Mediterranean climate of mild wet winters, followed by hot, dry and sunny summers. It is also native to Ireland, but there it has only a limited spread. There are thickets of strawberry tree around the Lakes of Killarney in the south-west, and a few outliers as far north as Lough Gill in County Sligo. The trunk has a flaky bark and a reddish-brown wood used only for carving souvenirs for tourists. The tree, though bushy, develops a sturdy main stem and may reach thirty feet in height.

Strawberry trees have dark-green and glossy-surfaced, leathery-textured leaves. Their flowers open in autumn, and look remarkably like those of the lily-of-the-valley. Each separate blossom is white and bell-shaped, and they hang downwards, on reddish stalks, in open clusters, well clear of the foliage. They have a pleasing scent and attract many bees. The fruit takes a whole year to ripen, and therefore decorates the tree at the same time as the flowers. It is round, soft, and strawberry red in colour and holds many seeds. Although it looks delicious, its taste is insipid, and the tree's specific name of *unedo* implies that people eat one, *only*. Strawberry tree is raised from seeds, which sprout in the spring after the fruit ripens. Its Irish names are *caithne* and *suglair*.

JUDAS TREE, *Cercis siliquastrum*

The Judas tree derives its name from an old belief that Judas Iscariot hanged himself from one of its branches after betraying Christ, though he is hardly likely to have found one high enough! It carries its crown of black-barked branches low down and clothes them in neatly rounded, bluish-green, rather kidney-shaped leaves that develop rich purplish-brown tints in autumn. The flowers are remarkably pretty and unusual, for Judas tree is our only tree to bear flower-clusters directly on the wood of bare leafless branches, instead of among finer twigs and foliage.

They open late in May, just as the leaves do, and their colour is a vivid lilac pink. In form they resemble sweet peas, but they differ in detail since Judas tree belongs to an exceptional group of the sweet pea family; both are Leguminosae, but sweet pea is a "butterfly flower" in the Papilionatae, whereas Judas tree belongs to the Caesalpiniodeae—a group important in the tropics but rare in the cooler north. The flowers are followed by conspicuous crimson seed pods, though with us the seeds within them are seldom fertile.

Judas tree will only thrive in the mild climates of the south and west. It is native to Mediterranean lands and will not flower in cold northern or eastern districts. It benefits from side shelter by taller trees or buildings, but the brilliance of its early blossoms is a fair reward for all the care it demands. Epicures may like to know that fresh-picked flowers taste delicious in salads!

Chamaerops see PALMS

Cordyline australis

This remarkable exotic tree is best known by its Latin name, as all the others are confusing. Most people call it a "palm" tree because of a superficial resemblance to the true palms, while some call it a "dracaena", which is the Latin name of a closely related genus. "New Zealand cabbage tree" is misleading, too, for although it does come from New Zealand, nobody could conceivably eat its foliage in mistake for a cabbage! *Cordyline australis* grows tall leafless trunks that are truly woody, and increase in height and girth like a true tree; they are usually undivided, though occasionally forked. At the top of each trunk it bears a tuft of stiff evergreen leaves, sword-shaped and pointed. At first they stand erect, then they droop downwards. *Cordyline* is related to the yuccas and is ranked with them in the lily family or Liliaceae. It occasionally flowers and sets seed but is usually increased by branch cuttings; stout woody sections of a branch are buried in peat in a warm, moist greenhouse, where they slowly send out shoots and roots.

Cordyline australis is hardy only in the mildest coastal districts of the British Isles and south-west Europe. There it is valued for the unique atmosphere it conveys, suggesting some tropical land. Although we grow a New Zealand species, others are found in south-eastern Asia, with allied kinds in the Canary Islands, so the illusion has some substance behind it. The West Coast of Scotland is quite mild enough to suit its needs, and rather remarkably there is a good specimen at Tongue, on the exposed North Atlantic coast of Sutherland.

SMOKE TREE, *Cotinus cogyggria*

The smoke tree is a pretty ornamental that draws its name from its conspicuous tufts of fruit; they look like puffs of smoke arising from the foliage. It is also called, though less aptly, the wig tree, because the fruit-heads have a vague resemblance to a lawyer's wig. It forms a neat low treelet or bush that is fully hardy and can stand a good deal of shade. The long-stalked leaves are small, neat, and oval, while the flowers, which open in June, are very small indeed and seldom attract attention. The feathery fruit masses develop about August and are most showy late in autumn, when the leaves are turning to a purplish-brown. Each separate seed is tiny, but it has a tuft of loose white hairs, intended to aid its dispersal by the wind, and it is the mass of seed-hairs that gives the illusion of smoke. The purple-leaved smoke tree, 'Foliis Purpureis' is even more effective, because of the stronger colour contrast; it is one of our best dark-leaved small trees. Smoke tree is native to south-east Europe, the Caucasus and the Himalayas.

DOVE TREE, *Davidia involucrata* Plate 18b, facing p. 245.

This lovely tree was discovered on the borders of China and Tibet by the great French missionary and naturalist Père David. The second half of its scientific name, *involucrata*, refers to the remarkable involucre of two white bracts that serve, instead of petals, to attract pollinating insects to the flowers. When a dove tree is in bloom in May, these white bracts stand out in a bold display, as though a flock of snow-white doves were alighting amid its bright-green foliage, and this explains the English name. A less romantic title is handkerchief tree, from the likeness of the white bracts to a lot of handkerchiefs hanging on a line!

Dove tree is reasonably hardy, but is usually grown in the side shelter of other, taller trees. It never becomes very tall, and except for its brief bright display has no special features to claim it a place in the garden, so on the whole it is best reserved for the larger property.

EUCALYPTUS TREES *Eucalyptus* species Plate 16c, facing p. 221.

So far nobody, repeat nobody, has found a eucalyptus tree hardy enough to grow out of sight of the sea—and it must be a southern or western sea —anywhere in northern Europe. The reason for this is that Australia, the homeland of all the varied and fascinating members of the genus *Eucalyptus*, lies in a latitude corresponding to that of Spain—a good ten degrees nearer the equator than Great Britain. The Gulf Stream helps a lot, and our best collection of *Eucalyptus* species is surprisingly far north, in the Forestry Commission's Kilmun Arboretum, near Dunoon on the sheltered coast of Argyll. At that favoured spot they will come through winters like that of 1965 when all the roads were icebound, because warm westerly breezes always blow again off the Atlantic, after a few days of snowfall. By contrast, the hardiest known Australian mountain species, planted at the Commission's Alice Holt Research Station, near Farnham on the Surrey-Hampshire border, perished to the last tree under the prolonged frost of the 1963 spring.

People often ask why the "eucalypts", which is a handy forester's name for the group, are not more widely planted. The answer is that they *are*

—but don't survive! If you have ground to plant in Devon or Cornwall, Brittany or the Channel Islands, press on with your planting of a highly decorative and unusual group of trees. Otherwise proceed at your own risk, and anticipate a literally dead loss.

Eucalyptus trees are evergreens, and their leaves are usually grey-green in colour owing to a waxy coating that helps to hold in moisture under the fierce Australian sun. Their leaves are placed on the twigs in such a way that the sun's rays strike *through* the foliage, so that the crown of the tree casts little shade. The young, or juvenile, leaves on each tree are usually very different from the more adult foliage. Often the juvenile leaves are paired, and the bases of each pair embrace the twig; older leaves on the same tree may be solitary, alternate, and long stalked. This complicates identification. Eucalyptus bark is pale grey; it breaks away in flakes, exposing pale yellow underbark below. The flowers are borne in clusters and are quite pretty, having showy tufts of golden stamens. The fruit is an oval capsule or box, holding many small round seeds. In the few spots where eucalypts thrive in Britain, they grow fast, flower freely, and set fertile seed. Eucalyptus trees are hard to transplant, and it is best to raise the seedlings in pots, so that soil can be moved along with their roots; planting is best done in spring. The characteristic scent of their essential oil is well known.

The main attraction of the eucalypts is their elegant blue-green foliage, which is often gathered for flower arrangements and indoor decoration. Much is imported by air from the South of France to London. Some gardeners in Devon and Cornwall treat their eucalypts as foliage plants, cutting them hard back before winter sets in, so as to encourage a strong growth of coppice shoots next spring.

The species usually grown in British gardens is *Eucalyptus gunnii*, which has handsome grey-blue, round to elliptic, juvenile leaves, and sage-green, sickle-shaped adult ones. Another relatively hardy kind is *E. urnigera*, with apple-green leaves; while *E. parvifolia*, with small leaves, is said to be remarkably frost-resistant and able to tolerate chalk soils, though none is ever grown in my own frosty and chalky district!

FIG, *Ficus carica*

The fig is usually grown as a fruit tree, either within a greenhouse or else trained along a south-facing wall where it receives full sun. Sometimes it is grown as a decorative bush or small tree, out in the open, and it will succeed in this way anywhere in the south of England, or under similar warm climates. The stems are smooth and grey, while the leaves—which form its main attraction, are pale green and very variable in shape, even on the same tree. They are large, and more or less deeply lobed, or even divided into segments. Their quaintness and the angular arrangements of the branches give the fig tree a character of its own, recalling the warm south. The fruit, which rarely ripens on an open-grown tree, is green and pear-shaped. The fleshy object that we eat is really a swollen stem that once held many hidden flowers, and now contains many seeds. Botany books relate the long and complex story of how cultivated figs can be pollinated by gall-wasps from wild figs, but in practice the modern cultivated kinds obligingly ripen their fruits without the help of any exceptional insects.

HOLLIES, *Ilex* species

The wild European holly tree, *Ilex aquifolium*, is a good illustration of a "Mediterranean climate" broadleaved evergreen. It is happiest in regions with a mild, rainy winter, where it can make good use of limited, though adequate, warmth to build up its food reserves by using winter sunlight. In the spring, its shoots grow longer, and during the summer it can, if the weather gets very dry, survive any amount of drought because its tough, leathery, waxy leaves are designed to restrict water loss. In *north-west* Europe it seldom has to face summer droughts, but it keeps its evergreen habit. In *north-east* Europe it cannot thrive, because the winter cold is too severe, and for the same reason it is not very happy in the north-eastern states of North America.

Any tree that remains in leaf when other trees are leafless is sure to be attacked by browsing animals. To save its life, the wild holly develops very prickly leaves on all its lower branches. Higher up, where sheep and deer cannot reach, there is no need for this protection, so the leaves are spineless. Certain cultivated hollies, however, are cultivars that never bear spines. A few, on the other hand, are exceptionally spiky.

Most holly trees are either wholly male or wholly female. Both sexes bear pretty white, waxy, bell-shaped flowers, which are individually small but attract the eye when they open in May amid the dark glossy foliage. Male flowers develop four stamens; female flowers have a single ovary that ripens to the well-known red berry by midwinter. Birds raid the bushes, and spread the seeds; these will only germinate in the following spring if they have passed through the digestive tract of a bird. Otherwise they have to be stored, still in the berries, in damp sand for fifteen months after ripening, before they will sprout. Good nurserymen guarantee the sex of their holly plants, as they increase stocks by layering or budding; most varieties can only be obtained in one sex.

Holly wood is white, hard, heavy, and close-textured. Craftsmen use it for carving, and it makes good draughtsmen or chessmen; dyed black, it passes as a fair substitute for ebony. It is also used for walking sticks and whip handles. The best of all firewoods, it will burn as soon as felled, without any seasoning. Even the green foliage will blaze up, for it holds little water and is coated with wax. A holly tree caught in a forest fire flames fiercely like a torch. But growth is slow, and demands are only casual, so holly is never planted for its wood.

Modern landscapists regard holly as rather a dull tree, but the Victorians, with less range of choice, found it a godsend. It is hardy, stands town smoke and sea winds, and will endure a large degree of shade. It can readily be trained into a close dense hedge, which cannot be seen through, while it is spiny enough to hold back farm livestock. Many varieties are available, and this enabled planters to avoid undue monotony. At one time over a hundred kinds were catalogued, but not all have survived. Some of the more distinct kinds are described below. There are many combinations of unusual leaf form with foliage colour or fruit colour.

Spiny-leaved Hollies

Highclere holly, also called broadleaved holly, or *Ilex* 'Altaclarensis' is a cross between wild holly and the Azores holly, *I. perada*, which was first found on the Highclere estate in Berkshire. It is always male, and forms a vigorous and imposing tree.

The hedgehog holly, *Ilex* 'Ferox', bears spines all over its leaves, on the top as well as the sides. An irritating curiosity. Male, and therefore never bears berries.

Ilex 'Polycarpa' also called 'C. van Thol' breaks the rules by bearing both male and female flowers, with abundant red berries.

Smooth-leaved Hollies

I. 'Camelliaefolia' is a beautiful pyramidal form of Highclere holly, with nearly spineless leaves; it is a female and berries well.

'Pyramidalis', a form of the common wild holly, has bright green spineless leaves, a pyramidal growth habit, and fruits very freely. The Scotch holly, various known as 'Scotica', 'Dahoon', or smooth-leaved holly, is the most spineless of all; female.

Variegated and Coloured-foliaged Hollies

The moonlight holly, *I.* 'Flavescens', a female sort, is tinted yellow all over its leaf surface, in shades of gold and canary. 'Golden Milkmaid', also called 'Aureo medio-picto', has *gold centres* with green edges. In contrast, the commoner 'Golden Queen', or 'Aurea Regina', has green centres to its leaves, with *golden edges*. Cultivar names can be misleading; both the 'Milkmaid' and the 'Queen' are male; if you want a *female* golden holly you must buy 'Golden King'!

A good silver-edged cultivar is the broadleaved silver holly, 'Argenteo-marginata', which is female.

Berry-colour Varieties

These are naturally female. *Ilex* 'Bacciflava' or 'Fructu-luteo' has yellow berries, while 'Amber' bears large bronzy-yellow ones. Black-fruited hollies, 'Fructeo-nigro', and white-fruited ones 'Fructeo-albo', are known, but are seldom propagated to-day.

Leaf-stalk Colour Varieties

Ilex 'Hodginsii' is a broadleaved, almost spineless, male kind, with curious purple leaf stalks. 'Madame Briot', an exotic French female, bears golden leaves on black stems.

Weeping Hollies

There is a good choice between 'Pendula', with normal dark green leaves, 'Perry's Gold Weeping', a gold-variegated kind, and 'Argentea Pendula', which has leaves variegated with silver. All three are females.

The usual holly in American gardens is the native species *Ilex opaca*. This has, if anything, even more varieties than the European kinds.

LABURNUMS, *Laburnum* species

Laburnums are both rewarding and refreshing trees, hardy, sure to bloom. bringing bright pennants of colour boldly displayed, and quite unlike anything else in the garden. They are long-lived and may form trunks over three feet round, yet they always remain small trees that need no pruning and rarely spread out of hand. The choice of kinds is limited. Nearly all have golden flowers, borne in such profusion every spring that the German name for the tree, "golden rain", sounds particularly apt.

The so-called Scotch laburnum, which is native to southern Europe, is *Laburnum alpinum*; its great merit is that it flowers late, prolonging the season into June.

The common laburnum, from central Europe, which flowers earlier, in late May, is *L. anagyroides*. This has a weeping form, 'Pendulum', and an upright form called 'Pyramidalis'. There is also a form with golden leaves, which is better forgotten; nobody wants to pile gold on gold, or to lose the contrast with green foliage. The most lavish displays of blossom come from a hybrid between the two species, *L.* 'Vossii'.

Those who seek a curiosity may care to try *L.* 'Adamii', which is a graft hybrid containing the elements of a purple-flowered broom and a yellow-flowered laburnum; the two colours appear at random in the same flower-clusters.

Laburnums have an attractive olive-brown bark, and their small round leaves, each with three leaflets, are attractive all the summer through. The black seed pods hold small hard round seeds, which are poisonous. Laburnum has dark red-brown heartwood at the centre of its trunk, with cream-coloured sapwood around it; it is only used for decorative carving or, on occasion, for musical instruments.

SWEET BAY, *Laurus nobilis*

The sweet bay is a dark-leaved evergreen that is often cultivated as a climber or as a formally-trained treelet in small gardens. Cottagers like it because its leaves have a spicy aromatic scent and flavour which adds zest to soups and fish dishes; for this reason a bay leaf will often be found included, at no extra charge, in tins of Portuguese sardines. Sweet bay comes from Greece and never looks truly happy under the colder skies of the north, though if given shelter it thrives in most districts. It grows slowly, and can be formed into a dense, dark hedge, or trained into ball or bird shapes by a skilful clipping that respects appropriately-placed buds. Sweet bay is one of the few trees that can stand having their roots imprisoned in tubs.

Bay flowers are so small that they often go unobserved. They are yellowish or white, and have four sepals and four petals. Each tree is either male or female; male trees have 12 stamens in each flower, and yield no fruit. Female trees have a simple ovary which later ripens one seed within a berry—at first green, later black.

The Latin name of sweet bay implies "the noble laurel", for its leaves were used to form the wreaths that adorned the victors at Olympic Games and similar contests in ancient Greece and Rome. From the word *baccalaurus*, meaning the "berried laurel", we draw our terms baccalaureate, Bachelor of Arts, and ultimately "bachelor".

LIQUIDAMBAR, *Liquidambar styraciflua*

This beautiful tree comes from the eastern seaboard of North America where it is known as sweet gum, because its bark, if wounded, exudes a sweetly-smelling resinous juice. Its scientific name, meaning "the liquid amber tree from which incense flows", also records this idea. Liquidambar forms a tall, rough-barked tree and yields a good furniture timber that is imported to Europe under the name of satin walnut, though it is not related to the walnut tree. Liquidambar is reasonably hardy in north-west Europe, where it is grown solely for its attractive foliage. Right from the start a liquidambar clothes its slender trunk in leaves of a pleasing mid-green; they are deeply lobed, usually with three lobes but occasionally with five. Liquidambar thus resembles a maple, but its leaves are alternate, not opposite. As autumn draws on, these leaves develop a marvellous range of glowing red tints, from scarlets through crimsons to purple. No other tree can match it for richness and range of autumn hue.

The flowers of liquidambar are catkin-like, and open in June at the branch-tips. They form separate male and female catkins, both on the same tree, and both shaped like balls on long stalks; the male has several balls along the stalk, the female only one. Female catkins ripen to round fruit-heads, which open to release winged seeds. Neither flowers nor fruit are really conspicuous.

MAGNOLIAS, *Magnolia* species

The large flowers of the genus *Magnolia* make it particularly desirable wherever a bold effect is needed. Some kinds come from America, but most are natives of China or Japan. All, when grown in Europe, make a complete contrast with the native trees and shrubs, and suggest the exotic opulence of far foreign lands. A feature common to them all is the open, lily-like flower, composed of many upturned petals that have been likened to a goblet or chalice. Within this lie many stamens, while the central ovary is made up of many separate carpels, an arrangement that botanists consider primitive in the scale of natural plant evolution The fruit is, in many kinds, swollen and fleshy, and can be an attractive feature when autumn comes.

The musical name *Magnolia* commemorates a French botanist, Pierre Magnol, who lived at Montpellier. The cultivar name of the most popular sort, 'Soulangeana', which runs so melodiously with *Magnolia*, records another French flower lover, M. Soulange-Bodin, who first raised this hybrid in his garden at Fromont, near Paris. Plant breeders have naturally been busy with these very desirable shrubs, and 'Soulange-ana', which is a cross between *M. denudata* and *M. liliiflora*, is now regarded as the type of a varied group.

You must be even more careful than usual when choosing a magnolia; some are evergreen, others not, while some kinds are far hardier than others.

From America come two tree forms, which are occasionally seen in arboreta though rarely planted in gardens. *M. acuminata* is called the cucumber tree, because its large red fleshy fruit resembles a cucumber. *M. tripetala* is known as the umbrella tree, because its exceptionally large leaves radiate outwards from the stem like the ribs of an umbrella; this effect is best seen by looking up the trunk from below.

The magnificent magnolia that is often seen ornamenting the walls of great country houses is *M. grandiflora*, from eastern North America. Its stems are stout and woody, yet it takes kindly to training and appreci-ates the sun's heat reflected from the brickwork nearby. The large stiff oval leaves, glossy dark green above and clad in rusty hairs below, are handsome and evergreen. There is a main blaze of pure white flowers, exceptionally large, in autumn, but on occasion blossoms may open at other times of the year. Once established, this climber appears to last as long as the mansion that it adorns, becoming a token of long-sustained affluence and gracious gardening. In the milder districts it can be grown as an isolated bush or small tree.

Two favourite magnolias are small deciduous trees that open their blossoms on leafless branches in early spring. One is the starry-flowered magnolia, *M. stellata*, from Japan, which has pretty star-shaped white blossoms. The other is the Chinese yulan, *M. denudata*, with fewer but much larger flowers, shaped like water-lilies; they are pure white in colour. *Yu-lan* is a Chinese poetic name meaning "jade orchid", and is more fanciful than accurate. During the Sung dynasty (A.D. 960-1260) it was called *Ying-ch'un*, meaning "meet the spring".

Like all flowers that open before winter has gone, spring-flowering magnolias run the risk of severe damage by late snow, hard frost, or gales. This makes a sheltered situation desirable, even for trees that are otherwise hardy. Few are really happy on chalk; a lime-free soil is preferable.

Other magnolias flower later, in April and May, after their finely-proportioned oval leaves have expanded; they carry their huge flowers high, so that they are clearly seen against their green background. The typical 'Soulangeana' is without equal; each petal bears a bold blotch of dark purple, within its surround of white, which stresses the refined oval outline of petal and flower alike. There is a superb tulip-flowered kind, with rose-purple petals that are white within, called 'Lennei' and also a good white race named 'Alba'. The black magnolia, *M.* 'Nigra', is now considered to be a cultivar of *M. liliiflora*, one of 'Soulangeana's' two parents. It is indeed unusual, if too sombre for most people's taste, and might well be chosen when a dramatic colour effect is demanded. It begins to bloom in late April, and opens occasional flowers at intervals until midsummer.

Another noteworthy kind is *M. campbellii*, the Himalayan pink tulip tree, which is only truly at home in the warmer districts. *M. delavayi*, an evergreen with enormous leaves and creamy-white flowers seven inches across, is also a tender species. *M. kobus*, a small tree which bears white flowers in rich profusion, is a very hardy Japanese kind; it is often used as a stock for the grafting of the choicer varieties.

PALMS, *Trachycarpus fortunei* and *Chamaerops humilis*

Palm trees give the keynote to the whole tropic scene, and provide the people of the torrid equatorial lands with many kinds of food and much of their commonly used building materials. Very few indeed will grow out of doors in the cold north, but these few are often cultivated, in part for their rarity and exceptional appearance, but mainly, one suspects, to remind returned wanderers of sunnier climes.

Palms belong to a strange, though very large group of trees, the Palmaceae in the natural order Monocotyledones. The wood of their stout stems is quite different from that of our common northern trees, and although they grow steadily taller, these stems seldom become much thicker. Most kinds never branch, and all of them bear their leaves in huge tufts at the top of the trunk. Palm leaves are generally huge; there are two contrasting patterns for them. Some are compound and feather-shaped or *pinnate*, with many leaflets; others are simple but spread out like an opened fan, and these are called *palmate*. When the leaves fall, they leave conspicuous fibrous bases attached to the tree trunk. Palm flowers are borne on special shoots, and are enclosed within a strange oval leaf called a spathe. Though large, they are green and unattractive; some in each group are male, others female. The fruits are nut-like but vary much in size and substance; both dates and coconuts are palm fruits.

The palm that is usually grown in Britain is the Chusan palm, *Trachycarpus fortunei*, which comes from the mountains of western China. It has fan-shaped leaves, and when they fall they leave behind a very woolly brown stem ridged with leaf-bases. People always handle this palm as though it were very delicate, planting it in the close shelter of taller trees;

yet is is perfectly hardy anywhere in the south or west of the British Isles. It grows very slowly, however, and many years must elapse before it gains real tree stature; six inches a year is about its maximum rate and thirty feet its greatest height. Individual leaves may reach two feet long by three feet wide; they are evergreen and each lasts for several years. A palm under snow looks odd, but the Chusan kind will survive unharmed.

The European palm, *Chamaerops humilis*, grows wild on waste lands along the south coast of Spain, forming a low short-trunked treelet rarely more than six feet high. It is evergreen, with fan-shaped leaves on spiny stalks. It is hardy in sheltered situations in southern and western Britain.

PARROTIA, *Parrotia persica*

This curious tree is occasionally grown in sheltered south-western gardens for its odd winter flowers and bright autumn leaf colours. The flowers, borne in clusters, are individually small, but make a brave show in February with their conspicuous tufts of red stamens. The leaves have a long oval shape, and a waved outline; they start to colour in August and become crimson and gold before they fall. Parrotia forms a low, much-branched tree. Its native home is in the mountains of Persia and the Caucasus; there it forms almost impenetrable thickets, for its branches become grafted together wherever they cross and touch, and the separate trees become united.

STAGHORN SUMACH, *Rhus typhina*

This very conspicuous dwarf tree from North America adds a blaze of bold red to the borders in autumn. It puzzles many gardeners because it flowers and fruits yet never sets seeds. The explanation is simple— staghorn sumachs are either male or female, and the male is seldom grown in gardens because its green flowers make no particular show of colour; it can, however, be bought as "Viridiflora". Female trees are easily increased by the sucker shoots that spring up readily from the spreading roots. Some gardeners in fact find the tree's suckering habit rather a nuisance, but the sumachs are tough, reliable trees that stand up to town smoke and poor soils.

Staghorn sumach forms a much divided stem, up to twenty feet tall. Its compound leaves are exceptionally long, up to two feet, and are built up of fifteen to twenty leaflets. They are clad in crimson hairs in spring, become mid-green in midsummer, and blaze with scarlet, crimson and purple in late autumn. If a stem is cut back, the leaves on the fresh young root-shoots are quite exceptionally large, up to three feet, and each leaf looks like a huge shoot; in parks the tree is sometimes deliberately "stumped" to obtain a display of exotic leafage in a broad flower border.

The inflorescence of a female staghorn sumach begins to grow out from the foliage in July. It is deep crimson in colour, and has a velvety covering of soft hairs; the resemblance to a growing stag's horn "in velvet" explains the tree's odd name. After the flowers have opened, this red tuft ripens into a broad, crimson, pointed plume that waves above the tree's crown like a banner, until it finally fades in late autumn.

ELDERS, *Sambucus* species

As a wild tree, the common elder, *Sambucus nigra*, has an odd distribution along hedgerows and in waste places. It never grows tall and it needs full light, so in woodlands it eventually gets shaded out by bigger trees. But it is very easily spread by birds, and particularly by starlings, which eat its glossy purple berries and later void their seeds, often many miles away from the point where the parent trees grew. Elder thrives on soils rich in nitrogen, which include rubbish heaps, rabbit warrens, and the heaps of waste bedding that badgers remove from their earths or setts. Elder is the only tree that no rabbit will willingly eat. Badgers like to clean their claws on its rough bark, but do not otherwise damage the growing tree. Elder-berries can be eaten raw, but their taste is insipid; they make tasty pies when cooked, and can be fermented into wine, though little of this random harvest is gathered in to-day.

Most people are content to regard elder as a wildling that gives a brief burst of snowy blossom every June, followed by garlands of purple berries in October. It only really merits cultivation under exceptionally severe circumstances where no other decorative tree will grow. One of these is town smoke, for it resists the worst possible pollution, even flourishing on railway banks adjoining chemical works in the middle of Manchester. Another adverse circumstance is exposure to salt winds; though young elder leaves are sometimes blackened by salt, the tree can thrive on the face of exposed cliffs just above the water line. To provide variety there are golden-leaved elders, called 'Aurea', elders with double white flowers called 'Plena' and cut-leaved elders such as 'Laciniata'. All of these are easily propagated by simple stem cuttings, which root readily.

The red-berried elder, *S. racemosa*, is a distinct species which has been introduced from Scandinavia to Scotland to provide covert for pheasants, and berries for them to eat. It has finely-divided leaves and never grows taller than a shrub. Red-berried elder is also common and conspicuous amid the Alps.

LILACS, *Syringa* species

The common European lilac, *Syringa vulgaris*, grows wild in Romania and other countries bordering the lower Danube. It has long been grown in England as a cottage garden tree, cherished for its abundant trusses of mauve blossom which open unfailingly every June. It has pleasing pale-green, heart-shaped pointed leaves, and curious stringy bark. A feature of all the lilacs is the repeated forking of their branches, since nearly every twig ends in two buds, not in one. Despite this branching habit, common lilac can make a tall tree, up to twenty feet. It has a hard tough wood, pale brown in colour, stained in places with the same mauve shade as the flowers. Lilac is a tough and hardy tree, which shoots up repeatedly if cut back, and it shows great tolerance of town smoke.

The true common race is seldom planted to-day, for it has been supplanted in the nurseries by a range of named cultivars, all of exceptional beauty. These are increased in one of three ways, namely rootgrafting or budding on to a stock of the common kind, or layering so that they put down their own roots.

Good single lilacs include the white 'Vestiale', the dark red 'Souvenir de Louis Späth', the yellow 'Primrose', the purple 'Prodige', the pink 'Lavansensis', and the blue 'Maurice Barres'. 'Charles X' is the best lilac-coloured cultivar.

Similar colours are found in the double strains, such as the white 'Monique Lemoine', the mauve 'William Robinson', the dark red 'Charles Joly', the lavender 'Condorcet', and the lilac-blue 'President Grevy'.

The Preston hybrid lilacs were raised in Canada by Miss Preston, who crossed two seldom-cultivated species, *Syringa reflexa* and *S. villosa*. They flower a fortnight later than the common species, which makes them useful for extending the season. Their panicles of blossom are more open and elegant, but equally large. Named cultivars in this new group include the pinkish-lilac 'Hiawatha', the purple 'Viola' and the unusual, two-coloured 'W. T. Macoun', which has large loose panicles of pinkish flowers that are white within.

Several species of lilac from southern Europe, Persia and the Far East, are also grown by connoisseurs. Hungarian lilac, *S. josikaea*, is a tall and vigorous shrub with large glossy leaves and deep violet-mauve blossom. Persian lilac, *S. persica*, has narrow leaves and fragrant lavender-coloured flowers. Rouen lilac is probably a hybrid between the common and Persian kinds, despite its name of 'Sinensis', meaning Chinese! It is a glorious tall shrub that carries drooping trusses of large, fragrant, flowers of a deep rich lavender shade. Yunnan lilac, *S. yunnanensis*, is a Chinese species with sweet-scented pink flowers, which it opens on slender panicles in mid-June.

TAMARISKS, *Tamarix* species

Tamarisks are desert shrubs and small trees that come from the arid zones around the Mediterranean Sea. They draw their name from the Hebrew word *tamaris*, which also means a sweeping broom. In fact, they are excellent examples of the "broom-like" foliage found on our native broom shrub (*Cytisus scoparius*), and also on a great number of other woody plants that have to live under very dry conditions. All the tamarisk leaves are reduced to thin scales or needles which are closely pressed against the twigs. The advantage of this is that it reduces the loss of water from the whole plant. Tamarisks have, in addition, an amazing tolerance of salt, whether it reaches them as spray blown off the sea's waves, or is found in the soil. In a seaside garden they are invaluable for forming the first line of defence; they will grow right down on a shingle beach, as may be seen at Bognor in Sussex. Elsewhere they prove hardy and happy in any well-drained soil.

Tamarisks are sub-evergreen. Their twigs remain green well into winter and eventually small bits of them fade and are shed as rather untidy fragments, not as separate leaves. The feathery, pale-green foliage and reddish stems are very attractive, and provide an airy effect not given by any other tree. Tamarisk flowers are borne in little tufts near the tips of the leafy branches, about midsummer. They are pink in colour, and individually very small. Small brown berries, holding dry seeds, are ripened later, but attract no attention.

The species usually planted as a seaside tree is *Tamarix gallica*, which comes from south-west Europe. In gardens, *T. tetrandra*, which comes from the Mediterranean and has more showy plumes of bright pink flowers, is more usual. A third species, *T. pentandra*, does not flower until autumn; it then displays feathery masses of rose-pink flowers above its blue-green foliage.

Trachycarpus—see PALMS

YUCCA, *Yucca* species

The yuccas rank as trees because they develop a truly woody stem below their spreading clusters of greyish-green evergreen sword-shaped leaves. They come from the desert zones of the southern United States, Mexico, and Central America, and their leathery-textured, stout, wax-covered foliage is designed to store water under a very dry climate. The sharp edges and spines on their leaves discourage browsing animals. Yuccas belong to the lily family or Liliaceae, and their white flowers reveal this relationship. These flowers are carried on long upright stalks, in clusters, and droop downwards. There is a popular belief, luckily only half-true, that a yucca grows for seven years before blooming, blooms only once in its life, and dies as soon as it has set seed. What happens is that some specimens flower only at intervals of several summers, while a few, mainly overseas, do in fact exhaust all their reserves by setting seed—just as an annual plant does, and die after doing so. All yuccas need several years to become established, before they will flower.

Yuccas are grown where it is desired to create an effect of exotic sub-tropical vegetation, for their unusual form recalls at once the hot south-lands. All need dry, well-drained soil, and an open situation exposed to sunlight. Yuccas are most often seen as centre-pieces in small raised gardens; they dominate the scene so effectively that other trees and shrubs can scarcely be blended in with them.

There are many kinds of yucca that differ little in appearance, but a good deal in hardiness. *Yucca filamentosa*, from the south-eastern United States, is a "stemless" form in which the woody stem is so short that the leaf rosette appears to spring directly from the ground; it puts out side-growths at ground level and can be increased by transplanting them. This species sends up tall flower spikes, from three to five feet high, a few years after planting. The Adam's needle yucca, *Y. gloriosa*, comes from the same region and forms a small tree with a trunk up to eight feet high; this is topped by a tuft of straight stiff leaves, and bears on occasion a creamy-white flower spike four feet tall and a foot across. *Y. recurvifolia* is similar, but its leaves sweep down towards the ground; it has proved very resistant to town smoke. The grandest of the yuccas is the Californian *Y. elata*, which is hardy only in the mildest parts of the British Isles. It can grow twenty feet tall, topped when it flowers by a ten-foot flower spike, crowded for most of its length with large white blossoms.

17. Rose-tribe Trees and Shrubs

THE great natural tribe of plants called the Rose family, or Rosaceae, includes a large number of trees that are of major value for ornamental planting, as well as our main fruit trees. Very few of these grow large enough to yield timber; cherry wood and "fruit wood" obtained from pear trees are the only kinds commonly seen in commerce. In this book on tree planting for timber and ornament, we will not look deeply into the fruit-grower's craft, although his skills have an important bearing on the raising of decorative sorts of apples, cherries, and almond trees.

The Rose-tribe is one of the few groups of trees that consistently bear large and showy flowers to attract pollinating insects, and this makes it outstandingly valuable to the gardener. Most of its members also ripen large and showy fruits, which gives a second spell of interest in the autumn. There are one or two leading evergreens in its ranks, but in most species the foliage is deciduous, with attractive autumn colouring. The small size of the mature trees is also an advantage, for it results in a minimum of pruning.

Common features of all the many kinds of tree included in the Rose-tribe are, according to botanical theory, these: there are five sepals enclosing five petals, which are large and showy, and stand free from each other; within them comes a group of numerous stamens, and within these again an ovary composed of a single carpel, or of two to five carpels fused together. Abundant nectar is produced by nectaries at the base of the blossom, to attract the bees, and orchard trees are a leading source of nectar for honey-making. Cultivated varieties of Rose-tribe trees do not always follow this orthodox plan. For example, some sorts of double cherry have no stamens, ovary, or nectar, and set no seed; such sterile forms can only be increased by grafting, or by taking cuttings.

One of the fruit-grower's problems is the self-sterility of certain kinds of fruit tree. If all the trees in an orchard are of a single cultivar, they may fail to ripen fruit, because the pollen cannot effectively fertilise the ovules of trees of the same sort. The fruit grower gets over this by planting trees of another, proven kind at intervals through his orchard, and these trees, called "pollinators", provide effective pollen. Self-sterility is seldom a problem to the grower of ornamental varieties, who is not dependent on his fruit-crop anyway. Nor does he have to worry much about the periodicity of heavy fruit crops, which is a serious problem to the orchardist. Apples, plums, and cherries are apt to give a heavy crop one year, and no crop at all the next! Nothing will persuade them to be more careful with their food reserves—if the weather proves favourable they exhaust them in a bumper crop, and take two years to recover from it.

Fruit growers maintain their high yields with the aid of an exacting programme of spraying, to check insect pests and fungal diseases. The grower of ornamental fruit trees, with smaller returns in view, seldom has time for this. Happily, most of the decorative kinds are disease-resistant and suffer little from insect foes, though some maladies, including the silver-leaf disease of *Prunus*, may spread from the orchard to the shrubbery.

Most cultivated Rose-tribe trees are grafted, and fruit growers pay great attention to the stocks they use. The stock can affect the growth of the scion it supports, making it tall or short. It must also be compatible, which usually implies that it is a very closely-related tree. The scions are drawn from "foundation stock trees" of the fruiting kind. (Note that these "foundation stock trees" yield *scions*; another group of "foundation stock trees" is used to propagate *stocks*.) Because the scions are "adult" branches rather than "juvenile" ones, they start to flower and bear fruit at an early age. Ornamental trees are usually "grafted adults", and this maturity enables them to blossom within a year or two of planting out. If grafting is done on to a tall upright stem, the resulting tree is called a "standard"; but if it is done on a lower stem a "bush" results.

We shall not attempt to deal with the cultivated roses themselves in this chapter. They demand a book of their own, in fact a whole library. Some of the more vigorous briers can be handled like ordinary shrubs, being left to fend for themselves without the exacting tending and pruning that the rose usually demands—and rewards exceedingly. A few roses can be naturalised on woodland edges, and one of the toughest of these is the Ramanas rose, *Rosa rugosa*, which comes from Kamchatka, at the far north-eastern corner of Asia. This forms a much-branched clump of spiny stems, with long leaves compounded of many leaflets, and it bears large flowers of a striking mauve shade, that contrast with its bright golden stamens. Its fruit is large and conspicuous, being a flattened globe, coloured crimson-scarlet, tipped by long green persistent sepals.

THE PRUNUS GENUS

Many Rose-tribe trees are divided into genera according to the structure of their fruit. One of the largest genera is *Prunus*, which can be known by its large single stone within a soft pulpy fruit-mass. It includes several groups of trees distinguished further by the character of their foliage, flowers and fruit, and therefore best considered separately.

LAURELS, Evergreen *Prunus* species

The common laurel, or cherry laurel, *Prunus laurocerasus*, comes from the Balkans and Asia Minor, where it is well adapted to the Mediterranean climate. Its large, leathery, pale green and evergreen leaves make good use of sunlight during the winter rains, yet conserve moisture during the hot dry summers. Cherry laurel is tough and completely hardy, and will thrive on very dry soils, including thin ones over chalk. It makes an excellent evergreen hedge, and stands clipping well, though it needs ample room because of its bold branching. If clipped as a hedge it never flowers, but where it is allowed to grow taller it bears pretty spikes of white flowers, heavily scented with the smell of almond paste, and rich in nectar. These develop into small black cherries, which are no good to eat but soon attract the birds. A good bush for shrubberies, the sides of driveways, and as pheasant covert. The leaves, when crushed, have a strong smell of bitter almonds, due to minute amounts of poisonous hydrocyanic (or prussic) acid; they will poison insects if placed in a closed bottle and are sometimes used as "killers" by entomologists.

Portugal laurel, *P. lusitanica*, which comes from Portugal and southern Spain, is a similar bush but has a darker aspect. Its leaves are a very dark green, and its stems always have a reddish tinge. It never grows so vigorously as the cherry laurel, but is fully hardy and reliable. As it will stand deep shade, it can be planted below tall deciduous trees and will still thrive. If it is left unclipped, Portugal laurel forms a handsome tree which bears white hawthorn-scented blossoms, followed by purple stone-fruits.

ALMOND, *Prunus amygdalus* and allies

Almonds originate in the Near East, and are widely grown in southern lands for the delicious and nutritious kernels within their hard seed-stones. The outer coating of the seed is green, tough, and leathery, no good at all to eat. The almonds used in confectionery are obtained by cracking the hard, pitted stone that encloses them. The strains of almond that are grown in northern lands ripen seeds, but never yield a worthwhile crop. We grow them solely for their beauty and the cheerful surprise they give us when their pink blossoms burst from leafless twigs in early March. They herald the coming spring as no other tree can do, and then carry a pleasing crown of long, shining mid-green leaves all the summer through.

The common race is satisfactory, but exceptionally large rose-pink blossoms are borne on the cultivar 'Pollardii', which originated in Australia, about 1904, as a hybrid between almond and peach. Those who seek very early blossom should plant 'Praecox', for it opens pale pink flowers two weeks ahead of the type. There is a double-flowered strain called 'Roseo plena', with pink blossoms. There are also white almonds, which seem rather pale and pointless for a tree that glories in crisp, delightful pinks.

Dwarf almonds are comparatively new and rare. They are bushes for the border rather than real trees, though sometimes grown as standards. The dwarf Russian almond, *P. tenella*, forms a low shrub, rarely reaching four feet, and bears bright pink blossoms in April. The cultivar 'Fire Hill', also called 'Gessleriana', develops upright stems that are completely wreathed in rosy crimson flowers each April. *P. triloba*, which is usually grown in its double-flowered forms, 'Multiplex' or *flore-pleno*, carries bright-pink rosette-shaped flowers along its many branches during March and April. It is best treated as a climber, given some shelter and trained along a south-facing wall. The Chinese dwarf almond, *P. glandulosa*, forms a bush about four feet tall, and bears conspicuous, large single flowers, pink or white, early in April; there is a double white form called 'Alba plena', which blooms profusely.

PLUMS, *Prunus spinosa* and allies

Plums bear their large and showy flowers singly, not in clusters like those of the cherries. The common wild sloe or blackthorn, *P. spinosa*, is occasionally used to form hedges, but is frankly a very troublesome tree. It is apt to throw up a thicket of suckers from its roots, calling for repeated cutting back. Its white blossoms open on bare black twigs in a cold, late spring, but during a normal season they come out at the same time as the bright emerald green young leaves, making a delightful contrast. The bitter fruit, called the sloe, has a beautiful silvery blue sheen over its purple-black skin.

The common form is best admired in the hedgerow; for the garden there is a choice of two cultivars. 'Plena' bears double white flowers, while 'Purpurea' forms a compact bush with bronze-red leaves.

The Myrobalan plum, *P. cerasifera*, which comes from the Near East, has been widely used for spineless hedges, since it stands clipping well; its twigs have a peculiar shade of verdigris-green. If allowed to form a tree, it bears white blossoms followed by red or yellow "cherry-plums".

Two cultivars of this tree are very widely planted for their unusual, dark foliage, which makes a striking contrast with their bright pink flowers in spring. Both are hardy but not too vigorous in growth, and make excellent street or garden trees. The most popular is the copper-leaved plum, *P. cerasifera* 'Atropurpurea', which still appears in many lists as "*Prunus pissardi*", being so-called from its discovery by Monsieur Pissart, the French gardener employed by the Shah of Persia, in 1880. 'Nigra' has blackish purple foliage too dark for some people's taste, and opens its pink blossoms very early, before the leaves have expanded.

Prunus 'Blireiana', a hybrid between the copper-leaved plum and the Japanese apricot, *P. mume*, forms a small purple-foliaged tree that smothers its leafless branches with bright double pink flowers in late February. *P.* 'Cistena' the purple-leaf sand cherry, is an upright-branched shrub with deep red leaves, white blossoms, and blackish-purple fruits.

PEACH, *Prunus persica*

The luscious-fruited peach is a tree for warmer climes than we know, having originated, in all probability, in Persia. A few hardy strains will open their soft-skinned rose-and-yellow fruits when trained against a south-facing wall, but as a free-standing orchard tree the peach is unreliable even in southern England. Ornamental peaches, chosen for the gay glory of their flowers, can prove most rewarding trees in the milder south and west.

'Clara Meyer' bears large double carmine-rose flowers profusely in April. 'Windle's Weeping' is an unusual tree that bears broad leaves on drooping branches; it should be grown as a standard.

BIRD CHERRIES, *Prunus padus* and allies

The native bird cherry, *P. padus*, is seen at its best beside some madly-rushing Highland torrent in early June. It is common in Scotland, infrequent in Wales, and unknown in the south and east of Britain. The Bird cherries bear their snowy white blossoms in long open spikes, and they are followed by small black fruits—no good for people to eat, but relished by the wild birds. Three of the varieties merit a place in the garden. 'Albertii' grows strongly to form a pyramidal tree up to twenty-five feet tall, which flowers very freely. 'Watereri', also called 'Grandiflora', has still larger flowers and grows equally tall. From Korea comes the geographical form *seoulensis*, which opens welcome fresh green leaves in the dull days of February.

GEAN, *Prunus avium*

The gean is the common wild cherry of the northern European woods, where it makes a fine timber tree up to one hundred feet tall and twelve feet round. It makes a brave show of blossom when its snowy white flowers, grouped in bunches, open in May. As a rule, the leaves open at the same time, rather bronzed in colour, becoming dark green later. Exceptionally, when spring is late and cold, the flowers open on leafless branches, like some random fall of snow. The ordinary wild gean is occasionally planted in woodlands on the chalk hills of southern England, as a source of a valuable, beautifully figured brown timber, having a warm golden-green tinge, which is used for furniture and as a veneer. The double form 'Plena' is a magnificent tree for the larger garden; it grows tall and cannot easily be restrained by pruning. Both forms have an attractive purplish-brown bark, carrying prominent breathing pores. The dark red cherries of the wild gean have a large stone, with little flesh over it; they are sweet, but hardly worth gathering, though the wild birds relish them and soon strip the trees bare.

The gean is one of the parents of most garden cherries, which accounts for their considerable height as compared with other orchard trees. The sour cherry, or Morello, *P. cerasus*, is another ancestor of the cultivated races; it comes from Asia Minor and is sometimes found wild as a garden escape. Its variety 'Semperflorens' is occasionally cultivated as an ornamental tree, because of its engaging habit of opening flowers at intervals, all through spring and summer.

JAPANESE CHERRIES, *Prunus serrulata*, *P. subhirtella*, and allies

The gardeners of Japan, working over long centuries in total isolation from the West, have selected and developed a marvellous range of ornamental cherries. These are now available everywhere, as cultivars that often bear Japanese names. The brilliant outburst of bloom each spring is celebrated in Japan as a national festival. At Cherry Blossom Time everyone visits the parks and gardens to rejoice in the brief glory of pink, white, mauve or rosy-red flowers, massed in rich clusters on branches not yet fully hidden under foliage. One of the peculiar beauties of the Japanese cherries springs from the red, bronze or copper tints of the young leaves, contrasting with the floral colour; the gleaming bark is a further attraction.

So many separate kinds of Japanese cherries are stocked by nurserymen that here we can only describe a few of the best-known and most exciting cultivars. A good catalogue will enable buyers to find just what they feel best suits their need—or meets their mood. Nomenclature is confusing. Many cultivars have a botanically "correct" name, an old-established Japanese name, and a popular English name as well, so several of these synonyms are perforce included here. Most sorts have a well-defined flowering season, but for the group as a whole the total season runs from late March to mid-May. A careful choice will ensure a long spell of bloom, one kind succeeding another, and therefore the usual peak period—for southern England—is given also; farther north all kinds open later than stated.

Most popular of all is *P. serrulata* 'Kanzan' (late April) a very vigorous and reliable cherry with double pink flowers, carried in extravagant profusion. It pours all its reserves into blossoming, and never sets fruit. All that can be held against it is that it is perhaps *too* widely planted. Its sugar-candy pink is seen along every suburban road in late May, and there seems little to be gained in adding further examples when variety is so easily achieved by using other colours.

'Amanogawa' (May) holds a unique place for planting where space is limited, for example on a terrace. Springing from a low rootstock, it forms a slender upright column of one, two, or more thin stems which clothe themselves from head to foot in blush semi-double blossoms. It needs reasonable care, demanding both sunlight and side shelter, for its

PLATE 17 *Elms*

Above English elm, *Ulmus procera*, first planted along new hawthorn hedges by 'enclosing landlords' two centuries ago, has ever since maintained itself by sucker shoots from its roots. Tall trunks with billowing masses of foliage give shelter and grand-scale scenic effects.

Below Scots or wych elm, *Ulmus glabra*, never produces sucker shoots. Its branches spread widely from a single trunk, forming a graceful dome-shaped crown.

slender stems must not be exposed to the wind. Because it never spreads, people are apt to pop it in a corner and then neglect it, often allowing it only a square foot or so of soil between paving stones. Stronger competing shrubs or plants should always be cut back to give 'Amano-gawa' ample light; and a mulch of hop manure, applied every second winter, will maintain vigour where there is little soil for rooting.

In contrast of form, there are several cherries that weep gracefully, and these must be bought as rather expensive standards, to give them the necessary height. *P. yedoensis* 'Perpendens' (late March), also called 'Shidare Yoshino', is an exquisite drooping form with single, blush-white blossoms. *P. subhirtella* 'Pendula' (early April) the weeping spring cherry, opens multitudes of small pale pink flowers that smother its long, slender, drooping branches. *P. serrulata* 'Rosea' (late April), which is also called 'Kiku Shidare Zakura' or 'Cheal's Weeping' cherry, forms a small tree with arching branches that carry deep pink, very double blooms; its leaves are glossy.

The spring cherries are so named from their habit of flowering early, often in March. The typical race is *P. subhirtella*, with pink blossoms. Desirable cultivars are 'Fukubana' (late March) with semi-double rose-madder flowers borne in rich profusion; and 'Stellata' (early April) also called 'Pink Star', which has dainty pinkish-white star-shaped blossoms, and forms a small compact bush. The autumn cherry, which is also known as *P. subhirtella* 'Autumnalis', 'Jugatsu Zakura', or 'Miquel-iana', is remarkable for its long and unusual flowering period. In a warm district, given shelter, it will open semi-double white flowers at intervals right through the winter, from October to March. It has a pink-flowered form called 'Autumnalis Rosea'.

For those who prefer the chaste outlines of a single blossom to the thronged masses of petals in the double forms, *P. yedoensis* 'Yoshino' (late March) is an excellent choice; it has blush-white, almond-scented blooms, and grows vigorously. 'Yoshino Pink Form' is equally desirable for its lovely soft pink flowers.

PLATE 18 *Flowering trees*

Above left The American june-berry, *Amelanchier canadensis*, bears clouds of delicate white blossoms in April, before its leaves have fully spread. The maroon-purple berries ripen, as its name suggests, in June, and the foliage turns rich crimson in autumn.

Above right Handkerchief tree, *Davidia involucrata*, from China, drapes its branches with rows of white leafy bracts, recalling handkerchiefs, late in June. Also called dove tree, since these bracts suggest a flock of white-winged doves.

Below The white-flowered horse chestnut, *Aesculus hippocastanum*, from Asia Minor, bears stately spires of blossom, clear of its lustorous foliage, in May. Our boldest decorative tree, it needs ample space for an effective display.

ROWANS, WHITEBEAMS, and SERVICE TREES, *Sorbus* species

The genus *Sorbus* is made up of small Rose-tribe trees that bear white flowers in clusters, followed by bunches of brightly coloured berries— red, orange, yellow, or brown, that each hold several seeds. They are colourful trees, with fascinating leaf patterns and gay autumn tints.

The rowan, *Sorbus aucuparia*, is also called the mountain ash, because its compound leaf resembles that of an ash tree, though there are no other points of resemblance. It is a very hardy tree, growing far up the hills in Scotland, Scandinavia, and the Alps. Its wood is tough, but the stems are never stout enough for modern commercial use.

Rowan trees have ancient associations with magic and witchcraft. Their Norse name, *rφn*, is also the root of the word "rune", for the old runic alphabet, and numerals were carved on rowan wood before stone was used. Rowans were planted around every Scottish croft to ward off evil, and to-day the easiest way to find deserted steadings, which have crumbled down to ruined ruckles of stones, is to look out for lone rowans surviving on the Highland braes.

Rowan bears a compound leaf, in which every leaflet has an indented edge, which gives a feathery appearance to the foliage as a whole. It blooms each May without fail, and by late July its crown is decked with orange berries that persist until the birds strip them from the trees in late autumn. There are yellow-berried races such as 'Xanthocarpa' (also called 'Fructu-luteo' and 'Fifeana'). 'Beissneri' bears red berries and has finely-cut fern-like foliage. The berries are too sour for eating raw, but if plenty of sugar is used they can be made into rowan jelly, a spicy seasoning for venison or winged game. *S. cashmeriana*, a Himalayan species, has elegantly-divided leaves and carries *white* berries far into the winter.

Whitebeam, *Sorbus aria*, still bears an old Saxon name meaning "white tree", from the colour of its foliage. It has a very local distribution, being common on chalk downs but scarcely seen anywhere else. In spring, the young leaves, which are oval in shape and have toothed edges, are clad all over in white hairs, which help to check water loss on the very dry soils where whitebeam grows. This whiteness is very vivid on the under side, and there is a spell in early May when the goblet-shaped clusters of up-turned, half-open leaves look like white lilies on the grey branches. Gradually the upper surface of each leaf turns to mid-green, but even when the leaves fade in autumn their undersides remain white. Fallen leaves show an odd contrast of white and brown. Whitebeam flowers are white, and larger than those of rowan; the fruits are also larger but equally bitter, while the tree as a whole is more robust.

There are several unusual cultivars or hybrid forms of whitebeam, which are more often seen in gardens than is the wild tree. Swedish whitebeam, *S. intermedia*, which is occasionally found growing naturally in Scotland, is generally held to be a cross between common whitebeam and rowan. Its leaf lies part-way between the two, being neither simple nor compound, but deeply lobed. Its fruits are bright red. It makes a pleasing small tree and has the great merit of being quite unaffected by town smoke; it will even thrive in the heart of Glasgow. The Fontainebleau whitebeam, *S. latifolia*, is a more vigorous cultivar that grows to timber size, and demands a roomy spot. Its leaves are broad, with two lobes to their lower part, and the fruits are large and orange-brown.

The oddly-named service trees differ from the rest of the *Sorbus* genus in bearing fruit that is sweet enough for people to eat raw, even though the berries are too small to merit plucking. "Service" is derived from a Latin name for beer, *cerevisia*, which in turn comes from *ceres* and *vis*, meaning "the strength of the grain". The explanation is that the berries really *were* added to beer to give it a cider-like flavour. True service tree, *Sorbus domestica*, is sometimes grown for its feathery foliage of compound leaves, and for its pretty fruits. These may be apple-shaped or pear-shaped.

The wild service tree, *S. torminalis*, is a remarkable small tree that is found as a rarity in southern England and Wales, but more commonly on the Continent. Its bark is hawthorn-like, divided into small squares, and this gives it the local name of "chequers tree". The leaf is shaped just like that of a maple, with five lobes and a smooth edge. The berries are brown, with a gritty pulp that tastes like a pear. An intriguing tree to plant if you want to puzzle your visitors, but seldom stocked by commercial nurserymen.

Vilmorin's service tree, *S. vilmorinii*, which is named after a great French nursery firm, comes from China and has recently gained a well-merited place as a small ornamental tree. It grows about fifteen feet tall, and has dark green, fern-like, finely cut foliage. The white flowers are succeeded by bright red berries in autumn, but as winter comes on the fruit colour changes to white, tinted with rose-pink.

Another genus of Rose-tribe shrubs closely allied to *Sorbus* is that called *Aronia*. They are closely related, and have given rise to several hybrids, classed by botanists in the hybrid genus *Sorbaronia*. Typically, they bear clusters of white flowers, followed by black berries, and have much-dissected leaves that give fine autumn colours.

PEARS, *Pyrus* species

Pears differ from apples in the well-known elongated oval or "pear-shape" of their fruit, which is convex or bulging at the base, instead of concave or hollowed-out. Their flowers are always white, and appear a whole fortnight ahead of pink-tinged apple blossom. Pears flower freely and so early that they deserve a place in the ornamental park, as well as the orchard. Pear wood is a warm reddish-brown, very even-grained and stable. At one time it was widely used for mathematical instruments, such as T-squares and set-squares used by draughtsmen, but it has now been supplanted by plastics. Wood carvers still use it for sculpture, under the name of "fruitwood".

The European wild pear, *Pyrus communis*, forms a tall slender tree, with a grey bark broken into small squares. Its brown twigs carry occasional long spines, but all the cultivated races are spineless. The fruit is hard and woody, mellowing only slowly to something just palatable when raw. Wild pear makes a brave show of white blossom on the edge of a wood in late April.

The willow-leaved weeping pear, *P. salicifolia* 'Pendula', is a remarkably ornamental tree from the Balkans, with silvery, willow-like leaves and cream-coloured blossoms. It is usually grown as a standard tree, reaching twenty feet in height. The branches stretch out from the trunk and then descend, to end in silvery-green downy twigs, which bear scattered spines. The fruits are oddly shaped, small, and green, and they do not ripen until they have fallen. Willow-leaved pear is increased by grafting, as it seldom comes true from seed.

APPLES, *Malus* species

The enormous range of cultivated apples has originated from a few species of small trees that grow wild in Europe and Asia. Hybrids have arisen between them, and these, together with chance variations that give a more delicious fruit, a brighter flower, or a new foliage colour, have been seized upon by zealous gardeners and propagated by grafting on to common stocks. To simplify this profusion of varieties, we can classify all the apples into five groups—

1. Wild species.
2. "Crab-apples" grown as ornamental trees.
3. Eating apples.
4. Cooking apples.
5. Cider apples, grown for making alcoholic drinks.

Here we shall only be concerned with the first two groups, though an orchard of the more useful apples is a thing of beauty in its own right.

The common wild crab-apples, *Malus sylvestris* and *M. pumila*, form low trees with a rounded crown and spiny branches. The "crab" in their name is derived from an old Norse word, *skrab*, signifying a scrubby tree. The fruits are small, round, yellow, and very sour, but they make the best crab-apple jelly, with a sharper tang than the cultivated kinds that are often used instead. The very tough wood was once used in cudgels, for driving fence stakes, or as mallet heads. Wild crabs give a gay display of blossom; the flowers appear pink in bud, for their outer surfaces are a rose-red shade; as they open this colour blends harmoniously with the whiteness of their inner side. Any crabs that chance to grow along hedgerows or forest rides merit preservation for this spring enchantment, as well as for the food their fruits provide for game birds and deer in autumn. But in the face of the competition from so many cultivars, the native wild sorts will seldom be chosen for garden planting.

The species *M. pumila* is distinguished from *M. sylvestris* only by its downy shoots, buds, leaves, flower stalks and sepals. It comes from south-eastern Europe, but has become established in English woods as an escape from gardens. A variety of *M. pumila* called 'Niedzwetzkyana', which comes from Turkestan, has its leaves, young wood, flowers, and even the flesh of the fruit tinged with red. It is an ancestor of most of the red and purple-leaved crabs so widely grown to-day.

Ornamental crab-apples have three attractive features—blossom, fruit, and foliage colour. Some give satisfaction with all three; others merit selection for a peculiar excellence in a single feature. Crab-apples, like roses, have now hybridised so freely that it is futile to try to unravel their ancestry.

Malus baccata mandschurica, the Manchurian crab, bears fragrant white flowers and red fruits like cherries.

M. 'Purpurea' is the finest purple-leaved kind, which also bears crimson-purple fruits. Its flowers are rosy crimson. *M.* 'Eleyi' resembles it closely, but flowers earlier. There is also a weeping form, *M.* 'Purpurea Pendula'.

From Japan comes *M.* 'Floribunda', the Japanese crab, which carries a profusion of crimson buds and ice-pink blossoms on long arching stems.

'Gibb's Golden Gage' bears waxy, translucent, golden fruits. 'Golden Hornet' has similar decorative apples, which ornament the branches long after leaf-fall. 'John Downie' ranks as a "fruiting crab", because its large, oval, bright yellow-and-red apples are sweet enough for eating, and have a refreshing flavour; it also makes a delicious jelly; nevertheless it is usually grown solely for ornament.

The 'Robusta' crabs have cherry-like fruits without calyx cups at the base. 'Red Siberian' and 'Yellow Siberian' are striking kinds named after their fruit colours.

The Iowa crab, *M. ioensis*, has beautiful large fragrant flowers, up to two inches across, white in colour with a pinkish tinge. It has a double-flowered form called *M. ioenis* 'Flora Pleno'. Another fine double-flowered form is *M. coronaria* 'Charlottae' which bears violet-scented, shell-pink flowers, and broad leaves that develop rich autumn hues.

The 'Wisley Crab' is a handsome and vigorous cultivar with large bronze-red leaves, big wine-red fragrant blossoms, and large deep-red fruits. 'Lemoinei' excels it in the brightness of red blossom and bears a profusion of reddish-purple autumn fruit.

HAWTHORNS, *Crataegus* species

There are two kinds of hawthorn native to northern Europe, including the British Isles. Common hawthorn, *Crataegus monogyna*, has only a single stone in its fruit, and only one style on the ovary at the heart of the flower. Midland hawthorn, *C. oxyacanthoides* (also called *C. oxyacantha* in nursery catalogues), has *two* little stones in each fruit, and *two* styles on its central ovary. Both species are the parents of very hardy and reliable

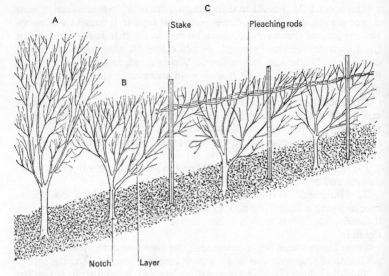

FIGURE 76. Laying and pleaching a hawthorn hedge. A, untouched hedge, becoming gappy. B, hedge bush trimmed to proper height, and main stem *laid*, by cutting it half through at notch near foot, then bending it sideways. At C, stakes have been added to give rigidity; *pleaching rods* have been intertwined along hedge top to stop *layers* jumping out of place.

ornamental trees that bear both bright flowers and handsome autumn fruits. Other names for the hawthorns are may tree, from the month in which they blossom, whitethorn in contrast to the darker twigged black-thorn, and quickthorn or quick from their use in the living or "quick" hedges that gradually replaced the old "dead-hedges" around enclosed fields. Their close growth and spiny branches enable them to hold animals back.

Hedges are usually formed from common hawthorn, raised from seed. The berries are first stored for eighteen months in damp sand, which causes their pulp to rot away. Only after this long dormant spell are they ready to sprout in the seedbeds. One-year-old seedlings are transplanted to another bed, where they spend a further year or two before being used, at a height of nine to eighteen inches, to form a young hedge. They are usually planted in a double row, nine inches apart, with nine inches between two ranks, the plants being staggered so that each falls opposite a gap in the next row. A young hedge needs protection from grazing livestock for several years, and at first it also needs weeding. After about six years the young hedge is formed into a stock-proof barrier by pruning, cutting and laying the longer shoots in a sloping direction, then adding upright stakes every three feet or so, and finally, by "pleaching". Pleaching means the intertwining of long hazel rods to form a horizontal border running from one upright stake to the next, so that the "cut and laid" shoots of the living hedge cannot spring up and get out of place.

An established hedge has to be re-cut and re-laid every five years or so, to keep it low and stockproof. Despite the work involved, hedges provide a cheaper and better field boundary than any wall or fence. They give shelter to livestock from sun and wind, and they slow down the wind's speed without creating troublesome eddies.

Hawthorns trimmed as a hedge seldom flower, but blossom is always plentiful on free-standing trees along hedges or in fields, and on patches of hawthorn scrub. Birds that eat the red haws, or berries, swallow the seeds and void them later. Natural seedlings form thickets of scrub, through which oaks and other trees slowly force their way up to form new woodlands.

Cultivated hawthorns are usually cultivars of the Midland kind, *C. oxyacanthoides*. They are grafted on stocks of ordinary races, or else increased by cuttings, which take easily. Those who prefer single flowers, grouped in rich clusters, may like to grow the pink 'Rosea' or the scarlet 'Punicea'. With the densely-petalled double kinds you have the choice of 'Plena', double white, 'Rosea Flore Pleno' double pink, or 'Coccinea Flore Pleno' which is also known as 'Paul's Scarlet Thorn'.

Common hawthorn, *C. monogyna*, is more noteworthy for curious variations of form, fruit or flowering-time. The Glastonbury thorn, known as 'Biflora' or 'Praecox', is supposed to have originated as a remarkable tree planted—according to ancient legend—in Roman times by Joseph of Arimathea where Glastonbury Abbey now stands in Somerset. It bears flower clusters on bare branches during mild spells in midwinter, even on Christmas Day, but these seldom yield fruit. It flowers again in May, the normal season, and this flower-spell results in berries.

'Aurea' bears yellow berries, 'Pteridifolia' has much-divided fernlike leaves, and 'Inermis Compacta' is an odd dwarf race with stout, stiff branches that carry no spines at all. 'Pendula' has weeping branches that carry white flowers, and there is a similar pink-flowered form called 'Pendula Rosea'. 'Stricta', also called 'Fastigiata', grows upright like a Lombardy poplar, while 'Tortuosa' is a curiosity with twisted, corkscrew-like branches.

Those who like a particularly choice hawthorn, out of the ordinary, should plant the oriental thorn, *Crataegus orientalis*, from China. This forms a small tree with greyish, downy, deeply-cut leaves, and downy shoots. The white flowers are packed into close bunches, and are delightfully fragrant. The haws are highly decorative, being large, appleshaped, and coloured vermilion, tinted with orange; they hang on the tree far into the winter.

A great variety of foreign species, hybrids, and cultivars of thorns have been planted, at one time or another, in European and American gardens.

Some have little merit beyond rarity or curiosity. The cockspur thorn, *C. crus-galli*, which comes from North America, bears remarkably long and stout thorns like the spurs of a fighting cock.

Two hybrids are particularly favoured by park planters in industrial districts, because they remain vigorous despite the worst conditions of poor soil and polluted air. Both have simple leaves, rather like those of a plum, and this puzzles many people who do not immediately recognise them as hawthorns. Plum-leaved thorn, *C. prunifolia*, bears vicious spines that discourage vandals. It has tough leathery leaves that are dull green above, paler below; they turn to a brilliant crimson in the autumn. Its flowers are white and fragrant. The large haws that follow them are downy-surfaced and bright red, but fall at the same time as the leaves—in October.

Lavallées thorn, a hybrid bearing the names 'Lavallei' and also 'Carrierei', is the second tough character. It is spineless, and its leaves turn from dark green to bronzy shades before they fall. The ripe haws are oval, orange-red flushed with a deeper red; they persist on the bare branches all through the winter.

The thorn-medlar, or Smith's medlar, *Crataego-mespilus grandiflora*, is a fascinating natural hybrid between the common medlar and a wild hawthorn, which has been cultivated since the eighteenth century. The tree looks just like a hawthorn in form and bark pattern, but its leaves have the oblong shape of the medlar's, while the flowers, exceptionally large and showy, are borne in clusters of four or five only. The fruit is olive green, ripening to russet, but is no good to eat.

PLATE 19   *Dwarf conifers for small spaces*

Above left Creeping blue spruce, *Picea pungens* variety *procumbens*, spreads widely close to ground level and is best placed in the rock garden.

Above right A slow growing form of the typical blue spruce, *Picea pungens*, which maintains a compact pyramidal crown of shining blue-green foliage.

Centre leftt Creeping savin, *Juniperus sabina* variety *prostrata*, is a hardy juniper from the Alps now widely planted for permanent low cover, for example, on the 'islands' of traffic roundabouts where views must remain clear.

Centre right This conical, slow growing form of the common juniper, known as *Juniperus communis* variety *compressa*, is an ideal kind for the small rockery. It bears silvery-blue foliage and suggests a far taller tree.

Below left Snake spruce, *Picea abies* variety *reflexa*, is a freak form of the common Norway spruce in which the branches hug the main stem, which bends down to ground level; the branches then continue to spread out over the ground surface.

Below right Conical spruce, *Picea albertiana conica*, comes from the cold tundra of northern Canada, where its close-packed foliage and conical outline enable it to withstand drying winds without undue water loss. It makes a fascinating tree for either the rock garden or the small formal bed, but grows very slowly. These four-foot specimens in Bedgebury Pinetum, Kent, are thirty years old.

COTONEASTERS, *Cotoneaster* species

The colourful cotoneasters are shrubs or creeping woody plants that come, for the most part, from the mountains of China and the Himalayas. Their old name of 'rockspray' aptly suggests their typical growth form, trailing over cliffs in rugged gorges, and the shorter kinds are most at home on the rockery or the wall garden. Some are evergreen, and are appreciated for a year-round tapestry of dark glossy foliage. Others are deciduous, but delight us with bright crimson or deep orange tints before their leaves fall. None has showy flowers, but most display attractive red or orange berries, borne profusely all along their trailing or arching stems.

Cotoneaster simonsii, a semi-evergreen from the Khasia Hills of eastern India, has deservedly become a popular hedge shrub, for it forms a dense screen ornamented each autumn with large orange berries. *C. adpressus* is a good rock-garden trailer, with bright-red fruits and small leaves that turn scarlet before they fall. *C. microphyllus*, from the Himalayas, has small, dark, glossy *evergreen* leaves and large red berries; it is often used for draping over walls. *C. salicifolius*, a "willow-leaved" species, is a tall evergreen shrub which bears heavy crops of berries every autumn. *C. tomentosus* from the European Alps is an upright shrub with round leaves that are white and downy beneath, and large brick-red fruits. *C. integerrimus*, a small shrub with pink flowers and red berries, is a rare British native, recorded only from the Welsh coast.

FIRETHORNS, *Pyracantha* species

The "fire" that causes these hardy shrubs or wall trees to glow comes from their berries rather than their flowers or foliage. They are adaptable to quite small borders beside houses, and tolerate sunless situations such as the foot of a north-facing wall. Each spring they put forth long vigorous shoots bearing glossy leaves, dark green above, paler below, oval in outline, and pleasingly irregular in size. These are followed by clusters

PLATE 20   *Propagation: two contrasting methods*

Above Grafting the scion of a selected strain of Corsican pine on to a rootstock of Scots pine. The operator, who is using the 'veneer side graft method', is tying the scion to the stock with raffia. Before so doing, he carefully prepared the two living surfaces that must meet and join. Grafting is widely employed for increasing stocks of selected strains of decorative trees, particularly broadleaves. Here it is applied to a valuable, but scarce timber-producing strain needed for tree breeding.

Below Young trees for timber production are usually raised from seed. This seedbed in a South Wales forest nursery has been prepared by cultivating the soil, throwing up a raised bed with the plough, firming down with a roller and finally marking shallow drills. While one girl spreads conifer seed along each drill, others cover the seed with coarse lime-free sand to protect it from drought, birds and mice until it germinates, three weeks later.

of small, hawthorn-like, white blossoms. The bunches of berries, green at first, ripen in early August to vivid scarlet or orange; they hang on the twigs until late autumn, when they are stripped by the birds. *P. coccinea*, from southern Europe, is the commonest species; there are several handsome cultivars.

JAPANESE QUINCES, *Chaenomeles* species

These shrubs or wall trees are well-known to everyone for the unrivalled brilliance of their early spring blossoms, which open in March on bare branches. The leaves are glossy green and leathery, and look as though they should be evergreen, but they fall each autumn. Most varieties ripen large yellow, fragrant quince-like fruits, which are quite edible and make a good jam, though few growers trouble to harvest them. The Japanese quinces have suffered more than most plants from name changes; many people still call them by their old name of *Cydonia japonica*, often shortened to "Japonica". Botanists now regard them as cultivars or varieties of *Chaenomeles japonica* and *C. speciosa*. The typical *C. japonica* (once called *C. maulei*) is hard to beat for a bright orange-flame shade; *C. speciosa* 'Cardinalis' is a striking deep salmon pink. Other colours range from white to crimson, scarlet, vermilion, and brick red, and some forms have double blossoms.

JUNE-BERRY, *Amelanchier* species Plate 18a, p. 245.

The *Amelanchiers* are hardy shrubs or small trees that become thoroughly at home in a shrubbery or even along a woodland ride. They bear white flowers in long racemes, opening in spring before their leaves are fully open. The whole bush then looks as though it had been swept by a snowstorm, and this has earned the group their common name of "Snowy Mespilus". They ripen their fruits early—hence the name of june-berry; their clustered berries are usually purple or black. When autumn comes their soft green foliage assumes gorgeous crimson and orange tints. *Amelanchier canadensis*, from eastern Canada, is the best known species. *A. ovalis*, which grows wild in central Europe, has its young shoots clad in white woolly down.

MEDLAR, *Mespilus germanica*

The medlar is a quaint tree that is occasionally found in cottage gardens or along hedgerows as an escape from cultivation; its original wild home was probably in the Balkans. In form it is much-branched and apt to grow crookedly; some strains bear stout thorns, others are spineless. The leaves have a peculiar oblong shape, rather like an oval that has been extended too far. The large solitary flowers have five white petals, interspaced with very long, slender, green sepals; there are many golden stamens and five styles, and the centre of the flower, where abundant nectar is secreted to attract honey-bees, consists of a golden, downy, disc.

Medlar fruits ripen from green to brown late in autumn. They are easily known by the long sepals at their tip, surrounding a curious hollow cavity. The flesh of the fruit is too hard and sour for eating until it begins to decay; then, for a day or two, it softens and yields a delicious, unusual flavour. A tasty jelly is made from it, which enables people to relish the medlar's taste at any time of year.

QUINCE, *Cydonia oblonga*

Quince, like medlar, is really a tree for the collector of old-world orchard or cottage-garden kinds, having unusual charms. It makes a small much-branched tree with grey bark and oval leaves. In May it opens large, solitary, white or pink blossoms, having elegant petals that are narrower towards their base; the narrow sepals are sharply reflexed. In October the resulting fruit ripens from green to yellow. In shape it is most peculiar, looking like a distorted pear, or—in some varieties—a mis-shapen apple. Quince fruits have a pungent, piquant, flavour and a scent of amazing strength; if stored near apples or pears they will pass on this fragrance, and small slices of the flesh give an unusual and attractive flavour to preserves or apple-pie. Quinces are too strongly-flavoured to be eaten raw, but they make an excellent jam or jelly.

STRANVAESIA DAVIDIANA

This widely-planted low shrub comes from China. It spreads vigorously, forming low thickets, which make it a good space-filler. The leaves are lance-shaped, long and leathery, and are evergreen. In autumn, a pro-portion of them fade, turning bright red, and these hang for long on the branches, giving a lively contrast with the persisting green foliage. The flowers, borne in bunches, are white, and the ensuing branches of crimson berries are carried on long stalks, well clear of the leaves.

SHRUBBY CINQUEFOILS, *Potentilla* species

Though the shrubby cinquefoils, as their name suggests, are never more than low bushes, they merit inclusion here for their profusion of blossom. Each separate flower resembles a large single rose—indeed many people mistake them for roses. Their flowers—nearly always yellow but occas-ionally white, appear in constant succession from late spring to late autumn. The foliage, made up of many small five-lobed leaflets, is finely textured and green or greyish-green in colour. Most of the cultivated strains are forms of *Potentilla fruticosa*, a European species which can be found wild—though rarely—on limestone rocks in north-east England and western Ireland.

SPIRAEAS, *Spiraea* and *Sorbaria* species

The spiraeas are now ranked in two genera, those with simple leaves being called *Spiraea*, and those with feathery-compound leaves *Sorbaria*. Both are easily known by the plume-like flower-heads, built up of very numerous small blossoms. The majority are low shrubs or woody herbaceous plants, most at home in the flower bed. The willow-leaved spiraea, *Spiraea salicifolia*, has become naturalised on many country estates; it is a low shrub with erect shoots carrying plumes of bright pink flowers in June and July. One of the few really woody kinds is the tree spiraea, *Sorbaria arborea*, from China; this reaches a height of fifteen feet, bears large pinnate leaves, and displays enormous banners of cream-coloured blossoms in late summer.

18. Broadleaved Shrubs and Hedge Bushes

In a book on trees there can only be space for a broad and brief account of the leading shrubs that are likely to be used in any scheme of ornamental planting, or in hedgerows and shelterbelts. But it is essential to include them, partly because there can be no clear-cut dividing line between "shrub" and "tree", but mainly because trees are rarely planted in isolation, save in large timber-producing forests. Without a foil of bushes to set off the taller and grander display of arboreal foliage and blossom, a tree planting programme can give, with the passage of time, a bare-stemmed and starkly geometrical result. It can also create unpleasantly windswept and draughty surroundings, because the open spaces below the trees will not only fail to stop air currents, but will actually carry an accelerated air stream. Hence every tree planter should know a good deal about the shrubs and bushes that ought to be planted as part of any landscape scheme.

In their wild state, the woody plants that we grow as garden shrubs form a low underwood in taller forests. They never develop single tall upright trunks that claim a place in the upper canopy of the timber trees. This is fortunate for two practical reasons—they need little pruning to restrain them, and they can thrive in a great deal of shade.

Because shrubs are long-lived, and need relatively little space, it is possible to accommodate a bewildering variety of species and cultivars in a garden of only moderate size. Plant collectors have combed the forests of all the temperate and sub-tropical lands to enrich our shrubberies, while plant breeders market numerous fresh cultivars every year. A complete collection is beyond the resources of the world's largest arboretum, and if a complete list *could* be made, it would become out of date in a few seasons. Here we have selected thirty-three of the leading genera, with representative species for each, as a pathfinder through a thicket of bushes that all claim a tree-lover's attention. All the taller shrubs that grow wild in the British Isles have been brought in, and the arrangement is alphabetical, by the name of each genus. Those shrubs that belong to the Rose-tribe, or Rosaceae, are described in Chapter 17, page 239, while the bushy conifers are dealt with in Chapter 20, page 296.

Most of the shrubs in common cultivation are grown "on their own roots", which means that they are propagated from seed, or by cuttings or layers, rather than by grafting or budding. This means that every shoot, no matter how low down it emerges, will be true to its kind and name. Rhododendrons, azaleas, and camellias are major exceptions to this practice; their cultivars, and even their species, are usually budded

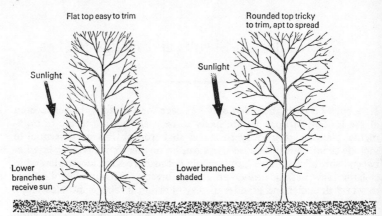

FIGURE 77. Hedge-trimming shown by cross-sections. *Left*, good work, hedge tapers upwards, all branches get sunlight, foliage is held almost to ground level. *Right*, bad work, top of hedge has been allowed to spread, making trimming difficult; bottom branches, deprived of light, are feeble and foliage is gappy.

on to stocks of the commonest suitable kind, and only these stocks are grown from seed.

Certain widely planted shrubs are capable of establishing themselves in the woodlands and becoming naturalised. The thickets they produce are often welcomed by the gamekeeper because they provide self-sustaining covert for pheasants. But if the process gets out of hand those shrubs that run wild can prove a serious embarrassment to the forester. They may prevent the easy establishment of timber trees and prove almost impossible to eradicate except at great cost. Rhododendrons are the most troublesome invaders.

AUCUBA, *Aucuba japonica*

Most people know the common variegated form of this shrub, the cultivar 'Variegata', by its dark, evergreen, paired leaves which are curiously mottled with gold. It was widely planted in Victorian times, as it suited the prevailing fashion for intricate patterns, and withstood the worst coal smoke of the busiest towns. If not too harshly treated or pruned, it occasionally bears quaint little purplish-brown flowers, which are followed by clusters of bright scarlet berries. This particular race is always female, for certain aucuba cultivars are of one sex only; they are increased by cutting or by layering.

In the wild Japanese shrub, which is rarely seen in cultivation, the leaves are green throughout. A good all-green variety is 'Longifolia' which bears slender bright-green leaves that create a sub-tropical effect;

it is available in both sexes, and the female race bears abundant berries. 'Crotonoides' has large broad leaves, densely mottled with gold, and looks even more exotic; this kind, too, can be obtained either as a male or as a female shrub.

BARBERRIES, *Berberis* species

The word "barberry" means the "barbed berry (bush)", and along the twigs of every barberry you will find these barbs—sharp spines, always in threes, at the base of every leaf. This is a most useful feature for recognising a shrub as a member of the very varied *Berber* ۱ genus. Typically, the barberries form dense bushes built up of countless long thin and flexible branches that arch over, building up a low oval form. Some are evergreen, and are valued for deep glossy green foliage, in view the whole year through. Others lose their leaves in winter, and at that season show only their bare, fawn-coloured, spine-bearing twigs; most of these deciduous barberries give a brilliant display of autumn colour.

A few barberries bear really showy flowers, yellow, orange or red, carried in neat clusters. Most have attractive berries, in a whole range of colours, which linger until the birds find them just ripe to eat. When you choose a barberry, from among the multitude offered by nurserymen, you must keep in mind all these possible attractions of foliage, flower and fruit. The native species of Britain and northern Europe, *Berberis vulgaris*, is rarely cultivated, since it has no special merits; it is a deciduous bush with small golden flowers and red berries.

One of the best of the evergreens is *B. darwinii*, which comes from Chile. Its flowers are deep orange, and its autumn berries resemble small blue plums covered with waxy bloom. *B. stenophylla*, a related evergreen, has boldly arching branches carrying drooping clusters of large yellow flowers which open early in April. *B. thunbergii*, a deciduous species, forms a compact bush with red and yellow flowers. Each autumn it flames with fiery orange as its leaves fade, while its scarlet berries enhance the impression of a "burning bush". Its variety 'Atropurpurea' has purple foliage all the summer through, giving a unique colour that can occasionally be placed most effectively in landscape work, but is dull in the mass.

Most of the barberries make good hedge shrubs, if you can stand their prickles!

BUDDLEIAS, *Buddleia* species

About the year 1890, the great Irish botanist and plant collector, Augustine Henry, when exploring in the Chinese province of Hupeh, encountered a low shrub with arching branches and compound leaves, which bore marvellous spikes of purple blossom. He introduced it to Europe, and there it proved a hardy and reliable flowering shrub that will readily become naturalised on waste land, especially where the soil holds ample lime. Given sunlight, it flowers freely, and its nectar-rich blossoms have a peculiar attraction for certain kinds of brilliantly-patterned butterflies, notably Red Admirals, Tortoiseshells and Peacocks; for this reason it is sometimes called the butterfly bush. Plant breeders have developed a number of more boldly coloured cultivars of the wild buddleia. Among the best are 'Royal Red', 'Empire Blue', 'Black Knight' and 'White Cloud'—all aptly described by their names. These are increased by cuttings which strike readily. They are cultivars or hybrids of the wild Chinese species, *Buddleia davidii*. The name of the genus commemorates Adam Buddle, an early English botanist, while *davidii* records Père David, a French missionary who discovered many rare plants and animals in China.

The golden-ball buddleia, *B. globosa*, also called the orange-ball tree, is a distinct species which comes from Chile. In habit and foliage it resembles the purple-flowered kinds, but its flowers are very distinct. They open in May, in tight, round globular clusters, and are bright orange-yellow in colour.

BOX, *Buxus sempervirens*

Box is a neat little evergreen tree that grows on dry limestone sites in the hills of southern and central Europe. Its natural range extends to England, but here it is a very scarce and local tree; it is well established as an undershrub below oaks on the chalk soil of Box Hill in Surrey, and has also been found wild at Box near Bath, in the Cotswold Hills of Gloucestershire, and near Chequers in the Chilterns. The wild form has a slender trunk with a grey bark, patterned in squares. It opens small greenish-white flowers in May, some being male, others female. The autumn seedpods are papery capsules with curious horned tips, holding small black seeds. Natural seedlings are occasionally found on Box Hill. Box wood is remarkably hard, heavy, and dense, with an even texture and a bright orange-yellow colour; it is used for wood carving, mathematical instruments, and the finest of wood engraving blocks. Nowadays the small amount actually used is imported from Turkey.

Box leaves are small, oval, glossy mid-green above and paler below, and are ranked in pairs along slender twigs. They stand dense shade and remain healthy and green even when closely crowded together. This makes box highly suitable for neat, low, close-clipped hedges, and also for topiary work; it is one of the few broadleaved evergreens that can endure the close training required. It can also be kept very low, and box hedges only one foot in height are often featured in formal gardens. Box is perfectly happy on lime-rich soils, but dislikes town smoke. For the low edges of formal beds a special strain called 'Suffruticosa' is generally used; this is increased by dividing the clumps, whereas other strains are propagated by cuttings. There are also golden-leaved and silver-edged varieties of box, but none is particularly attractive.

BROOMS, *Cytisus*, *Sarothamnus* and *Spartium* species

Brooms are sub-evergreen shrubs which have greatly-reduced leaves and are adapted to life in dry places. Their twigs are tough and switch-like, and can in fact be used as sweeping brooms. They remain green all through the year and do much of the work of photosynthesis that, in a normal plant, is done by the leaves. Some strains of broom never open leaves, but in others, such as our common wild broom, small leaves with three leaflets appear at joints along the twigs in late spring. Broom flowers are shaped like those of sweet peas, and they are borne very profusely. The seed is a hard black grain, which develops within a black pod like that of a garden pea; as the pod becomes fully ripe it splits open with a sharp "pop", twisting as it does so and sending the seeds flying. Many brooms are short-lived shrubs, and after a few seasons you must be ready to replace them with fresh seedlings. The choicer kinds are grafted on a common stock.

The wild broom, *Sarothamnus scoparius*, is rather a local shrub, being common only on dry sandy soils, in districts with much summer sun and little rain, such as the east coast of Scotland. It makes a brilliant blaze of gold at midsummer, and is worth encouraging on wayside embankments. Unfortunately it is inflammable, so it cannot safely be left to flourish on the forester's firebreaks.

Spanish broom, *Spartium junceum*, forms a bold bush with whip-like branches of a glossy dark green, which throws out bright bunches of large, deep yellow, richly scented flowers in July. It thrives on chalk soils and tolerates salt winds.

The more decorative garden brooms are usually catalogued by nurserymen under the genus *Cytisus*; many are hybrids, and often have the common wild broom as one parent. 'Andreanus' has crimson and yellow flowers and gives a blaze of contrasting colours. The Portugal broom, *Cytisus albus*, gives a profusion of white blossoms in May and June. Pineapple broom, *C. battandieri*, is a striking small tree or wall shrub from Morocco, which has silky grey laburnum-shaped leaves, and opens cone-shaped torches of pineapple-scented gold yellow flowers each July, but it is not very hardy.

CAMELLIAS, *Camellia* species

The camellias are evergreen undershrubs that grow wild in the steaming hillside forests of Japan, China and the Indian Himalayas. They belong to the same family as the tea bush, which grows in the same region and has a like habit of growth. In early spring camellias open delightfully symmetrical flowers with soft velvety petals, in shades or patterns of white, pink, and red. Under cultivation, camellias were first treated as greenhouse plants, and some species and cultivars are in fact only hardy under glass. Recently there has been a vogue for so-called hardy camellias. At best they are only half-hardy in northern Europe.

If you have a garden near the west or south coasts of Britain, are able to provide light overhead or side shelter from tall trees, and are on a lime-free soil, then it is worth while to experiment with these delectable trees out of doors; but they prove disappointing where those conditions cannot be met. It is particularly necessary to provide shelter for the tender flower buds in early spring.

The wealth of attractive cultivars offered by nurserymen, who propagate them by cuttings, is apt to give a false impression of easy cultivation. Most of the fascinating named sorts are derived from the Japanese species, *Camellia japonica*, which is hardier than the Chinese kinds.

CEANOTHUS, *Ceanothus* species

These very lovely blue-flowered shrubs come from the Pacific Coast of North America, and are sometimes called Californian lilacs. Most are sub-evergreen, holding part of their foliage through the winter. Unfortunately they are not fully hardy in the north. Away from the coast they need the protection of a south-facing wall and even so may fail to survive an exceptionally severe winter. One of the best of the many species and cultivars available is 'Autumnal Blue', which flowers twice a year—in June and again in October.

DOGWOODS, *Cornus* species

Dogwoods are one of the few groups of shrubs that always carry their leaves in opposite pairs. Their name has no connection with four-legged dogs, but is derived from "dag wood", a "dag" being a spike or skewer. The same root is found in our word "dagger" and also in the timber handler's "dog-spike", but the largest dog you can cut from a dogwood bush will only make a meat-skewer. The Latin name, *Cornus*, implies a horny-textured wood. The petals of a dogwood flower form a neat tube, and there are always four sepals, four petals, and four stamens. The fruit is a berry.

The common wild dogwood of northern Europe, *Cornus sanguinea*, is very common on chalk and lime-rich soils, though scarce anywhere else. Its specific name, *sanguinea*, means blood-red, and aptly describes the colour of the twigs, and also that of its fading leaves in autumn. Its elegant white flowers are carried erect in little clusters and open in June. The black berries are quite an attraction in October, but they are soon stripped by the birds, who void the seeds later and so enable the dogwood to spread rapidly over waste land, especially on chalk downs. If you are a forester establishing a young plantation, or a nature conservationist trying to maintain the lowlier plants of a chalk grassland, you may find wild dogwood a nuisance. It coppices readily when cut back, and sends up suckers from its roots. But in other circumstances it is useful, for it binds the earth of exposed cuttings made through the chalk. It is pretty enough to merit preservation along hedgerows, though more showy kinds are likely to be chosen for the garden.

Cornelian cherry, *Cornus mas*, is a very neat small tree, native to southern Europe, that is grown in gardens for its appealing spring flowers. These are very small and would be ignored in summer, but when they open their golden bells in the bleak days of February, they are welcomed as harbingers of returning warmth. The fruit, which resembles a golden cherry, ripens in September and though small is quite good to eat. Plate 16b, p. 221,

Certain dogwoods, which bear only small and unattractive flowers, attract insects to them by displaying four large petal-shaped bracts at the base of each bloom. One of these is the North American flowering dogwood, *Cornus florida*, which opens creamy white bracts in May; its autumn foliage glows with a warm rosy pink. The Japanese dogwood, *Cornus kousa*, shows still larger white bracts somewhat later, in June, and ripens curious strawberry-shaped pink fruits, on long stalks, in late July.

Other dogwoods are grown for the brilliant colours of their leafless stems, as a winter-garden feature. These are treated as coppice, being cut back in spring each year to promote a vigorous growth of bushy shoots. Red-barked dogwood, *C. alba*, from the Far East has rich red stems, while its variety *sibirica*, the Westonbirt dogwood, is a brilliant crimson. Yellow-barked dogwood, *C. stolonifera flaviramea*, provides a strongly contrasting colour.

HAZEL, *Corylus avellana*

Hazel is a very common wild shrub in most parts of the British Isles, and also in the neighbouring countries of western Europe. It sometimes forms a small tree with a much-branched woody stem, but is far more often found as a bush with numerous stems springing from a low stump or stool. In England a huge area of hazel coppice was deliberately planted centuries ago so that it could be cut over at intervals of seven years. It provided a steady crop of thin poles, for every year one seventh of each great coppice was harvested. These poles were worked up by craftsmen into hurdles, temporary hedges, or wattles for wattle-and-daub house walls, or they were used for rough basketry, fish traps, or barrel hoops. Some went for pea-sticks, bean rods, thatching spars or clothes props, while much was used as firewood on cottagers' hearths or in bakers' ovens.

To-day most of these uses have ceased, and skilled craftsmen are so few that foresters can find no profitable sale for hazel stems. So they are busy converting the old coppices to crops of taller timber trees. Removal of the old coppice growth has proved exceptionally difficult. Hazel springs up vigorously from stumps, and its tangle of branches is almost indestructible by mechanical means; it will not burn, and it stands a great deal of shade. The practical solution is the poisoning of the unwanted stools by using one of the modern synthetic brushkillers, such as commercial formulations of "2, 4, 5 T". Hazel must be killed outright before the land is free for planting with a useful and profitable kind of tree.

In the garden, hazel is occasionally grown as a nut-bearer, to yield either the round cob nut or the oval filbert, according to its species. The wild tree is a capricious cropper, and it is therefore a good investment to buy an orchard strain such as the 'Emperor Cob' or the 'White-skinned Filbert'. Filberts have their fruit in a long tubular cup, and belong to a separate species, *Corylus maxima*, native to the Balkans. Nut trees need fertile soil and ample space to ensure full sunlight. Branches should be thinned out at intervals of a few years, and pruning back may be needed to restrain the shrub in size.

Four kinds of decorative hazel are occasionally cultivated in gardens. The best is purple-leaf filbert, *Corylus maxima* 'Purpurea', which forms a dense shapely bush of a dark purple-green shade. In contrast, there is a golden-leaf cobnut, *C. avellana* 'Aurea'. The tree hazel, *C. colurna*, comes from Turkey and is planted mainly for its bright show of golden lambs-tail male catkins in spring, before the leaves open. Female catkins of hazel are seldom noticed, as they look just like buds, with only a tuft of red stigmas protruding to mark them out. Corkscrew hazel, *C.* 'Contorta', is a freak with wildly twisted twigs; it gives an excellent catkin display whilst still leafless in February.

Cytisus—see BROOMS

DAPHNE, *Daphne* species

Few people suspect that the exquisite little daphne bush, *Daphne mezereum*, is a native British plant. It grows, as a rarity, in a few lime-stone woods in west and north-west England. Though never more than a few feet high, it always assumes a tree-like form, and makes the ideal "treelet" for the very small garden. It is deciduous, with grey stems that suddenly come alight with bright lilac-pink, fragrant blossoms in the cold dull days of February. Later there comes a show of bright red berries, holding the seeds from which this tiny tree is raised. A note of caution here, the berries are poisonous, and so are the bark and leaves of most of the daphnes.

The well-known cultivar *Daphne* 'Somerset', also called 'Burk-woodi', is a semi-evergreen of more bushy habit. It bears pink, fragrant flowers all along its branches in May and June. The spurge laurel, *D. laureola*, grows wild in beechwoods on chalk and limestone in southern England. It has dark green glossy evergreen leaves, and stands deep shade. The flowers are greenish yellow, and the berries black, but spurge laurel is usually grown for its decorative foliage, very effective in floral arrangements.

ESCALLONIAS, *Escallonia* species

South America is the homeland of all these wonderful evergreens, which have become deservedly popular in all seaside districts because of their resistance to salt winds. Their leathery leaves, of a glossy dark green hue, are packed closely on branches that can easily be clipped and trained to make a dense screen or hedge. This is particularly valuable where flowering plants, less tolerant of salt spray or wind, have to be given protection near the seafront.

Escallonia macrantha, which comes from Chile and has rosy crimson flowers set deeply amid its foliage, as though for protection, is the most widely planted species. There are now many cultivars derived from selections and cross-breeding, and these bear larger flowers on panicles set clear of the foliage, where they can be better seen. 'Slieve Donard', which has large blooms of apple-blossom pink, is among the best-known.

Little is known about the hardiness of escallonias inland, though they certainly succeed in the warmer southern districts. They are readily increased by cuttings.

SPINDLE TREES, *Euonymus* species Plate 16f, p. 221.

The native spindle tree, *Euonymus europaeus*, is found wild on lime-rich soils, and is sometimes cherished in gardens; its wood was once used for spindles in hand spinning. It has slender grey-barked stems and square green twigs, carrying pretty oval leaves. Each bush is either male or female, and the spindle tree can prove disappointing in cultivation since both are needed for cross-pollination. If you are lucky enough to have a fertile female tree, its autumn fruits are a real joy; the little pods ripen to a brilliant pink, then open to reveal the bright orange of the fleshy seed coat. At the same time the leaves are turning to rich crimson, orange, or purple-brown tints, the whole providing a wonderful symphony of autumn colour. *E. latifolius*, from central Europe, grows more vigorously and bears larger fruits.

In contrast, the shrub that commonly goes by the name of "euonymus" is the dullest plant known to man! It was formerly widely planted in seaside gardens, before escallonias came in, because it tolerates sea salt. Botanically it is *Euonymus japonicus*, and no doubt it bears flowers and fruits when allowed to reach full size in Japan. But when treated as a hedge in Britain its dark green leathery foliage does little except trap smoke, dirt, and dust. Some very ugly variegated strains, allegedly silver or gold, are available for those who really relish the horrific.

FATSIA, *Fatsia japonica*

This peculiar shrub from the rain-drenched mountains of Japan has been widely planted because it conveys, better than any other hardy plant, the atmosphere of a tropical jungle. It is an evergreen hygrophyte, or rain-loving plant, with leathery leaves adapted to shed surplus water. These leaves are exceptionally large, up to eighteen inches each way, and are divided into about nine broad lobes. The flowers, which are borne in upright umbels, are green and inconspicuous; they are just like those of an ivy plant, to which this singular bush is closely related. Fatsia was very popular in Victorian times, as it succeeds in small villa gardens, resisting smoke and also sea winds; it was also cultivated in conservatories, and as a pot plant. Fatsia was formerly called *Aralia*, and also, mistakenly, the "castor oil plant". Though now out of fashion, it can still be planted to good effect. It is increased by cuttings, struck in a warm greenhouse.

FORSYTHIA, *Forsythia* species Plate 16a, p. 221.

The forsythias or golden-bells are undershrubs from China which have the engaging habit of opening a wealth of bright golden, bell-shaped blossoms on leafless twigs in March. This cheerful welcome to the spring is followed by a spread of dark green willow-shaped leaves that remain rather dull, though pleasing enough, all summer through. Forsythias grow vigorously and on fertile ground need constant pruning back to hold them within bounds. If any of their long trailing stems strikes the ground, it is apt to layer naturally, striking root and forming a fresh bush. Alternatively, forsythias are easily increased by cuttings.

Many of the strains of forsythia cultivated to-day are hybrids between two eastern species, *Forsythia suspensa* and *F. viridissima*, and collectively they are called *F. intermedia*. 'Lynwood Gold' is one of the most free-flowering, carrying many broad-petalled blossoms along its branches. 'Beatrice Farrand' has the largest blooms of all, one inch across, in an unusual deep yellow colour. 'Arnold Dwarf' remains low, but spreads widely.

ALDER BUCKTHORN, *Frangula alnus*

Alder buckthorn is a low undershrub that grows on damp, peaty soils, in the woodlands of Britain and western Europe. Its greenish flowers are seldom noticed, but the berries, which ripen through green to red and then black, are a pretty sight in autumn. Charcoal made from the wood of the small stems is used for the highest grade of gunpowder.

FUCHSIAS, *Fuchsia* species

Fuchsias, which come from South and Central America, and also from New Zealand, are among the most beautiful and distinctive of flowering shrubs. Many kinds are too delicate to succeed outside a cool greenhouse, but happily there is one species, with many varieties, that is reasonably hardy. This is *Fuchsia magellanica* from Chile, which in its typical form has drooping flowers with red sepals around a violet tube of petals, with pretty red stamens protruding beyond. The fruit, a black oval berry holding many seeds, is seldom gathered, though it is quite good to eat. In the mild coastal districts of Cornwall, Wales and Ireland, this fuchsia grows rampantly and even runs wild on walls and waste ground; it can there be trained into a very decorative and unusual hedge. Though fuchsias are not evergreens, they have a long season in leaf; the leaves are grouped, in threes, along red stalks that always look attractive; flowers appear continuously all the summer through, while the neat oval flower buds have a charm all their own.

In colder inland or eastern districts fuchsias behave quite differently. It is hopeless to try to persuade them to make hedges or to reach real shrub size. Each winter the frost cuts them back to ground level. Yet they are seldom killed, and next summer they reappear like a herbaceous perennial, growing rapidly and flowering freely before being cut back again.

A half-hardy species, the New Zealand *F. excorticata*, reaches small-tree size in the mildest districts, but will not succeed elsewhere. Its leaves are borne singly, it has woody stems with flaking bark, and it opens purplish flowers which are yellow at the base.

GARRYA ELLIPTICA

Garrya elliptica is a highly decorative evergreen from California, which flowers in midwinter; hardy in most districts, it grows vigorously in south-western gardens. Male bushes are usually planted, because they become festooned with long grey conspicuous catkins that make a brave show in a dull season. The catkins of female bushes are less obvious, but they are well worth growing for their hanging chains of black berries.

WITCH HAZELS, *Hamamelis* species Plate 16d, p. 221.

Though unrelated to the common hazel, the witch hazel does have a hazel-like leaf and it forms a bush of similar size and shape. Its charm lies in its early outburst of gay little golden flowers, which appear in December in the milder districts, though delayed till February in colder spots. Each flower has strap-shaped petals, springing from a reddish centre. In the Chinese species, *Hamamelis mollis*, the petals are straight, but in the Japanese kind, *H. japonica*, they are curiously waved, and the central calyx is purple. Several named cultivars are hybrids between these two. Oil of witch hazel, used in eye lotions, comes from the North American species, *H. virginiana*, which flowers in autumn, before leaf-fall.

HIBISCUS, *Hibiscus* species

To tropical gardeners the hibiscus is as familiar as the rose. It flourishes in climates that the rose cannot endure, and gives a succession of beautiful blossoms, of every hue and combination of colour, the whole year round. Few species are hardy enough to thrive in Europe, and the only one commonly grown is *Hibiscus syriacus*; this, despite its name, comes from India and China. It forms an open much-branched shrub with pale green leaves, daintily toothed and lobed. Late in the summer, towards August, the oval buds along the stems burst to release beautiful bell-shaped flowers, like hollyhocks, and this bold show is often prolonged well into October. But it may not happen every year, for this opulent sub-tropical shrub is always greedy for sunshine to ripen its wood and renew its food reserves, and it needs a few years to become established. Blue is its finest colour, but plant breeders have now developed cultivars in white, pink and purple, some having maroon or purple centres; there are also impressive double kinds.

SEA BUCKTHORN, *Hippophaë rhamnoides*

Sea buckthorn is really a desert shrub, adapted to grow on very dry or salty soils. Its leaves are long and slender, and clad in silver scales intended to check water loss. The twigs are very spiny, to discourage every sort of animal, from a goat to a camel, from eating it. In winter, when the bush is leafless, its spiny character is well seen. A thicket is almost impenetrable, for sea buckthorn spreads by sending up suckers from its straggling roots. This makes it particularly valuable for binding together drifting sand dunes, or the shingle of river banks. Each bush has flowers of one sex only. Female bushes bear attractive orange-coloured berries in autumn, and these are eagerly sought by migrating birds, which may void the seeds many miles from the place where they ate the fruit. In this way, no doubt, sea buckthorn has spread from Asian deserts to alpine stream-banks, and to the sandy shores of Denmark and England.

Sea buckthorn is frequently planted in seaside parks and gardens, or on sand dunes, because of its tolerance of salt winds and drought. Occasionally it is grown in inland gardens, for the unusual silvery colour of its slender leaves.

PRIVETS, *Ligustrum* species

The native wild privet, *Ligustrum vulgare*, is a sub-evergreen shrub with leaves that change from glossy dark-green to dull orange-brown in midwinter, and then fall. It has white flowers in June—pretty but too small to be showy, and long spikes of glossy black berries in late autumn. Wild privet turns up naturally along hedgerows, especially on chalk downs in the southern counties, and is sometimes planted to give covert and food for pheasants.

Hedges are always made with the Japanese oval-leaf privet, *L. ovalifolium*, which is fully evergreen and has a very neat habit of growth. The monotony of miles of suburban privet hedges has often been deplored, and is happily much less oppressive than hitherto. It arose when our towns were far smokier than they are to-day. Privet, which is easily increased by cuttings, proved the best evergreen for withstanding both soot and infinitely repeated cuttings. Golden privet, the cultivar 'Aureomarginatum', has green centres to its otherwise yellow leaves, and gives a brighter effect, yet never loses an aura of artificiality. If you let a privet hedge grow up, the leading stems will eventually become small trees, twenty feet tall, which bear plumes of white flowers, spoilt by a rather sickly smell; the wood is white, horny-textured, and very hard.

WINTER JASMINE, *Jasminum nudiflorum*

This exquisite winter-flowering shrub, which is usually grown as a climber against a south-facing wall, can also be treated as a free-standing bush. The long whip-like green branches build up into a dome, which bears bright yellow tube-shaped flowers on bare twigs in the shortest days of winter. Elegant three-lobed leaves follow in the spring. Winter jasmine, which comes from China, is fully hardy and is easily increased by allowing twigs to touch the soil and take root.

HEDGE HONEYSUCKLE, *Lonicera nitida*

Most members of the genus *Lonicera* are climbers or shrubs with fragrant flowers and gay yellow berries, but the hedge honeysuckle seldom gives us either. It is easily the best shrub for a really fine and dense evergreen hedge, which will stand any degree of close clipping. It comes from China and is readily propagated by cuttings. If allowed to grow tall, it forms a graceful shrub with small flowers and translucent, lilac-purple berries.

MAHONIA, *Mahonia* species

The mahonias are low evergreen shrubs, resembling barberries, but having all their leaves pinnately compound, and lacking spines on their stems. The genus is named after Bernard M. Mahon, an American horticulturist. *Mahonia aquifolium*, which comes from western North America, has been widely planted as game covert on many English estates. It forms dense thickets, spreads readily from sucker shoots, and is quite happy below the shade of broadleaved trees. The rich yellow flowers, which open early in spring in long racemes, are followed by bunches of very decorative purplish-black berries; the glossy dark green leaves often turn scarlet in winter, but do not fall.

For the garden, a finer choice is the Japanese *M. japonica*, which has remarkably large pinnate evergreen leaves and an early spring display of lemon-yellow flowers in drooping racemes; like most shrubs that bloom before winter has really gone, it needs some shelter to lessen damage to flowerbuds. *M. bealeii* is similar, but carries its flower-spikes, which open in February, erect; I have found it hardy and vigorous on thin soil over chalk in an exceptionally cold district. Both these ornamental mahonias have blossoms shaped like lilies-of-the-valley, with the same delicious scent.

MOCK ORANGE, *Philadelphus* species

These lovely white-flowered shrubs are also called "orange blossom" and "syringa"; the latter name is confusing, as it is also the Latin name for the lilac genus. There are two foundation species, *Philadelphus coronarius* from southern Europe and *P. microphyllus* from Colorado and neighbouring states in North America. Most of the cultivars grown to-day are hybrids between these too, but some are descended from Chinese or Japanese species. All are tall branching shrubs, with white blossoms which open profusely in June and July. Their fragrance, as well as their shape, recalls the true orange blossom, which cannot be raised outdoors in northern Europe. 'Belle Etoile', which has very fragrant flowers, white save for a maroon flush at the centre, is one of the best single-flowered strains; 'Virginal' is the finest double-flowered kind. The mock oranges bloom most freely after hard cutting back of old growth after flowering has ceased; this encourages the young shoots that will carry next year's flowers. They are easily increased by cuttings.

PURGING BUCKTHORN, *Rhamnus cathartica*

Purging buckthorn is a quaint shrub or small tree that springs up from bird-spread seeds on chalk downs, and sometimes gets included in hedges. Its small, neat, oval leaves are deciduous, and appear in pairs. There are three kinds of shoots—ordinary long ones, spiny ones that account for the "thorn" in its name, and short ones that are curiously ribbed like the horns of a roebuck, which explains the "buck". The flowers are very small and green, and each bush carries flowers of one sex only. Female bushes bear attractive clusters of small glossy black berries in the autumn; these berries are purgative and were once widely used in herbal medicine.

RHODODENDRONS AND AZALEAS, *Rhododendron* species

A few years ago botanists decided that two groups of very widely-grown flowering shrubs, that had hitherto enjoyed separate generic names—*Rhododendron* and *Azalea*, must henceforth be grouped in the former genus only. Gardeners and nurserymen have found this lumping together very inconvenient. They have a clear conception of rhododendrons as large evergreen shrubs with clusters of big bell-shaped flowers grouped closely together in crowded upright spikes. Azaleas, by contrast, are smaller bushes with open inflorescences, and in many species the leaves fall each autumn, after first turning to lustrous shades of orange, brown and russet. So most nurserymen continue to divide the genus, in their catalogues, into the two well-established sections of *Rhododendron* and *Azalea*.

Most of the species in this big genus hybridise readily. Innumerable hybrids and cultivars have been raised and marketed by plant breeders, and one or another of these is more likely to be chosen for garden planting than an original wild kind. A good catalogue will bewilder you with its wide scope for choice, and bedazzle you with its coloured pictures, for rhododendrons can now be obtained in every hue of the rainbow. These delectable kinds are easily propagated by budding on to common stocks, which are raised from seed. In this brief account we can only mention the common members of each group, which are likely to be naturalised in woodlands.

No sort of rhododendron or azalea will thrive on a chalk or lime-rich soil. Treatment with any soil-modifying medium is quite useless when one is growing deep-rooted shrubs, though it may possibly work with shallower-rooted plants. The roots of these shrubs must be stopped, by a physical barrier, from going down into the underlying lime-rich layers, while alkaline water must likewise be kept away from them. This means in practice that you must either be content to grow the shrubs in tubs, or else sink a strong permanent container, made of concrete, into the ground to isolate a large body of soil. Drainage holes must be provided, and the container must be filled with a lime-free acid soil including peat. The ordinary geological map, by the way, is not a good guide to surface soils; many areas mapped as "chalk" have a thick layer of sand, clay or gravel over them, and heaths and rhododendrons are perfectly happy in such soils. Those lucky people who claim "We grow lovely rhododendrons although we are on chalk," are really growing them in an utterly different medium.

People usually associate rhododendrons with the Himalayas and western China, where adventurous plant hunters found many of the choicest kinds. But the common or pontic rhododendron flourishes much nearer home, throughout Turkey and the neighbouring lands. Its scientific name of *Rhododendron ponticum* means "the tree of Rhodes from the land of Pontus", a region south of the Black Sea. It is a typical Mediterranean evergreen, and like most of that group is fully hardy in north-west Europe. It was introduced to Britain in 1763, grown first as a precious garden bush, and later naturalised on a vast scale in the shrubberies of every country estate, bar those on the lime-rich soils. Its virtues are its hardihood, toughness, evergreen foliage, and display of lilac blossoms every June; it provides good low shelter, both for people and pheasants.

Unfortunately, in mild western and southern coastal districts, from North-west Scotland down to Land's End, rhododendron soon runs completely wild. Seedlings spring up everywhere from the very fine seeds, and soon grow up into impenetrable thickets wherein no planted tree, useful or ornamental, can hope to survive. Rhododendron resists all the usual economic chemical weedkillers, and if you attack it with bull-dozers you simply churn it up into masses of stumps that sprout again, plus thousands of cuttings that take root. The only way in which the forester can regain control of the situation is to nurse up, at high cost, a crop of conifers that cast a dense shade. Douglas fir or western hemlock will eventually kill out the invading rhododendron, but pines or any broadleaved tree merely encourage its growth by their light shade.

The common naturalised azalea is nowadays called *Rhododendron luteum;* it was once called "*Azalea pontica*", because it, too, comes from the Caucasus and the land of Pontus. It bears pretty yellow flowers, very sweet-scented, in May, and the autumn colours of its deciduous leaves are rich shades of crimson, purple, and orange. The evergreen azaleas, such as the Kurume hybrids, originate from low shrubs found high on the mountains of Japan.

FLOWERING CURRANT, *Ribes sanguineum*

All the common currant bushes bear flowers, but one species has won the name of "flowering currant" because it opens blooms of a vivid rose-red shade in April before its leaves are fully expanded. It comes from western North America, and was very generally planted in Victorian times because it was one of the few shrubs then known that flowered so early. It has also a fine disregard for town smoke. Some people find its colour irritating, yet it has often struck the only cheerful note in a drab industrial landscape. Its currants, which are black with a bluish bloom, are too small to be worth eating. Golden-foliaged forms such as 'Brocklebank', double-flowered ones like 'Plenum', and large-blossomed strains like 'King Edward VII' are now available.

There are also many other species of *Ribes* that have claimed a place in the shrubbery for beauty of flower or fruit. The cultivated gooseberry, *Ribes grossularia*, the red currant, *R. rubrum*, and the black currant, *R. nigrum*, can all be found occasionally as wild or naturalised shrubs in the woods, but none has any ornamental merit.

Sarothamnus—see BROOMS

Spartium—see BROOMS

SNOWBERRY, *Symphoricarpus albus*

The snowberry, native to North America, has been widely planted in British woodlands as pheasant covert. It is now quite naturalised and spreads freely both by its underground stems and its seed. Snowberry flourishes on woodland fringes, or below light-foliaged trees, and sends up a thicket of twiggy stems, carrying oval, pale green leaves and very small pink flowers. The berry, which is smooth and white, looks just like a little snowball; it ripens in autumn and hangs on the leafless twigs all winter through. Bare twigs holding berries are often plucked for indoor decoration or flower arrangements. The cultivar 'Laevigatus' has large berries like marbles. Birds eat them, people don't.

GORSE, *Ulex* species

Three kinds of gorse, also called furze or whin, grow wild in Britain and western Europe. All are evergreens that have had their leaves transformed into spines, and this enables them to resist browsing by sheep, cattle, and deer. Their greyish-green stems and spine leaves are covered in a waxy coating to check water loss, and this makes them highly inflammable. Foresters find wild gorse a troublesome weed, costly and tiresome to cut back from young trees, and dangerous because it brings with it a high risk of heath fires. Farmers hate to see it spreading over pasture land. But lovers of scenery, and artists, are enthralled by its brilliant blazes of bold yellow blossom, spread luxuriantly over landscapes of brown heather, rolling away towards hazy blue hills.

Recently, landscapists have taken an interest in the gorse as ornamental bushes, good for covering bare dry banks, even those near the sea. Common gorse, *Ulex europaeus*, flowers most freely from February to May but is seldom without the odd flower all round the year. Western gorse, *U. gallii*, is smaller, more spreading, and has its main flowering spell in autumn. Dwarf gorse, *U. nanus*, makes a compact bush only a few feet high. There is also a very effective double gorse, 'Flore Pleno' which is a cultivar of the common kind.

Though gorses are weeds on waste land, when cultivated they prove hard to raise. Seed is sown in pots and covered a quarter of an inch deep; then the seeds are "scorched" by lighting a fire of wood-wool or shavings on top of the soil; next they are watered with lukewarm water to promote germination. This curious heat treatment is in line with the forester's experience that gorse seed stays dormant in the soil for very many years, and only springs to life after a forest or heath fire. Cultivated gorse bushes cannot stand transplanting with bare roots; they have to be moved at once from the pot to their final position.

VIBURNUMS, *Viburnum* species

The *Viburnum* genus consists of low shrubs, some evergreen, others not, which grow wild in the woodlands of the Northern Hemisphere, right across Europe, Asia and North America. All have their leaves in opposite pairs, and tube-shaped flowers carried erect in flattish bunches; their fruits and berries ripen from green, through red, to black. Over fifty species are in garden cultivation with at least as many varieties, so it is only possible to describe the most popular ones here. Viburnums usually have "naked" buds, not enclosed within the usual scales; hence you can see the form of leaf and flower all through winter, long before they are due to open. Most kinds have white flowers, usually very fragrant.

Wayfaring tree, *Viburnum lantana*, is very common on chalk hills, but rare anywhere else. It is easily known because its stems and leaves are clad in a white woolly down, which helps to lessen water loss on very dry soils. In winter its slender brown downy twigs, ending in large naked buds, are very distinctive. These twigs are pliable, tough and hard to break; they are sometimes used for tying brushwood and account, with the whitish twigs and foliage, for the tree's old English name of "hoar withy". In June the wayfaring tree opens conspicuous clusters of white flowers. These are followed in autumn by attractive berries—green, white, red and finally black at various stages of ripening. Alas! if you gather them for display indoors you will be disgusted by their smell of rotting fruit.

Guelder rose, *Viburnum opulus*, is so called because its best-known variety, the snowball tree, was first cultivated in the Gelderland province of Holland. The wild bush, which grows sparingly in woods on many soils, is attractive enough to merit its well-established planting in gardens. The elegant leaves are five lobed, and become a bright orange every autumn. The umbels of white flowers have large-petalled sterile flowers all round the rim, with smaller fertile flowers at the centre. In autumn the red, translucent berries glow like gems, hanging on the twigs well into winter and becoming more conspicuous as the leaves fall.

Snowball tree, *V. opulus* 'Sterile', is a freak Guelder rose with every flower in the umbel completely sterile; the flowers thus form a white ball. Since they never set seed, there are no gay autumn berries, and the tree has to be propagated by layering.

V. carlesii, which comes from Korea, is the finest of many introduced species; its pink buds expand into large clusters of sweetly scented blossoms in April and May. *V.* 'Burkwoodi', a hybrid raised from it, is sub-evergreen in the milder parts of the country and bears fragrant blossoms even earlier, from February onwards to April. *V. rhytido-phyllum*, from China, is grown mainly for its large evergreen leaves, which are deeply wrinkled and give a hint of tropical luxuriance; it has white flowers and large bunches of berries, first red, then ripening to black.

Viburnum fragrans, another Chinese species, is widely grown for its engaging habit of bearing flower clusters through the depths of winter, from November to February. These open in little groups on bare leafless twigs, and are as sweet-scented as the name suggests. Laurustinus, *V. tinus*, by contrast, is an *evergreen* winter-flowering kind, which comes from the Mediterranean region. Its dark green, glossy leaves provide a fitting background for its small clusters of white blossoms, which are pink when in bud, and pleasantly scented. Laurustinus is fairly hardy, but its flowers benefit from side shelter. It can stand a great deal of shade, and tolerates both smoke and sea winds.

19. Tall Forest Conifers

THE coniferous or cone-bearing trees play the leading part in present-day planting for timber production, though they are less important in landscape work. Nearly all of them are evergreen and this means that they are unsuited to planting in or near industrial towns and cities where the air is polluted by smoke and fumes; the larches are the only common conifers that lose their leaves in winter, but even they are unhappy in smoky surroundings.

All conifer timber is known as *softwood*, although one or two conifer woods, such as pitch pine, are quite hard. It is this relative softness, as compared with the *hardwood* of the broadleaved trees, that has ensured the much wider use of conifer timber in modern industry. Timber-users to-day want a material that is easily handled and has *moderate* strength; work that calls for great strength is entrusted to metal or concrete. Because the fibres of softwoods are longer than those of hardwoods, the paper-makers always prefer the coniferous softwoods, which ensures their use in an enormous modern industry that consumes two-fifths of the world's timber harvest. Conifer crops yield larger volumes of timber in a lesser number of years than do the broadleaved trees. They thrive on poor land unsuited to food production, and under harder climates All these facts explain why commercial timber growers, and national forest authorities, nowadays concentrate their efforts on conifer planting.

The conifers include mighty Californian redwoods and wellingtonias which are the world's tallest and largest trees. Most of them, when skilfully grown and tended in open surroundings, develop an unmatched grace of form and line, the outcome of centuries of evolution towards a natural life form adapted to the play of sunlight, wind, rain and snow. Wherever the air is clear enough, they make magnificent garden trees, but space must be available too, for most of them are intolerant of pruning and promptly die if lopped or topped.

Some, but not all, conifers show a marked periodicity of growth in their main stems and major branches. A whorl of side shoots is produced each spring from a node, which marks the close of the previous season's growth. The section of a trunk or branch between these points, called an *internode*, bears no side shoots, or only small ones.

The naming of conifers is a puzzle to the non-botanist, because many foreign kinds have been introduced and are now widely grown both in garden and forest. All the conifers have a general resemblance to each other, and at some time or another people have called most kinds "fir". In timber-growing and gardening it is essential to be more precise. Luckily, there is close agreement between British and American practice in the choice of English names for each botanical genus, while most of the genera can easily be told apart by their foliage alone.

A brief note on these identification features is therefore given for each genus. The first point to notice is whether the leaves stand out clearly from the twigs as distinct *needles*, as in the pines and spruces. Alternatively, they may hug the twig, for a part or all of their length, so hiding it; such leaves, found in the cypresses and their allies, are called *scale-leaves*.

PINES, *Pinus* species Plates 3b; 4a; 6a.

The true pines are easily known because their *needles* are nearly always grouped in *twos*, *threes*, or *fives*; other arrangements are found only on the early shoots of very young seedlings. All pines are evergreen, and their needles are tough and leathery. The number of needles in each cluster is constant for each species of pine, and this helps identification.

The Scots pine, *Pinus sylvestris*, is native over most of Europe, including the British Isles, and much of northern Asia also. It is widely grown as an ornamental tree in North America, and there, though not in Europe, it is used for indoor decoration as a Christmas tree. Scots pine is easily known by its rather short bluish-green needles, and by the orange-red bark that develops on all the older branches. On still older trunks or limbs a thick pinkish-brown bark, divided by fissures into broad plates, is formed. The contrast of bluish foliage with reddish bark makes Scots pine a uniquely attractive evergreen. Plate 6a, p. 181.

Young Scots pines have an attractive conical outline, and throughout the summer their long pale green new shoots make a lively contrast with the darker and older blue-green foliage below. Older trees enter into a less comely "pole" stage, but still older trees, from their fiftieth year on, develop a marvellous rugged crown, more like that of a broadleaved tree than a typical conifer. This grandeur may endure for as long as one hundred years, but Scots pine is seldom a really long-lived tree. In the

PLATE 21 *Afforestation*

Above Ploughing peaty moorland in Galloway, south-west Scotland, for the large-scale planting of spruce woods. These poor hill pastures have been abandoned by sheep farmers because of long-term deterioration in their capacity to carry stock. Drainage is needed to give trees roothold, and this is achieved by giant ploughs, pulled by powerful crawler tractors. The spruces will be planted in, or through, the long ribbons of peaty soil thrown up by the ploughshares. *Below* Replanting cleared woodlands in Monmouthshire. Each planter carries his trees in a waterproof sack on his back, leaving both hands free. He judges distance apart with the spacing stick and forms planting notches with a spear-shaped spade.

lowlands, one hundred and fifty years is its practical maximum, though I have seen a three hundred-year-old tree felled in the royal forest of Balmoral, on Deeside in the Scottish Highlands.

Scots pine is one of the world's leading timber-yielding trees, used under various trade names for all kinds of building construction, telegraph poles, railway sleepers, mine props, box making, board making, and paper manufacture. Enormous quantities are imported to Britain annually as "redwood" or "red deal", or in manufactured forms as paper, paper pulp and man-made board. In British forestry the Scots pine, our only native timber-producing conifer, has always played a leading part. It is very hardy and thrives on most soils and in most situations; the only circumstances that limit its good growth are town smoke, thin soils over chalk and limestone, and exposure to salt-laden gales from the sea. Other conifers yield timber in larger volumes in less time, but none is so reliable and easy to grow.

The only significant ornamental varieties of Scots pine are dwarf or shrub ones.

The lodgepole pine, *Pinus contorta*, is native over a wide extent of western North America, from Alaska and Alberta down to California; there are many local races adapted to the hard conditions of cold, drought, or exposure, under which this relatively small "pioneer" tree is able to compete, successfully, with the giants of the Pacific Coast forests. Certain of these *provenances* of lodgepole pine have proved very valuable in British forestry. "Coastal" ones grow vigorously on poor heaths and peat bogs in Ireland and the west of Scotland, provided they are helped by a few ounces of phosphate when first planted; these new strains have greatly extended the profitable area for timber growing. "Inland" provenances compete with Scots pine on less severe land farther east, growing faster and so yielding saleable poles earlier, at greater profit.

Lodgepole pine has therefore become an important tree for the timber grower. It has no particular merit as an ornamental tree, though its soft green foliage is pleasing and restful to the eye. It can easily be told apart

PLATE 22 *Transplanting forest trees*

Above Two-year-old spruce seedlings are lifted from their nursery beds and set in a transplanting board. This fixes correct depth in soil and distance apart, and enables sixty trees to be planted in one action.

Centre Boards, filled with trees, are carried to a trench dug with a plough in well-tilled soil. The canvas screen shields tree roots from dry winds while the boards are being filled.

Below A tractor next draws a transplanting plough along the row of boards. In one pass of the plough, the train of implements it carries throws soil against the tree roots, firms it down and cuts a new trench for the next row of trees. The boards are then removed for re-filling. Note, *right*, the regular, repeated rows of small trees, which will now grow larger for one or two years, before going out to the forest for final planting.

from the Scots pine by its dark, often black, bark, its greener needles, and the tiny prickles on its cones. Cones are borne even on young saplings and often persist on the branches for many years.

Corsican pine, now called *Pinus nigra* variety *maritima* (but formerly variety *calabrica*) is a magnificent tree from the sunny island of Corsica which has proved a highly profitable timber producer in the sunnier regions of south and east England, and along the eastern Scottish coast. Elsewhere it misses the hot summers of its Mediterranean home, and fails to thrive. Corsican pine forms a perfectly upright tree with a graceful open crown of grey-green foliage, borne on slender branches; its bark is pale grey. Identification is easy, for its long *twisted* sage-green needles are unique. It thrives on dry sands and tolerates lime-rich soils. The lower branches of the Corsican pine are soon shed, and the shapely bole and windswept crown form strong scenic features where a single specimen, or small group, is grown for landscape effect. Otherwise the Corsican pine is a tree for the timber grower with an expanse of poor heathland, or sand dune, to afforest in a region of low rainfall. Plate 4a, p. 129.

Austrian pine, *Pinus nigra* variety *nigra*, is a gaunt, craggy tree, which has a part to play in shelterbelts under very very difficult conditions. It tolerates limestone soils and exposure to sea winds, and resists the wildest gales. The close spacing of its branches, which is an advantage in a shelter tree, is a serious fault for timber production, for every branch means a knot; Austrian pine is, therefore, never planted for timber, nor even as an ornamental specimen. Its place is on the hilltops, as a screen against sea gales or bitter winter winds.

Maritime pine, *Pinus pinaster*, comes from the Mediterranean shores and the Atlantic coasts of Spain and Portugal. It is widely grown for timber in southern Europe, and is the leading source of resin. This is obtained by tapping the living tree, in summer, with sharp-edged tools, which cut right into the wood and expose the fine resin canals. Vast commercial forests of maritime pine have been established on the Landes sand dunes of south-west France, between the Pyrenees and Bordeaux, and there are many smaller woods in Britanny. In the British Isles the maritime pine is only considered hardy in the south, and along the western coasts; around Bournemouth it has become naturalised on heathlands. We do not grow it for timber, nor for resin, but it makes a grand specimen tree, with a rust-red deeply furrowed bark, long dark green leathery needles, and huge bright brown cones.

Stone pine, *Pinus pinea*, is occasionally grown in southern coastal gardens as an unusual ornamental feature, because of its broad-spreading, low crown, which is very resistant to sea winds. It is native to the Mediterranean zone, and particularly to Italy, where it is grown widely-spaced in orchards to yield edible and nutritious seeds. These seeds, which are well-flavoured and very large for a conifer, are known as "pine kernels", pignons, pignolias, or pinocchi; they are widely used in confectionery and vegetarian diets.ate 3b, Pl p. 128.

Mountain pine, *Pinus mugo*, comes from the high Alps, where it is valued for its snow-holding and soil-holding properties; it is sometimes planted to help lessen the risk of avalanche damage. It rarely grows larger than a straggling, rounded bush, and never yields timber. It is popular with landscape architects to-day because it can be relied on to fill a small space with a hardy, evergreen tuft of foliage. This is darker green than that of Scots pine, and the shrubby form of mountain pine also marks it out; a key identification feature is the black ring round the knob of every cone-scale.

Monterey pine, *Pinus radiata*, is an important ornamental and shelter tree in the coastal zones of Ireland, western Britain, and western France, but it is not hardy inland. In Spain, and many subtropical countries such as East and South Africa, Australia, New Zealand and Chile, it has become a leading timber-producer. Its original home is a small strip of land around the Monterey peninsula of southern California, where rugged veterans face the Pacific gales. Identification is easy, for it is one of the few pines, grown in the north, that bear their needles in *threes*. These needles are long, soft, and emerald green. The bark of mature trees is thick and rugged, and the cones, which hang on the trees for many years, are large and lop-sided.

Although Monterey pine withstands any amount of drought when once established, it is very difficult to transplant. Some nurserymen raise seedlings in pots and supply the potted plant ready for planting, complete with its ball of soil; but this is expensive. Alternatively, the large first-year seedling can be transplanted after only one year in the seedbed, and the resulting two-year-old (or 1 + 1) transplant can be set in its final position next year. Once established, Monterey pine grows rapidly, increasing in height by two to three feet a year. This quick growth, its dense crown of emerald green foliage, and its ability to resist salt winds on dry, sandy seaside sites, makes Monterey pine invaluable as a coastal shelter tree.

There are two five-needled pines that merit planting in ornamental collections, though no pine of the five-needled group has, at present, any prospects for timber production. The Bhutan pine, *Pinus griffithii*, from the cold climate of the high eastern Himalayas, bears elegant, exceptionally long and drooping needles, tinged with bluish-grey, and form a fine specimen tree. From Japan comes the Japanese white pine, *Pinus parviflora*, which has rather short, somewhat twisted needles carried in fascinating clusters ; they are bluish-green in colour, with clear white resin bands. It ripens many cones, quaintly shaped like short bananas, with white pearls of resin encrusting their scales. As grown in Britain, it makes a bush rather than a tree, and its best position is in a shrubbery or Japanese garden, where it displays attractive features all round the year.

The North American white pine, *Pinus strobus*, is a completely different tree, which forms natural forests in the eastern States and south-east Canada, and yields a smooth but strong timber suitable for joinery and furniture making. Under the name of "Weymouth pine" it was formerly widely grown in Britain, but its cultivation under the British climate is nowadays ruled out by two enemies. The white pine Blister rust, *Cronartium ribicola*, is a fungal disease that spreads from *Pinus strobus* to blackcurrants and then back again, causing blisters on the stems and killing the tree. The Weymouth pine aphid, *Adelges strobi*, feeds on the bark, below tufts of white fluff, and finishes off any pines that survive the rust!

It is now believed that both these troubles reached our shores accidentally, being imported on living white pines of other species, to which they do little or no harm. The rust probably came from Switzerland on the Swiss stone pine, and the aphid from Asia on some Asiatic species of five-needled pine. Nowadays strict quarantine measures are enforced on living conifers, to keep similar pests and diseases out, but little can be done about those that have become established.

From the Alps we get the Swiss stone pine, *Pinus cembra*, which provides the wood used by Swiss carvers to make the bears and similar figures so attractive to tourists. In the lowlands it grows very slowly, seldom more than six inches a year, and rarely bears cones or ripens the large seeds, like wheat grains but better flavoured, which are gathered and eaten in Switzerland.

LARCHES, *Larix* genus Plate 2b, p. 113.

The larches, which are the only common and widely grown group of conifers to shed their leaves in autumn, are of great value both for ornamental planting and as timber producers. Their main merits for garden planting are hardihood, rapid growth in youth, graceful form when mature, and a striking march of seasonal colour. Early in spring, before the broadleaved trees have broken bud, the larches push forth tufts of bright emerald green needles, which mellow to deeper greens by midsummer. Their autumn tints range from pale gold to orange, and even in winter the bare twigs show a lively shade of straw-yellow or rust-red. The rose-pink "larch roses", which are really female flowers, are surprisingly pretty when they open in May, and the brown cones that succeed them are also quaint and decorative.

Larches thrive on all reasonably fertile soils, but can only grow well in full sunlight. The shade they cast is light, even in summer, so plants can be grown quite close to isolated specimen trees.

In the woods, the larch's need for full-light means that the crop must be widely spaced, at five to six feet apart. It must later be heavily and repeatedly thinned out, to allow ample space for each tree to expand its crown of branches and leaves. The total timber crop is, in consequence, a light one. But larch grows so fast, and gives yields so early, that economists assure us that it pays the forester well. Larch timber is stronger than that of most other conifers, so it can be put to more exacting uses and fetches a higher price. It is particularly serviceable on country estates, for fencing, gates, farm buildings and general repairs. Poles can readily be sold for fence work, or else, provided their bark is left on, as rustic poles for garden screens and pergolas. The heartwood of larch is naturally durable, but since most planks and poles contain some sapwood, it is always advisable to give them preservative treatment if they will be exposed to damp in use. Rustic poles can be butt-treated, the bark being removed from the base, but left intact elsewhere.

Three kinds of larch are grown in Europe, namely the European larch, *Larix decidua*, the Japanese larch, *L. kaempferi*, and the hybrid between them, *L. eurolepis*. Woods of rather scrubby European larch grow high on the Swiss Alps, where they play a useful part in holding the winter snow, which lessens the risk of spring avalanches; they also check soil erosion caused by frost, rainstorms and mountain torrents. At one time, seed from these "High Alpine" provenances was used to raise trees for British plantations, in the belief that such a race would prove hardy and thrive on poor soil. But the climatic differences were too great, and the young trees were badly damaged by a stem-canker disease. Nowadays seed is taken from good stands in Britain, or woods on the relatively low mountains of Czechoslovakia. Larch of such "lowland" provenances is vigorous and virtually free of canker.

There are few estates without larchwoods, or at least some fine European larches in their mixed woodlands, or in shelterbelts. The distinguishing characters of the European larch are straw-coloured twigs, pale green needles, and straight cone-scales.

Japanese larch, which grows wild on the slopes of Mount Fuji, has also been extensively planted because of its vigorous early growth and freedom from canker. It thrives best in the high rainfall regions of the British Isles, where winters are mild, notably in Ireland, Wales and the west of Scotland and England. It is a good tree to choose where quick cover is needed, as its fast early growth lowers weeding costs. So it is often planted on old coppice land or amid tall bracken. Recent tests at the Forest Products Research Laboratory have shown that, despite its quick start, its timber is equal in strength to that of the European kind. Japanese larch is easily recognised by its rust-red twigs, blue-green needles, and cone scales with reflexed tips, which make each cone look like a pretty little rosette.

Hybrid larch first arose accidentally, about 1909, on the Atholl Estate at Dunkeld in Scotland. The chance pollination of female flowers on Japanese larches by pollen from male flowers on European ones, produced vigorous and unusual progeny. Like many hybrids, it shows exceptional vigour and hardiness. Because of its speed of growth, it is preferred by many foresters, but the supply of planting stock is limited. Only the first-cross shows full hybrid vigour, and seed for raising this is obtained, in practice, only from specially planted "seed orchards". In these, European and Japanese larches are grown in alternate rows to favour cross-pollination.

Hybrid larch has no particular attraction for the ornamental tree planter, unless he is seeking an exceptionally quick-starting tree that will grow three feet taller each year. It is not easy to identify, since its characters lie midway between its European and Japanese parents; its long annual shoots help to mark it out.

Few other larches are distinct enough to merit planting in gardens, except for their scientific interest. In North America the usual species grown is the native tamarack, *L. laricina*, remarkable for its small cones. Several weeping strains of larch are known, some being varieties of European larch, others of Japanese larch, and others again having an American origin; but all need grafting and none is particularly desirable.

Golden larch, *Pseudolarix amabilis*, is a small Chinese tree sometimes cultivated for its elegant foliage which turns a pleasing golden shade each autumn. It is slow-growing and needs lime-free soil.

SPRUCES, *Picea* genus   Plates 2a; 19 a, b, e, f; 22, 23d.

Spruces, which are familiar to everyone in Britain and northern Europe as the typical Christmas trees, are easily distinguished from all similar conifers by one simple feature. All their needles are borne singly, never in groups, and if you pull one off its twig, a little stalk or peg comes away with it. But if it is left to die naturally (as it does after about four years on the living tree), or is left to wither, it leaves the woody peg behind. The older, leafless twigs of spruces are ridged with such pegs.

Spruces, of one species or another, are found throughout the colder regions, and on the higher mountains, right round the Northern Hemisphere. They form a leading world source of softwood timber, which is known as "whitewood" because of its uniform pale cream colour. Spruce wood is only moderately strong, and shows no natural resistance to decay, but it is light in weight, and easy to work, and is therefore used in enormous quantities for box making, joinery, and everyday furniture, also in building construction where it will not be exposed to damp. Spruce is easily the best wood in the world for paper making; its annual rings hold a high proportion of springwood fibres, which "collapse" during the paper-making process into long flat ribbons that interweave with one another to make a strong, smooth-surfaced paper; its chemical characteristics are also good, and its pale colour is a further advantage.

Demands for industrial use are so strong and assured that spruces play a large part in modern afforestation plans. They thrive on poor soils in districts of high rainfall, producing large volumes of timber rapidly. In Ireland, Wales and the western and northern uplands of England and Scotland, spruces are nowadays planted on a greater scale than any other tree. But they are not well suited, as timber yielding trees, to the warmer and drier lowlands, and they cannot tolerate dry acid-soiled moorlands where only heather, birch and pine can thrive. As ornamental trees, however, they can be grown on reasonably fertile soils in most districts.

Foresters always plant spruces in a different manner from other trees;

their roots are kept shallow. In a garden or an old woodland the best way to do this is to slice off a surface layer of soil, about three inches thick, and then spread out the spruce roots, as level as possible, on the flat surface below; the soil that was removed is then returned and stamped *very* firm indeed. On grassland, *turf planting* is best; this involves the cutting out of a slice of turf, one foot square by about two inches thick, from a point adjacent to the position of planting. This turf is then *inverted*, that is, turned upside down and placed on the actual planting point. Using the spade, a slit is now cut through one side of the turf, half-way across, and the spruce plant is "threaded" through this. Its roots are spread out *below* the inverted turf but *above* the untouched grass beneath. The two opposed layers of grass, which now hold the spruce roots, soon wither, but always remain moist, and it is rare for any spruce to fail when turf-planted. See figure 43, page 109.

Foresters who plant grassy moors or peat bogs on a large scale get the same results by ploughing the land, in such a way that the slice of turf turned up by the ploughshare provides a continuous strip of shallow planting points, at the desired distance apart—usually five feet.

Spruces grow slowly at first, but rapidly later. The special treatment they need when grown as Christmas trees is outlined in Chapter 22.

The Norway spruce, *Picea abies,* which is native to Scandinavia, the Alps, and other mountain ranges throughout Europe, is the traditional North European Christmas tree. In the woods it has an old-established place as a reliable timber-producer, limited only by its need for a moist site quite free from heather, from smoke pollution, and from exposure to salt-bearing sea winds. It is rarely grown as a garden tree for long; people are apt to lift it for Christmas decoration and it seldom gets the care needed to ensure regrowth after its return to the garden bed. In practice it is hopeless to grow Norway spruce in parks, on roadsides, or at similar spots easily accessible to the public; vandals are sure to take their toll on dark December nights!

There are a number of dwarf garden strains of Norway spruce; these are described in Chapter 21, page 309.

Oriental spruce, *P. orientalis,* comes from the Caucasus and makes an attractive alternative to the common kind, where an ornamental tree is needed. Its needles are remarkably small and short, and form a lustrous texture of bright green foliage.

Serbian spruce, *P. omorika,* is found wild only in a small zone of limestone forest near Sarajevo. It forms a very slender tree with a narrow crown, soaring upwards in spire-like fashion, and so claims a place in landscape work. It is hardy and vigorous, and produces timber so quickly that it will be widely grown in plantations, as soon as more seed becomes available. Plate 2a, p. 113.

Sitka spruce, *P. sitchensis,* comes from the West Coast of North America; it is found from Alaska south to California, and is named after a small Alaskan seaport. It can be known at once by its beautiful silvery-green foliage, which glistens in the sun, and by the sharp point at the tip of each needle. Definitely a forester's tree, it is planted by the million in western Britain, where it exceeds all other trees in rate of timber production and shows complete resistance to gales and wind-borne salt. Where rainfall is below forty inches a year, it is less vigorous, but still makes a pleasing specimen. You are unlikely to lose it at Christmas time, for its sharp-pointed needles make it both undesirable and unmarketable for indoor decoration.

Blue spruce, *P. pungens* 'Glauca', is a garden form of the wild Colorado spruce which grows under cold winters and hot dry summers in the southern Rocky Mountains of America. It is increased by grafting and rarely grows beyond bush size. Its silvery-blue shade is a protection against the extremely bright sunshine that threatens to dry out leaves at a high elevation in a near-desert climate. It is due to resins which lessen water loss, and also throw back the sun's rays. Plate 19a, p. 252.

The West Himalayan weeping spruce, *P. smithiana*, is a stately tree that proves quite hardy in Britain and is often seen in the older arboreta. Its smaller branches droop symmetrically, and the individual needles, which are remarkably long and round, likewise lie evenly spaced all round the twigs. In this spruce, weeping is a natural form designed to shed the snows of its mountain home; it is raised from seed, without grafting.

Brewer's weeping spruce, *P. breweriana*, is another kind that droops naturally, but in another fashion. Each side branch is inclined slightly downwards and bears a curtain of finer twigs that falls vertically, carrying bluish-green needles that continue the downward trend. Seen in the sunlight, stirred by the wind, this sheet of foliage shimmers with a silvery light, like the bright face of a waterfall. This exquisite tree, which comes from the high mountains of Oregon, is still scarce and rather costly to buy; it well merits more frequent planting.

Three spruces that form great natural forests in North America, and contribute a huge output of lumber and paper pulp, are the white, *P. glauca*, the black, *P. mariana*, and the red, *P. rubens*. None has proved really at home in Europe; white spruce is sometimes grown in shelter-

PLATE 23 *Tree-felling, traditional and modern methods*

Above left In the traditional method of tree-felling, the base of the trunk is first 'rounded up' with the axe, as shown here. An 'undercut' is next made on the side towards which the tree is to fall, called the 'face' of the tree.

Above right Two men next draw a cross-cut saw across the opposite side, called the 'back', until the tree, already leaning slightly forward, starts to fall. This larch is just tilting forward.

Below left Using the modern power-driven chain saw, a single worker, wearing a safety helmet, does all these operations alone. Here he is 'rounding-up', removing a buttress root before under-cutting and cross-cutting.

Below right The fall of the tree. A great spruce crashes down in Glenbranter Forest, Argyll.

belts, but proves far inferior to the Sitka spruce. None has any particular decorative merit.

SILVER FIRS, *Abies* species

The silver firs resemble the spruces in having single needles, ranged in flat planes along the twigs. But there are no pegs at the base of a silver fir needle, and if you pull it away, a smooth round scar remains. The cones, which are large and upright, fall to pieces soon after they ripen in autumn.

The European silver fir, *Abies alba*, thrives on the Alps and other hill ranges of central Europe and is commonly planted in the lowlands too. The white resin bands on the underside of the needles give this tree its names in three languages—*Weisstanne* in German, *sapin argenté* in French and silver fir in English. Its timber is widely used on the Continent and is occasionally imported to Britain as "whitewood", a name it shares with the spruces. The tree itself was grown for timber in the British Isles until the present century, but it is no longer planted because it suffers severely from a minute aphid, *Adelges nordmannianae*. This insect is found on the Continent but, under the somewhat different climatic conditions, does only trivial harm there. Silver fir makes a handsome specimen tree, indeed it has provided our largest (though not our tallest) known conifer, a giant, 168 feet tall by 20 feet round, on the Duke of Argyll's estate at Inveraray in Scotland. But aphid damage is so frequent that it is scarcely worth planting to-day.

Grand fir, *Abies grandis*, which comes from the west coast of North America, is a good tree to use in its place, whether timber or beauty be the aim. It has long deep-green needles neatly ranked in a level plane, and forms a shapely tree with a pyramidal outline. It does best under a mild, rainy, western climate, but is hardy and grows on any soil except dry chalk or sand. In the west, it yields timber at as fast a rate as any other tree.

Noble fir, *A. procera*, has exceptionally attractive foliage. All its needles are swept upwards and forwards, giving a rich texture like some lustrous fur. They are blue-green in colour, with an overlay of silvery wax, which gives their surface a lively sheen. In Denmark, this conifer is preferred to all others as a Christmas tree. Noble fir grows slowly when young, developing a markedly conical shape that some may consider too formal. As it gains timber size, its trunk develops a strong taper. The bark

PLATE 24 *Planting*

Above How not to do it. Unsympathetic planting of square blocks of conifers across the rounded contours of a Scottish Border hill.
Below By contrast, at Glenbranter Forest in Argyll. Vast woods of spruce and pine have been successfully blended with a winding valley and a sweeping hillscape.

is smooth, and of an unusual, effective shade of silver-grey. The cones are fascinating structures of spirally-ranked scales, each accompanied by a long, pointed bract; but this "feathercone", like all silver fir cones, soon falls to bits. Mature trees have a stately grandeur, matching the tree's name. In western districts, where a few plantations are grown, Noble fir has proved a rapid timber-producer.

Several other silver firs are grown in arboreta. The most distinct are the Greek fir, *A. cephalonica*, a vigorous tree with very sharp-pointed needles, and the Spanish fir, *A. pinsapo*, which has blunt needles all round, its twigs and looks like a bottle-brush. Veitch's silver fir, *A. veitchii*, comes from Mount Fuji in Japan, where it is known as *shirube*. Its blunt, densely-packed needles are glossy dark green above and silvery white below. Hardy and fast-growing, it has deservedly gained a place in landscape work as a shapely green-and-silver conifer.

DOUGLAS FIRS, *Pseudotsuga* species   Plate 4c, p. 129.

The Douglas firs are named after David Douglas, a Scottish botanist who sent seed of the principal species to Britain, from British Columbia, in 1824. The genus *Pseudotsuga* has needles set singly; they are not on pegs, and if pulled away they leave a smooth round scar. Foliage specimens can be told apart from those of the similar silver firs by their buds, which are pointed and free from resin, and have papery scales. The cones are distinct; they hang downwards and do not break up when ripe, while each scale bears a conspicuous three-pointed bract.

The green or Oregon Douglas fir, *P. menziesii*, comes from British Columbia and the neighbouring regions of Alaska, Canada, and the United States. It holds an important place in planting for timber, throughout central and western Europe as well as in North America and even in New Zealand, because it yields a remarkably strong wood at a surprisingly fast rate. Because of its pine-like character, with a broad band of strong summerwood in every annual ring, this timber is often imported under the name of "Oregon pine" or "British Columbian pine". In Britain, Douglas fir thrives well and grows fast wherever soil is deep, well-drained, moderately fertile and not too rich in lime; it does particularly well on former broadleaved woodland. It is best planted at six feet apart to allow for its rapid start. But it is not a success on poor or ill-drained soils, while in exposed places where it cannot gain a deep root-hold in well-drained subsoil, it is apt to be blown over.

When grown as an ornamental tree, the green Douglas fir demands ample room. You must reckon with an annual height-growth of three feet a year, with a branch spread to match. The ultimate height may be the record-breaking 181 feet reached by a specimen at Powis Castle, near Welshpool in mid-Wales; and the girth may go up to 20 feet, found on a tree at Dunkeld, Scotland. In British Columbia it may scale 350 feet tall and 50 feet round! Definitely a tree for the park or greater garden. Where there is less room, the best kind to plant is the blue or Colorado

Douglas fir, *P. glauca*. This comes from the high dry mountain forests of northern California, and its needles have a shining blue waxy coating, designed to throw back sunlight and hold in a limited supply of water. It is hardy and pleasing to the eye, but never grows fast or tall; a foot a year is a usual speed, and heights seldom exceed fifty feet.

HEMLOCKS, *Tsuga* species

Hemlock trees get their odd name from a supposed resemblance between the smell of their crushed foliage and that of the hemlock plant, a poisonous weed found along European rivers; it was given them by the early English settlers who first found these trees in North America. The key feature of the group is the irregular length of the needles—long and short ones alternating all along the twigs.

Western hemlock, *Tsuga heterophylla*, is native to British Columbia and the neighbouring American states, and is the most vigorous kind in western Europe. Grown as a specimen, it has no rival for grace of form. Its crown becomes a well-proportioned pyramid, with sweeping branches that each show individual characters of shape and line, and bear foliage rendered both lively and lustrous through the differing lengths and angles of the needles. Cones are borne freely, and these ornament the green tapestry as bright fawny-brown ovals. The summit of the tapering crown is always a long solitary leading shoot that bends over gracefully and droops downwards.

Despite the fact that its final bud points earthwards, the western hemlock grows steadily taller, often by as much as three feet in one year. The drooping leader, found in most hemlocks, is often said to be a protection against snow damage. Yet the crown as a whole collects a lot of snow, and looks surprisingly lovely when its upper surfaces are outlined in glistening white.

Western hemlock is one of the fastest timber producers, yielding a pale cream wood of moderate strength that has much the same uses as spruce —box making, joinery, and paper pulp. Hemlock is particularly useful in the replacement of worn-out broadleaved woodland by a high-yielding conifer. Young trees tolerate a fair degree of shade, and start growth rapidly when interplanted among broadleaved trees, or even underplanted below a light canopy. The flexible nature of the long drooping leading shoot saves it from much casual injury, through careless weeding or the whipping by other shoots.

Hemlock seedlings need special care in the forest nursery. They are very small and each one has only three seed leaves. They always need two years in the seedbed, and during their first year they must be protected with an overhead screen of laths; this saves them from being killed outright by hot summer sun, and also from being lifted from the soil by a succession of hard winter frosts.

Eastern hemlock, *T. canadensis*, is the common wild kind in eastern Canada and the north-eastern United States, where its wood, which is far inferior to that of the western kind, is used for paper pulp, box making, and minor construction jobs. It branches low down and its form is usually poor, but it can be used in landscape work where a shapeless low evergreen is needed to fill a gap. Carolina hemlock, *T. caroliniana*, provides by contrast a neat and shapely small tree, with distinctive rounded needles. Mountain hemlock, *T. mertensiana*, is an exceedingly beautiful small ornamental kind, having silvery green needles ranged all round its slender and often drooping twigs. It comes from the higher valleys of the Rocky Mountains, from British Columbia south into California.

WESTERN RED CEDAR, *Thuja plicata*

This beautiful evergreen comes from British Columbia and the neighbouring western American states, where its timber was used by the Indians for every kind of constructional work—from houses and dug-out canoes to totem poles. They preferred it to all others because it is strong, light in weight, and, under their climate, naturally durable. Many trees and timbers are called "cedar", with or without some qualifying term, but this is the only one nowadays extensively imported to Europe. It is the "cedar" of bungalows, sheds, greenhouses, and roofing shingles. Bright reddish-brown when freshly sawn, it mellows naturally to a pleasing silver grey. Despite some timber merchants' claims, it is *not* durable indefinitely out-of-doors in the British climate. It should be treated every five years or so with a brush coating of a good preservative of a suitable shade. Otherwise the fungi of decay will eventually gain a hold.

Western red cedar bears fern-like foliage, in flattened fronds, with *scale-leaves* pressed against the twigs. The younger twigs are hidden, and so are the buds, but as the twigs age the older scale-leaves fade to bright reddish brown, and eventually fall. Many cypresses have similar foliage, as described in the next chapter, but western red cedar can be distinguished by three pointers:—its twig tips are swollen and "solid" to the touch, they have the reddish tinge characteristic of the whole tree and the leading shoots are always upright; the bark of young branches is a distinctive red; the little cones consist of a few slender scales united only at the base, and are quite unlike the round globes of the cypresses.

Unfortunately the western red cedar suffers, in its early seedling stage, from a serious fungal disease, the *Keithia* disease caused by *Didymascella thujina*. A chemical antidote is now available, and stocks are also raised in isolated, disease-free, nurseries, or else from cuttings, which costs more. After the seedling stage, the tree is remarkably free from diseases or pests, and thrives on any reasonably fertile soil in the lowlands, and even on high chalk downs; it tolerates lime-rich soils.

Western red cedar is planted on a small though increasing scale for timber production. It is a high yielder, and the straight, strong, light poles that are removed as thinnings are easily sold. If the lower branches are pruned away while still bearing live green foliage, they can often be sold at a good profit to wholesale florists, for they are widely used in making wreaths. Western red cedar is also a good tree for hedges and high screens; it stands clipping and can be kept neat and narrow. It makes a good individual tree for the lawn of a small garden. If trained as a slender pyramid it holds its foliage right down to ground level, and it can be topped to hold it down to any desired height, without appearing odd.

The name "arbor-vitae", meaning "tree of life", from evergreen foliage without apparent buds, is often applied to this tree—"western arbor-vitae", and its relatives when they are used in ornamental planting. The "American arbor-vitae", which comes from the eastern United States and is there known as "eastern white-cedar", is *Thuja occidentalis*. In Europe it is a slow-growing tree of compact habit, with foliage that turns an attractive bronze shade in winter. The Chinese arbor-vitae is *T. orientalis*. This has a rather dense framework of small, much bent branches, which tend to lie in one plane; its intricate irregularity makes a decorative contrast to the two American kinds. There are a number of ornamental cultivars of all three species, providing a range of yellow, green and bronze shades, and a few blues; there are also dwarf, columnar, and rounded bush forms, and some varieties with peculiar foliage.

CEDARS, *Cedrus* species Plates 2d; 3a; 13a.

Many trees, both broadleaved and conifer, have been called "cedars" because of their fragrant wood or fragrant foliage; those of the genus *Cedrus* comprise four magnificent conifers that grow wild only on high mountains in Asia or North Africa. They are the only conifers that bear *evergreen* needles in tufts on short shoots along their branches; in other words, their main foliage consists of *grouped* needles that are dark green and tough. Their leaf pattern is like that of the deciduous larches, and like those trees they bear single needles at the branch tips. Cedar cones are large and barrel shaped, with flattish scales and a hollowed-out top. They stand upright on the branches, and take two years to ripen; then they slowly break up and release large winged seeds. Cedar flowers open in autumn, about September, and the tapering oval male flowers, heavy with golden pollen, are then conspicuous and attractive.

Cedar timber is fragrant, strong and naturally durable, but it is rarely seen on the world timber market. Merchants and users apply the name "cedar" to a wide range of woods, besides those of this *Cedrus* genus. Most true cedar wood is used in the countries where it grows, the classic example being the building of the Temple by Solomon, King of Israel, with Cedar of Lebanon timber bought from Hiram, King of Tyre. Though trial plantations have grown well, cedars are seldom planted for their wood. They are grown, both in Europe and North America, solely as ornamental trees.

Cedar of Lebanon, *Cedrus libani*, is nowadays found wild only in small, protected groves on Mount Lebanon and other high mountain ranges in Syria, the Lebanon and Turkey. It was introduced to Europe about 1650 and there are many grand specimens, with stout trunks that suggest an age much greater than their three hundred years.

The Lebanon cedar is remarkable for the flat character of its masses of foliage. Young trees grow in a pyramidal shape, but older ones develop level planes of green. No other tree strikes so marked a horizontal note in the view, and landscape architects often select the Lebanon cedar for this feature, even though it takes twenty years to become apparent. The flat surface is built up of a myriad of twigs. If you walk below the cedar's crown and gaze upwards, you will be surprised by the intricate texture of its branchwork, interwoven like a tapestry.

The deodar or Indian cedar, *C. deodara*, which comes from the high Himalayas, is a tree of more slender outline and grace of form, with side branches that droop elegantly at their tips. It makes an attractive specimen, and is hardy, though slow-growing. Cyprus cedar, *C. brevifolia*, which is only occasionally cultivated, resembles the Lebanon kind but bears shorter needles; it comes from the high Troodos Mountains of Cyprus.

The Atlas cedar; *C. atlantica*, is native to the great Atlas mountains of North Africa, which are snow-capped in winter though parched by the sub-tropical sun in summer. Its branches always strike outwards and upwards at an acute angle to the trunk, giving its crown an open and rather restless outline. The blue Atlas cedar, variety *glauca*, displays this striking habit effectively, and possesses in a marked degree the blue coloration, caused by water-retaining resin and wax, that all Atlas cedars possess in some degree. This colour is an adaptation to life in a difficult climate, where the limited amount of soil moisture gained from winter's snowfall must be conserved through summer's heat. The silver-blue spires of foliage on a well-grown blue Atlas cedar look truly delightful as they glisten in the summer sun. This is a tree that defies drought and is happy on a chalky or lime-rich subsoil; one that casts a light shade and can be accommodated in a small garden. It is costly, one must admit, but it is a rewarding tree to raise and may well be a first choice wherever a blue-foliaged conifer is required.

CALIFORNIAN REDWOOD, *Sequoia sempervirens*

This remarkable conifer is easily known by its thick, rather soft, red bark, and needles set in two ranks on *brown* twigs, together with leafy buds; its foliage is much like that of a yew, but yew has green twigs. It forms widespread forests in California, mostly in the fog belt along the Pacific coast. There the finest groves, including a three hundred and sixty-eight foot high specimen believed to be the world's tallest tree, are preserved in National Parks. Less impressive woods are harvested for timber, then replaced by natural regrowth or by planting. The few trial plantations in Europe, including a magnificent group owned by the Royal Forestry

Society at Leighton Park near Welshpool in mid-Wales, show amazingly rapid rates of timber production. But so far this redwood is not grown commercially for timber outside California; it needs a good, sheltered site, and considerably more care than do our everyday timber trees. Most seeds prove infertile and it is costly to raise, either from seed or from cuttings.

Californian redwood was widely planted in European arboreta, shortly after its introduction in 1845. The resulting specimens, now around one hundred and twenty years old, are tall stately trees with irregular crowns not unlike those of a broadleaved tree. None exceeds the 135 feet found at Cuffnells Park, Lyndhurst, Hampshire; this is probably due to the harsh winds experienced in Britain, which damage exposed leading shoots. Ornamental planting is nowadays only done occasionally; small redwoods have no particular decorative merit, and ample room is needed for future giants. A tree, then, for a picked site, where it may possibly stand as a focal point in the landscape for as long as 2,000 years, an age often recorded in California!

WELLINGTONIA or BIG TREE, *Sequoiadendron giganteum* Plate 6, p. 181.

Americans call this magnificent evergreen the Big Tree or mammoth tree, for it is in fact the largest—though not the tallest—tree in the world. The largest recorded veteran, named "General Sherman", in the Sequoia National Park, California, is 272 feet tall and 75 feet round; it holds 50,000 true cubic feet of timber, and weighs about 1,500 tons! It is also one of the world's oldest trees; counts of annual rings on stumps have shown that some Big Trees exceed 4,000 years.

In Europe, this tree is generally called the wellingtonia; it was given the early scientific name of *Wellingtonia* in honour of the Duke of Wellington, who had died just before it became known! As a wild tree it grows only in the inland districts of California, in valleys hidden amid the Rocky Mountains and the Sierra Nevada range. This explains why it escaped discovery by the European settlers until 1841, when John Bidwell stumbled across a grove near the Sacramento River. Because of their rarity, nearly all the ancient giants are now preserved in National Parks, and though the Big Tree yields a good timber little is available commercially. In an age when less reverence was paid to natural beauty, some tourist promoter cut a hole through one of the largest Big Trees, so that folk could drive their cars through it.

Seed of the wellingtonia reached Europe in 1853, and though only a small proportion is ever fertile, the mid-Victorian nurserymen soon had specimen trees on sale. Timber planting has never progressed beyond the experimental plot stage, but tall specimen trees are very frequent in European arboreta. Many are approaching one hundred years old, exceed one hundred feet in height, and have impressive girths. Records are 162 feet tall at Endsleigh in Devon—probably the tallest tree in England—and 29 feet round at Crichel in Dorset.

Large wellingtonias are easily known by their very thick, soft, reddish-grey bark on strongly tapering trunks. The foliage consists of *scale-leaves* closely pressed against the twigs, so as to hide them, but each leaf ends in a free, sharp point. Young wellingtonias form most attractive small decorative trees; they have a symmetrically pyramidal shape, and the leaves last for so long that the whole tree is a pale greyish-green, with no brown branches exposed to view. They keep this pleasing shape and colour for about twenty years. Once they grow more than twenty feet tall, the owner must decide whether to sacrifice them or let them develop into mighty giants, greedy for space and light. I have never heard of any gardener bold enough to lop or top a stately wellingtonia.

JAPANESE CEDAR, *Cryptomeria japonica*

This beautiful evergreen is widely grown in Japan, where it is called *sugi*, both as a timber-producer and as an avenue tree or ornament to a temple garden. It bears long, round needles, that curve to follow the trend of the twigs, which they also hide from view. It looks rather like a wellingtonia, but may be distinguished by the longer, more isolated needles; the hard, fibrous mid-brown bark contrasts with the softer bark of the wellingtonia.

Outside its native land, the Japanese cedar is considered a difficult tree to raise, and it has made little headway as a timber-producer; transplanting needs particular care, and it is not considered hardy in the colder districts, nor in any way adapted to poor soils. Large specimen trees, most of them around one hundred years old, are fairly common in arboreta, and a little decorative planting is still done.

The Japanese have developed several curious varieties and cultivars of *Cryptomeria*, some being more bizarre than beautiful. One of them, the variety *elegans*, is very widely used by landscape planters in most temperate and sub-tropical lands. This form has long, lax "juvenile" needles standing well clear of the twigs, loose irregular branches that build up a dense crown having no definite shape, and no clear central trunk. It forms a rounded bush rather than a tree, and rarely grows more than twenty feet tall. In summer its foliage is a soft bluish-green, but in winter it turns to an attractive rusty-bronze, changing back again next spring. This exceptional conifer fills a definite need for a low tree or shrub that will contrast with the hard lines of buildings and the more definite uprights of taller trees. It can also be depended on to remain reasonably low and small in spread. As a rule it is increased by cuttings, though it occasionally bears cones and comes true from seed.

SWAMP CYPRESS, *Taxodium distichum* Plate 1b. p. 112.

This graceful tree grows in the swamps of the south-eastern United States, where it yields a useful and naturally durable timber. It is occasionally planted for ornament in Europe, and is naturally set beside a lake or stream, though it will thrive on any deep, well-watered soil that does not dry out in summer. It is unique among the conifers in being able to tolerate water-logged ground, and it can only do so by sending up curious knee-roots called "pneumatophores". These project above the ground level and carry air down to the main root system below. They are common in America, but rare elsewhere.

Swamp cypress is a deciduous tree, and bears its flat needles on short twigs that fall, all in one piece, in autumn. In spring they are a bright pale green, but they darken later. In autumn they change to a fiery orange, which makes the tree look like the proverbial "burning bush" of the Bible. This foliage has a soft texture, and a mature swamp cypress shows a flowing outline like that of a broadleaved tree. Altogether it is a highly decorative conifer that deserves consideration wherever there is reasonable room along the waterside. If the site is waterlogged, it is essential to plant the swamp cypress on a mound of earth above the general level, as it cannot *start* growth below the water-table. Once started, it will even grow in the still waters of a pond, as shown by a well-known specimen in Kew Gardens.

DAWN CYPRESS, *Metasequoia glyptostroboides*

This charming Chinese conifer is sometimes called "the living fossil", because it was known to geologists, through specimens preserved in rocks, long before living trees were discovered. In 1944 a Chinese botanist named Tsang Wang, who was engaged on a survey of timber resources, came across small wild groves and numerous cultivated trees in a land-locked valley fifty miles south of the town of Wan-hsien in Szechwan. The Chinese call this tree the *shui-hsa*, or water fir, and it gives its name to the *Shui-hsa-pa*, or Water Fir Valley. Seed was later sent to Chinese, American and European botanic gardens, and then it was found that the dawn cypress, despite its great antiquity, can easily be propagated by cuttings. It is nowadays fairly readily available from commercial nurserymen.

Dawn cypress resembles swamp cypress (*Taxodium*) in bearing its needles on short twigs that fall each autumn. But it differs from that tree, and indeed from any other living tree in the world, in bearing its buds *below* the leafy twigs; usually any bud grows *above* a leaf base. The feathery foliage is pale green in spring and golden orange when it fades in autumn. The trunk has a pinkish-brown bark and soon develops an outline of hollows and bulges, which looks quaintly attractive throughout the leafless winter months. In summer the soft green foliage forms a graceful pyramid, well suited to form a focal point for a small garden. Growth is steady, though not rapid, but so far few cultivated trees exceed thirty feet. It tolerates dry soils, but prefers moist ones.

INCENSE CEDAR, *Calocedrus decurrens*

This outstanding tree is unique among conifers for its upright habit. It forms a slender column of lustrous dark green foliage, completely hiding its trunk, up to eighty feet tall. This foliage is fragrant, and on a hot day gives forth a pleasing odour recalling that of an Eastern incense. All the twigs are completely concealed in long, flat, *scale-leaves* that bear short points at their tips. This is an evergreen that no planner of the grand landscape can ignore, though it is rather too vigorous, and perhaps a little too sombre, to set in a smaller space. There are many fine examples in our larger collections, and always they strike an emphatic note, contrasting with more rounded or level tree forms.

Incense cedar comes from the mountains of Oregon and California, and its shape and foliage pattern, together with the aromatic waxes that provide its fragrance, are adaptations to a climate of snowy winters followed by arid summers under a blazing sun. It is fully hardy in western Europe. The wood is fragrant, strong, and even-textured, and the pinkish-brown heartwood is naturally durable. In America it has a wide range of indoor and outdoor uses, the most exacting being in lead pencils, which need a wood both strong and smooth to the touch.

MAIDENHAIR TREE, *Ginkgo biloba*

This fascinating tree is always ranked with the conifers, though it really belongs to a far more ancient group of plants. It is the only tree living to-day that has survived unchanged from the Carboniferous era; fossils of almost identical trees are frequently found in seams of coal. Its name is derived from the slight resemblance of its foliage to that of the maidenhair fern (*Adiantum*). The leaves, quite unlike those of any other tree, are frond-like; they broaden out towards the tip, with curious veins that fan out in the same way; each leaf is divided by a shallow notch, which explains the specific name of *biloba*, or two-lobed.

Maidenhair trees are either male or female. Nurserymen prefer to stock the male sex, which bears catkins, rather than the female one. The latter bears a plum-like fruit that has a foul-smelling pulp, though its kernel is quite good to eat. But flowering and fruiting only occasionally take place in Europe. Whatever the sex of the maidenhair tree may be, it forms a tall, thin, grey-barked trunk with slender branches, and twigs bearing knob-shaped buds. It is deciduous, and in spring these buds put forth a bright-green tapestry of fresh young leaves. Their autumn tints, as they fade and fall, are a gay golden yellow.

Maidenhair tree is hardy and it succeeds on any reasonably fertile soil; it also tolerates town smoke. But it grows slowly and is rather expensive to buy. Young trees are usually raised from cuttings, and their sex is therefore known. It makes a good choice for those who want an unusual, and remarkably decorative, small and slender tree, and who do not care about it looking rather bare when leafless in winter. Old trees may reach ninety feet.

The native country of the maidenhair tree is southern China, but only a few wild groves are known, notably those at Chang-hua Hsien in Chekiang province. It has long been cultivated throughout China and

Japan, mainly in temple gardens, and it has been grown in Europe since 1730.

MONKEY PUZZLE, *Araucaria araucana* Plate 1a, p. 112.

However impressive the forests of the monkey puzzle, or Chile pine, may appear on the slopes of the snow-topped Andes, it never looks at home in any lowland garden or broadleaved wood. Yet it was zealously planted by Victorian tree lovers in gardens, parks and woods, great and small, throughout the land. Everyone knows it at sight by its very regular branches, clad right to their tips in large, triangular, sharp-tipped scale-leaves. These leaves last for years and slowly change from bright green through dull green to dirty black before they finally fade and fall off, leaving behind ragged bark which scales off, leaving white branches.

This tree is called "monkey puzzle" because it looks so hard to climb, but as no monkeys live in its high, bleak, and snowy homeland, the puzzle has never been tested. Under cultivation, mature trees bear large male flowers, or small globe-shaped, female ones—usually, though not always, on separate trees. The huge cones take three years to ripen, but in the Andes fruiting is so regular that the Araucanian Indians expect an annual harvest of the large nutritious seeds. The scientific names of the monkey puzzle honour this warlike tribe, who for long resisted the Spanish Invaders. The timber, which resembles the closely related "Parana pine" that is often imported from Brazil, is used in Chile as a general purpose softwood. No timber-producing plantations have been established elsewhere.

The monkey puzzle was discovered in 1780 by Don Francisco Dendariarena, whilst exploring the southern Andes in search of shipbuilding timber. In 1795 a famous Scottish botanist, Archibald Menzies, kept some seeds that he had been given to eat at a Chilean banquet, sowed them on board ship, and installed the resulting seedlings in the greenhouses of Kew Gardens, near London. But this tree remained a rarity until William Lobb, and other collectors, sent home larger consignments of seed in the 1840's. Young trees, which grow slowly, did not look too absurd in the mid-Victorian garden scene, for that depended largely on formal lay-outs and regimented mass-plantings. But as they grew larger, and no less regular in outline, fashions changed. Few planters would welcome one of these bizarre evergreens on their front lawn to-day.

Nobody can ever reconcile the stark geometry of a monkey puzzle's crown with the random branching of a broadleaved tree, nor even with the graceful curves of a larch or spruce. It is not out of place in a botanic garden, but nobody should dream—save in some nightmare—of planting it anywhere else!

20. Shrub and Hedge Conifers

MANY kinds of conifer that grow in the wilds are bushes, rather then trees. Others, which are typically tall trees, have shrubby varieties that retain their low habit when propagated by cuttings. Many of these shrub-conifers, selected for their pleasing form, attractive foliage, hardiness, and general good behaviour in the garden, have become very important in horticulture. They fill the need for an evergreen of compact habit and a predictable course of growth, a bush that will stay attractive all the year round and never become too large or ungainly in appearance. It should, if possible, be self-training, so that pruning, clipping, or lopping are not required.

The choice of genera for this chapter is an arbitrary one. It omits the taller timber conifers described in Chapter 19, while the very dwarf forms will be dealt with in Chapter 21. Some of the genera now described include timber trees, but none is regularly planted for use at present, either in north Europe or North America. Briefly, we will look at the true cypresses, the junipers, the yews, and a few allied groups.

A welcome feature of most of the bush conifers in this group is their unfailing supply of evergreen foliage suitable for indoor decoration. It is possible to harvest a regular crop of leafy branches, at suitable intervals, without checking the vigour of the tree. The loss is soon made good by regrowth, which closes over any holes in the general outline of the tree's shape.

CYPRESSES, *Cupressus* and *Chamaecyparis* species Plates 2c; 4b.

Many conifers have been called "cypress", an English word derived from Latin *cupressus* and Greek *cyparis*. Two of the so-called cypresses, that have no close relationship to the original Mediterranean trees, are the dawn cypress and the swamp cypress described in Chapter 19. The key features of the two genera that we can regard as "true cypresses" are *scale-leaves* which hug the twigs so closely that they completely hide the twigs and buds, combined with a round, woody cone, which is shaped like a little button or knob.

In their first year of life as seedlings, all cypresses bear pointed needles; but later in their first year, or early in their second year, they normally lose this *juvenile* character and develop *adult* foliage. Some of the decorative cultivars, however, retain juvenile leaves all their lives, and these sorts are increased by cuttings.

Those cypresses that have all their scale-leaves adpressed evenly on all four sides of each stem, forming a *square* leafy twig, are nowadays placed in the *Cupressus* genus. The other cypresses, which have the scale-leaves adpressed unevenly, so that a *flat* leafy twig results, are included in the genus *Chamaecyparis*. This name is an unhappy bit of botanical jargon—it means "dwarf cypress" but many of the trees so named are quite tall. The two groups are so nearly related, however, that an important hybrid has arisen between them—the Leyland cypress, *Cupresso-cyparis leylandii*, and this naturally bears an intermediate pattern of foliage. Let us look at the square-twigged *Cupressus* group first.

The Italian cypress, *Cupressus sempervirens*, merits mention because of its importance in classical history and the modern Mediterranean landscape. The typical wild form, which provided a strong, fragrant, and durable timber for Roman houses and ships, has an irregular, wide-spreading crown. The striking column-shaped form, with its close, sombre foliage, which is widely grown in Italian gardens, is the variety *stricta*. Neither is hardy north of the Alps.

Monterey cypress, *Cupressus macrocarpa*, which has been widely planted in northern gardens, resembles the wild Italian cypress but bears larger cones—round grey-brown globes the size of marbles, with a blunt knob on every scale. It is native to the Monterey Peninsula and a small strip of surrounding land in the far south of California. It is essentially a sub-tropical tree, and it proves a good timber-yielder when grown in Spain or East Africa.

At one time the Monterey cypress was widely planted in British gardens, but experience has shown it to be a most unreliable tree. It is only fully hardy along the western coastal fringe. In the east, or inland, it may thrive for a few years, but is then killed outright by a few days of hard frost, such as occur in any really severe winter. For southerly and westerly coastal districts, its great merits are its quick early growth, and its complete tolerance of salt-winds off the sea. It quickly provides a dense and sturdy screen, in the shelter of which more tender shrubs and plants may be raised. Transplanting is very tricky, and the extra cost of pot-grown plants will prove a sound investment. Monterey cypress can easily be trained into a close dense hedge. Both hedges and taller screens need regular attention, for they become straggly and gappy if regular clipping is neglected. Clip only in April or August.

Leyland cypress, *Cupresso-cyparis leylandii*, is a fairly new hybrid with tremendous possibilities for garden planting; and perhaps even for timber production. It was discovered, as long ago as 1888, by Mr. C. J. Leyland, a leading arboriculturist, and he found it—remarkably—on both of his large forest estates—Kyloe in Northumberland and Leighton Park near Welshpool in mid-Wales. The parents, in both places, were the Monterey cypress and the Nootka cypress, that is *Chamaecyparis nootkatensis* from Alaska. There are naturally several *clones* of this hybrid, differing slightly in character.

About 1950, commercial nurserymen, encouraged by the great Kew tree expert, William Dallimore, who had named and studied this exceptional tree, began to promote its use. It is easily increased by cuttings, but does not appear, so far, to flower or bear fertile seed. Leyland cypress has the good form of its Californian ancestor, and the hardiness of its Alaskan one, and a full measure of hybrid vigour which causes it to grow as fast as any evergreen. Quite easy to establish, it grows three feet taller each year, and forms a shapely oval pyramid of a restful mid-green. Its only fault is that it may soon grow too large for a limited position, but it is easily restrained by clipping. It is a good hedge bush.

Four cypresses with flattened, fern-like foliage are widely grown as ornamental shrubs. Frankly, it is very hard indeed for anyone, expert or otherwise, to distinguish these four species, especially when he is dealing with an exceptional garden variety or cultivar. If cones are present, things become easier, but many ornamental races rarely if ever bear seed, being increased by cuttings or by grafting.

The following brief key may help, though it only works well for the typical examples of each kind. For the rest, one is very dependent on the nurseryman's label!

Uneven leaf lengths

Lawson cypress, *Chamaecyparis lawsoniana*, which is by far the commonest kind, has the *side-leaves* along its branches distinctly *larger* than the *face-leaves*. All the leaves are *pointed*, and the cones are small, without sharp points.

Hinoki cypress, *C. obtusa*, has similar large *side-leaves*, but every leaf has a *blunt*, or obtuse, point.

Even leaf lengths

Sawara cypress, *C. pisifera*, has both *face-leaves* and *side-leaves* equal in length. All the leaves bear *sharp* points, and the cones are large—pea-shaped—with blunt scales.

Nootka cypress, *C. nootkatensis*, also has leaves of even length, but each cone-scale bears a distinct, curved, and sharp point.

In practice, Nootka cypress is usually identified by its rank odour when the foliage is crushed, and by its drooping habit of growth. Maurice Nimmo aptly says, "It always looks as though it needs a good watering." In the variety *pendula* this weeping habit is intensified to provide, through the long and gracefully drooping branches, a highly decorative effect. Nootka cypress comes from Alaska and British Columbia, where it is known as "yellow cypress" and yields a useful timber.

A rather similar tree, *C. thyoides*, is found wild in the eastern United States, where it is called the white cypress or white cedar, because of its pale green foliage. In America it is cultivated both for timber and for ornament, but in Europe it is seldom seen outside botanic gardens.

The two Japanese cypresses, Hinoki and Sawara, are the Tweedledum and Tweedledee of the ornamental bush conifers—almost exactly alike yet having distinct identities. Confusion is increased by the existence of similar cultivars of each species—you may for example, buy a dwarf golden-leaved form of either kind. There is really nothing to choose between them on the grounds of good garden behaviour. Both are hardy and long-lived, and most cultivars follow their expected habit of growth, and remain at a reasonable size over a long span of years; pruning or training is seldom necessary. These cultivars are the outcome of diligent selection by Japanese gardeners, who have tended these cypresses for centuries.

Recommended cultivars for the Hinoki cypress, *Chamaecyparis obtusa* (the one with sized, blunt scale-leaves), are—

'Crippsii', a slow-growing small tree bearing rich golden yellow leaves.

'Filicoides', the fern-spray cypress, a slow-growing form with flattened, fern-like branches.

'Nana', a dwarf, bushy form of slow growth, which carries dark green mossy foliage on flat tiers of branches.

'Sanderi', a dwarf form which has blue-green juvenile leaves throughout, and looks very like a heath; the foliage turns bronze in winter.

'Tetragona'. The name of this cultivar means "four-sided", and each twig has that appearance. It forms a much branched bush of slow growth, with smooth, green mossy foliage; each twig is tipped with bronze. There is a golden-leaved variant called 'Tetragona aurea'.

Good cultivars of the Sawara cypress, *C. pisifera* (the one with even-sized, sharp-pointed scale leaves), include—

'Plumosa', a dense conical shrub, clad in feathery foliage made up of soft juvenile leaves. Its colour is greyish green, and there is also a golden-leaved strain called 'Plumosa aurea'.

'Squarrosa', another form with juvenile leaves, which stand out from the twigs in an angular fashion; their colour is bluish-green.

'Filifera', rather a freak this, having long whip-like branchlets completely hidden in adpressed leaflets; they are undivided over most of their length, but fork near the tip. It forms a low, straggling bush.

Lawson cypress, *C. lawsoniana*, owes its Scottish name to its discovery, in 1854, by Andrew Murray, during the course of a botanical exploration promoted by Peter Lawson, an Edinburgh nurseryman. The Americans, who had discovered it already, still call it Port Orford cedar, after a seaport in Oregon. It grows wild within a small coastal region on the borders of southern Oregon and northern California, usually as a minor tree in the forests of Douglas fir and Sitka spruce. It yields a strong timber with a naturally durable heart-wood, but this is only available in relatively small sizes; some is used locally, but it has never featured much in world commerce. Several trial plantations of Lawson cypress have been established in Europe, but the trees have always shown a strong inclination to fork. Forked trunks are worth little or nothing to the timber trade, so foresters, with other trees available, have not persevered with this awkward evergreen.

Luckily, forking is not a serious fault in Lawson cypress when it is grown for ornament. It holds its foliage so low down that few onlookers notice whether a tree consists of one, two, or four separate upright trunks. The common wild form, which is easily raised from seed, is often used for hedging. It can be trained into a robust barrier of a pleasing bluish-green, holding a dense cover right to its foot. But the branches are so sturdy that, in practice, it is hard to keep it reasonably narrow; it is always tending to grow wider than the situation permits. Western red cedar, *Thuja plicata*, is a far better-behaved hedge shrub, and few people notice the difference between these two trees! (See page 288).

The foliage of Lawson cypress, like that of the western red cedar, is always in demand by florists, who use it for wreaths and as background greenery in floral arrangements. Pruned side branches, if of sufficient size and substance, can be sold to wholesale florists at a fair profit.

The cultivars of Lawson cypress are remarkably numerous and varied for a tree that was introduced to garden cultivation only a century ago. They are increased by cuttings, which strike fairly easily, or more rarely by grafting. Most nurserymen stock a good selection in adequate quantities. Several arboreta have a good display, which helps the intending planter to make a choice, and there is a wonderful group in the Cypress Valley at the Forestry Commission Pinetum at Bedgebury, near Hawkhurst in Kent.

To simplify description, we will here divide the leading cultivars by their leaf colour:

Blue Cultivars of Lawson Cypress

'Triomphe de Boskoop' is the most vigorous of the blue varieties; grows fast and forms a tall pyramid up to fifty feet high.

'Columnaris' provides a perfectly rounded close spire of rich blue foliage.

'Allumii' is more pyramidal in shape and grows at a moderate rate to medium size.

'Milford Blue Jacket' is claimed to be the bluest of them all.

'Silver Queen' is remarkable for the silvery-white sprays of its youngest branches, which later become bluish-green.

'Fletcheri', named after a leading nurseryman in the Chertsey district of Surrey, bears juvenile leaves and forms close, soft-textured, blue-green pyramids up to fifteen feet tall.

'Wisselli' is rather a gaunt tree, with blue-green foliage clustered on angular branches that give it a restless, twisted look. Some think it quaintly effective, others consider it an unhappy freak; both views are firmly held!

'Ellwoodii', the best of the slow-growing blues, having upright branches densely clad in feathery juvenile leaves; seldom exceeds eight feet.

Golden Cultivars of Lawson Cypress

'Lutea' is the most consistently yellow, and provides a strong contrast with the blue varieties.

'Lutea Nana' is the dwarf form of this, and forms a low rockery shrub.

'Minima Aurea' is a dwarf with a pyramidal form, and curiously twisted branches.

'Stewartii' is a tall and vigorous kind with pleasing rich yellow leaves.

Green Cultivars of Lawson Cypress

'Kilmacurragh,' which originated in Ireland, grows in a beautiful columnar shape recalling an Italian cypress, but bears more cheerful bright green foliage.

'Erecta Viridis' forms a pyramidal bush of an intense true green hue.

'Pottenii' is a slow growing, dwarf form with feathery sea-green foliage.

'Forsteckensis' is a dwarf globular kind, suited to the rock garden, with densely crowded branchlets giving the appearance of deep green moss.

There are also a number of variegated forms, which somehow never look healthy or natural. Most of them have white or yellow tips to green or blue-green branchlets. Exceptionally, as in the rock-garden form 'Pygmaea Argentea', silvery-white branch tips enliven dark, blue-green foliage with a charmingly decorative effect.

Within this range of cultivars—which could easily be extended by adding less distinct and more freakish kinds—the most exacting landscape planner can find trees for every situation and effect. Lawson cypress is very hardy and exceptionally free from pests and diseases, and shows fair tolerance of town smoke. You can hardly go wrong in choosing it as a garden shrub that will not fail to display bright foliage all through the year. But do read the catalogues carefully, weighing every word, to choose the form and colour that you really want for the spot you have in view.

The flowers of the Lawson cypress, like those of its allied kinds, are so small that many people get the impression that it is a flowerless tree; certain cultivars, in fact, seldom if ever bloom. The male flowers appear in spring at the tips of branchlets, and look like bright pink buds; after scattering yellow pollen they fade and disappear. Female flowers are blue clusters of scaly bracts, also borne on branch tips, which ripen in one season to small grey-brown round woody cones. The ordinary buds of this tree, which extends twig growth onwards, are never exposed to view, being completely hidden within the close-packed scale-leaves.

YEWS, *Taxus* species Plate 1C, p. 112.

Although the common European yew, *Taxus baccata*, occasionally grows to timber-tree size, and was once the source of the bow-staves used by medieval archers, it is never planted for timber production to-day. The main use of this tree and its American ally, *T. canadensis*, is in horticulture, as dependable evergreens which withstand any amount of clipping and training, rarely grow too large, and tolerate a greater degree of shade than do any other trees.

Yews have one serious practical drawback, in that their leaves, bark and seeds are poisonous. The risk to human life is small, for the only part of the tree that attracts a child, as something good to eat, is the pink flesh or *aril* around the seed, and this, fortunately, is harmless. The risk to farm livestock is considerable. One can find many examples of sheep, cattle, and horses which have regular access to growing yew trees, and occasionally browse their leaves, yet suffer no harm. But against this one must set instances in which valuable farm stock, suddenly given access to yews, have eaten too freely of an unaccustomed, toxic food, and promptly succumbed. Withered foliage appears to be particularly dangerous, though still attractive to animals; yew clippings, therefore, should always be disposed of in such a way that no beast can reach them. In brief, yews should never be planted in any situation where farm stock can reach them, nor can they be used for hedges designed to keep in livestock.

Yew hedges are usually established with transplants of the common wild yew. This is easily grown from prepared seed; after collection, the seeds must first be freed from their fleshy pink outer coat, and then be stored for eighteen months in damp sand. Yew grows fairly fast in youth, and a staggered row of trees, spaced two feet apart, will unite to form a close barrier, five feet high, within five years. Because the individual leaves can thrive with very little light, the side shoots fill all gaps in the clipped surface of a yew hedge, making it exceptionally close and dense. It is therefore a good barrier to trespassers, and a high screen of yew will also keep out noise and dust, as well as providing an effective sight-screen. Being impenetrable to light, it will also cast a heavy shade, and this factor should be allowed for in garden planning. Clipped hedges rarely bear berries.

Yew is the best of all trees for topiary, or the art of tree sculpture. The same ability to tolerate shade, and fill all gaps with foliage, enables it to build up the even surfaces required by the tree sculptor. If his hewing is a bit rough, the natural growth of the tree will soon round it off—which is more than can be said for a block of stone! But artificial shapes can only be maintained by repeated clippings, at least once a year, for the tree is always striving to regain its natural form.

Whether topiary is worth while is a matter of opinion. Purists who maintain that a tree is a tree *is a tree*, will never accept the delusion that it may be a peacock, and any representation of a human figure drives them mad! Yet any hedge form is basically unnatural, and we all accept hedges as desirable features in the landscape. The acceptance of artificial tree, hedge and bush shapes is largely a matter of proportion, and of fitness for surroundings. Arches, overhanging porches, and screens of yew can look entirely right in some old cottage garden, set against grey walls of Cotswold stone. They can make good use of restricted space, even filling borders too narrow for a flower bed. In the more open surroundings of a modern brick house they usually look absurd—as though somebody had tried to revive an ancient fashion in dress or manners.

If the common yew is allowed to attain tree size, it forms a low spreading tree with an irregular ribbed trunk, such as may be seen in many old churchyards. Our largest and most rugged yews all stand beside churches; the record for girth, 35 feet, is held by one at Ulcombe in Kent. Allowing for the probable rate of outward growth, these yews must be older than the church buildings—themselves ancient—beside which they stand. This implies that some of the earliest Christian churches were built close to old yews, already hallowed by tradition, which had served as meeting places for pagan worship. A few of these trees probably exceed 2,000 years in age.

The modern planter is more likely to want an upright form of yew, that will remain clothed in foliage down to ground level, and soon provide a simple pillar of foliage that casts little shade. Nothing at all will grow beneath the sombre crown of the common yew. Upright or fastigiate yews are generally known as "Irish" yews, because the best-known cultivar, called 'Fastigiata', was found by a farmer named Willis on the Florence Court estate in County Fermanagh in the year 1780. They are increased by cuttings.

Those who find the dull green of the common yew too depressing may prefer a golden yew, in either the normal or the upright "Irish" habit of growth. 'Fastigiata Standishii' is an excellent upright golden cultivar. Creeping yews such as "Repandens" may have a place near the rockery, though they readily become untidy and hard to control. There are no yews that "weep" in the accepted sense, but an elegant variety with drooping branchlets is the Westfelton yew, cultivar 'Dovastoniana'.

These exceptional varieties of yew rarely flower. Normally, a yew tree is either wholly male or wholly female. The male tree bears pretty pale yellow clusters of flowers in February, but you must secure a female tree to be rewarded by the display of crimson berries in late autumn, in the words of the poet Meredith:

> "Threading it with colour,
> As yewberries the yew."

There are varieties like 'Fructo-luteo' which bear yellow berries, equally effective in contrast with the deep evergreen leaves. Unless you buy one of these special sorts, which are naturally always female, you usually have to take your chance with the sex of a yew—few nurserymen guarantee it.

The plum-fruited yew, now known as *Podocarpus andinus* though formerly called *Prumnopitys elegans*, is a beautiful yew-like evergreen from the Chilean Andes. It has bright green foliage and large fleshy, yellowish-white fruits.

JUNIPERS, *Juniperus* species   Plates 19 c, d, p. 252.

The common juniper, *Juniperus communis*, is a low straggling shrub with a curiously broken distribution in Britain and western Europe. It has vanished entirely from large regions where the land is well cultivated. In England it can be found growing abundantly on the chalk downs east of Salisbury in Wiltshire, while in Scotland it forms great thickets below the northern pinewoods, notably those of the Rothiemurchus Forest in mid-Inverness-shire. Elsewhere it is very local, being completely absent from many counties.

Few junipers grow large enough to yield timber, and the only use of the common kind is as kindling for fires or as the source of the piquant oil of juniper used to flavour gin. This is obtained, by distillation, from the unripe green berries that hold the seeds. Junipers are unique among conifers in having cones with soft fleshy scales that attract birds, which spread their seeds; when ripe, these berries have an attractive blue colour. The other key feature of the genus is the arrangement of the needles in groups of three; this is not obvious at a glance, but becomes clear on close examination. Some species, however, bear adpressed *scale-leaves* instead of free needles, while others again have the two kinds of foliage intermixed. The male flowers of juniper are clusters of yellow anthers, which become, in some species, quite obvious and attractive. The whole shrub has an attractive fragrance, and in Poland the smoke of junipers is used to give a delicious taste to the best ham.

The common wild juniper succeeds on nearly any garden soil, from chalk to sand, but is seldom grown as it has few attractions beyond its grey-green foliage. In the wilds you may occasionally come across a taller, columnar juniper which aspires to tree form. This is cultivated as variety *suecica*, or Swedish juniper, and it is a good choice where a small upright evergreen is required. Irish juniper, cultivar 'Stricta', has a similar form but makes a denser column. Dwarf kinds include the variety *nana*, or mountain juniper, which slowly develops into a low compact bush, having broad leaves bearing conspicuous white resin bands on their undersides; it is found wild, though rarely, in northern Scotland. The still smaller cultivar 'Compressa' takes several years to build itself up into a blue-grey pyramid only one foot high, and is best sited in the rock garden. 'Aurea' bears golden-yellow shoots and young leaves at the tips of grey-green branches, turning bronze in winter; it forms a low, spreading bush. The variety *prostrata*, which is occasionally seen as a wild plant in low juniper scrub, creeps over the ground and forms a dense mat of fine-textured foliage; it can look very effective in a large rockery or wall garden, but its carpet of foliage appears awkwardly odd when it spreads over soil, rather than over rock.

Hybrid junipers, collectively known as *Juniperus × media*, provide a useful range of hardy and vigorous cultivars. They apparently arose in Europe through crossing between the Chinese juniper, *J. chinensis* and the

Swiss savin, *J. sabina*. The best known is the Pfitzer juniper, generally catalogued as *J.* 'Pfitzeriana', but also called the "Knap Hill savin", after a famous Surrey nursery near Woking. This is a wide-spreading shrub bearing branches that shoot out strongly from the centre, and droop gracefully at their tips. Its foliage is grey-green in colour and feathery in texture. The Pfitzer juniper is widely employed in landscape planting because it can be relied on to fill a set space to a low height, with foliage of a lively texture and a pleasing, if rather neutral, hue.

Two junipers have the engaging habit of bearing juvenile, pointed needles intermixed with adpressed scale-leaves, so that every branch has a variable character, according to the disposition of the leaf clusters. One of these is *J. virginiana*, which comes from Virginia and forms a handsome, pyramidal tree. In America it is called the pencil cedar because its pinkish-brown, fine-textured and fragrant wood is the best of all materials for making lead pencils. A rather exotic cultivar of this is the Dundee juniper, or 'Pyramidiformis Hillii' which forms a narrow column of grey-blue foliage, turning to plum-purple in winter.

The second juniper of variable foliage is the Chinese one, *J. chinensis*, native to Formosa and Japan as well as to the Asiatic mainland. The typical form makes a small pyramidal tree, but it is more likely to be seen as one of numerous cultivars developed by both oriental and western gardeners. Young's golden juniper, cultivar 'Aurea', is the best of the yellow-foliaged kinds, while 'Fortunei' is an exceptionally attractive blue-grey sort. The variety *japonica* is a dwarf one, with foliage consisting almost entirely of free juvenile needles; it rarely exceeds three feet in height.

A curious feature of the Chinese juniper, as cultivated in the west, is that it is nearly always a male tree, bearing abundant yellow male flowers but seldom, if ever, developing female flowers or berries. This masculinity is not typical of the genus as a whole; most junipers bear flowers of both sexes, followed by pretty clusters of lustrous blue-grey berries.

HIBA, *Thujopsis dolabrata*

Hiba is a fascinating evergreen bush from Japan, which is frequently grown in shrubberies for its bright green foliage and its engaging irregular shape; very rarely it tries to grow into a small tree, but specimens over fifteen feet high are unusual. You can recognise hiba by the grouping of its scale-leaves in definite sections of fours, which makes a branchlet look surprisingly like the interlocked vertebrae of a human backbone. The underside of each leaf, when exposed to view by turning a branchlet over, bears very broad and obvious white patches; these are covered in resin, which restricts the loss of water through the leaf's stomata.

Hiba cones are round in shape, and each scale bears a hook-shaped prickle. Its foliage is particularly useful for floral decorations; if removed in moderate amounts it is soon renewed by natural growth.

JAPANESE UMBRELLA TREE, *Sciadopitys verticillata*

The odd name of this tree is easily explained as soon as you see it. All its needles are grouped in whorls set at intervals along the twigs, and the leaves of each whorl project outwards, in all directions, just like the ribs of an umbrella or a parasol. Each leaf looks like a stout needle with a groove down its centre; it is leathery in texture and dark olive-green in colour, while the twigs are bright reddish-brown. Botanists have discovered that each "leaf" is in fact a pair of needles, which spring from a minute short shoot and have become fused together. Very occasionally the Japanese umbrella tree bears curious egg-shaped cones which reveal, by their shape, a remote relationship to the true pines.

The Japanese umbrella tree is only fully hardy in the south and west of Britain, and even there it benefits from the side shelter of taller trees. It grows very slowly, an increase in height of six inches a year being a fair average. Repeated branching causes it to form an irregular bush, but occasionally it develops a definite trunk and may make a straggly tree up to forty feet high. Its ornamental value lies solely in the quaintness of its geometrical foliage carried at regular intervals on leafless twigs. It looks exactly right in a Japanese garden, and also provides unusual material for indoor flower arrangements. Seedlings grow extremely slowly, and trees must be at least six years old before they are big enough for garden planting; hence these trees are rather costly.

21. Dwarf and Miniature Trees

PEOPLE grow small trees for one or more of three reasons. They may actually have little space available, they may take a delight in living plants and contrived landscapes that are less than life-size, or they may wish to create a comprehensive collection of different living kinds which would be beyond their resources of space, cash, and time if every example had to be full-scale.

There is one golden rule that applies to every collection of small trees—and indeed to small objects of every kind. *Everything must be in scale.* Never attempt to mix the miniature with the life size. Both will suffer by comparison, and so will the whole effect. The illusion of a common degree of scale must be preserved by keeping every tree, plant, and inanimate object in proportion with its neighbours.

DEGREES OF SCALE AND TIME

Basically there are two degrees of scale that are employed in practice. One is the very miniature indoor scale, developed by the Japanese under the name of *bonsai*. This involves the *artificial dwarfing* of otherwise normal trees by methods to be described later. The heights of the resulting trees are best measured in *inches*.

In contrast, there is the rock-garden scale, widely used by gardeners everywhere, in which the trees, though small, can be measured in terms of feet. For this purpose *naturally dwarf* trees are grown—trees that will never become full-size, no matter how well they are fed and watered. These are, of course, far easier to handle.

The time factors for tending dwarf trees, on either scale, are of course, quite different to those employed for normal trees. The forester and the general landscape gardener aim to keep their trees growing steadily taller and larger for many years; everything is planned with that in view. The forester will aim at growth in height at rates between one and three feet a year, maintained for as long as sixty years, and ended by the felling of the tree, or a slowing-off as it nears maturity. The landscapist may be content with somewhat slower growth, because in restricted surroundings he will have to lop or prune those trees that get too big.

On the rock garden scale, the dwarf tree grower plans to avoid both lopping and felling; he hopes that his trees will grow by a few inches annually to heights of two or three feet at the most, and then somehow remain static forever! The Japanese miniature gardener aims to hold trees only a few inches tall at the same dimensions for scores of years even for centuries; but he can only do so by the minute pruning of both shoots and roots—one might call it "mini-pruning".

For both these gardeners, time must stand still.

When people are buying small trees, they usually insist, rather perversely, that they shall be fairly big! To ensure that the tree they plant is well-rooted, and unlikely to become smothered by weeds, they choose one with some substance. This means that the price is fairly steep, because it takes the nurseryman much longer to grow a dwarf tree to a certain size, than it does a normal tree.

NATURALLY DWARF TREES

Trees that remain small when given normal conditions for growth arise in two different ways. In nature, many kinds of trees have a great geographical spread, from regions of normal climate, where they grow tall, to places with adverse climates where they can only survive and reproduce their kind at smaller dimensions. On the cold tundras around the Arctic Circle, on the upper slopes of high mountain ranges, and in dry deserts with great extremes of heat and cold, only stunted trees are found. During millions of years of evolution, distinct species or varieties of trees have developed, which can make efficient use of their harsh surroundings, but have lost the power to grow to full size. They are able, however, to bear flowers and fruit in the normal way. You can therefore grow them from seed, secure in the knowledge that nature has set its own limits to their stature.

The dwarf birch, *Betula nana*, the dwarf juniper, *Juniperus communis* variety *nana*, and the mountain rhododendron, *Loiseleuria procumbens*, are examples from the Scottish hills of trees and shrubs with this hereditary limit to their size, combined with normal reproduction by seed.

The second group of trees that remain small are the "freaks". Among the millions of trees that grow up just like their parents, there are always a few stunted individuals whose genetic make-up has gone wrong. They cannot develop normally, and in the wilds they are usually soon suppressed and crowded out by taller neighbours. Ingenious nurserymen spot these exceptional dwarfs from time to time, bring them into cultivation, and increase them by taking cuttings, or else bv grafting. Few of them bear normal flowers or fruit, so they can only oe kept in continued existence by human aid.

In the average garden or nursery that features naturally dwarf trees, examples of both kinds—the freaks and those developed by evolution—are usually grown together. But they behave differently, the freaks having no normal course of flowering, fruiting, or ageing.

Some of the freaks arise as "sporting" branches rather than as seedlings. A normal tree may send out a side branch of a peculiar habit of growth, and if grafting material, or cuttings, are taken from this, they continue to grow in the same exceptional way. The abnormal branch clusters called "witches brooms", which arise through insect attack or fungal disease, often include branches that, when propagated, continue life as dwarf trees!

The rock garden is usually chosen as the home for dwarf trees, and it is a good place for several reasons, some practical, some visual. Where the spaces between the trees are filled with rocks, weeding is reduced, and no large herbaceous plants intrude to destroy the impression of the trees as the leading elements in the view. Trees planted in the gaps root very happily in the cool soil below the stones, while all the rainfall is concentrated into the gaps. The slopes can be varied, to give hills and hollows, and prostrate varieties of tree can be trained to creep over flat rock faces, or even to droop over precipices. The low rock plants that are usually chosen to accompany the trees do not intrude, but provide charming and fitting contrasts of colour and form.

The rock-garden environment really succeeds because it is close to nature. Many dwarf trees are, in fact, most at home among crags, scree and shingle high in the mountains.

Good drainage is important for success. A subsoil of sand or gravel is ideal, whereas clays are unfavourable. The elevation of the ground above its surroundings, as is usual in rock-garden construction, usually ensures drainage that is sharp enough; any waterlogged hollows are best filled with bog plants!

Since you are not aiming to grow trees fast, fertilisers will seldom be needed. Should trees hang fire, a mulch of leaf mould or hop manure is the simplest and safest means of supplying needed nutrients and so re-starting growth.

DWARF CONIFERS Plate 19, p. 252.

Coniferous trees are far more popular in the rock garden than are the broadleaved trees, for several good reasons. Being evergreen, they are attractive throughout the year. Their very regular pattern of growth helps them to fit more neatly into a small space than does the more free and random branching habit of the broadleaves. The numerous cultivars that are offered by commercial nurserymen, mainly by specialists in this field, give good scope for choice, and each remains very true to type.

As a general rule, the more shade-bearing kinds of conifer form the better dwarf trees, because they will grow happily with their needles crowded closely together. Spruces, for example, prove better dwarf subjects than do the pines or the larches, because the latter trees must have ample light around every leaf, and that calls for ample space also.

Specialists have recorded over sixty freak dwarf forms of the Norway spruce, *Picea abies*, but the differences between many of them could only interest a crank! Distinct forms that attract the more general collector include the following cultivars:

'Clanbrasiliana', a flat rounded bush, shaped like an inverted pudding basin, rarely more than six feet high; discovered at Moira, near Belfast, about 1770, and named after Lord Clanbrasil.

'Humilis', a very dwarf and dense cushion of dark green leaves.

'Repens', a creeping form most at home in the rock garden.

A very attractive and unusual dwarf spruce is *Picea albertiana conica*, which is a natural dwarf from the cold tundras of northern Canada. It makes an erect treelet with a regular conical shape and dense even foliage, and increases in height at a very slow rate indeed. Plate 19e, p. 252.

Dwarf forms are found in most of the cypresses, and good ones include the dwarf Lawson cypress, *Chamaecyparis lawsoniana* 'Minima' and its golden equivalent 'Minima Aurea'. The Japanese Hinoki cypress, *C. obtusa*, also has a 'Minima' cultivar that is exceptionally small; so does the Sawara cypress, in its 'Nana' cultivar.

In the rather similar genus *Thuja*, very desirable dwarf trees are:

Thuja occidentalis 'Robusta Nana', with crimson-tinged foliage and short, thick branchlets having recurved tips; and the very lively 'Ellwangeriana Aurea', tipped with gold in summer and bronzed in winter.

T. orientalis 'Minima Glauca', which is bluish-green in summer but turns to a bronzy green in the winter months.

T. plicata 'Rogersii', a pyramidal dwarf with golden and bronzy foliage.

Dwarf junipers can be obtained in several fascinating forms. *Juniperus communis* 'Compressa' is a tiny bluish-grey race that takes many years to reach a height of one foot, while 'Prostrata' creeps over the ground to form a mat of foliage only one foot high. Even the mighty sequoias, the world's tallest trees, have their pygmy races that can be accommodated in the rock garden.

JAPANESE MINIATURE TREES or BONSAI

The art of growing miniature trees in pots is peculiarly Japanese in origin, though it has now spread to the Western world. It is centuries old, and apparently began with the practice of growing exceptional trees —natural dwarfs—in pots where space was limited in the small Japanese house. Techniques were developed to hold each little tree at a set size, while still keeping it healthy. These have been perfected to the point where perfectly normal trees can be kept small indefinitely and be trained into attractive shapes.

Many people in the West have completely wrong ideas of the methods that the Japanese use for "dwarfing" their *bonsai* or miniature trees. They imagine that they keep them small by using poor soil, applying no fertilisers, providing the minimum of water, and pruning the roots at intervals to check upward growth.

Actual practice is quite different. It is true that the roots are pruned, but this is only done in order to promote more active growth of the bushy type desired. Good soil is used, and fertilisers are added, while the trees are given ample water at frequent intervals. A miniature tree living in a pot has to be kept growing vigorously at all times, or it will perish. The problem then is how to keep it growing without letting it get any bigger!

The main step taken to keep bonsai small is pruning, repeated more often, and done with greater skill, than is usual for any larger tree. It is usually done by pinching with the fingers, but fine shears are also used, for any stems that have become tough and woody. During the growing season, a tree sends out many soft green shoots from its buds, which normally extend its spread by several inches, or even feet. The bonsai trainer *stops* these, after an inch or so of growth, by pinching them off with his fingers. If growth is renewed by small side buds below the

Prune shoots short monthly during growing season

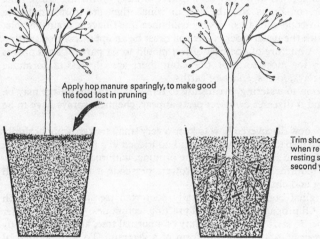

Apply hop manure sparingly, to make good the food lost in pruning

Trim short roots back when re-potting in resting season every second year.

FIGURE 78. Artificial dwarfing of a bonsai miniature tree.

pruning point, he prunes again, as often as becomes necessary during the growing season. In the winter he tidies the tree up by a further pruning of resting shoots. These pruning processes are much like the clipping of a hedge, except that they are directed towards forming an open tree-like shape, instead of a close wall of green leaves. Growth goes on steadily, but the crop of shoots is "harvested" almost as fast.

This removal of prunings slowly but inevitably exhausts the limited amount of plant nutrients within the soil of the pot, so it becomes necessary to renew this soil at intervals. In practice, bonsai are re-potted about once every two years. Like any other tree, they tend to form long slender roots that make further transplanting risky. Therefore at each re-potting these slender roots are systematically pruned back. The tree then forms a mass of short bushy roots which are excellent for the uptake of water and plant nutrients, and help it to survive the shock of the next transplanting. No matter how long a bonsai may live, this re-potting must be repeated every few years.

In between the successive re-pottings, the miniature tree also needs added nutrients. The Japanese use rape-cake, a residue from the extraction of rape-seed oil. This is an organic material holding about 5% nitrogen, 2.5% phosphorus and 1.5% potash. It is applied in small crumbs, followed by watering, and has long-lasting effects, since it releases its nutrients slowly. A satisfactory alternative is hop manure—another organic substance that holds the food once stored in a growing plant.

Water is applied to bonsai very freely; a daily sprinkling is the rule. Both their containers and the soil in which they are grown must be designed to cope with this. Every container must have a drainage hole, covered with the usual crock. The soil must be an open-textured potting compost. A mixture of one part of leaf mould to six parts of sand proves satisfactory for most sorts of trees, but there are all sorts of formulae involving clays, loams, and rare earths.

In addition to watering, syringeing to remove dust from foliage may be needed, and if diseases or insect pests appear, chemical sprays have to be applied.

We have now discovered how to keep a very small tree growing healthily in a restricted space—well watered and nourished in a freely draining soil, and restrained in size by repeated fine pruning, with root trimming whenever it is required. How do the growers persuade it to grow into such fascinating and charming shapes?

The original bonsai were naturally contorted trees, and many such races are still propagated by skilful grafting techniques. But it is simpler and cheaper to start with the seedling of a normal tree, and to force it, by artificial restraints, to adopt the form of a veteran. To the commercial grower, time is money, and he cannot raise trees that look centuries old, at a profit, unless he can do it in four to five years! The method used is to bend and twist the stems and branches of the growing treelets into bizarre shapes by coiling wire around them; for certain styles they are even bent around short sticks. This must be done at just the right stage, whilst the wood is becoming firm but has not yet got too rigid. It calls for careful judgement, to bend the twig without breaking it. Once the twig has become "set" in its new shape, through the hardening of its woody tissues, the wires and sticks are removed, leaving an appearance of gnarled but natural growth.

To a Western gardener such tedious manipulation of a growing tree may seem unnatural. But the Japanese have developed it to a fine art. They keep in mind the high standards of perfection to which tiny trees can be brought, according to styles of design and grouping that have become traditional. In their hands a tree becomes a plastic substance like clay in the potter's hands, to be trained into an exquisite design. For example, the branches springing from a single prostrate stock may each be persuaded to take on the form of a tree, so that a miniature wood is created from a single seed. There is a sense of satisfaction in taking in the whole of a tree, or a grove of trees, within a close-up view, even though we know the whole thing to be an illusion. It all accords well with the Japanese décor of exquisite pottery containers and polished wood supports.

What trees are grown as bonsai? Among the conifers, the Japanese favour pines and spruces, but these trees cannot be imported to the British Isles, because of quarantine restrictions designed to protect timber crops. It is sad, but true, that these tiny trees suffer from just the same diseases and pests as do taller trees of the same genus. Junipers, and cypresses of all kinds, are not kept out by any quarantine ban, and they can be trained into patterns almost as intricate as those of pines and spruces. Coniferous bonsai are of course evergreen; it is quite exceptional for them to bear cones when kept so small.

Deciduous broadleaved trees are often grown as bonsai in Japan; though they are seldom seen in the West. The dwarfing treatment does not impair their ability to flower, and some even set fruit. Decorative cherries, and apricots, and even wisterias, can be persuaded to blossom when raised in remarkably small containers. Viburnums can be induced to bear branches of scarlet berries, while pomegranates only a few feet high may bear their bright orange fruits.

Now that the Japanese have revealed the secrets of the bonsai-raising art, anyone can do it! But it is safe to prophesy that most of the masterpieces will continue to come from Japan, whose gardeners are happy to express their personality and artistic skill in designing trees just a little more perfect than you can find in nature.

22. Shelterbelts and Christmas Trees

A belt or screen of trees provides the cheapest and most effective means of slowing down the force of the wind and giving shelter to crops, farm livestock, buildings, and people. Once a belt has been established, it grows steadily larger, and also renews its branches and leaves without help. The design of a tree's crown, which is intended by nature to filter air through a screen of leaves, is very satisfactory from the dynamic point of view. A wall or a fence gives rise to eddies, whereas a tree screen produces a "cushion" of slowly-moving air, free from gusts. This slower air stream can be detected a long way from the belt itself, and on flat land the wind is still being appreciably slowed down up to a distance of *twenty times* the height of the belt. Thus, a shelterbelt sixty-six feet tall shelters land for a distance of 440 yards, or one quarter of a mile, on its leeward side. There is also a small shelter effect on the opposite side, for twenty yards or so in the windward direction.

In practice, this means that farmers can shelter a large expanse of land by giving up only a small fraction of it to shelter belts. A width of one chain, that is twenty-two yards, is fully effective, and gives shelter for a distance of twenty chains. On the great plains of the United States, and also on the steppes of Russia, networks of shelterbelts have been planted. They occupy about 10 per cent of the land, but increase yield from farm crops and livestock by about 30 per cent, so there is a substantial net gain.

Most planters, however, will only be concerned with a single belt, or a group of two or three belts protecting a single field, a park or garden, or a group of buildings. Correct siting is the first essential. The belt should run at right angles to the main flow of the wind that it is designed to check. On very exposed ground it is best to set it in a slightly sheltered position, so that the young trees themselves do not have to face the full windblast until they have become established. But anywhere else, the higher the belt is placed, the better. The ground must be soundly fenced on all sides. Where artificial drainage is needed, it must be very thorough; trees are more likely to be blown down because the soil is waterlogged at their roots, than for any other reason. Damp soil has little resistance to the turning forces of the wind.

CHOICE OF TREES

The choice of trees to use for shelter depends very much on the type of land that is to be planted. The principles are the same as those for timber crops. Any *thriving* tree crop will provide shelter, whereas an unthrifty one will not do so, no matter how desirable its choice may have appeared

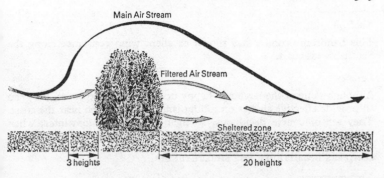

FIGURE 79. How shelterbelts work: Cross-section. The main air stream is deflected *above* the belt. A filtered air stream passes slowly through it. Effective shelter results, on flat ground for twenty times the height of the belt in its lee and three times the height in front. (Not drawn to scale.)

on theoretical grounds. It goes without saying—though it is sometimes overlooked—that only evergreen trees can give full shelter the whole year round. Deciduous trees like the beech can give only partial shelter in winter, though even this can prove well worth while.

In practice, certain trees are far more likely to be chosen than others. Characteristics of some of the most generally grown shelter trees are set out below.

SUITABLE SHELTERBELT CONIFERS

Scots pine

Reliable on moderately exposed land free from lime. Particularly successful on sands and sandstones on the eastern side of Britain. Unsuitable for extreme exposure, chalk or lime soils, heavy clays, or seaside belts.

Lodgepole pine

A remarkably hardy conifer, far more tolerant of wet western conditions and peaty soils, than is the Scots pine.

Austrian pine

Stands any amount of exposure, and tolerates most soils, including limestones and chalk. A good seaside tree.

Sitka spruce

Easily the best shelter tree for the worst exposures in western Britain. Withstands the worst salt-laden sea gales. A very effective species on the sea-boards of Scotland, Wales and Ireland. Unsuitable for the drier east.

Noble fir

This handsome conifer has shown excellent wind resistance along the Scottish west coast.

Larches

Although none of the larches is happy under extreme exposure, they can all provide effective shelter on rolling land that is not too near the coast. They are of course deciduous, so their effectiveness in winter, when shelter is most needed, is less than that of evergreen trees.

CONIFERS UNSUITABLE FOR SHELTERBELTS

Norway spruce

This has none of the hardihood and salt-tolerance shown by Sitka spruce. It cannot take the full brunt of the wind without becoming distorted.

Douglas fir

A poor shelter tree. Its crown is distorted by gales, and it is more apt to be windblown than is any commonly planted conifer.

There is so far no indication that the "rarer" conifers, such as western hemlock and Lawson cypress, have any particular merit as shelter trees. It is best to avoid using all untried species, on any scale, in situations where certain shelter is needed over a long span of years.

BROADLEAVED TREES SUITABLE FOR SHELTERBELTS

Beech

Wherever a broadleaved tree is desired for shelter in inland districts, beech is usually chosen. It is very windfirm, and is equally at home on high chalk downs, on limestones, on sands, or on sandstone soils. It is not, however, a good tree for coastal exposure.

Sycamore

The best, and almost the only reliable broadleaved shelter tree for coastal exposure, or the higher western hills. Remarkably windfirm, but needs reasonably fertile soil. Its fine performance near farmsteads, where it has been widely planted in north-west England and Wales, is largely due to farmyard manure!

Elm

Elms have a remarkable tolerance of salt-laden sea winds, and thrive along the exposed coastline of southern England.

BROADLEAVED TREES UNSUITABLE FOR SHELTERBELTS

Oak, ash, and birch are all alike unsuitable, for they are light-demanders that open out their branchwork above and lose it low down, as soon as they have gained height. The same is true of poplars, and there are no other broadleaves that really merit consideration as shelterbelt trees.

WIDTH AND SPACING

A shelterbelt one chain—that is sixty-six feet—wide is adequate to effect the necessary diversion of the wind-stream. Shelterbelts of twice this width are sometimes advocated on the grounds that half of the belt, by width, can be cut down and replanted at some future date, leaving half still

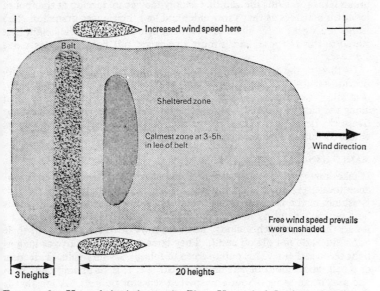

Increased wind speed here

Belt

Sheltered zone

Calmest zone at 3-5h.
in lee of belt

Wind direction

Free wind speed prevails
were unshaded

3 heights

20 heights

FIGURE 80. How shelterbelts work: Plan. Upward deflection of main air stream gives a sheltered zone for twenty times the height of the belt in its lee and three times the height in front, with about 70 per cent of free wind speed. Calmest zone is three to five heights behind the belt; wind speed here is less than 40 per cent of that in open. Wind speed is *increased* at ends of belt.

standing for a further thirty years or so, when its own turn for treatment will come round; but that is looking very far ahead, and one seldom sees the plan put into practice. There is no practical advantage in making belts wider than two chains (or 132 feet); greater width does not lead to any better diversion of the air stream, and may even cause it to return to ground level rather sooner than occurs behind a narrow belt.

Spacing of shelterbelt trees should be fairly wide; six feet is a reasonable distance and seven or eight not too wide. When people see small trees going out, they tend to think that the closer they are set together, the more effectively they will slow down the wind. But in practice the main work is done by the tree's crown of branches, not by its trunk, and what is needed is a barrier of well-branched trees, each standing somewhat apart from its neighbours, and holding a deep crown of foliage. By planting widely, thinning out, which is always a problem with shelterbelts, can be postponed for a long spell. The successive rows of trees should always be "staggered", so that each tree stands opposite a gap in the two adjacent rows.

It is a great advantage to combine a shelterbelt with a hedge. A row of tough hawthorns fills the gap that is only too apt to develop at the foot of taller timber trees as they grow older and lose their lower branches. The hedge must get its due share of attention, being trained to the height best suited to this purpose, and it must always get full light on at least one side.

In theory, the gap below the tall trees can be filled by low, shade-bearing shrubs. In practice, anything planted within a belt thrives badly, if at all. The necessary cover to close the gap should therefore be sited along the side of the belt. Where fencing can be maintained to keep out livestock, beech is a better choice than hawthorn, because it holds its withered foliage low down, right through the winter.

MAINTENANCE

It takes many years for a belt to develop to the stage when any maintenance measures, other than the care of fencing and drains, are needed. Brashing, or the removal of dead side branches from growing conifers, is best postponed for as long as possible, or omitted entirely. It will be found that the branches along the outer rows of trees, at least on their outer sides, do not die off at all. They remain green and alive as long as light reaches them. This outer screen of foliage is a very valuable feature of a belt, and should be left undisturbed. Yet it is surprising how often one sees it cut away—from a misplaced sense of tidiness. A job that is sound practice for a timber crop may be quite wrong for a shelterbelt.

Thinning is likewise a job that can be left for a long time, provided the original spacing was wide enough. Some natural losses are sure to have occurred, and over much of a belt's length these may well suffice. It is exceptionally difficult to choose trees for removal from a narrow belt, without leaving open gaps that the wind can whistle through. Even the suppressed trees, which a timber-raising forester might cut down out of hand, may be playing a useful part in slowing down the breezes.

Optimists often claim that farm shelterbelts have a double function— to provide shelter and to produce timber. In practice it is very hard to gain either benefit without detriment to the other. The owner should therefore make a firm and clear decision as to which comes first.

Grants towards the cost of shelterbelt planting, where shelter is the primary object, are given by the Agricultural Departments for each country in the British Isles. If, however, there is a timber-producing side to a project in Great Britain, a Small Woods grant can be claimed from the Forestry Commission. This is of course alternative to the shelterbelt grant, and not additional to it. For details, see page 332.

CHRISTMAS TREES

The Christmas trees sold so plentifully each December are of two types, and each arises in quite a different way.

The larger trees, which are sold without roots, are the top lengths of thinnings taken from evergreen conifer plantations early in December. At other times of the year, there is no sale at all for these top lengths, and they are simply left to rot on the forest floor. It is therefore a good plan to concentrate the thinning of suitable young conifer woods into the winter months, and to arrange the sale of this valuable by-product to the decorative foliage trade, well ahead. It is unusual for whole trees to feature in the "big tree" market, for unless they are open-grown they lose their lower branches early on. In plantations, only the top-lengths of the trees remain sufficiently well-clothed or "furnished" with foliage. Just before Christmas these tops are often worth more than the larger butt length of the tree, which is used as a pit prop, as a sawlog, or for pulpwood.

The most acceptable kind of large Christmas tree is the traditional Norway spruce; Sitka spruce is *unacceptable* because of the sharp tips to its needles. Silver firs, such as noble fir and grand fir, are welcomed by buyers, and so is Douglas fir. Other kinds of evergreen conifer are hard to sell because their appearance is so different from that of Norway spruce; the pines, for example, have branches that are too widely spaced to allow the desired concentration of foliage. "Top-length" Christmas trees are usually six feet or over in length, and the wholesale prices range from two shillings per foot-run upwards. A really big tree is worth several pounds, but is seldom prepared except to a special order. The only preparation needed to fit "top-length" trees for sale, is to bind their branches, loosely around the main stem, with binder twine, for convenience of transport, and even this is not always done.

The other, much more numerous kind of Christmas tree is the short, rooted one, from eighteen inches to six feet or so in height, which is specially raised in a Christmas tree nursery. Many optimistic people imagine that all that need be done is to find an odd patch of ground, fill it with small Norway spruce trees, and then await a golden harvest a few years later. In practice, considerable care and planning are needed. Quarantine restrictions prevent the entry of any Christmas trees from abroad, so all the trees sold are raised within the British Isles. So far the demand has always been equal to the supply, and this is an encouraging situation for those who wish to invest in a relatively short-term tree crop. No Government grants are available for Christmas tree growing; profits are taxed normally, but growing trees are exempt from Capital Gains Tax.

The public's preference for Norway spruce is so strong, in Britain, that no other tree is ever planted commercially. The land selected must be reasonably fertile and well-drained, but it need not be flat. Norway spruce does not succeed at all on certain kinds of ground; it is hopeless to try to grow Christmas trees commercially on dry heaths or any ground that naturally carries heather, on thin soils over chalk or limestone, or in districts where air is polluted by industrial smoke or fumes, or in places directly exposed to the sea. But former broadleaved woodland and abandoned grassy pastures are both very suitable.

An important practical point is that the crop is very vulnerable to theft. It is risky to establish Christmas trees in remote situations away from supervision. If an occupied house is near at hand the risk is far less.

The ground must be securely fenced against livestock and rabbits, in the same way as a timber plantation, and where necessary it should be drained. Norway spruce is normally turf-planted, and the cheapest way to provide the turfs is to plough the ground partially, at intervals of eighteen inches. Alternatively the turf can be cut with the spade.

The usual planting distance is eighteen inches apart each way. In theory, this means that 19,360 trees can be established on every acre of land, but in practice, after allowing for tracks and boundaries, 16,000 is a more likely figure. The usual size and age of tree planted is a sturdy 2+2 transplant, that is, a tree that has spent two years in a seedbed and two years in a transplant bed; it should be about fifteen inches high. Smaller trees may not all succeed, and larger trees are too costly. Planting stock should be bought at wholesale rates from a forest nursery, and it is best to inspect it in advance. Planting is done in autumn, winter, or spring, by the turf-planting method described in Chapter 19 for Norway spruce.

After-care is important. The trade demands symmetrical trees of a pyramidal shape, with even their lowest branches carrying every possible needle. A Christmas tree plantation is soon invaded by grasses and other weeds that check the regular growth of the spruces, and suppress the even growth of their side branches by overshading them. Weeding must therefore be thorough and sustained, and it will often be necessary to weed twice during one season. This requires much labour and forms one of the main costs of the enterprise.

The alternative to hand weeding, with the reap-hook or short scythe, is the application of chemical weedkillers. These can be applied quickly and cheaply, but they bring with them a risk of damage to the crop. The more potent chemicals scorch the foliage of Norway spruce just as readily as they kill weeds, but if a guard is used little damage is likely to be done to the side branches of the Christmas trees. One solution is to apply weedkillers of the paraquat type, which kill off the grasses, the most troublesome of the weeds concerned; other weeds that survive can then be tackled at reasonable cost with the reap-hook.

The harvesting of a crop of Christmas trees is best done in stages. From about the fourth year after planting onwards, that is when the trees are eight years old in all, a high proportion of the crop will reach a size that is fit for market. The whole crop should then be thinned out, taking suitable trees at intervals along the rows and leaving the survivors with more growing space than they had before. The first harvesting should be a heavy one—all trees in alternate rows, plus every other tree from the remaining rows. As the remaining trees grow older, they rapidly become larger and so fetch substantially higher prices. The last large trees need not be taken out until ten or twelve years after the crop was established. Eventually the land must be cleared in readiness for the succeeding crop.

Fertilisers are seldom used to promote the growth of Christmas trees. They carry the risk that they will cause "leggy" growth, with too long a gap between each successive whorl of foliage; purchasers prefer compact trees with successive branches close together. If repeated crops exhaust the soil, the best source of nutrients is a dressing of spent hops.

The sale of the crop should be negotiated well ahead of the pre-Christmas harvest. The purchasers, who are usually wholesale greengrocers, require the trees to be dug up, counted and bundled, all ready for transport, during a very short spell of days. There is a big labour requirement here, but overall the crop is profitable. Prices range from one shilling per foot of height wholesale, for the smallest trees, to three times that figure for tall, well-foliaged ones.

Purchasers who aim to keep this year's tree for next year's festival also, by planting it out in their garden at New Year, are nearly always disappointed. The long exposure that the roots always suffer, particularly in a heated house over Christmas, dries them out and prevents them from making an effective living contact with the soil. This is a good thing for the grower, who is assured of a repeated market, year after year.

Leading Arboreta open to the Public

ENGLAND

LONDON
Royal Botanic Gardens, Kew, Surrey, off the South Circular road just south of Kew Bridge.

SURREY
Wisley Gardens, owned by the Royal Horticultural Society, north of the main London-Portsmouth road, A3, between Cobham and Ripley.

KENT
Bedgebury Pinetum and Forest Plots, run by the Forestry Commission. Off the main London-Hastings road, A21, north of Flimwell, close to Hawkhurst, Kent; take B2079 to reach car park.

SUSSEX
Wakehurst Place, Ardingly, managed by the Royal Botanic Gardens, Kew; west side of B2028.
Sheffield Park, near Lewes, owned by the National Trust; east of A275.

HAMPSHIRE
New Forest: (a) Bolderwood Grounds, off the Cadnam-Ringwood road, A31, beside unclassified road signposted "Lyndhurst", 2 miles west of Stoney Cross.
(b) Ornamental Drive, south of Lyndhurst-Bournemouth road, A35, three miles south-west of Lyndhurst.

WILTSHIRE
Stourhead, near Mere, Wiltshire (National Trust). On by-road north of A303.

GLOUCESTERSHIRE
Westonbirt Arboretum, 2 miles south-west of Tetbury on the Bath road, A423 (Forestry Commission).

SOMERSET
Royal Victoria Park, Bath.

OXFORD
    The University Parks. just east of the Banbury Road, have a better
tree collection than the small University Botanic Garden.

CAMBRIDGE
    University Botanic Garden, Trumpington Road, on the south side of
the city.

WALES

BODNANT
    Between Conway and Llanrwst, Clwyd, on east side of A496.

SCOTLAND

EDINBURGH
    Royal Botanic Gardens, Inverleith Row, on the north of the city.

DUNOON, ARGYLL, STRATHCLYDE
    Younger Botanic Gardens, Benmore House, on A815, 3 miles north of
Dunoon Pier (Younger Benmore Trust).
    Kilmun Forest Plots, by Kilmun Kirk. on A880, 3 miles north of
Dunoon, on Kilmun road (Forestry Commission).

CRARAE, ARGYLL, STRATHCLYDE
    Crarae Forest Garden, Crarae, east of Minard on the Inveraray-Loch-
gilphead road, A83 (Forestry Commission).

ROSS-SHIRE, HIGHLAND
    Inverewe, near Gairloch, on A832 near Poolewe bridge (National Trust
for Scotland).

IRELAND

DUBLIN
    Glasnevin Botanic Garden, on the north of the city.

TOLLYMORE, COUNTY DOWN
    Arboretum at Tollymore Forest Park, near Newcastle (Forestry
Division, Ministry of Agriculture for Northern Ireland).

Notes: Many properties owned by the National Trust, and the Scottish
National Trust, have important collections of ornamental trees; details
will be found in the Trusts' guides.
    Other ornamental tree collections, in private ownership, are accessible
to the visitor, from time to time, when gardens are opened in aid of
charities. The gardens concerned are listed each year in handbooks
entitled *Gardens Open to the Public* and *Scottish Gardens Open to the
Public*, generally available from booksellers.

Sources of Further Information

JOURNALS AND ORGANISATIONS THAT ISSUE THEM

Arboricultural Association Journal, c/o Arboricultural Association (The Association of British Tree Surgeons and Arborists) at: Merrist Wood Agricultural College, Worplesdon, Guildford, Surrey, GU3 3PE.

Commonwealth Forestry Review, Commonwealth Forestry Society, 11 Keble Road, Oxford, OX1 3QG.

Forestry, Institute of Foresters of Great Britain, 6 Rutland Square, Edinburgh EH1 2AV.

Forestry and Home-Grown Timber, Benn Bros., Ltd., 74 Drymen Road, Bearsden, Glasgow.

Forestry Abstracts, Commonwealth Forestry Bureau, South Parks Road, Oxford.

Irish Forestry, Society of Irish Foresters, c/o J. Dillon, Royal Dublin Society, Ball's Bridge, Dublin 4.

Journal of the Institute of Landscape Architects, 12 Carlton House Terrace, London, S.W.1.

Journal of the Royal Horticultural Society, Vincent Square, Westminster, London, S.W.1.

Quarterly Journal of Forestry, Royal Forestry Society of England, Wales and Northern Ireland, 102 High Street, Tring, Hertfordshire.

Scottish Forestry, Royal Scottish Forestry Society, 12 Abercromby Place, Edinburgh. EH3 6LB.

The Timber Grower, Timber Growers' Organisation, National Agricultural Centre, Stoneleigh Park, Kenilworth, Warwicks. CV8 2LG.

Trees, Men of the Trees, Secretary, Miss M. A. Blackburn, Crawley Down, Crawley, Sussex.

LIBRARIES

Government Libraries with a specialised interest in trees, forests and timber include those of:

British Museum (Natural History), Cromwell Road, S.W.7.

Princes Risborough Laboratory, Building Research Establishment, Dept. of the Environment, Princes Risborough, Bucks.

Forestry Commission, Alice Holt Lodge, Wrecclesham, Farnham, Surrey.

Nature Conservancy Council, 19 Belgrave Square, London, S.W.1.

Royal Botanic Gardens, Inverleith Row, Edinburgh.

Royal Botanic Gardens, Kew, Surrey.

Science Museum, South Kensington, London, S.W.7.

Other leading libraries are those of:

Commonwealth Forestry Institute, South Parks Road, Oxford.

East Malling Research Station, East Malling, near Maidstone, Kent.

Royal Forestry Society of England, Wales and Northern Ireland, 102 High Street, Tring, Hertfordshire.

Royal Horticultural Society, Vincent Square, Westminster, London, S.W.1.

Royal Scottish Forestry Society, c/o University Department of Forestry and Natural Resources, Kings Buildings, Mayfield Road, Edinburgh.

Timber Research and Development Association Limited, Chiltern House, Stocking Lane, Naphill, High Wycombe, Bucks.

OTHER USEFUL ADDRESSES

Association of Professional Foresters of Great Britain, Brokerswood, Westbury, Wilts.

Royal Institution of Chartered Surveyors, 12 Great George Street, London, S.W.1.

Forestry Commission, 231 Corstorphine Road, Edinburgh, EH12 7AT.

Research Station, Alice Holt Lodge, Wrecclesham Farnham, Surrey GU10 4LH

Forestry Division, Ministry of Agriculture for Northern Ireland, Stormont, Belfast.

Forestry Division, Department of Lands, 88 Merrion Square, Dublin, Eire.

Scottish Woodlands Owners' Association, Ltd., 6 Chester Street, Edinburgh. EA3 7RD.

Tree Council, Dept. of the Evironment, 2 Marsham St., London SW1P 3EB.

Trees to Choose or Avoid
For Particular Situations and Features

TREES are remarkably tolerant of varied soils and sites. The full list of possible choices for the average garden or woodland that does not have an exceptional exposure or subsoil, can be very long indeed. Yet there are many circumstances in which the planting of a particular sort of tree can only lead to costly failure, where some other kind is equally sure to thrive.

Sometimes the difference between success and failure is related to the choice of species from among a group that are outwardly much alike. For example, Norway spruce cannot tolerate salty sea winds, yet the very similar Sitka spruce suffers no harm at all from them. Austrian pine will grow to maturity on almost pure chalk, yet its near relative the Scots pine will turn a sickly yellow, and may die, as soon as its roots reach the deeper, lime-rich layers.

The following lists have been drawn up to help people avoid the more obvious failures, and to choose the most certain successes. They are not exhaustive, and for each situation there are scores of satisfactory alternatives. The trees listed are simply those that spring to mind as the most certain "winners" or "losers" for each class of land or requirement of growth. In each list, broadleaved trees are shown first, followed by conifers, which are shown in *italics*.

1 AUTUMN COLOUR
Outstanding are:

Azaleas	*Metasequoia*
Liquidambar	*Swamp cypress*
Maples	
Sumach	

2 CHALK AND LIMESTONE SOILS

Reliable	**Unsatisfactory**
Ash	Azaleas (impossible)
Beech	Rhododendrons (impossible)
Birch	

continues overleaf

Chalk and Limestone Soils—continued

Reliable	**Unsatisfactory**
Box	Strawberry tree
Elm	Liquidambar
Forsythia	Japanese maples
Maples other than Japanese	
Oak	
Privet	
Walnut	
Whitebeam	

Lawson cypress	*Douglas fir*
Western red cedar	*Scots pine*
Austrian pine	
Corsican pine	
Yew	
Atlas cedar	

3 EVERGREENS

Box	Lucombe oak
Escallonias	Turner's oak
Cherry laurel	Holly
Portugal aurel	Rhododendrons
Holm oak	Strawberry tree
Privet	

All conifers *except* larches, swamp cypress, *Metasequoia*, and maiden-hair tree, are evergreen.

4 EXPOSED UPLAND SHELTERBELTS

Reliable	**Unsatisfactory**
Beech	Poplars
Sycamore	

European larch	*Douglas fir*
Austrian pine	*Norway spruce*
Sitka spruce	

5 HEDGES

Reliable	**Unsatisfactory**
Beech	Ash
Hawthorn	Birch
Hornbeam	Oak
Privet	

Hedges—continued

Reliable	Unsatisfactory
Western red cedar	*Douglas fir*
Lawson cypress	*Silver firs*
Western hemlock	*Larches*
Norway spruce	*Pines*
Yew	

6 RAPID GROWTH

Rate of growth depends very much on soil fertility and climate. The following trees grow exceptionally fast when conditions are satisfactory:

Tree of heaven
Poplars
Willows

Leyland cypress
Monterey cypress
(not hardy in north-east)
Larches
Monterey pine (not
hardy in north-east)
Sitka spruce (on
western seaboard)

7 VERY SANDY SOILS

Reliable	Unsatisfactory
Birch	Ash
Rowan	Maples
	Oaks
Pines	*Spruces*

8 SCREENS

Reliable	Unsatisfactory
Cornish elms and other narrow-crowned elms	Normal broad-crowned strains of most broadleaved trees
Limes	
Lombardy poplar	
Lawson cypress	*Normal broad-crowned strains of*
Leyland cypress	*most conifers*
Also, fastigiate, i.e. narrow-crowned varieties of most forest trees.	

9 SEASIDE EXPOSURE

Reliable	Unsatisfactory
Elms	Beech
Escallonias	Common oaks
Holm oak	Hybrid poplars
Grey poplar	
Sycamore	
Tamarisk	

Austrian pine	*Douglas fir*
Corsican pine	*Scots pine*
Maritime pine	*Norway spruce*
Monterey pine	
Sitka spruce	
Stone pine	

10 SHADY PLACES

Reliable	Unsatisfactory
Azaleas	Ash
Beech	Birch
Box	Oak
Holly	
Hornbeam	
Rhododendrons	

Western red cedar	*Larches*
Lawson cypress	*Pines*
Western hemlock	
Norway spruce	
Yew	

11 SMOKY TOWNS

Reliable	Unsatisfactory
Ash	Most evergreen
Elder	broadleaved trees
Holly	
Plane	*All conifers*
Privet	
Sycamore	
Tree of heaven	
Swedish whitebeam	

12 SPRING BLOSSOM

The following trees regularly flower in early spring, before their leaves appear.

Cornelian cherry	Certain magnolias
Forsythia	Norway maple
Wych hazel	

13 WATERSIDES

Reliable	**Unsatisfactory**
Alders	(Trees of any kind
Elms	grow well unless
Poplars	the soil moisture
Willows	is stagnant)

Swamp cypress
Metasequoia

Economic Aids for Timber Growing

As mentioned in Chapter 5 on "Trees and the Law", anyone who plants any substantial area of ground with trees may qualify for cash grants under various plans, made by the Exchequer because of the long-term importance of timber to the national economy.

GRANTS FROM THE AGRICULTURAL DEPARTMENTS

These are limited to farm shelterbelts but may prove more generous than those given under alternative schemes. They are only made where planting forms part of a Farm Improvement Scheme approved by the Ministry of Agriculture, Fisheries and Food or, in Scotland by the Department of Agriculture. The grant may amount to 25% of the actual cost, or up to 50% on Hill Land.

GRANTS FROM THE COUNTRYSIDE COMMISSION

These are made, usually to Local Authorities, to cover up to 75% of the cost of tree planting schemes aimed at preserving or enhancing the natural beauty of the countryside. They are also available to private landowners in connection with country parks, picnic areas, or other places of public access.

GRANTS FROM THE FORESTRY COMMISSION

Since 1920 the Forestry Commission has offered grants, under various schemes to private landowners to encourage tree planting for timber production combined where appropriate with the improvement of the landscape, shelter for farms, and opportunities for recreation. Between 1947 and 1972 a remarkably large area of private woodland, some 1,450,000 acres, or roughly half the available total, was brought into long-term schemes for Dedicated and Approved Woodlands. Appropriate planting and management grants are being continued for the land already within these schemes.

From 1st October 1974, further land may become eligible for grant aid, provided the owner accepts an obligation to secure sound forestry practice, good land use, environmental benefits and provision of such opportunities for recreation as may be appropriate. In considering applications the Commission will consult agricultural departments, planning authorities and other interests. The minimum area considered is 2½ acres. If more than 25 acres are involved, a legally binding dedication of the land to forestry, effective for the life of at least one tree crop, is required.

The current (1975) rate of grant for trees of all kinds is £18·21 per acre. Where a scheme involves hardwood trees planted to establish a hardwood crop and give a predominantly hardwood appearance to the landscape, a supplementary grant of £50·59 an acre is payable. Rates of grant are subject to review from time to time.

Details are available from the Forestry Commission, 231 Corstorphine Road, Edinburgh, EH12 7AT, or its local offices.

Similar schemes differing in detail, operate in both Northern Ireland, and the Irish Republic. Addresses for further information appear on page 326.

AN ATTRACTIVE INVESTMENT

Because of such aid and encouragement, investment in timber growing has been expanding steadily over the past twenty-five years. Over 1,300,000 acres are now under ordered management in various schemes agreed by landowners and the Forestry Commission, and 50,000 fresh acres are planted annually. The Commission must, of course, approve grant schemes in advance, and arrange inspections by its regional officers, before payments are made.

People who do not own extensive woodlands, but wish to invest capital in timber growing, are now able to do so by means of syndicates or similar co-operative arrangements with other investors.

Quite apart from grants that help meet costs, timber growing is an attractive long-term investment because it puts money into a growing crop. This crop, once established, increases in size and value at a rate comparable to the compound interest on the capital invested. The crop itself continues in existence as a tangible asset that holds real value despite inflation. It is an asset that can nowadays be realised at any time, either by felling to secure the timber, or as a going concern for other people who wish to invest in woodlands. Qualified forestry consultants are now available to guide those investors who have little previous knowledge of forestry, while competent contractors can establish plantations, or market timber, at agreed economic prices.

Containerised Trees, Paperpots and Tubed Seedlings

Three recently developed methods of raising trees for planting aim at extending the effective planting season and reducing losses due to transplanting. The most popular is the use of **containers** which are temporary pots made from waterproofed fibre or paper, for the sale, transport and establishment of ornamental trees, usually for garden planting. By comparison with the standard method of raising 'bare-rooted' transplants of similar size, container practices are costly. But they are convenient to the purchaser, who is prepared to pay higher prices for small numbers of trees, with a greater assurance of success. These trees are displayed at garden centres with handy car parks, all ready and priced for immediate collection. Take-away trees, in fact.

Although these trees are sometimes advertised as 'container grown' scarcely any are actually raised in that way. It would be too costly to use a sufficiently robust container in place of the usual flimsy kind. Instead, they are raised by conventional methods in ordinary nurseries, and 'containerised' a few weeks before sale. Provided that good composts are used, that roots are made firm at the outset, and that the trees are subsequently sheltered and watered until established, all goes well. Buyers should beware of any trees that look as though they have been casually or hurriedly handled. It is safer to buy containerised trees in late spring or early summer, from May to July, than earlier. If growth has begun, roothold must be satisfactory. One cannot be sure of this earlier, whilst the trees are still dormant.

Paperpot methods are the concern of large-scale planters of forest trees, usually conifers, who hope to cut down costs as well as planting losses. The little pots are made of thin paper, designed to resist breakdown in soil for a few months only. They come in an assembly of many units that opens up like a concertina. Placed in a greenhouse with planned control of temperature and humidity, they are filled with a compost of organic material and soil, plus artificial fertiliser. One seed is sown per pot. Under the ideal conditions that are provided it develops, within eight weeks or so, into a robust seedling four to six inches high. Each batch of pots is then taken to the forest and separated into single units. These are planted with a special tool, like a metal spade with a large upright stem. Using this tool, the operator opens up a hole in the soil just the size of one paperpot. A pot, complete with its little tree, is then inserted into the top of the tool. It shoots straight down the upright stem and plants itself in the ground automatically! The Japanese thought up this one.

Tubed seedlings, also called *tubelings* are still smaller trees grown in plastic tubes, little bigger than cigarettes. Each tube has a split side so that when the tree stem evetually grows larger, it splits open the tube without injuring itself. Tubed seedlings are raised in greenhouses and planted out during summer, usually on ploughed land. The method originated in Canada, where it extends the planting season from a short spring to a long summer. In the British Isles it can only be used on peaty soils, because elsewhere our alternating frost-and-thaw sequences in spring lift the tubes out of the ground.

Bibliography

THE following list is a selection of leading textbooks, each of value in its particular field, that are readily available from booksellers or libraries. No single book can tell the whole story; it is necessary to refer to several to find a full range of illustrations of all tree features and forms. The dates and prices quoted are those of the latest edition.

ALDOUS, J. (1972). *Nursery Practice*. Forestry Commission Booklet No. 43, H.M. Stationery Office, £1. 50. A full, well illustrated guide.

BEAN, W. J. (1967). *Trees and Shrubs Hardy in the British Isles*. Murray £27 (approx, reprinting) for 3 vols. The standard account of every sort of ornamental tree and shrub grown in Britain. Comprehensive, but inadequately illustrated. (Vol. I £8, Vol. II £9, Vol. III in press).

BEDDALL, J. L. (1950) *Hedges for Farm and Garden*. Faber, £2·10. A practical account of tending every sort of hedge for shelter and scenic effect.

BOOM, B. K. and KLEIJN, H. (1966). *The Glory of the Tree*. Harrap, £4·20. Readable survey of the leading ornamental trees grown in Europe, illustrated with excellent colour photographs.

CABORN, J. M. (1965). *Shelterbelts and Windbreaks*. Faber, £2·50. A thorough study of the planting and care of windbreaks, and their effects on crops and livestock.

COLVIN, B. and TYRWHITT (1950). *Trees for Town and Country*. Lund Humphries, £1·65. Written for landscape architects and town planners, describes how each kind of tree may be fitted into site and scene. Good drawings and photographs.

DALLIMORE, W., JACKSON, A. B. and HARRISON, S.G. (1966). *Handbook of Coniferae and Ginkgoaceae*. Arnold, £10. Standard botanical textbook on the conifers of the world, including all the kinds cultivated in Britain.

EDLIN, H. L. (1964). *Wayside and Woodland Trees*. Warne, £1·60. The key handbook for quick identification of all native trees and those introduced for timber. Fully illustrated with drawings, photographs, and colour plates.

EDLIN, H. L. (1966). *Know Your Conifers*. Forestry Commission Booklet No 15, H.M. Stationery Office, 30p. Photographs, drawings and descriptive text covering the kinds grown for timber, but not the ornamental species.

EDLIN, H. L. (1970). *Trees, Woods and Man*. Collins, New Naturalist Series No. 32, £3·00. The history of natural and planted woodlands in

Britain from prehistoric times to the present day, and their importance for man's need of timber, fuel and shelter. Fully illustrated, with colour photographs.

EDLIN, H. L. (1969), *What Wood is That?* Thames & Hudson, £3·00. An illustrated manual of timber identification, with 40 actual wood specimens.

EDLIN, H. L. (1973). *Trees and Timbers*. Routledge and Kegan Paul, £2·00. A project book in the 'Local Search' series, to guide students in the best methods of finding out facts about trees, woods, and timber-using industries. Photos and drawings.

EDLIN, H. L. (1973). *Woodland Crafts in Britain*. David & Charles, £3·95. A fully illustrated record of the rural crafts that use wood as their raw material, from pre-historic times until their decline in the present century.

EDLIN, H. L. (1974). *Observer's Trees*. Warne (*in press*). A complete revision of a handy pocket book describing 50 common species. Colour paintings of trees in summer, and winter silhouettes, plus flower and fruit details; photos of bark and bole characteristics, drawings of seedlings.

EDLIN, H. L. and DARTER, CHRISTINE (1969). *Know Your Broadleaves*. Forestry Commission Booklet No. 20. H.M. Stationery Office, 80p. Straightforward account of forty-two leading kinds illustrated by 126 large pictures in black and white. Fine photos of trees in summer foliage. Christine Darter's drawings show exceptionally clear details of winter twigs, buds and flowers.

EDLIN, H. L. and NIMMO, M. (1974). *The World of Trees*. Orbis Books, £2·50. A display of colour photos featuring eighty of the most picturesque broadleaved and coniferous trees found in Britain, Europe, and North America. Text relates seasonal changes, landscape values, life histories, and timber uses for each group.

EDLIN, H. L. and NIMMO, M. (1956). *Treasury of Trees*. Countrygoer Press, Buxton, £3·75. Photographic studies of leading garden and forest trees, with descriptive text.

HADFIELD, MILES (1957). *British Trees*. Dent, £1·50. Historical and botanical accounts of all common ornamental and timber trees, broadleaved and conifer. Excellent line drawings of leaves, twigs, flowers, fruits and seedlings, but no photographs or pictures of growing trees. Emphasis is on horticultural history.

HADFIELD, MILES (1967). *Landscape with Trees*. Country Life, £3·15. Poetical survey of the place of trees in the landscape of the British Isles, from the earliest prehistoric days to the great planting landowners and the modern foresters. Fine photographs of woodland and park.

HART, C. E. (1967). *Practical Forestry for the Agent and Surveyor*. Estates Gazette, £3·15. Outlines established methods of planting, tending and harvesting timber crops, with helpful financial data and information on taxation, costs and prices.

HART, C. E. and RAYMOND, CHARLES (1974). *British Trees in Colour*. Michael Joseph, £4·00. Sixty beautiful colour paintings show foliage, flower, and fruit or cone detail. Sixty line drawings illustrate typical bole and branch patterns in winter—but unfortunately all the broadleaved trees are leafless. Sound descriptive text.

HILEY, W. E. *et al.* (1967). *Woodland Management.* Faber, £6·30. Outlines the principles and methods to be followed for profitable timber raising on private estates.

HYDE, H. A. (1961). *Welsh Timber Trees.* National Museum of Wales, Cardiff, 90p. Comprehensive and well illustrated descriptions of timber trees grown in Wales; omits ornamental trees and the smaller native kinds.

JAMES, N. D. G. (1965). *The Forester's Companion.* Blackwell, Oxford, £1·25. A handy pocket book packed with facts and figures for everyday reference in the woods.

JAMES, N. D. G. (1972). *The Arboriculturalist's Companion.* Blackwell, £3·15. A handy compendium of practical hints for the growers of trees in parks, streets and gardens. Illustrations are inadequate.

JOHNSON, HUGH (1974). *The International Book of Trees.* Mitchell Beazley, £9·95. A massive 288-page quarto volume, lavishly illustrated with several hundred splendidly reproduced and well-chosen colour photos of magnificent trees, plus flower, fruit and foliage details, also paintings and diagrammatic illustrations. The text is a miscellany of curious lore; serendipity throughout.

JOHNSTON, D. R., GRAYSON, A. J., and BRADLEY, R. T. (1967). *Forest Planning.* Faber, £6·50. A concise guide to large-scale forest management.

LATHAM, B. (1964). *Wood from Forest to Man.* Harrap, 90p. A popular, readable, and well-informed book on the growth of timber in forests, and its many uses in industry.

MAKINS, F. K. (1948). *The Identification of Trees and Shrubs.* Dent, £2·25. An atlas of line drawings to enable any common tree or shrub to be identified by botanical details. No general text.

MILES, ROGER (1967). *Forestry in the English Landscape.* Faber, £5·25. A critical study, by a landscape architect and forester, of the way in which woods can be fitted into the rural scene. Good photographs and drawings.

MINISTRY OF AGRICULTURE (1960). *Farm and Estate Hedges.* H.M. Stationery Office, 14p. Outlines practices suitable for farmers.

MINISTRY OF AGRICULTURE (1969). *Shelterbelts for Farmland.* H.M. Stationery Office, 28p. Simple account of establishment and maintenance, well illustrated.

MINISTRY OF HOUSING AND LOCAL GOVERNMENT (1968). *Trees in Town and City.* H.M. Stationery Office, £1. A guide, intended mainly for local authorities and their staff, to the planting of trees along roadsides, and in parks or squares. Well illustrated.

MITCHELL, ALAN (1974). *A Field Guide to the Trees of Britain and Northern Europe.* Collins, £2·95. The definitive guide to the identification of all species and varieties in regular cultivation today. Describes 800 kinds, most of them illustrated. Excellent colour plates show foliage, flower and fruit detail, also conifer tree forms. 600 line drawings feature identification pointers, also broadleaved tree forms. Comprehensive keys and indexes. Dimensions given for leading specimens. All trees have English names— often for the first time ever! Clear descriptions in plain, often vivid, words.

MITCHELL, ALAN and DARTER, CHRISTINE (1972). *Conifers in the British Isles. A Descriptive Handbook.* Forestry Commission Booklet No. 33. Her Majesty's Stationery Office, £2·25. This hefty 322-page quarto volume, planned for the specialist, describes 43 genera, 270 species and 217 varieties cultivated in British collections today. Measurements of height and girth are given for leading specimens, with locations. Many keys. 203 drawings, largely of foliage, by Christine Darter, aid identification. 24 photos illustrate tree forms.

OVINGTON, J. D. (1965). *Woodlands.* English Univerisities Press, £1·10. Readable account of natural and planted woods, and their associated plant and animal life, on an ecological basis. Well illustrated.

PEACE, T. R. (1962). *Pathology of Trees and Shrubs.* Clarendon Press, £5·25, Oxford. The standard scientific work on tree diseases.

PIRONE, P. P. (1959). *Tree Maintenance.* Oxford University Press, New York, £6·50. The standard American work on tree surgery, the pruning of street trees, and their treatment as sources of scenic values and shade.

PROCKTER, N. J. (1960). *Garden Hedges.* Country Life, £1·25. Practical account of choice of tree or shrub, establishment and maintenance. Illustrated.

ROBBIE, T. A. (1955). *Teach Yourself Forestry.* English Universities Press, 38p. Sound introductory account for students, estate agents, and land-owners.

ROWE, W. H. (1949). *Tree and Shrub Growing.* Faber, £1·25. A practical guide for gardeners, with cultural hints for all usual kinds.

SHEAT, W. G. (1948). *Propagation of Trees, Shrubs and Conifers.* Macmillan, £2·75. An exceptionally full account of the best methods of increasing trees of all kinds, by seed, cuttings, etc., based on experience gained at Kew Gardens.

TANSLEY, A. G. (1950). *The British Isles and their Vegetation.* Cambridge University Press, £8 for 2 vols. Includes classic studies of semi-natural woodlands, but ignores all modern foresty and ornamental planting.

VEDEL, H. and LANGE, J. (1960). *Trees and Bushes in Wood and Hedgerow.* Dent, £1·95. Beautifully illustrated in full colour, with a descriptive text, this book covers nearly all native trees and those grown in woodlands, but no purely ornamental kinds.

WILKINSON, G. (1973). *Trees in the Wild.* Stephen Hope Books, £3·50. Charming colour photos of trees, nearly all cultivated (!) in countryside surroundings, with descriptive text.

WOOD, J. B. (1966). *Growing and Studying Trees.* Blandford Press, 75p. A broad general account of woodland life and the forester's work. Well illustrated, mainly in colour.

Index

Figures in italics refer to illustrations